CHINESE URBAN LIFE UNDER

The Changing Social Contract

One of the most dramatic changes in the lives of average, urban Chinese since the introduction of market reforms in the 1980s has been the erosion of the "iron rice bowl," the social contract between the communist government and the Chinese people. The promises of socialism – job security, medical benefits, housing, education, and other elements of social welfare – have gradually given way to the promises of the market. In this book Wenfang Tang, a political scientist, and William Parish, a sociologist, team up to explore the social aspects of China's economic transformation, the shrinking role of the Chinese government in social welfare, and the politics and difficulties of that transition.

Tang and Parish examine the trade-off – the loss of communal egalitarianism – for the market reforms that give freer reign to individual aspirations in China. Their study, based on a unique set of national social surveys completed over ten years, beginning in 1987, presents a rare glimpse into how the Chinese population is experiencing the shift from a planned to a market economy. The authors give voice to workers, civil servants, intellectuals, and women, who report their grievances and joys at home, work, and in the public sphere. This book offers fresh data on emerging patterns of economic inequality, labor–management relations, political participation, and gender inequality in China. Using comparative data from similar surveys in the more market-based Taiwan, the authors illuminate the future directions in which Chinese society may be headed.

Wenfang Tang is Associate Professor of Political Science at the University of Pittsburgh.

William L. Parish is Professor of Sociology at the University of Chicago.

CHINESE URBAN LIFE UNDER REFORM

The Changing Social Contract

WENFANG TANG
University of Pittsburgh

WILLIAM L. PARISH
University of Chicago

CAMBRIDGE
UNIVERSITY PRESS

PUBLISHED BY THE PRESS SYNDICATE OF THE UNIVERSITY OF CAMBRRIDGE
The Pitt Building, Trumpington Street, Cambridge, United Kingdom

CAMBRIDGE UNIVERSITY PRESS
The Edinburgh Building, Cambridge CB2 2RU, UK   http://www.cup.cam.ac.uk
40 West 20th Street, New York, NY 10011-4211, USA   http://www.cup.org
10 Stamford Road, Oakleigh, Melbourne 3166, Australia
Ruiz de Alarcón 13, 28014 Madrid, Spain

First published 2000

Printed in the United States of America

Typeface Times Roman 10/13 pt.   *System* QuarkXPress [BTS]

A catalog record for this book is available from the British Library.

Library of Congress Cataloging in Publication data

Tang, Wenfang, 1955–
Chinese urban life under reform: the social contract/Wenfang
Tang, William L. Parish.
p.   cm. – (Cambridge modern China series)
Includes bibliographical references and index.
ISBN 0-521-77085-8
1. City and town life – China.   2. China – Social life and
customs – 1976–   I. Parish, William L.   II. Title.   III. Series.
DS779.23.T365   1999
951'.009732 – dc21-99–30393
CIP

ISBN   0 521 77085 8   hardback
ISBN   0 521 77865 4   paperback

Contents

Acknowledgments

The idea of writing a book about Chinese urban reform began in 1990 when Wenfang Tang had several conversations with the deputy director of the Economic System Reform Institute of China (ESRIC), Wang Xiaoqiang, about ongoing urban social surveys conducted by ESRIC. Subsequently, Wang Xiaoqiang helped us establish cooperative ties with the staff at ESRIC. A National Science Foundation grant (INT-9215268) allowed Wenfang Tang to secure all the ESRIC survey data since 1987, and supported the development of new surveys until 1992. During this process, Yang Guansan, director of the China Social Survey Network at ESRIC, provided extraordinary leadership skills and indispensable technical expertise even when ESRIC was going through a difficult time after the 1989 urban protests. Several years have gone by since the initial stage of this project. While expressing our sincere appreciation for their early help, we can only apologize for the slow pace of our computers in crunching the vast quantity of data they provided (Chapters 3, 5, 7, 8, 10, 11).

In time, we came to use data from several other sources, and we give thanks to people who helped with those additional data sets. Analysis of labor–management relations (Chapter 6) was made possible with the help of Feng Tongqing, Zhao Wei, and Li Ruirui at the Labor Institute of China. Elizabeth Li and her collaborators also provided a supplementary data set that helped enrich the analysis of labor–management relations. The data analysis of gender and family (Chapters 9 and 10) was achieved through a collaborative effort with the Universities Service Centre, Chinese University of Hong Kong, with William Parish serving as a Project Associate of the Centre during the period of analysis. We are grateful to the Director and Vice-Director of that Centre, Professor H. C. Kuan and Jean Hung, for assistance in this part of the project and for their skilled shepherding of a marvelous research collection on China. We are also grateful to the principal investigators in China for making this data set available for scholarly use outside of China. The comparisons with Taiwan (Chapter 11) relied on the generous policy of providing public use data sets by the survey research group at Academia Sinica, led at the time by Professor Chiu Hei-yuan. We are grateful to Professor Chiu for setting a precedent in East Asia of providing public use data sets, and for his generous support of this and other projects. We are also grateful to the scholars who made the 1988 Chinese Household Income Project (CHIP) (Chapter 4) income data set available through public sources.

Several people have given generously of their time and energy in helping to write and edit the book. Though her name as coauthor heads only Chapter 9, "Gender and Work," throughout the book Sarah Busse has labored mightily in helping us to think and write more clearly. A tough schoolmaster, Sarah has prodded and probed, even getting us to throw away or rewrite whole sections that weren't "up to snuff." As a Russian specialist, she provided considerable contextual material from the Soviet and East and Central European socialist experience. James Farrer, coauthor of Chapter 10, "Gender and Family," gave generously of his time when he was busy completing his wonderfully rich ethnographic dissertation on romance and self-identity in Shanghai. A "right-brain" person more given to poetics than statistics, James is to be admired for enduring our linear ways of analysis and thinking. His rich insights from three years of living in Shanghai help provide some of the human interest in that chapter. Marsha Tsouris and Nancy Matrozza at the University of Pittsburgh also helped with editing several chapters.

At the University of Chicago, several other graduate students have given tremendous help with different parts of the analysis. These include Charles Chi-hsiang Chang, computer jockey and data analyst par excellence and an expert on the Taiwan portion of our data, and Fang Li, general pinch hitter who has written an excellent dissertation of his own on private entrepreneurs.

Because this book was a long time in gestation, many friends and colleagues had opportunities to comment on draft chapters and gave feedback on chapters during conferences and seminars at several universities. By now, we fear that we have forgotten some of the most astute commentators on early versions of chapters. Nevertheless, with the usual warning about how none of these people are responsible for the final product, we want to thank those we can remember. For gracious comments on one or more underdeveloped chapters, great thanks and bows of appreciation go to Yanjie Bian, Monte Broaded, Deborah Davis, Barbara Einhorn, Li Lulu, Nan Lin, Thomas Metzger, Ethan Michelson, Ellen Pimentel, Thomas Rawski, Bert Rockman, Irwin Schulman, Tianjian Shi, Donald Treiman, Tang Tsou, Andrew Walder, Wang Fenyu, Martin King Whyte, Dali Yang, Yu Xie, Ming Zhang, and Dingxin Zhao.

In addition to the National Science Foundation grant, Wenfang Tang received financial support from several other sources, including the Committee on Scholarly Communication with the People's Republic of China (1993), the China Study Endowment, and the Asian Studies Program at the University of Pittsburgh (various years). The Department of Political Science at the University of Pittsburgh provided research assistantship over the entire project period. A National Fellowship (1997–98) at the Hoover Institution, Stanford University, enabled Dr. Tang to work continuously on the manuscript. During parts of the project, William Parish had support from the Luce Foundation, the National Science Foundation (SBR-9515173, SBR-9515143), the Chiang Ching-kuo Foundation, Academia Sinica in Taiwan, and the Social Science Collegiate Division at the University of Chicago.

William Parish benefited greatly from collaborative research, friendship, and insights from people at several Chinese institutions. At the Sociology Institute at the Chinese Academy of Social Sciences, he has had the great pleasure of working closely with Shen Chonglin, Zhe Xiaoye, Chen Yingying, and Zhang Houyi. Listing some of these people as coauthors of several articles in our references only begins to indicate their contributions. Other friends in China have been wonderful sounding boards for evolving ideas, even when they had little hint of what use would be made of their observations.

We enjoyed working with Elizabeth Neal and Mary Child at Cambridge University Press. We are also grateful to William Kirby and the anonymous readers for their comments and suggestions. Our family members and friends supported us throughout the project. Finally, we dedicate this book to Chinese urban residents – the real subject of this book – including the tens of thousands who took the time to reply to the surveys analyzed in this book.

Part I

INTRODUCTION

1

Socialist and Market Social Contracts

OVER the last two decades, China has gone through a massive economic transformation. This book tries to capture the social and, to a lesser extent, the political aspects of that transformation. The transformation involves a fundamental redefinition of the social contract the government has with society.[1] The socialist social contract promised an egalitarian, redistributionist order that provided job security, basic living standards, and special opportunities for those from disadvantaged backgrounds. In return, the state demanded sacrifices in current consumption, a leveling of individual aspirations, and obedience to all-knowing party redistributors.[2] In time, some of the demands wore thin, particularly when economic inefficiencies accumulated and the sacrifices in current consumption failed to translate into long-term growth or into improved housing and consumer goods.

The new, post-1978 market social contract makes a different set of demands and promises. In return for abandoning the ideal of communal egalitarianism and security of jobs and other benefits, the market contract promises that giving free reign to individualistic aspirations will produce better jobs and greater consumption. Freedom from communal dictates by all-knowing redistributionist party superiors will allow the

1. In the voluminous contractarian literature, perhaps the emphasis on the moral obligation of citizens to obey an egalitarian social contract (Kant 1970; Rawls 1971) is the theme most relevant to socialist societies – though Rousseau's (1950) suggestion that citizens should be socialized from an early age into ethical values consistent with the social contract also seems relevant. China's emphasis on "virtuocracy," promoting the ideologically committed and societal guidance by the ideologically committed, provided an extreme implementation of some of these contractarian ideas.
2. Earlier applications of the idea of a social contract to socialist and postsocialist societies include Bialer (1980), Lapidus (1983), Breslauer (1984), Hauslohner (1984), Connor (1988), Hewett (1988), Kennedy (1991), Cook (1993), Berliner (1994), and Cheek (1994).

economy to adapt readily to changing domestic and international markets. While some may be left behind, the growing economic pie means that the vast majority of people will benefit.

As late 1980s student demonstrations against inflation and government corruption showed, much of this shift from old contract to new can provoke resistance. Once the transformation begins, many interest groups find that they miss parts of the old social contract.[3] In Eastern Europe and the Soviet Union, where economic downturns were more severe, the public often protested against problems with the transformation by voting Communist parties back into power.

This book examines the difficulties of transition, with an emphasis on promises kept and promises betrayed during the socialist period and with an emphasis on the politics of transition. We do this with a unique set of social surveys conducted over the most difficult of transition times, between 1987 and 1992. The surveys include repeated semiannual surveys, allowing us to monitor changing responses to reform (see Appendix B). The data sets also include surveys of political participation and surveys on specific population groups. The special population surveys let us examine how the changing social contract influenced women, workers, and civil servants. Finally, we have a pair of surveys comparing public attitudes in Taiwan and China, letting us examine popular reactions to market and socialist social contracts in two societies with shared cultural origins but radically differing economic systems. This final, "one culture, two systems" comparison helps pull together many of the observations made from regional and group comparisons within China.

SYSTEMIC DIFFERENCES

Two central issues guide the analysis: the systematic consequences of socialist and market systems and, second, the politics of transition. The first issue concerns how different social contracts shape people's lives. The second issue is about the winners and losers during market transformation. We begin with systematic intended and unintended consequences of the socialist system.

3. E.g., Millar and Wolchik (1994), Kluegel and Mateju (1995).

Systematic Consequences

To give a set of names to the debate, the issue of systematic consequences can be thought of as a debate between Janos Kornai (1980, 1992, 1995) and Alex Inkeles (1968). Kornai, the famous Hungarian economist, argues that socialist systems, wherever they were put in place, had a systematic set of secondary consequences that shaped all areas of life. Many other authors, of differing political persuasions, join Kornai in emphasizing the differences between socialist and market systems.[4] Though the emphases vary by author, one of the presumed systematic consequences of a top-down planned economy is vertical dependency. With many goods distributed not through open, market principles but instead through redistributionist channels, people were indebted to redistributing bureaucratic superiors. This tendency was exacerbated by an emphasis on large production units and by the lack of alternative employment possibilities outside work units organized in a single, pyramid-shaped hierarchy. The result, Wiles (1977) and others suggest, is the very alienation from work that Marx decried as an evil of capitalist societies. In large, state-owned work units, despite individualized bargaining enhanced by patron–client ties, workers were not in control of their own fates. This produced feelings of hopelessness, powerlessness, and passive strategies of protest (Havel et al. 1985; Kaminski 1992). To the extent that people did pursue their interests, this was typically conducted through particularized contact in hierarchically organized corporatist systems. This particularized, person-to-person contact through informal channels could become corrupt in times of political relaxation (Chirot 1972; Hough 1977; Eisenstadt and Roniger 1981, 1984; Jowitt 1983, 1992; DiFranceisco and Gitelman 1984; Shi 1997). When particularized contact failed, people retreated into passive grousing among a small coterie of close kin and friends (Smith 1976; Kaminski 1992, p. 252). With some exceptions, the list of consequences included high levels of equality within a given society. Even when elites got additional in-kind benefits in housing and other goods, overall inequality remained modest (Ellman 1989). So much so, suggests Lenski (1994), that morale among elites and

---

4. E.g., Hayek (1944); Hollander (1973); Lindblom (1977); Wiles (1977, ch. 12); Ellman's (1989) chapter on the "Results of Socialist Planning"; Kornai's (1992) chapter on the "Coherence of the Classical Model"; Szelényi (1996).

skilled workers suffered. Moreover, with an emphasis on blue-collar work and a slowing in growth, mature socialist societies failed to provide the job and income opportunities that they initially promised. Morale sagged in response, particularly among blue-collar workers (Connor 1979, 1991). We explore whether these types of systematic consequences appeared in China.

Based on his 1950s work on the Soviet Union, Alex Inkeles suggests that while there are some obvious differences, industrialization is a great homogenizer that obscures differences among social systems. When societies industrialize, education, stratification, family systems, and even personality begin to converge (Inkeles 1950, 1960, 1968, 1974, 1976; Inkeles and Bauer 1959). More education, the freer flow of information through the media, and work in large, complex organizations creates a new, autonomous, assertive personality type that in time demands changes in both market and socialist top-down, authoritarian socialist systems.[5] While agreeing with many of these tendencies, other authors note that the change process occurs not in a smooth, linear progression but in tumultuous, episodic events that may be painful to all participants. With increasing information from abroad and rising aspirations, the more educated and those in close contact with information and ideals coming from abroad can come to expect much more than their governments can deliver. Social and political instability may be the result (Huntington 1968; Portes 1976). If true, then, parallel with tendencies in many market societies, the more educated and those in contact with media containing new ideals from abroad will be among the most discontent in Chinese society and the most likely to consider political actions outside official, corporatist channels.

Consistent with the theme that there are many commonalties among all complex societies, other authors note that socialist and market systems produced similar prestige rankings of occupations (Treiman 1977) and broadly similar patterns of occupational mobility (e.g., Connor 1979). Even the neo-Marxist critics often agree, arguing that in actually

---

5. Kohn and Slomczynski (1990) show parallel processes of personality formation in Poland and the United States. Almond and Verba (1963) provide a classic statement in the political modernization school, which emphasizes bottom-up pressures from more informed, participant citizens. Though emphasizing change at a later state of development, Ingelhart (1990) notes how increasing education and resources contributes to increased political mobilization.

existing state socialism – disparagingly labeled "state capitalism" – the structures of inequality, dominance, and personal motivation mimicked patterns in market societies.[6]

Part of the answer to this debate is, of course, that it is a matter of degree. Often the differences were not qualitative but instead quantitative – or a matter of degrees of difference. For example, in examining state-owned corporations in France, Michel Crozier (1964) reports a host of consequences, including worker repulsion to personalized dependency and problems of motivation once one moves toward a more rule-bound organization of work. Despite some variations among societies, the impressive aspect of the "bureaucratic phenomenon," according to Crozier, is its similarity across societies, with key differences being only of degree, not kind. Socialist states effectively reproduced Crozier's set of unanticipated consequences of the bureaucratic organization of work, only on a societal scale.

Capturing degrees of difference is always difficult, both because there are few truly comparative studies and because people who live within each system are often insensitive to the peculiarities of their own social lives. Observations that have been most useful in capturing these subtle differences often arise from people who have left one system for the other. However, these analyses are risky. Those who have left might be special in some way, either because only people who were different chose to leave or because they were changed by the process of leaving and relocating in a different society. Nevertheless, accounts from emigres are suggestive. In earlier years, popular media and interview accounts report culture shock among emigres who left East Germany, Russia, and China for the capitalist West or hyper-capitalist Hong Kong. Emigres deplored the social costs of individualist competition and the loss of close, supportive ties among workmates, neighbors, and friends.[7] Similar to Tönnies's account of early market transformation in the West, people in new, cold, "*gesellschaft*" settings longed for the warm, "*gemeinschaft*" relations they had left behind. Much as in the early emergence of the market, individualistic mobility and competition created a new set of less personalistic social relations.

Besides losses in warm personal relations, in the early 1980s, Russian

---

6. Lane (1985, pp. 85–88) reviews the state capitalism literature.
7. WGBH (1983); Whyte and Parish (1984), ch. 11; Gill (1986).

emigres in the United States reported a loss in social support mechanisms. Once out of the Soviet system, emigres reported that subsidized
housing, education, and health care were important aspects of Soviet life
that they missed. When emigres were asked what lesson the United
States might learn from the Soviet Union, socialized medicine led their
list of suggestions (Millar and Clayton 1987). During the early 1990s in
the postsocialist states of Europe, many residents remained attached to
old egalitarian values.[8] Of course, there were less flattering images as
well, with employers, coworkers, or neighbors in West Germany, Israel,
and Hong Kong finding their socialist brethren excessively passive,
waiting on someone else to provide for their wants rather than striking
out on their own.

In this book, a series of new surveys lets us observe a great natural
experiment. Like during early market and industrial transformation in
the West, people in the midst of market transformation are more sensitive to differences between old and new systems. This is the same type
of transformative moment that produced an antimarket backlash in the
West. There, the utopian communes of the early and mid-1800s were one
counterreaction to the growth of the market (e.g., Kanter 1972). Marx
was only one of many people who commented negatively on the spread
of the cash nexus in human relations. Simmel, Durkheim, Weber, and
many other social scientists made a career of analyzing the changes
caused by the spread of the market. More recently, following themes
about "the great transformation" by Karl Polanyi (1944), E. P.
Thompson (1971) and Charles Tilly (1975) have noted how the market's
erosion of the old "moral economy" of communal sharing was a wrench-
ing experience in early modern Europe.

Once again, with the decline of idealistic socialism, characterized by a
panoply of subsidized housing, food, and other benefits, and the rise of
the market in these same societies, we have a chance to capture people's
reactions as old socialist, communitarian contracts are shelved to be
replaced by more individualistic, market social contracts. By capturing
people's reactions at the very onset of reform, we hope to get a better
sense of what each of these social contracts meant for people's everyday
lives. Also, using similar survey instruments in marketized Taiwan and

---

8. E.g., Duch (1993), Berliner (1994), Dobson (1994), Millar and Wolchik (1994), Kluegel
   and Mateju (1995), Mason (1995), Zaslavsky (1995).

socialist China, we hope to get a clearer sense of how people in a common cultural tradition react to different systems of economic opportunity.

Negative Consequences

On the negative consequences side of our study, we will examine the consequences of the socialist contract for authoritarianism, life chances, and job satisfaction. Our study of authoritarianism considers the degree to which people could participate in spite of one-party rule. We will note that as they matured, socialist states increasingly sought feedback from below, both to help produce better policies and to deal with spontaneously arising interest group pressures.[9] The question is whether citizens used the corporatist system of institutionalized contact through official channels (such as contacting supervisors, mass organizations, or ombudsmen, or writing letters to the editor) to solve their problems. Furthermore, we ask whether that system of institutionalized contact continued to work for most people and whether among the young and more educated other means of interest articulation were coming into play. Our studies of both worker participation and general political participation deal with this issue (Chapters 6 and 8).

Also, in passing, we will consider whether democracy and free expression were very high on people's demands for change. During the 1989 student demonstrations many foreign observers concluded that this was a major demand (e.g., Schell 1988; Ogden et al. 1992; Calhoun 1994). In contrast, some studies of postsocialist societies in Eastern Europe suggest that democracy was not a major concern of many people (e.g., Mason 1995, p. 56). By observing how people ranked complaints during the upheavals of the late 1980s, we hope to get a better sense of the priority of democracy in people's list of demands. Also, in comparisons both among subgroups within China and between Taiwan and China, we will try to get a better sense of the forces that increased people's sense of political efficacy, or the ability to influence political decisions, and how that might be changing (Chapters 5 and 11).

9. E.g., Daniels (1971), Skilling (1971), Chirot (1972), Hough (1977), Nathan (1985), Lieberthal and Oksenberg (1988).

Our study of life chances examines whether at the height of the social-ist era in China, the promise of greater opportunity was realized. Perhaps more than in any other socialist society, China in its 1966–76 Cultural Revolution decade enacted an affirmative action program for the chil-dren of peasants and workers. Studies of other socialist societies suggest that as these societies mature and economic growth slows, socialist states fail in their promise to provide more mobility opportunity for the for-merly dispossessed – or for anyone, for that matter.[10] Studies of China also suggest that the Cultural Revolution's attempt at change by brute force was often counterproductive (e.g., Parish 1984; Whyte and Parish 1984; Davis 1990, 1992b; Deng and Treiman 1997). We will revisit this issue with fresh data, asking about both past trends in education and job opportunities and the new opportunities that may or may not be pro-vided by the spread of the market in the late 1980s and early 1990s (Chapter 3).

Our study of job satisfaction asks how people responded first to the socialist system and then to changes during market transformation. This builds on an earlier literature about workers in European socialist states and in China. Part of that literature is involved in a debate about the relative dependency and bargaining power of workers.[11] We revisit this debate, suggesting that much as in early industrialization in the United States, workers object to personalized dependency on supervisors (e.g., Edwards 1979). Combined with the need to wait many years until senior-ity created modest pay increases, the system of institutionalized control and weak financial incentives led to a generalized dissatisfaction with income and work opportunities -- even as these same workers express satisfaction with interpersonal relations among coworkers and with the fringe benefits attached to work. We examine these issues in discussions of popular reactions to reform, of reactions of workers and of civil ser-vants, and of workers in China in comparison to workers in Taiwan (Chapters 5–7 and 11). In the conclusion we return to themes from Marx and others about how growing dependency in large factory settings pro-

10. E.g., Connor (1979, 1991); Dobson (1980b); Matthews (1982); Lapidus (1983); Erikson and Goldthorpe (1994), p. 300.
11. Sabel and Stark (1982), Walder (1986), Kennedy and Bialecki (1989), Lu (1991), Burawoy and Krotov (1992), Burawoy and Lukacs (1992), Lin (1992), Crowley (1994), Fish (1995).

duces alienation among workers, first in the early industrial revolution and more recently in socialist factory settings.

Generalized Dependency

One of the major themes that emerges in this book is the generalized role of dependency and its debilitating influence on people in all walks of life. As already noted, this is a common theme in writings on European socialist states. Perhaps even more so than in Europe, Chinese socialist institutions forced people to live and work within large organizations, with hierarchical chains of command (Xu 1994b; Li 1995; Shaw 1996). The secondary consequence was to convince not only workers but also professionals and bureaucrats that one needed personal connections to superiors in order to get ahead in life (e.g., Yang 1994). "I didn't have the right personal connections" became an easy explanation of why one did not get ahead in life. People who were promoted were often suspected of having special connections. Non-party intellectuals, in particular, saw party members as having special access and special privileges. In part they did. The systematic way of maintaining party loyalty was through "principled particularism," with the party faithful and political activists being given more access to resources (Walder 1986). However, among the general population the suspicion often grew that party members with only modest educational qualifications were using their special access for personal gain and that those outside the party could have little control over policy decisions or the distribution of public resources. Most galling of all was the feeling that much of the exercise of party and bureaucratic authority was arbitrary – similar to Edwards's (1979) description of the reaction of workers to the arbitrary use of power by intermediate supervisors in the early industrialization of the West. By the 1980s this led to increasing complaints that China was ruled by a system of "personal whim" rather than predictable, uniformly applied "law." Or, in the parlance of Talcott Parsons, this was a system based not on universalistic rules but on particularistic social ties. We want to trace these types of behaviors, asking both whether party members and others had special access to policy making and to privileges and how the public reacted to the system of personalized dependency that this system tended to create.

Egalitarianism

Another theme emerging from this research concerns egalitarianism. In urban areas, socialist states were highly egalitarian – even if party and bureaucratic elites tried to compensate for their low salaries with in-kind benefits. Reviewing the legacy in Europe, Gerhard Lenski (1994) suggests that occasional hyperemphases on egalitarian income distribution had the negative byproduct of increasing school dropout by students unconvinced that education had a payoff in the labor market and of morale problems among professionals, engineers, and skilled workers who remained at very modest incomes. Our question will be whether these tendencies were also evident in China, and whether the return to market principles begins to reduce both hyperequality and the reduced incentives that can accompany that equality.

THE POLITICS OF MARKET TRANSFORMATION

The past decade has produced a proliferation of articles about the politics of market transformation, with a concentration of articles around the issue of whether redistributors (administrators) or producers (entrepreneurs, workers) are winning in the political battle for resources in reforming socialist and postsocialist states. The debates harken back to work by the Hungarian sociologist Ivan Szelényi, now at UCLA (1978, 1988). Echoing Karl Polanyi's 1944 work on the great transition from a communitarian, redistribution-based society to a market based, producer-based society, Szelényi implies that one of the biggest effects of market transformation is to reduce the rewards of former redistributors – administrators who, while redistributing societal goods among social groups in the socialist society, also pocketed a little extra for themselves. With the decline in redistribution, producers who actually do something for the market will begin to reap the greater rewards.

Beginning with this starting point, Nee (1989, 1992, 1996) suggests that China exhibits many signs of this market transformation, with the educated, entrepreneurs, and others close to production quickly overtaking local administrators in economic rewards. An opposing bargaining school disputes this claim, suggesting that effective bargaining by administrators continues, and that as late as the early 1990s both old redistributors (e.g., administrators) and new producers (e.g., entrepreneurs) could share benefits in an increasingly prosperous China (e.g., Logan and Bian 1993; Bian 1994a; Bian and Logan 1996). Recently, Szelényi and others studying Eastern Europe argue for a more differentiated analysis, paying attention to erosion from below (small entrepreneurs coming from society), erosion from above (state managers taking over spontaneously privatized state enterprises), and early- and late-market transformation (e.g., Róna-Tas 1994; Szelényi and Kostello 1996).

With new data from enterprises in Shanghai, Guthrie (2000) disagrees with the direction much of this debate takes. The debate assumes that if the market is truly liberalized, producers closest to the market will be the most highly rewarded. Guthrie suggests, in contrast, that often those closest to the market and the most subject to new competitive pressures will be the least rewarded. Failure, rather than success, may be the surest sign of the progressive spread of market forces. Following Walder (1992), Guthrie suggests that one must focus on micropolitics and the degree to which local administrative bureaus have the resources and attention span to closely monitor and subsidize local firms. We deal with the issue of market transformation in three new ways.

Market Rewards

First, we revisit the issue of market rewards. Our analysis validates much of what has been done before, with attention to income returns to human capital (education, experience), to administrative/redistributor jobs, to administrative rank of firm, and to private entrepreneurs. Compared with the standard analysis, however, we do several things differently. First, our data provide a monetary value on benefits (including housing and other fringe benefits). Much of the debate about continued administrative bargaining, which ostensibly shows the continued weakness of market forces, has been about these additional sources of incomes. By providing a monetary value for these extra sources of income, we help deal with the issue of whether these additional benefits are actually significant. Second, through comparisons to income returns according to education, experience, job, and type of work unit in Taiwan and other market societies, we deal with whether China's patterns are distinct when compared with "actually existing" market societies. Along with Guthrie (2000), we conclude that current work on market transformation is undertheorized. The bipolar distinction between producers and redistributors is simplistic. Intellectuals and others have been major winners in income in recent years, suggesting that additional forces are important. Similarly, the increasing returns to education are often less the result of the corrosive effects of the market than of intellectual groups winning the bargaining battle to get educational credentials certified as a ticket to better jobs. This, then, returns us to a discussion of credentialing and segmented labor markets in ways that are familiar to scholars working on actually existing market societies in the West (Chapters 3–5 and 11).

Attitudes

Second, we deal not just indirectly with the circumstantial evidence of changing income reward patterns but also directly with people's reactions to reform. We examine the attitudes of different types of "redistributors." If the market transformation arguments are correct, administrators in charge of political work should be distressed. Administrators and managers of a more technical bent, in more applied work, should be quite pleased with their new work situation. This is the technical transformation view that Róna-Tas (1994) suggests for Hungary. We examine whether this bifurcation of interests between different types of administrators occurs in China (Chapter 7).

As Polanyi (1944), Kluegel and Mateju (1995), and others suggest, if the market is to progress, many attitudes must change. We examine whether people are more accepting of reform, of pay rates, and of monetary acquisitiveness when they live in more rapidly growing areas, such as in the southern sunbelt with considerable light industry and foreign investment as opposed to the northeastern rustbelt, with its concentration of old state-owned heavy industry. If transformation is spreading, then people in places able to take advantage of the new nonstate economy should be pleased with their situations and the progress of reform, while people in other locations should be much more distressed with the progress of reform. If market transformation began to accelerate in the early 1990s, then attitudes in the early 1990s should be quite different from what they were in the late 1980s. We consider these issues when we examine popular reactions to reform and how these reactions compare with reactions of people in highly marketized Taiwan (Chapters 5, 7, 11).

Another way to state the objective of this part of the inquiry is that we pay close attention to group or class interests. Whether different group interests are being served will be judged not just by surface appearances of whether this or that group is getting more income but by their direct reports of whether their work situation, their income, and government reform efforts satisfy them.

Gender

Finally, we examine the consequences of market transformation for gender relations. The socialist social contract made many promises to women. Even if the results were less than ideal, in education, work, and income, many parts of this promise were kept. Whether the promise will continue to be kept under the new market social contract is highly uncertain. In both Europe and China, observers suggest that once freed from top-down administrative control, employers will hire fewer married women with young children. For women, freedom from the administrative admonition to work will mean that women who worked more out of necessity than personal volition will retreat to the home (e.g., Einhorn 1993). New market tendencies, with an emphasis on consumption, including women as beautified consumer objects, will have diverse effects. The advertising-fed drive to increase consumption might keep women in the labor force as they strive to keep up with their neighbors in buying sofas, TVs, and other consumer durables. Simultaneously, the increasing wages for men and a growing gap between male and female wages could encourage more women to withdraw from the labor force.

We examine these possibilities with data on women's position in both the labor market and at home. The material on women in the home examines whether high levels of work and income increased women's bargaining power in the home. In the West, increased female paid employment was unrelieved by husbands helping in the home. Gary Becker's (1981) model of husbands and wives rationally calculating their joint advantages seems poorly realized in market societies. No matter how much women work and bring income into the home, the cultural frame of women as producers in the home and men as producers outside the home continues (e.g., Berk 1985; Pleck 1985; Berado, Shehan, and Leslie 1987; Brines 1994). Nevertheless, Chinese society could be different, with an official ideology calling for gender equality and with women more nearly approaching men's incomes in most families. We examine the possibility of a unique pattern of domestic bargaining both with data on chores in homes in China and with comparable data on homes in market Taiwan. The striking set of comparisons says much about the differences between market and socialist systems and about the possible losses Chinese women might suffer if China moved more toward the Taiwan type of market system.

The remaining sections of this book are organized as follows: Chapter 2 in Part I provides an overview of the historical background that brought China to the post-1978 reform period. This is followed by a detailed section on group interests (Part II), which considers in succession the issue of economic returns among different groups (Chapters 3 and 4); attitudes among different occupation, education, and regional groups (Chapters 5–7); and evolving patterns of political participation (Chapter 8, with some of Chapter 6 also being relevant). In Part III, we consider the consequences of the transition for women both at work and in the home (Chapters 9 and 10). Part IV reviews the issues raised in earlier chapters, this time with comparisons to highly marketized Taiwan.

2

The Urban Social World

BEFORE studying group interests and market, we lay out four important background characteristics of the social world within which system changes occur. First, given the dramatic twists and turns of Chinese political history over the last four decades, much of Chinese society has a strong geologically layered quality. Within the lifetime of many of the people we study, there are very different experiences according to age or cohort. The oldest people will have come of age during the early 1950s, the golden age of Chinese Communism. Some middle-aged people will have come of age during the 1966–76 Cultural Revolution, a period that caused a strong revulsion against extreme idealism and political appeals among some – much like Crane Brinton's (1938) description of the French Revolution and other similar revolutions, where a strong thermidor reaction followed the extremes of a period of revolutionary radicalism and terror. Finally, the youngest groups came of age during the reform period, when things were very different from the period of high socialism. So, the geologically layered nature of Chinese urban population will be one of the important characteristics of Chinese society to keep in mind.

Second, China is now evolving from a caste to a class system of social organization. Chinese leaders may not have intended this, but over the years, desired or not, their policies produced a caste of privileged urbanites against a rural caste of have-nots. Those boundaries are beginning to soften, and society is adjusting slowly to this new reality. Most of this book is focused on the urban caste, that special group which was once entitled to a highly subsidized urban lifestyle.

Third, we want to describe some of the major institutional legacies of the socialist social contract. Unlike the redirection of an irrigation channel from one field to another, which can often be done by moving a single board, the rearrangement of the social contract from a socialist, planned to a market, open mode is a much messier process. There are many more separate "rivulets of water" or institutions that must be changed, and many more interest groups behind each rivulet, eager to return the water to old paths. This is the aspect of socialist societies that causes Kornai (1992) to suggest that gradual reform in socialist systems is impossible. China's rapid progress over the last fifteen years seems to prove the more pessimistic predictions about reform wrong.

Fourth, consumption and media patterns are changing rapidly. Urban China is turning into a consumer society, with the ordinary citizen pursuing different goals than just a few years ago. Given the rapid increase in TV programming (including satellite broadcasts from Hong Kong and elsewhere), books, newspapers, and magazines, and the ability to fax and e-mail around the world, the chance for forming a critical stance on major issues of the day is much greater than ever before.

HISTORICAL ERAS

Although the physical and behavioral environment from centuries ago continues to influence Chinese life today, the geologically layered quality of the Chinese urban experience began from the very different experiences of different cohorts. For the oldest, those experiences began in the pre-1949, pre-socialist era.

Pre-1949

The pre-1911 Chinese empire included an elaborate urban structure. Built almost exclusively around administrative centers, China's widely dispersed cities and towns were nodes of administrative and commercial activities. Well-known examples of such administrative centers include Xi'an, Nanjing, and Beijing. Unlike contemporary Chinese cities, imperial cities were minimally distinguished from the surrounding countryside, and seasonal and lifetime flows of population from countryside to cities and back again were tremendous (Skinner 1977). Most of today's cities, and much of the rank size distribution of large and small urban nodes, trace back to this ancient history.

Western contact, starting most intensely with the Opium War of 1842 and its aftermath, affected Chinese cities. As opposed to the even growth of cities and towns across the Chinese landscape, coastal cities were given a fresh boost from foreign trade and the presence of special foreign extraterritorial zones in the major cities. Shanghai, a new city, was perhaps the epitome of everything good and bad about these new trends. At once the home of opulence and poverty, of hyper-Westernism and traditional Chinese working-class neighborhoods, Shanghai came to represent many of the dangers of bourgeois traits that Communist leaders sought to avoid in later decades. It was only in the 1980s and 1990s, with the reopening of China to foreign trade and foreign invest-ment, that these old, coastal cities began to return to the growth patterns established before 1949. Examples of other port cities that developed under Western contact include Qingdao, Tianjin, Guangzhou (Canton), and Hong Kong.

The First Five-Year Plan

The chronological layers in the Chinese urban experience involve several distinct periods after 1949, starting with the first five-year plan, which moved China's cities sharply away from old patterns of development. With the help of Soviet advisors, China established its centrally planned economic system in the mid-1950s.[1] Following Stalin's model of eco-nomic development, this new system set economic development goals in five-year plans, starting with the first plan for 1953–57. The Stalinist model emphasized heavy over light industry and industrial development over agriculture. Fully 63 percent of the total state investment during the first five-year plan went into capital construction, of which almost two-thirds went to the ministries of heavy industry, fuel industry, and the machine building industry. Agriculture, including water conservation, received only about one-twentieth of total capital construction invest-ment. Subsequent plans followed much of the initial, heavy industry-intensive model with most of the investment funds going to cities. Initially, China experienced rapid industrialization, a high rate of growth, and an expansion of employment opportunities in cities. Including all sectors, annual industrial growth averaged an astounding 18 percent from 1953 to 1957 (SSB 1993a, pp. 97, 413). In line with the Stalinist model borrowed from the Soviet Union, urban living standards were

---

1. For additional references to the political and economic history that follows, see Riskin (1987) and Lieberthal (1995).

highly subsidized. With the return to political stability and social order after a century of political turmoil and social unrest, many people could feel that this was the "golden age" of Chinese socialism. Even when they disagreed with specifics, many groups felt that they should go along with the new social and political programs (e.g., Link 1992). In later years, older people remain among the most satisfied with the current political and social order. Some of that satisfaction traces back to this cohort's formative experiences in the early 1950s, when they were in the early years of their adult work life.

The Anti-Rightist Campaign

The optimism, satisfaction, and unity among Chinese of all backgrounds was not to last. In an episode that pitted the party against intellectuals, a legacy of distrust was created that persists to this day (e.g., Link 1992). When Mao said, "Let a hundred flowers blossom, let a hundred schools of thought contend" in 1956, he thought that the intellectuals would be mobilized and follow the party as the peasants did in the revolution. The intellectuals (artists, writers, scientists) were expected to help the Communist Party purify its organization and membership by criticizing bureaucratism and pro-Soviet revisionism and orthodoxy. The intellectuals not only responded, but quickly went beyond their initially designated targets. After criticizing bureaucratism, corruption, and individual party leader's work styles, they began to question the legitimacy of the party's leadership. They criticized the party for betraying its revolutionary tradition, monopolizing political power, and leading China into repression and dictatorship. Fearing things had gotten out of hand, the party responded in the summer of 1957 by labeling the most outspoken critics "right-wingers" or "rightists." By 1958, some 400,000 to a million intellectuals, including many party members, were labeled rightists.[2] Many were demoted, stripped of normal privileges, and sent for varying lengths of time to remote areas to engage in physical labor. In the early 1980s, feeling the need for intellectuals in its new modernization drive, the party apologized to intellectuals and restored the former jobs and privileges of rightists. Though many intellectuals remained highly nation-

2. Estimates of the number of people labeled rightists range from 400,000 to 700,000 (Fairbank 1986, p. 293) to over a million (Meisner 1986, p. 200).

alistic and prone to Deng Xiaoping's call to build a new, modernized country, many old hurts could not be forgiven (Link 1992). Rebuilding of trust was no mean task, and as we shall see, into the 1990s, it continued to affect the reactions of intellectuals.

The Great Leap Forward

The Communist victory in China was based on mass mobilization, using politically mobilized peasants to stave off militarily superior Japanese aggressors during World War II and then Chiang Kai-shek's Nationalist soldiers in the 1946–49 civil war. After 1949, Mao believed that the same approach could be used in economic development. The magic power of the people, once mobilized, would be more effective than new technology and managerial innovations. By relying on the power of people, China could surpass major industrial countries within a short time. In the countryside, people's communes were established where peasants worked and lived collectively. In urban areas, everyone was mobilized to participate in industrial production. They were told that if everyone contributed, China would make a great leap forward into Communism where no one would ever have to worry about not having enough material goods. Since the basis of industry was iron and steel, people collected any metal parts that they could find in their household and set up iron-casting furnaces in their backyards. Eager to please their supervisors, local cadres often exaggerated production figures. By 1959, most of these "backyard steel mills" had been shut down due to insufficient quality control.

The Great Leap Forward was a political setback for Mao. Its real beneficiaries were the urban areas. The industrial bias increased, particularly in heavy industry. The number of employees in urban state and collective enterprises doubled in a few short years in the late 1950s and early 1960s. Part of this increase drew on a sudden mobilization of women into new neighborhood-run collective enterprises, the successors to the backyard steel furnaces.[3] The long-term result was a rapid increase in the labor force under central and regional planning, and a shift of virtually all able-bodied women into the urban labor force. In this

---

3. SSB (1993a, p. 97). According to another estimate, state enterprise employees tripled from 7.48 million in 1957 to 23.16 million in 1958 (Yang and Li 1980).

sense, the Great Leap Forward had a long-lasting impact on urban life in China.

The Cultural Revolution

Beginning in 1966 and ending with his death in 1976, the Cultural Revolution was Mao's last grand attempt to keep Chinese socialism on a populist track. In a backlash against the inevitable bureaucratization inherent in the Stalinist model of development, anything related to hierarchy and traditional authority was attacked – including not only bureaucratic leaders and their organizations but also Confucian values, literature, and art – anything seen as impeding China's march toward a utopian revolutionary future. Much like during its revolutionary predecessor, the reign of terror and virtue during the French Revolution, the human toll was enormous. Many families were separated and the entire middle to upper levels of administration and management were destroyed. Traditional values, family, and social order were threatened.

In the short run, the Cultural Revolution achieved many of its intended effects. At its peak, it provided many opportunities for political newcomers. Many top-level managers were replaced by blue-collar workers, peasants, and soldiers, resulting in greater upward mobility. China also achieved a high level of social and economic equality. Today, one often thinks more of the subsequent popular backlash against the hyperpoliticization of the Cultural Revolution. But some legacies remain, including a longing for egalitarianism that sometimes surfaces in worker discussions and a sense of permanent loss among middle-aged people whose education and careers were sacrificed on the altar of revolutionary utopianism.

The Reform Era

The reform era began in 1978 with the Communist Party's decision in the National Party Congress of that year to launch a new drive for economic modernization. Following a few years of successful reform in agriculture, the party tackled the much more difficult problem of urban reform in 1984. During the second period (1984–89), urban reform programs, even when introduced piecemeal, were sweeping, eventually including changes in enterprise structure, prices, finance, banking, housing, labor markets, welfare, pensions, and wages. As we shall see, these economic reforms were matched, sometimes haltingly, by reforms in the bureaucracy, polity, and mass media availability. By late 1988 and early 1989, the economy was overheated. An uncontrolled investment drive created surplus demand and inflation. Bureaucratic profiteering was rampant. Following an economic austerity program and the crackdown on urban demonstrations in 1989, economic and political reforms slowed. In the third period of reform (1989–92), state control of the economy was strengthened and political freedom was reduced. In 1992, after Deng Xiaoping's widely publicized speech during his southern tour, China entered the third period of post-Mao reform (1992–97). Deng's speech emphasized renewed efforts at market reform and political control, a neoauthoritarian approach typical of some East and Southeast Asian countries. In the initial stage of the post-Deng era (1997 to present), China's new leaders are continuing this developmental model. Thus, by the late 1990s, China has experienced several stages of reform, and urban life is quite different from what it was two decades ago.[4]

FROM CASTE TO CLASS

Beneath the episodic changes in political and economic policy that help set one era and one cohort off from another, there was a much slower set of changes in the basic institutions that underlay urban life. The story of the evolution of these institutions and how they shaped life chances helps complete the story of the environment that shapes urban life both before and after reform.

Classical Administrative Measures

The first five-year plan introduced institutions with many unintended consequences. One of these helped produce what might be called urban aristocracy, which was similar to the Latin American experience. Historically, countries in Latin America have had some of the most socially and economically distorted policies of all developing countries. As Collier and Collier (1991) report, these policies began with a series of critical junctures in the early 1900s, when a politically precocious urban working

---

4. For an account of the reform era under Deng Xiaoping, see Baum (1996).

and middle class caused so much turmoil that the government was forced to respond. The response was to provide government-guaranteed protection and benefits in return for labor peace and social order. The resulting distortions in policy created a labor aristocracy with incomes much higher than would have occurred from market forces alone. To support the artificially inflated urban living standards, agriculture was stripped of resources. The resulting gulf between urban and rural living standards attracted hordes of people into cities. Once they got to cities, however, the migrants found that a heavily regulated, highly subsidized formal sector provided few jobs for migrants. The result was a large informal sector that came to account for as much as half the labor force of most large cities. Living in slums and surviving by their wits in an unprotected economy of jitney buses, illegal storefronts, and streetside peddling, this despised sector nevertheless contributed significantly to Latin American growth.[5]

Adopting many Soviet programs wholesale in the first five-year plan, Chinese planners quickly created an urban labor aristocracy that was very expensive to maintain.[6] Though take-home salaries were highly constricted, urban workers in the formal state sector had access to many subsidized benefits, including almost cost-free housing, medical care, pensions, subsidized staples, and other perquisites, that soon made real urban incomes almost double nominal take home pay. Peasants soon got the news, and flooded into cities in the middle and late 1950s, particularly when agriculture collapsed in the 1958–61 Great Leap Forward (see Fig. 2.1).

Realizing the expensive quandary they had created, by 1958 planners passed laws establishing a sturdy "bamboo wall" between two great new castes in society. On the one side were those born of agricultural parents – with parental status defined by one's position in 1954 when the unified

---

5. See DeSoto (1989), Dornbusch and Edwards (1989), Nelson (1990), Braun and Loayza (1994), Loayza (1994), and Banerji et al. (1995).
6. For more detailed references to the history that follows, see Whyte and Parish (1984), Kirkby (1985), Kojima (1987), Kwok, Parish, and Yeh (1990), Naughton (1995), Chen and Parish (1996). For an overview of contemporary urban issues in English, see Gudin and Southall (1993) and Davis et al. (1995). In Chinese, see Xiaoye Zhe's (1989) concise summary in the useful series of booklets on social issues by Yunkang Pan (1989), Lu and Li (1997), the annual "blue cover" series on social issues by the Sociology Institute of the Chinese Academy of Sciences, e.g., Jiang, Lu, and Shan (1995) and Ru, Lu, and Shan (1998).

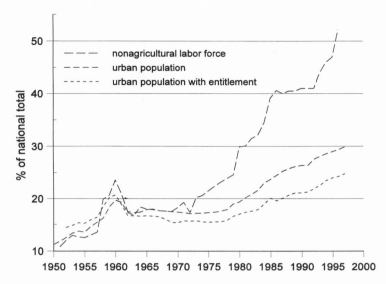

Figure 2.1 Urbanization in China by year. Source: PRI 1987, 1993, 1996; SSB 1994a, 1995a, 1996, 1997a, 1998c.

grain purchasing and marketing mandate was enacted. On the other side were those born of nonagricultural parents. If one was born on the privileged, nonagricultural side of the bamboo wall, one was entitled to a host of urban benefits, including attending urban schools, being part of the urban job assignment process, subsidized housing, subsidized grain, and hardship allowances. Typically, those in the urban job assignment process got a job in the state sector, which brought with it additional benefits, including free health care, disability insurance, pensions, and a host of other allowances.[7]

When they realized the budget-busting possibilities of these extensive entitlements, planners made several administrative adjustments. One,

7. The many benefits of urban entitlement led to several changes in behavior. Entitled urban registration often became a criterion for marriage decisions, with marriage to an urbanite sometimes (not always) providing an urban "green card" for rural residents to move into cities. In the popular consciousness there is also a hierarchy of cities. Residency in more developed cities such as Beijing, Shanghai, Tianjin, and Guangzhou, for example, brings access to better jobs and benefits, and, thus, these places are more desired and fought over than less developed cities like Xi'an or Lanzhou.

starting in 1962, was to enforce the 1958 migration law, which allowed migration to cities only after a long approval process. That approval process was more rigorous in China than in any other socialist state, given the continued tight control over jobs by the labor bureau, the increasing rigor of the household registration system run by the neighborhood civil and police offices (see below), and the increasingly long list of rationed goods that could be secured only when one had a legal permit to live in the city. In short, China took the Latin American urban protection program and the program that the Soviet Union wanted to implement and did it more effectively. Very few people were allowed to either move into cities or to gain urban entitlements (see Fig. 2.1).

The second administrative step, starting about 1963, was to take away revenue from towns and small cities. Many towns and small cities were deincorporated and forced to return to a near-rural status that gave them few autonomous revenue rights. Among the remaining towns and cities, much of the control over local revenues was stripped and passed to higher levels. The result of both measures was that many towns and cities went into a fifteen-year hibernation. The consequences were extraordinary, and very different from anything that the European socialist states had experienced. As a percent of the total population, the urban population virtually stagnated in the fifteen years following 1963 (see Fig. 2.1). Except for hidden subsidies, urban living standards stagnated as well. Nominal take-home pay was frozen for most workers, and investment in housing slowed. As a result, by 1978 cities were dreary places and there was growing discontent in the urban population. All this created an urban population eager to accept Deng Xiaoping's and other leaders' post-1978 call for economic modernization and liberalization.

The third administrative step was to send 16 million youth "down" to the countryside. Much as in Latin America, and exacerbated by the Stalinist-type emphasis on capital intensive investment in heavy industry, the successive five-year plans generated too few jobs. Then, with the increase of women into the labor force during and following the 1958–61 Great Leap Forward, urban youth found increasingly fewer jobs once they got out of school. Youth unemployment began to be a problem by the mid-1960s, and helped fuel the student discontent that energized the Cultural Revolution. Unfortunately for many idealistic youth, planners fortuitously found an ideological solution to their employment problem in the new program to send youth to the countryside to be educated by the peasants. Temporarily, this helped solve the employment problem and reduced the growth of urban expenses – though, by expelling urban youth, it also caused much consternation among urban parents.

A fourth administrative measure, which became popular later, was to encourage rural industrialization, so that peasants would remain in their rural homes while changing occupations. In the ideal plan of urbanites who wanted to protect their privileges, industrialization could thus proceed without the usual costs of urbanization. To some extent this plan succeeded. In the late 1970s and at an accelerating pace in the 1980s, the proportion of people in nonfarm work grew much faster than the registered population in cities (see Fig. 2.1). Whether this provides a long-term solution, or is only the calm before the storm, remains to be seen.[8]

By 1978, there was tremendous popular pressure to change many of these extraordinary administrative measures, particularly the first three. Before examining the post-1978 changes, we should explore further the unusual organization of urban life that allowed the tightly controlled system to continue for so long. Even now, as restrictions in cities loosen, significant parts of this organization remain.

Neighborhood and Work Unit Organization

The system of tight controls over migration could succeed only because, to a degree unusual even for socialist societies, China's neighborhoods and work units were both tightly organized. Either directly under the government of small cities or indirectly under the districts of larger cities, all residents are organized by neighborhood. Each neighborhood has a paired civilian neighborhood committee (*jiedao banshi chu*) and police office that work in close coordination. By 1990, China had 5,099 neighborhood committees in 447 cities.[9] Each neighborhood committee has a staff of about 50 people, controlling a population of approximately 20,000 in 3,000 to 5,000 households and 15 to 25 residents' councils (*jumin weiyuan hui*) (Li 1994). With few full-time employees, most staff

8. In Taiwan, successful early rural industrialization soon gave way to rapid urbanization. And, in China, rural industrialization is so concentrated in pockets that it will soon produce new towns and cities with many of the social infrastructure needs and social problems of older cities – absent only a population entitled to full urban benefits (see Blank and Parish 1990; Parish 1994). For recent developments, see Wang (1995a).
9. The total number of cities was 668 in 1997 (SSB 1998a, p. 363).

members in the residents' council are retired persons working part-time. Functions of the residents' council include supervising birth control, cleaning the sidewalks, and mediating interneighbor and intrafamily conflict. Other functions include providing services to the community, such as care for the elderly without pensions, the chronically sick who are bedridden, and the blind, the handicapped, and mentally ill outpatients. Another important function of the residents' council is to work with the public security bureau in crime prevention. It is common to see retired women with a red armband patrolling the streets in Chinese cities. Widely dispersed and knowing everyone in the community, these women help ensure that any stranger will be noticed and sometimes even questioned. Such a high level of mobilized neighborhood watch is one reason that China previously had low crime rates (Whyte and Parish 1984). It is the vigilance of these committees and the previously extensive rationing system administered through these committees that helped keep illegal migrants out of cities before 1978.

Among the new challenges in the late 1990s facing neighborhood committees and residents' councils is the shrinking state budget and the pressure to generate additional funds through self-initiated economic activities. They are spending more time regulating the economic and social activities of an increasing number of rural migrant workers. As more and more state sector workers are being laid off and are looking for new jobs, neighborhood committees and residents' councils are also taking over some of the welfare responsibilities traditionally performed by work units (see below).

The second arm of neighborhood organization is the public security bureau (*gonganju*), which has a branch office (*paichusuo*) in each neighborhood. A representative of the public security branch office is automatically a member of the neighborhood committee. The security officials take a leading role in mobilizing residents for crime control. The public security branch office keeps the official household registration of every resident (*hukou*). Under central planning, when food and other necessities were rationed and subsidized, urban residents could get ration coupons only with their urban registration cards.[10]

---

10. The household register, by the way, is also the sampling frame for all the surveys used in this book. This means, of course, that the surveys are capturing the formal, registered population and not recent migrants who are absent from the register.

Since virtually all adult males and females are at work, the work unit (*danwei*) is also very important in most people's lives.[11] Traditionally, each workplace was a self-contained unit, and each work unit played a vital role in almost every aspect of one's life. It provided employment for offspring under the replacement system (*dingti*), medical insurance, labor protection, pension, housing, and direct subsidies. The work unit acted as parent, caretaker, mediator, and even matchmaker. During much of the past several decades, it had not only assigned housing to its employees, and provided gloves, hats, shoes, soap, meat, rice, and cooking oil, but also granted permission to get married, to get divorced, and to have a child. An employee in China was much more involved with his or her work unit than an individual in the average market economy. Because work units had differential access to housing and benefits, there was considerable competition to get into the best work units (Bian 1994a). Besides being an economic and social unit, a work unit was also a political unit where government policy was implemented, loyalty to the party was promoted, political mobilization was carried out, public opinion was collected, and voting took place. As we shall see, the broad functions of the work unit created vertical dependencies between workers and their work unit superiors (see Chapters 5, 6, and 8).

The importance of work units began to fade in the 1990s. With more and more public sector workers being laid off, local governments and neighborhood committees are taking over the traditional welfare responsibilities. Assuming continued growth of the private sector, housing markets, socialized labor insurance and medical care, and multiple income sources, the role of the work unit will further decline. This will affect many behaviors and attitudes that originated in the dependency-inducing nature of traditional work units.

Migrants and the Informal Sector

Though significant aspects of the above system remain, much of the control of the system has lessened during reform. Previously, unless one was a legal, entitled member of a neighborhood and work unit, it was impossible to live in a city for very long. However, with the return of

11. The secondary literature on work units includes Xu (1994b), Li (1995), and Shaw (1996).

peasant markets to cities, and the gradual abandonment of rationing, citizens could again live in cities without a legal permit. The bamboo curtain began to have holes, as officials either gave temporary work permits or simply looked the other way. According to the 1995 census, for example, 13 percent of the city residents in Beijing, Tianjin, and Shanghai did not have local registration, and more than three-quarters of these out-of-towners were from rural areas (Census Office 1997, pp. 538–43). The urban/rural caste barrier, while still officially in place, had begun to weaken.[12]

Again, much like the informal sector in Latin American cities or the large communities of illegal migrants in other countries, the host communities had a love/hate relationship with the new flood of quasilegal migrants. With the acceleration of economic growth, including a huge construction boom, cities rapidly went from labor surplus to labor shortage, particularly in the more menial construction, transport, textile factory, and service jobs that the privileged urban residents disdained. This increased flow of menial laborers and service providers from the countryside was beneficial for residents.

Continuing the Latin American analogy, although the large 3.1 : 1 gap (SSB 1998a, p. 324) in living standards attracted a surplus of new peasant laborers into cities, cities were reluctant either to build the infrastructure or give migrants the legal access to urban amenities that would deter the emergence of social problems. Much like Latin America, the informal sector is growing rapidly. With no legal rights to urban housing, peasants in the city are forced to live an uncertain existence on construction sites, in marketing stalls, on the streets, in rented rooms, or in makeshift barrios on the edges of cities. Whole rural villages have relocated themselves to suburban barrios, where they sometimes have a law unto themselves. Police and other outsiders dare not enter. Thus, finally, with the relaxation of organization controls and growing labor demand in cities, the Latin American-type pressures that were set in place in the first five-year plan are coming to full fruition.

Much as in Latin America, there are periodic cries to expel the newcomers. Urbanites complain that migrants are using scarce public resources. Much like privileged urbanites elsewhere, those in China complain of the migrants contributing to bad sanitation and a perceived

12. For references, see Solinger (1995a, b).

explosion of crime.[13] In the traditional pattern, complaints about using local schools and medical facilities will soon follow. Dorothy Solinger (1995a) predicts that this flood of migrants will soon cause a collapse of the classical urban "public goods" regime, with its subsidized living standards for a select entitled population. However, the history of Latin American cities suggests that these types of dual regimes, with a sharp gap between the haves and the have-nots, could last for decades.

Of course, many of those in the daily city-directed flood of bicyclists and bus riders are not long-distance migrants but simply daily commuters from the surrounding countryside. These people, perhaps a third of all urban residents, though officially "in" the city are not "of" the city in that they do not share in the full entitled, nonagricultural status. But they, like many people who remain in small towns and villages, have increasingly abandoned agriculture, leading the total nonagricultural labor force to rise to half of all workers in China (see Fig. 2.1, large dashed line).

Though lagging behind the growth of nonagricultural employment, urban growth is accelerating (Fig. 2.1, medium dashed line). This growth was caused in part by the early 1980s rescission of the restrictive rules on town and city incorporation and revenue retention. With this liberalization of the rules, a horde of new towns and cities sprang up. And, with new revenue retention rules, these places once again came to life. The administrative machinations used to get revenue-enhancing incorporation as a city or town make it difficult to know with any certainty what the true urban population is in China today. But it appears to be near 30 percent, which is the figure we show in Figure 2.1.

Finally, the trend that continues to lag furthest behind is the figure for "entitled population," those urbanites who are entitled to full urban subsidies. There is continued quibbling about the rules (e.g., PRI 1993, p. 11). But to this point, central planners have resisted the efforts of most groups to get on the full urban entitlement program. As a result, the proportion of the population entitled to full urban benefits was still only about 25 percent in 1997 – or only about four-fifths of everyone who lives

13. For example, in a 1997 survey in Beijing, Shanghai, Guangzhou, Chongqing, and Xiamen, a majority of urban residents in these cities complained about the rising number of crimes related to rural migrants (65%, 65%, 62%, 50%, and 53%, respectively). See Yuan and Fan (1998, p. 195). For further examples of blaming migrants for water shortage, high prices, crime, and crowded transportation, see Solinger (1999).

in cities. Thus, urban caste membership persists, although with the increasing diversity of economic opportunities available in cities, being a member of the entitled caste means less now than it once did.

The Private Sector and New Class Positions

One additional reason caste position means less is that there is a new class of private entrepreneurs and workers, some of whom are doing extremely well with none of the usual state benefits. Before 1978, virtually the entire urban labor force was in state or collective work units. Subsequently, to help create more employment opportunities, the private sector was restored to legality. This sector started with self-employed workers and family enterprises hiring seven or fewer employees. This self-employed, or "private household" (*geti*), sector was in time joined by a newly legitimated private sector (*siying*), hiring eight employees or more. Now the slightly larger private firms are growing as rapidly as the smaller "private households." Besides this domestic private sector, there is a rapidly expanding joint venture sector. The joint ventures include collaborative investments not only by European, American, and Japanese companies but also by a host of companies from Hong Kong, Taiwan, and Macao. Faced with labor shortages and rising labor costs, these regions have been eager to move many labor-intensive operations to China. The result of these developments is that both domestic and foreign private sectors have grown rapidly. Though the traditional state and collective sectors remain the dominant employers, these sectors are shrinking. By 1996, domestic private endeavors and joint ventures together employed nearly 17 percent of the urban labor force, as compared with only 3 percent in the beginning of urban reform in 1984 (Fig. 2.2). And, among new hires, the trends are even more striking. As compared with only 6 percent in 1980, 50 percent of the newly hired in 1997 were in neither traditional state nor traditional collective enterprises but in newly emerging sectors (SSB 1998a, p. 156). Assuming these trends continue, the new class of private workers will become an ever more dominant force in urban life.

In the early days of reform, private self-employed households were looked down upon because of their low status as compared with the traditional public sector. Over two decades later, the self-employed, domestic private, and foreign joint venture sectors have thrived. People

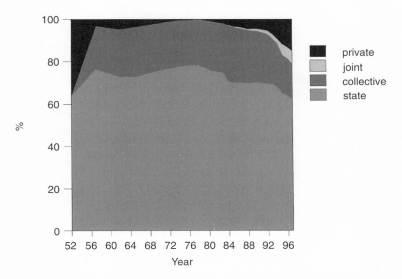

Figure 2.2 Urban employment by ownership and year. Notes: "Private" sector includes both private enterprises and self-employed (*geti*); "joint" firms include jointly owned, share holding, foreign funded, and other types of ownership. Source: SSB 1998a, pp. 130–31.

not only have the possibility of quitting their state jobs to work as street vendors or in small domestic enterprises, but they can also work for many joint venture and foreign companies that pay much higher salaries. The more successful of this new class of Chinese urban professionals (Chuppies) in private business and foreign companies travel by plane, go to fancy restaurants, drive luxurious cars, and live in extravagant apartments. The result is that more people are debating between a low-income but stable state job and a high-income but no-benefit and low-security private job. For many, the benefits and job security offered by the public sector seem too important to lose, but for many others the opportunities to make money in the private sector are too seductive.[14]

It seems, then, that the private sector cannot help but blossom in the

14. According to a 1993 survey, the prior occupations of urban private businessmen included professionals and administrators (34%), manual and service sector workers (33%), farmers (17%), self-employed (9%), and other (7%). Over half (56%) had been in the state sector (raw data).

years ahead. To the extent that it does, China will complete its move from administratively determined, inherited caste position to market-determined class position as a major determinant of life chances. We are familiar with this transition path in East Asia. It is precisely the path followed by Taiwan, where a dominant state-enterprise sector was eventually overwhelmed in efficiency, size, and prosperity by an initially informal, but now increasingly formalized, private sector (Amsden 1985; Ranis 1992). If successful, China could eventually move from its current Latin American model to a new Taiwan model of development. In the Taiwan model, the old state sector will not completely go away, but work in that sector will become increasingly less appealing and less a consideration in making calculations about how best to improve one's life chances (see Chapter 12).

THE SOCIALIST SOCIAL CONTRACT

China's classical socialist contract with the urban population promised basic living standards and a long list of other benefits in return for political quiescence. Unlike in developed market societies, the guarantee for basic living standards was provided not through unemployment benefits, public aid, or other generally available welfare benefits. In developed market societies, these kinds of last-resort safety nets provide some flexibility in labor markets, letting workers endure spells of unemployment while the worker moves from job to job or as the society experiences economic downturns. In socialist systems, in contrast, the social contract provided not a last-resort safety net but full employment for all entitled urban residents. Safety net-like benefits, including pensions, health care, and disability benefits, were not a universal human right but benefits that were earned through work in a formal, state-sector job.[15] As one moves away from lifetime, highly secure state sector employment, new institutions need to replace the old ones.

Job Security

China's use of employment security to ensure basic living standards was in part shared with the European socialist states. However, those states

15. E.g., Osborn (1970), George and Manning (1980), and Millar and Wolchik (1994).

long ago accommodated themselves to interfirm labor mobility, and more European housing and social services were provided by city-level administrative units. China was more extreme in limiting most people to lifetime employment in a single work unit, and in providing housing and many other social benefits through work units. Chinese employees had come to treat their work units as having lifetime obligations to the employee.[16] All that must now change.

In the 80 percent of urban jobs that were in the public sector, lifetime job security was the rule. Once one got a state job, it became an "iron rice bowl" (*tie fanwan*): No one could be laid off. Though an employee's malfeasance was disciplined within the work unit, the employee could not be fired. Even if one committed a minor crime and served a sentence in prison, one was in theory entitled to come back when the prison term was over. Job security not only applied to each employee, but at certain times could also be inherited by a single child entering the state work unit the parent had abandoned (see Bian 1994a). One set of consequences, of course, was a decline in labor flexibility, discipline, and incentives.

To help solve these problems, Chinese reformers introduced several new measures. In 1986, lifetime tenure was replaced by a new system of successive five-year labor contracts. Though many contracts still got renewed automatically regardless of performance and though older workers remained exempt from this new system, 52 percent of all state sector workers were on contracts by the end of 1997 (SSB 1998a, p. 148). The labor bureau's authority to make appointments was passed down to work units. And, as we see in the next chapter, the early retirement program of the early 1980s created many new vacancies at the top of work units in ways that encouraged intra- and interfirm labor mobility. Also, so as to delink welfare benefits from specific firms, thereby encouraging interfirm mobility, plans were under way in the mid-1990s to sell off work unit housing and to move pension plan management to units above the level of the firm. Consistent with these changes, interfirm labor mobility increased in the early 1980s. In one survey of state firms, while only half the firms had even had anyone successfully resign by 1980, a full three-fourths had suffered resignations by 1986.[17]

16. E.g., Tidrick and Chen (1987), Granick (1990), Lu (1991), and Xie (1991).
17. Calculated from raw data (Chinese Academy of Social Sciences 1986 Enterprise Survey).

Fearing a rapid expansion of welfare budgets, cities often pressured firms to stay open despite imminent bankruptcy. Firm managers, in turn, often feared completely open labor markets, since given the balance of scarcities in the labor market they could anticipate their skilled workers and technicians leaving for better-paying jobs, while they were stuck with the less productive, unskilled workers. The workers, of course, knew this and responded accordingly. For example, when asked in the mid-1980s whether the government should guarantee jobs, the proportion decreased regularly as one moved from those in blue-collar, manual jobs (61%) to those in white-collar, technical jobs (49%) (ESRCC 1986, pp. 94, 96).

Social Security

Changes were also occurring gradually in social security. Under the regulations in 1990, the work unit typically remained responsible for providing retirement pensions. After retirement, one receives 100 percent salary if one began working before 1949 and 75 percent if one worked continuously for twenty years or more.[18] As life expectancy increased and workers matured, pensions became more of a burden on work units. For example, on average, while 33 workers supported each pensioner in 1978, this figure had dropped to 13 for each pensioner in 1985 (Davis 1988). Currently, the government is experimenting with new retirement funds to which everyone must contribute. While three-fourths of all urban employees and retirees were still under the old pension system in 1994, one-fourth of them were already in new, experimental programs that pool pension funds among a much larger risk group. Work units are also required to contribute 1 percent of their wage expenditures to public unemployment insurance programs. Currently, over 90 percent of employees in state and collective enterprises are covered by unemployment insurance.[19] Thus, despite considerable wavering and many false starts, China's cities are gradually moving to a social security

18. Editorial Group (1990, p. 230). There are lesser amounts if one worked fewer years, but since virtually all men and women work continuously, most will get full benefits for having worked at least twenty years.
19. For an account of the halting character of these reforms by someone from the Ministry that handles welfare issues, see Chen (1995).

system more attuned with the labor mobility, unemployment, and other issues of a market society.

Public Housing

Although basic housing is made available to all, housing remains a serious problem.[20] The half of all housing owned by work units acts as a serious drain on firm budgets and manager time, with managers or their assistants listening endlessly to complaints from employees about housing conditions and housing assignments. Inter-firm mobility or the absence of mobility is often determined as much by housing availability as by other productivity considerations. With so much housing tied to work units, people working in rich work units are overhoused, while those in poor work units remain in near-slum conditions (Lee 1988; Bian 1994a). With only nominal rents in any kind of housing, true housing costs are multiple times what the average renter pays.

The system has several unanticipated consequences. Bribery of housing assignment committee members is reputedly common. High-ranking officials get more living space. Some get an apartment at each place they work. After three job changes, the family will have three apartments for the parents and their children. Given the only nominal rents, some people hold onto vacant apartments for long periods while other families have no place to stay. In common with other socialist states, apartment quality also deteriorates over time. Rents are so low that they typically cover no more than half of maintenance costs. The result is that both cosmetic and serious structural problems are often neglected until the housing is unlivable.

The final consequence is that despite massive housing investment since 1978, many residents remain dissatisfied with their housing. In a 1991 Economic System Reform Institute of China housing survey in forty cities, only 30 percent were satisfied with the current housing system, and fully 42 percent were dissatisfied. Among the dissatisfied, the reasons for dissatisfaction included corruption in housing assignment (45%), inferior housing (18%), lack of choice (15%), and unfair and irrational distribution (12%).[21] This high level of dissatisfaction persisted despite

---

20. For references in English, see Tolley (1991), Xie (1991), Chen and Gao (1993a), and Bian et al. (1995). For administrative assignment of housing, see Tang (1996c).
21. Raw data, ESRIC (1991). See Appendix B, Table B1.

the massive investment in housing that helped China recover from years of housing neglect. By 1991, there had been a significant recovery from the Stalinist-style underinvestment in housing that had caused floor space per capita to shrink from 4.5 to 3.6 square meters per person in 1978 (see also Table 2.1 for improvement in urban housing during reform). Yet much of the old discontent remained.

One proposal to solve these housing problems is to marketize housing – either by selling housing to employees at distress prices, as some work units are doing, or by gradually raising rents to near market levels.[22] Statistics show that these plans had a long way to go in the early 1990s. In the same 1991 Housing Survey, 42 percent lived in publicly owned housing, another 42 percent in work unit housing, 10 percent in private, 3 percent in rented, and 4 percent in borrowed housing.[23] Instead of shrinking, implicit rent subsidies expanded during the early years of reform. Only about 5 percent of monthly salary went to rent in 1993. Although rent increased from 0.41 yuan/m^2 in 1993 to 0.55 yuan/m^2 in 1994, the percentage of rent in total monthly salary was reduced by half because of the rapid wage increases. In 1978, about 83 percent of rent was subsidized. This figure rose to 96 percent in 1988 due to increased construction costs (Yang and Wang 1992, p. 59). In 1998, the government intensified its public campaign for housing marketization. To further reduce housing subsidies, urban residents were urged to purchase their apartments (*China Daily*, June 18, 1998).

Health Care

Health care provides one of the success stories from China's period of high socialism. Though subject to violent policy debates that caused radical swings in policy, there was enough continuing emphasis on preventive health (inoculations, sanitation, etc.) and on a wide array of para professionals and minimally trained physicians to make medical advice widely available and to radically lower the death rate in both towns and cities. More equitable food supply distribution and improved basic nutrition also played a major role.[24]

22. Although income from sales is minimal, work units can save on maintenance costs.
23. Raw data, ESRIC (1991). See Appendix B, Table B1.
24. For references, see Parish and Whyte (1978), Whyte and Parish (1984), and World Bank (1994).

Table 2.1. *Consumerism and Media Exposure by Year*

	1978	1985	1997
Income and consumption (urban)			
Indices[a]			
Disposable income per capita	100	160	312
Retail sales	100	239	2,031
Per capita living space (sq. meters)	3.6	5.2	8.8
Natural gas use (piped and bottled) (%)	14	22	76
Consumer durables per 100 households[b]			
Washing machines	6	48	89
Refrigerators	0	7	76
Sofas	89	132	205
Soft beds	. .	6	42
TV, black and white	32	67	26[d]
TV, color	. .	17	100
Media and communication (national)			
TV broadcast coverage (% population)	. .	. .	88
Radio broadcast coverage (% population)	. .	. .	86
Copies published (in millions)[c]			
Newspapers	140	200	187
Books	46	67	73
Magazines	11	26	24
Urban telephones (in 100,000s)	28	48	554[d]
Long-distance telephone lines (in 1,000s)	19	38	1,146
Mobile telephone (in 1,000s)	0	0	1,323

Notes: [a]For indices, 1978 = 100, and subsequent increases are adjusted for inflation. [b]Consumer durable statistics begin in 1980 or 1981. [c]Publication statistics begin in 1980. [d]1996 data. (. .) = not available.
Source: SSB (1998a, pp. 24–5, 128, 324, 325, 327, 568, 754; 1998b, p. 128, 1997a, p. 537; 1996, pp. 26, 533).

Despite these many successes, issues remain that must be confronted during reform. As in all low-cost medical systems, one nagging problem is how to control excess demand – people demanding time with the doctor and medicines that they do not really need. A related problem is how to improve the quality of doctors and facilities, when the administrators who fund the system continue to put caps on fees. More highly trained doctors are needed as the easily cured infectious diseases of the past are replaced by cancer, heart disease, and other long-term, technology-intensive problems.

In the early 1980s, China began a partial reform of the health care system. The core of the reform program was to improve the quality of care, strengthen medical training, increase foreign exchanges, purchase high-tech equipment from abroad, and increase funds for medical research. The result was improved care for a few in the best hospitals in urban areas and a rising cost of care. The rural–urban gap widened. Preventive care, including immunizations, was an unintended casualty. Most operational costs and part of the preventive care staff's income, previously fully supported by the state, had to come from direct or indirect user charges (World Bank 1994). The result was an increase in cases of infectious diseases, including cholera, hepatitis, hemorrhagic fever, typhus fever, rabies, and relapsing fever (Ministry of Public Health 1991, p. 112).

Realizing the problems of early reform, the Ministry of Public Health tried to reemphasize basic and preventive care, while not sacrificing the quality issue. The problems of the current health policy are high cost and underfunding. For work units that are under pressure to reduce their employees' medical benefits, the rising cost of prescriptions and high-tech treatment is an increasing burden. Concerned about the work units' ability to pay, the government has prevented hospitals from increasing their fees to a level that would cover hospital costs. Medical personnel are still underpaid and have few ways to increase their income. Though some reputable doctors serve a few hours a week in an "expert clinic" where the registration fee is doubled, the charges for treatment remain at government-regulated prices. The 1993 wage reform increased the salaries for top-level doctors, and a copayment system is currently under consideration. In some cities, a government-controlled medical fund, with contributions by employers, is being tried as an experiment. The government is reluctant, however, to relinquish health care to complete market competition. Ironically, with the rising cost of health care and the shrinking financial ability of the state to subsidize, the public health system is becoming increasingly selective about who is qualified for benefits. This process results in a stratification of health care access that in many ways parallels the market system that China has historically wanted to avoid.[25]

NEW TRENDS

Besides these old traditions that are now troubled and subject to possible reform, there are two new traditions that came to have a major influence on urban life by the mid-1980s. These are rampant consumerism and extensive mass media exposure, particularly to television.

Consumerism

One problem in motivating workers in all socialist societies is that even if the worker earned more, there would be little on which to spend the new earnings (Friedman 1962; Lindblom 1977; Nove 1983). In capitalist societies, producers soon learned the value of stimulating consumer desires. Working through advertising specialists, producers helped induce a high level of consumerism that answered many of their problems. Not only was there a near-insatiable demand for their products, but to get the products that would help them "keep up with the Joneses," workers were willing to work long hours to increase their income. Thus, rampant consumerism helped solve both marketing and worker incentive problems.[26]

In the Cultural Revolution decade, China tried to motivate workers with normative appeals for sacrifice on behalf of a greater national good. In the 1980s, though nationalism remained in the arsenal of appeals to workers, there was a shift to more utilitarian, remunerative appeals.[27] The

25. In 1992, coverage followed the administrative and entitlement hierarchy. Full medical coverage was as follows: administrators, managers, professionals, and retired state firm workers (88%), manual workers (75%), service workers (62%), private sector workers (4%), and farmers (5%). Much as in the United States, the uncovered could still report to many higher-class hospitals for emergency treatment, but this was only a partial victory on the side of equality (1992 public health survey, raw data).
26. For expositions of this thesis, covering both historical and contemporary Western experience, see McKendrick, Brewer, and Plumb (1982) and Schor (1992).
27. For popular accounts of the rapid shifts in consumption, the media, and popular culture, see Schell (1988) and Kristof and Wudunn (1994) (in English) and He and Tang (1989) (in Chinese). For an early account that borrows vocabulary from Amitai Etzioni

shift to utilitarian appeals was combined with a much greater emphasis on consumerism. The popular response was tremendous – goaded on, no doubt, by nearby Asian neighbors such as Hong Kong, Taiwan, and Japan that helped demonstrate what a mature consumer society could provide. Both foreign and domestic producers soon followed with colorful billboards and commercials in places once occupied by political slogans.

Many things that were impossible, even taboo, in the former anti-bourgeois society have now become commonplace. Ration coupons for life staples have been replaced by fancy supermarkets. Only a few years ago, a watch, a bicycle, and a stable job in the state sector with good benefits were necessary preparations for a wedding in urban China. Currently, a foreign degree, a job in a foreign or a private company, a car, and a private apartment are becoming highly desirable conditions for marriage. Gray and blue Mao jackets and green army uniforms are still worn, but now with mini skirts and Coca-Cola and Budweiser T-shirts. Disco dancing, which used to be described in the early 1980s in the *People's Daily* as harmful to one's bone development, has replaced t'ai chi.

The radical change appears in statistics on urban income and consumption (Table 2.1). Over the last fifteen years, urban income per capita almost tripled. Retail sales almost quadrupled. Important for family life, including the burden of chores and privacy of different household members, average floor space per family more than doubled. Cleaner bottled and piped gas often replaced the dirty soft coal burned for cooking and heating. First washing machines and then refrigerators have become common in many households. "Keeping up with the Zhangs" has become a new way of life. Though status concerns increased, improved objective conditions meant that family life was far more comfortable in the 1990s than at the end of the 1970s. These figures will be important for the discussion of family life in later chapters – including the statistics on soft beds and space with regard to the question of changing sexual mores.

In planned economies, the fantasy is that if people just sacrifice enough, sometime in the future there will be a time of abundance when there will be enough to go around for everyone. There will be no difficult

to discuss Chinese government vacillation among remunerative, normative, and coercive incentives, and the secondary byproducts of each approach, see Skinner and Winckler (1969).

choices between the haves and the have-nots. This fantasy is consistent with a society which produces constant shortages and an economy in which one of the most prized professionals is the deal maker who finds scarce supplies. The fantasy image, often captured in official art, is a field full of abundant grain or a city full of productive factories spewing out products by the ton.

In a market society the problem is precisely the reverse. The central problem is no longer shortages and underproduction but instead over-production. In this highly efficient production system, the anxiety is that no one will buy the products once they are produced. The new economic hero is the salesman or marketing agent.[28] And the new fantasy, stimu-lated by advertising funded by anxious producers, is that everyone will have a full array of consumer durables and other goods appropriate to his or her social status. The official symbol becomes the marketing bill-board and TV commercial. This is the goal to which China seems to be heading in record time.

Media and Communication

Along with the change in consumerism, there was a rapid change in media exposure and communication patterns. Inkeles (1974) suggests that increasing media exposure is one of the hallmarks of the modern age and that increasing media exposure is associated with an increasing flexibility of mind and ability to imagine things differently. Whether flexibility of mind changes so rapidly remains uncertain, but exposure to more kinds of media is occurring rapidly.

In the 1980s, media and communication facilities proliferated, and the popularity of different media shifted (Table 2.1).[29] As in other countries where television has spread, people were spending more hours a day watching TV. As the popularity of TV grew, people were staying at home longer, rather than going out to watch movies or converse with friends (Whyte and Parish 1984). If watching TV together can be called family togetherness, that increased after 1978. With increasing viewing time, the

28. In 1970s free-market Hong Kong, Chinese emigres who had been expediters, scouring much of China for scarce supplies, often had to change their profession in Hong Kong, becoming salesmen instead (personal interviews, William L. Parish).
29. Beginning references include Lull (1991) and the popular accounts by Schell (1988) and Kristof and Wudunn (1994).

old black and white TV, which seemed so precious in the early 1980s, was no longer enough. Color TVs soon supplanted black and white TVs. Whether color or monochrome, urban TV coverage was soon universal. In line with increased viewership, hours of programming increased dramatically, including critical dramas and comedies that made urbanites more critical of official behavior and public life. Some popular TV series such as *New Star* and *River Elegy* became national cause célèbres that even when later refuted in the official media only provided their critical message with a wider audience. Both TV and movies gave viewers a much wider view of the outside world and alternative cultural mores. Anti-American and antiimperialist movies on the Korean War were shown together with such American movies as *First Blood*, *True Lies*, *Forrest Gump*, and *Saving Private Ryan*, which heretofore were allowed to be shown only to those who were capable of making ideological judgments against them.

Although media and publication are still controlled by the government, newspaper, magazine, and book publication also escalated rapidly (Table 2.1). There was some falling off after 1985. Loss of public interest as people turned to TV, increasing paper costs, and loss of public subsidies all took their toll. But even so, many more publications were available in the mid-1990s than had been so fifteen years before. Newsstands in Beijing's subway stations now sell over forty different kinds of newspapers and magazines, as compared with three or four in the late 1970s. The wide range of topics in these newspapers and magazines included gossip on China's top leaders' private lives, bizarre legal cases, fortune telling, marriage counseling, sports, entertainment, business news, and consumer reports. The increasing availability of publications gave the public alternative stances on public issues. The official print media were used to criticize official corruption and waste. Some media had their own letters-to-the-editor departments with investigative reporters who went about the country inquiring into official misconduct and errant service providers.[30]

Communication also increased in other ways. Only a few years ago,

---

30. For samples of new letters to the editor, investigative reporting, and short stories, see Thomas (1980), Liu (1983), Siu and Stern (1983), Barme and Minford (1989), and Link, Madsen, and Pickowicz (1989).

several apartment compounds with several hundred households used to share a single pay phone. From 1978 to 1997, telephone availability in urban areas mushroomed (see Table 2.1). Beeper sales by Motorola and others began to rival sales in the United States. Cellular phone sales have exploded. Many households bought telephone and fax machines that could easily dial abroad. The rapidly increasing popularity of personal computers and home printers is breaking the government's monopoly in publishing. Home VCRs and video CDs make any official attempt to ban videos almost impossible. Residents near the Hong Kong border routinely watch Hong Kong TV programs and rarely tune their TV sets to Chinese channels.[31] To compete with Hong Kong, Chinese stations have had to increase their foreign programs. As a result, movie and popular music stars in Hong Kong and Taiwan, together with such names as Mohammed Ali, Michael Jordan, Madonna, and Michael Jackson, are known by almost every urban Chinese.

All of this new openness, though short of a completely free society ideal, has helped radically transform public consciousness. No longer must information and suspicions be passed back and forth nervously by word-of-mouth. With its own campaigns against corruption, waste, and abuse of women and children, the government has helped sensitize the public to many social problems. Call-in talk shows on sex, crime, and a host of other issues make the public more aware of issues and alternative perspectives on those issues.

All this should be kept in mind in later chapters as we discuss public opinion. Even as conditions improved in the 1980s, people often became more critical. Exposed to greater shared knowledge about social problems, people raised their expectations of what government should be doing to improve society. Using the media to help control bureaucratic corruption and other social problems, the government itself often contributed to the more critical atmosphere. In short, by the late 1980s, China had come to share in a problem common to many developing countries. As Samuel Huntington (1968) suggested for many developing countries, there is an uneasy balance between increased education,

---

31. For a detailed description of the coexistence of socialist, Western (Hong Kong), and traditional Chinese influences in leisure activities in Guangzhou, see Ikels (1996, ch. 6).

information, and expectations and the speed with which developing country governments are able to deliver goods and services that meet these new expectations. Without more education and information, the country will not develop. But when expectations outrun the government's ability to deliver, social and political turmoil can result. One issue for later chapters is how successfully the Chinese government dealt with this issue.

QUANDARIES OF REFORM

This cataloging of old traditions versus new trends, of social contract versus increased media and goods consumption, begins our discussion of the systemic consequences of moving from one system of social organization to another. In the rest of the book we trace out these consequences. One of the themes that we pursue is that the move from the old, classical socialist system to the new, market system poses a number of dilemmas. We emphasize two of them.

The first involves the difficulty of balancing normative, coercive, and remunerative appeals as one moves from one type of social contract to the other. The old social contract society not only provided a firm floor under living standards in return for political quiescence. It also reinforced that contract with normative appeals for sacrifice on behalf of the nation and the building of socialism. When it worked best, as in the early 1950s rebuilding of the country, people willingly provided many of the great personal sacrifices that were necessary in an investment-hungry socialist economy. When the normative appeals were not enough, the government could turn to political movements that combined normative and coercive elements.

In time, these types of appeals for a public good-based social contract began to wear thin, and to even cause a backlash among some people. The 1978 changes responded to this problem by abandoning normative and coercive appeals in favor of remunerative appeals. No longer are people to be motivated primarily by high-minded normative appeals or by fear of sanctions. Instead, higher personal income and consumption is supposed to be the major appeal for most people.[32] This switch to

32. On the costs and benefits of remunerative (monetary) appeals versus other appeals, see Skinner and Winckler (1969).

remuneration and consumption has many advantages. It is much simpler in many ways, not requiring an elaborate political study apparatus or agents who guard against ideological deviation. But it also has its own dangers. If the economy goes through a downturn, or if inflation causes real incomes to fall behind the promises of increased prosperity, as happened in the late 1980s, massive discontent can result (see Chapter 5). Also, the abandonment of normative appeals and the loosening of coercive controls leave the regime with fewer tools to control its own civil servants, with the potential result that bureaucrats may become involved in more anomic, self-serving, and corrupt activities that further delegitimize the regime (see Chapters 5 and 7). Thus, switching from one type of social contract to another is much like walking a tightrope.

The second dilemma is how to balance expectations and the ability to deliver economic and social goods. Huntington (1968) and Portes (1976) suggest that an excessively rapid rise in aspirations commonly cause problems in developing societies, making problematic the linear transition from tradition to modern societies (cf. Inkeles 1974). China has taken steps since 1978 that run into this very difficulty. To lay the groundwork for a more complex, open economy, education has been encouraged, particularly among administrators and clerical workers in public employment. Civil servants must engage in more training and pass exams to be promoted. The government thus begins to more nearly approximate the technically sophisticated bureaucratic–authoritarian states that have been so successful in Taiwan, Singapore, South Korea, and elsewhere in East Asia. The government uses media publicity of corruption and service failures to expose errant civil servants. Through letters to the editor and other similar reports, the public becomes involved in a bottom-up disciplining of increasingly far-flung bureaucracy. The gradual openness of the media encourages the freedom of thinking necessary to accelerate growth in a complex economy. The welcoming of information from abroad encourages new, more productive modes of thinking. But all these activities can be a two-edged sword, causing expectations to rise much more rapidly than the government can respond. Increased critical standards and knowledge of government failures may encourage not dynamism but cynicism about government performance.

It is the story about how different social groups respond to these types of quandaries that we pursue in the chapters that follow. As China moves from one system of social organization to another, there are both many opportunities to succeed and many opportunities for failure. What may be a successful program for one may be a disaster for another. Discovering the complexity of this transformation provides much of the drama of what follows.

Part II

GROUP INTERESTS

3

Life Chances: Education and Jobs

THIS chapter continues our theme of the way in which the shifting social contract has multiple consequences in individual lives. The classical socialist contract promised greater social equality and in addition often promised to right past wrongs by providing greater access to education and jobs for the previously disadvantaged. The emerging market system, while making no promise to right past wrongs or to guarantee equality of results, promises to provide greater equality of opportunity for all. Though income inequality may increase, under a market system everyone ostensibly has an opportunity to try for better education, jobs, and income. We want to examine how the promises of both the old and new system have been realized in China.

Typically, each system has several unintended consequences. Market systems often allow considerable inequality and permit the children of old elites to inherit their parents' status. Socialist systems, while equalizing incomes in urban areas, produced other kinds of inequality. Purportedly, socialist administrators in charge of redistributing economic resources reaped greater benefits for themselves and their families (e.g., Djilas 1957; Bettleheim 1976).[1] Parents in privileged work units provided special privileges to their children (e.g., Lin and Bian 1991; Titma and Tuma 1993; Bian 1994a; Lin 1995b). One line of argument suggests that with the transition to a market economy, many of these old administrative and work unit advantages will fade (e.g., Szelényi 1978, 1988; Nee 1989, 1991, 1992). We want to examine whether old advantages are fading, and whether they are being replaced by the kinds of inequalities that are more common to market systems.

---

1. Szelényi (1994) reviews the literature on the "new class" in socialist societies.

DEBATES RELATED TO EDUCATION AND JOBS

One central issue is whether societies are truly malleable. One school of thought suggests great malleability, with socialist systems and market systems being worlds apart (e.g., Kornai 1992). Another school sees great constancy across modern societies. Despite early increases in social mobility as new socialist systems staffed institutions with their own people, mobility soon slowed and old patterns of social mobility returned (e.g., Connor 1979, 1991; Dobson 1980a, 1980b; Matthews 1982; Lapidus 1983; Lin and Bian 1991; Erikson and Goldthorpe 1994, p. 300). Moreover, a specialized literature on social mobility suggests considerable constancy in mobility patterns across all types of societies (e.g., Featherman, Jones, and Hauser 1975; Grusky and Hauser 1984; Hauser and Grusky 1988; Erikson and Goldthorpe 1994). Even though rates of upward social mobility may increase as societies move first from agriculture to manufacturing and then from blue-collar manufacturing to white-collar service activities, old upper-class groups tend to reproduce themselves regardless of the social system. Variations in upper-class reproduction tend to be only at the margin.

China might be different. More than in the European socialist states, China took seriously the job of redoing the class order. Particularly in the 1966–76 Cultural Revolution decade, through discrimination against the children of intellectuals and other old elites and through affirmative action programs for the children of farmers and workers, the government tried to overturn old patterns of status transmission. Thus, there could be a sharper divide between the socialist and market era in China than elsewhere. If societies are malleable, China is an important test case.

As we examine malleability we need to note that issues of status transmission respond as much to political as to direct market pressures. Market transition is a transition in political interest articulation as much as is in the expression of market rationales (Parish and Michelson 1996). In market states, governments often fund education and legalize job credentialing under pressure from elite interest groups (Dore 1976; Collins 1979). Market states are more open to elite lobbying both because these societies tend to be more pluralist and because interest groups have more economic resources independent of top-down government control (Friedman 1962; Huntington and Nelson 1976).

Although political reform was slower than in former socialist states in Europe, China's political system was more responsive to political interest groups after 1978 than in the decades before (e.g., Lieberthal and Oksenberg 1988; Shirk 1993). It is thus difficult to separate changes caused by the invisible hand of the market from changes caused by the visible hand of self-interested social groups. This repeats a theme common to debates on the sources of income differences in Western market societies, with some scholars pointing to income differences caused by the influence of powerful societal interest groups and other scholars pointing to the functional needs of the market.[2] Thus, we want to pay attention to income differences that occur in more competitive market settings versus differences that occur in more protected sectors of the economy, where groups could seek income advantages unrelated to individual productivity.

Education

We first examine education. Education is central because in modern societies it is one of the major avenues by which privileged parents pass on their status to their children through an emphasis on educational credentials in job placement and promotion (e.g., Berg 1971; Collins 1979). In both the Soviet Union and China, the result has been vigorous policy debates about how to use and organize education. The debates have included disagreements over whether society should be primarily a virtuocracy or meritocracy, whether educational credentials were a subterfuge through which prerevolutionary elites passed on status to children, and whether the emphasis in education should be on producing a small coterie of highly trained technocrats or a mass of workers and farmers with basic education. Here we group those debates under the issues of levels of, uses of, and access to education.

Levels of Education. The debate about levels of education contrasts amounts to be spent on higher versus basic education or on academic versus applied education tracks. In developing market societies, the pressure for an emphasis on higher education comes from urban middle-class

2. For summaries of debates over structural versus market determinants of inequality within and across generations, see Smith (1990) and Baron (1994).

and upper-class parents who want to ensure that their children get access to the best jobs in society. The result in many of these societies is an over-investment in college education which leads to lingering problems of illiteracy (particularly among females), modest rates of education through junior and senior high school, and underemployment of college graduates (e.g., Psacharopoulos 1973; Dore 1976; Huntington and Nelson 1976; Bates 1981).

In socialist states, in contrast, the greater top-down control and the weakness of interest groups means more effective resistance to parental pressures. The result is typically one of ample education through high school, while college education is sharply curtailed. Moreover, except in the Soviet Union, most socialist countries directed high-school-age youth into vocational programs leading not to college but to manual and technical careers.[3] The result was a system that featured what Turner (1960) calls sponsored mobility, involving early tracking of students into elite and working-class academic paths. The emphases on basic versus higher education and on applied versus academic tracks was consistent with the socialist economy's emphasis on production. With as much as half the labor force in blue-collar, manual occupations, these societies needed many skilled production workers and few white-collar professionals and technicians.

China has experienced extreme shifts in education policy over the last four decades. The most extreme, antielitist policies emerged during the 1966–76 Cultural Revolution decade. In that decade, college education was stripped of funds, which were then redirected to basic education in villages and towns (Whyte and Parish 1984; Lavely et al. 1990; Pepper 1990; Seeberg 1990; Thogersen 1990; Rosen 1991; Zhang 1992b; Payne 1994; Parish and Zhe 1995; Tsui 1997). After 1976, however, educational funds were again shifted toward cities. The countryside experienced school consolidation. Many hastily recruited, poorly trained teachers of the Cultural Revolution decade were released. Pupils were required to travel farther to get to a secondary school. Intensive, exam-based, quality education was emphasized over simple quantity of education. While demand for college education increased, demand for basic education

3. For raw data supporting these generalizations, see the education statistics in the World Development Report for years both in the late 1970s and the mid-1990s (e.g., World Bank 1995). For secondary literature, see Fitzpatrick (1976, 1979), Dobson (1980a, b), Matthews (1982), Lapidus (1983), Connor (1991).

purportedly decreased. Parents discovered that their teenaged children were much more valuable working in family businesses and in other commercial activities. Dropout rates increased, with teenagers increasingly going to work in the fields, construction crews, transport teams, and other kinds of service activities (e.g., Taylor 1988; Pepper 1990; Thogersen 1990; Zhang 1992a).

Uses of Education. In China, there was a further policy debate about the uses of education. Though more extreme, this debate echoed earlier Soviet debates about the role of intellectuals in society (e.g., Szelényi 1994; Konrad and Szelényi 1979). In the 1966–76 Cultural Revolution decade, intellectuals and their children were discriminated against. Affirmative action programs helped ensure that the children of workers, peasants, and other nonintellectuals advanced in school and then obtained the best jobs (e.g., Parish 1984; Whyte and Parish 1984; Bian 1994a). Party loyalty and revolutionary fervor counted more than educational credentials and expertise. The quest for virtuocracy won over meritocracy.

By the late 1980s and early 1990s, new hires and workers in the nonstate sector were getting higher incomes if they had more education (Maurer-Fazio 1994). In comparisons of pre- and postreform patterns in large survey data sets, researchers were beginning to find increasing income rewards for people with more education (Bian and Logan 1996; Zhou, Tuma, and Moen 1996, 1997; cf. Xie and Hannum 1996). This suggests a gradual shift in the allocation of people to jobs. As in other market societies, education is increasingly rewarded, both because it provides more skills and because it is a convenient screening device when selecting people for jobs and promotion. This represents a sharp break with China's Cultural Revolution past.

Access to Education. The third education issue concerns which people will have access to education. Before the Cultural Revolution, the children of professionals continued to excel in the education system. A system that emphasized exams and magnet schools with more resources privileged the children of parents who themselves had greater education and resources. This advantage was drastically undermined during the Cultural Revolution. However, as might be expected, the children of administrators continued to do well when exam-based education pro-motions were replaced by administrative decisions about who would advance in school (Parish 1984; Whyte and Parish 1984; Deng and Treiman 1997). Furthermore, educational success, as in many other areas of life, was increasingly tied to work units. Work units had differential bargaining power, depending on how they ranked in the administrative hierarchy, which influenced their ability to obtain better services, includ-ing education. By the 1980s, educational success was heavily dependent on one's parents' belonging to a high-ranking work unit (Lin and Bian 1991). Thus, one issue for the present study is whether work unit status and parental administrative and professional status continues to shape educational futures.

Of particular concern is whether women are differentially affected by market reform. Though much of the existing literature is about the countryside, some authors suggest that as one moves toward a market economy in a traditional patriarchal society, parents will sacrifice their daughters' education for the sake of sons. This would repeat a pattern found elsewhere in East Asia, where parents can stint on daughters' edu-cation for the sake of sons' education – even sending a daughter out early to work so that a son can remain in school (e.g., Salaff 1981; Greenhalgh 1985; Wolf 1985).

Whether these tendencies inevitably reduce women's education is uncertain. In contrast to the effects of a retreating state, which provides parents more autonomy in decisions which would favor sons over daugh-ters, there is an improving economy, which provides more resources to fund schools. The result in some rural areas is that richer, more marke-tized areas provide more equal education for sons and daughters (Parish and Zhe 1995; Michelson and Parish 2000). Moreover, many new jobs require the credentials of a junior or senior high school degree (e.g., Judd 1994). In large cities, joint venture firms often use college degrees as a screening factor for selecting people for the best technical and manage-rial jobs. This new credentialing of jobs, then, may change the way parents and youth think about education. In short, the answer to the educational consequences of marketization may be that there is a race between cen-trifugal job opportunities that pull daughters (and sons) out of school and centripetal credentialing and school opportunities that keep daugh-ters and sons in school.

Job Mobility

The question of job mobility is closely related to the prior issue of access to education. As with education, socialist regimes promised equal access to desirable jobs. For a time, China took that promise one step further with an attempt to privilege people with working-class origins and the right political proclivities. With this system now abandoned, the question is whether opportunity is increased or decreased, particularly for those from working-class backgrounds.

Socialist states typically have distinctive patterns of job mobility. In the initial years of socialist rule, upward mobility is rapid. New bureaucratic positions have to be filled, as the government dispenses with much of the old leadership and builds new institutions of its own. Also, as the economy moves from an intensive, market pattern of development to an extensive, socialist pattern of development, new labor has to be employed. Both men and women are drawn into the labor force to staff the many new factories that a deferred consumption, high-investment regime creates. In Eastern Europe, the urban population was insufficient to staff many of these new jobs, with the result that farmers and the sons of farmers were drawn from the countryside to new manual jobs in industry. In these initial decades, sons and daughters found jobs that averaged much better than those of their parents' generation.

In time, however, the socialist pattern of development began to produce far fewer opportunities for upward mobility. The new administrative positions were already filled. Half of all new jobs were in manual, productive labor (e.g., Connor 1979, 1991; Dobson 1980b; Matthews 1982; Lapidus 1983; Whyte and Parish 1984, ch. 3; Erikson and Goldthorpe 1994, p. 300). China followed a similar trajectory through the 1970s, including frequent downward mobility for the children of high-status parents resulting from the Cultural Revolution. By the end of the 1970s many youth could not find jobs and many others took jobs of lower status than those held by their parents (see the previous chapter and Whyte and Parish 1984; Parish 1987, 1990; Davis 1990, 1992b; Bian 1994a; Chen and Parish 1996).

The 1980s reform era brought new work opportunities to Chinese cities (Davis 1992a). To increase employment and consumption opportunities, investment funds were shifted from capital-intensive heavy industry to labor-intensive light industry. More alternate forms of ownership were permitted, including more neighborhood licensed collective enterprises, self-employed (*geti*) endeavors employing seven or fewer people, and private firms employing eight or more people (legitimized in 1988), followed by joint ventures and other forms of employment. To get many septuagenarians out of the labor force, "golden handshakes" were offered to get people to take timely and early retirement (Manion 1993). One result of these policies was to bring the urban unemployment rate down from a high of more than 6 percent in the late 1970s to a low of only 2.2 percent in the mid-1980s. Another result of the liberalization of employment opportunities was to pull many quasilegal rural migrants into cities to do the tasks that urbanites scorned, including difficult manual labor in construction and transportation, unpleasant jobs in textile mills, and the growing number of menial service jobs in restaurants, stores, and hotels.

Our task in this chapter is not just to review these past trends with new data but also to examine the extent to which marketization provided new opportunities for the average urbanite. If those new opportunities are indeed present, we should see significant changes in patterns of job mobility. Jobs should be less in the control of the formal bureaucracy. For the first time in decades, there should be more intergenerational upward mobility, with children once again improving on the jobs of their parents. Many of these jobs should be in service sectors that more directly serve a growing market as China moves from being a producer society (the typical Stalinist model of development) to a consumer society (the typical capitalist mode of development).

In this chapter, we draw on five disparate sources of data. We use the 1988 Chinese Household Income Project (CHIP), a survey of some 8,000 urban households containing nearly 17,000 workers nationwide. Other material comes from a 1991 survey of 8,000 enterprise workers. We will also rely upon the 1992 Chinese urban social survey, with 2,300 people interviewed in 44 different cities. Finally, we will draw upon the 1995 census and more recent aggregate reports in statistical annuals. Where the data overlap in content, we have tried to compare the results from different sources, even if all the details are not reported here.

EDUCATIONAL CONSEQUENCES

This section begins an exploration of the educational consequences first of socialism and then market reform. Our focus here is on investment in different levels of education, on gender inequality, and on access to education by people from different family backgrounds. We wish to ascertain whether some of the socialist equalization goals were achieved, both in providing equal access to basic education for everyone and in giving special assistance to the children of workers and farmers. With the restoration of market influences in the 1980s, we want to know whether inequality in educational opportunities increased for women and for children from working-class backgrounds.

Levels of Education

Have investments in different levels of education shifted radically over time? By arraying people's current education by the year they would have turned age fifteen, we can approximate the amount of education available at different times. We pick age fifteen because over the last three decades many youth were stopping their education after junior high school, which would have made them about age fifteen when they and their parents decided whether to continue in school (Figs. 3.1 and 3.2).[4]

By the age fifteen measure, and restricting ourselves to men and women living in cities as of 1995, illiteracy shrank rapidly after 1949. By 1960, the vast majority of men and women were getting at least a primary education. For people now living in cities, the new socialist government had kept its promise to provide near-universal access to basic education. These trends were particularly favorable to women, with women's level of education beginning to approach (but not reach) that of men by 1960.

After a pause at the end of the 1950s induced by the Great Leap Forward, educational levels rose rapidly with the start of the Cultural Revolution decade in 1966. By the end of that decade, most males and females were getting either a junior or senior high school education. The

---

4. A potential difficulty with this procedure is that in the 1980s, many mid-career bureaucrats returned to school to get advanced degrees. Thus, in the analysis below, we distinguish people who earned advanced degrees in their youth from people who earned them as adults.

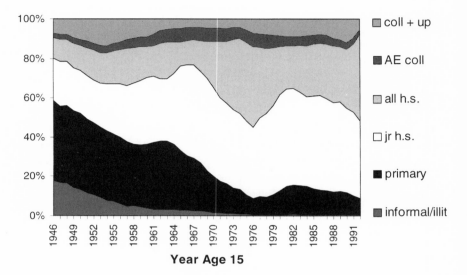

Figure 3.1 Male education levels by year. Notes: Data for current city residents. Illiteracy includes informal education. High school includes vocational and specialized high-school-level programs. Whether through adult study programs or normal programs, college includes technical (junior) college and above. Source: 1995 Census (Census Office 1997, table 2–3).

radical Cultural Revolution programs of shifting funds from college to secondary education and of promoting an open admissions policy had their intended effects.

There are two potential surprises here. One is that counter to the common complaint of intellectuals that the Cultural Revolution destroyed education, secondary school education expanded (cf. Bian 1994a). The second surprise is that these tendencies significantly affected not only rural children but also the urban youth represented in these statistics. Urban youth, particularly working-class youth, had a much greater chance to complete high school in 1976 than they did in 1966.

Urban education changed again after 1976. The results show that the consequences of school consolidation programs, the return of meritocratic exams, and a changing parental calculus were not restricted to the countryside. More urban youth stopped school either at a primary or junior high school level of education. Though these negative trends were

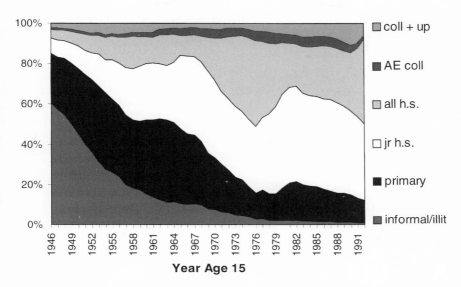

Figure 3.2 Female education levels. Notes and source: See Fig. 3.1.

soon reversed, full recovery to 1976 levels of secondary education enroll-ment did not occur until almost two decades later.[5] Hidden within the recovery was an increasing differentiation of secondary education, with different tracks for different types of students. In 1976, virtually all high school students were in the same type of high school. By the mid-1990s, over half of all high school students were in specialized vocational-track high schools (SSB 1998a, p. 684). This repeats a German and Eastern European pattern of tracking at an early age. This pattern is likely to recruit working-class children for vocational-track high schools and white-collar and professional children for academic-track high schools. In this sorting process, of course, exams once again play a central role. All this is familiar from many other market and nonmarket countries.

Finally, college enrollment has recovered from its Cultural Revolution low. Among urban males who got their college education when young, enrollment has more than doubled since the 1970s. Female enrollment

5. This pattern of shrinkage followed by gradual recovery after the mid-1980s also appears in annual statistics on the percentage of graduates advancing from one level of school-ing to the next (SSB 1996, p. 637; 1998a, p. 690).

has grown even more (ignoring the last several data points for younger people in Figs. 3.1 and 3.2).[6] In addition, because of the educational credentials required for promotion, many mid-career bureaucrats have obtained college and junior college degrees. To an extent, then, both the emphasis on credentialism for pubic-sector promotion and the increase in college-level enrollments after high school have nudged China toward a developing market country pattern. Though in comparison to market country patterns Chinese college education remained modest, the opportunities for college education are much greater than they had been in the past.[7]

Gender Equality

In urban areas at least, the return of the market meant not less but greater gender equality in education. In national enrollment data, women began to enroll more frequently in both high schools and colleges. In regular academic high schools, women's share of total enrollment increased from 40 percent in 1980 to 46 percent in 1997. Over the same period, women's share of college enrollment moved from one-fourth to over one-third (SSB 1998a, p. 692). These are nationwide statistics, including both rural and urban areas. The more rapid convergence of male and female college enrollment in cities (Figs. 3.1 and 3.2) suggests that daughters were advantaged on several dimensions, including the higher incomes of urban parents, fewer siblings competing for parental resources, more colleges in cities, and new pink-collar jobs that required college education. Thus, while all daughters were helped by trends since 1978, urban daughters were particularly advantaged. Instead of harming daughters, market trends helped daughters more than sons.

6. Ignore the last few data points because these people are in their teens and not old enough to have graduated from college.
7. Nationwide, including both rural and urban youth, 2 percent of China's relevant age group were in college. This was less than half the 5 percent of low-income developing market societies – which is the group with which China was most comparable. In middle-income developing countries, college age enrollment was a much higher 19 percent (World Bank 1995, pp. 216-17; SSB 1996, p. 631). World Bank analysts suggest that Chinese college enrollment ratios remained too low relative to China's economic needs.

Trends in Access to Education

We want to complete this section by returning to the question of access. Which children have access to high school and college? Were intellectual parents able to pass along advantages to their children? Were children of parents in high-status units privileged? Were youth in rapidly growing cities pulled out of school by the attractions of the labor market?

We begin with rudimentary data on trends in parental influence on a child's education. In most societies, things learned at home are useful for the child in school, producing a near-universal schooling advantage for children raised by more educated parents. Typically, whether the society is market or socialist, each extra year of parental education produces about a half-year's additional education among children (Treiman and Yip 1989; Ganzeboom and Treiman 1993). The question is whether China was able to alter this common pattern.

Data from urbanites suggest that China was indeed able to alter the pattern. We have data both on average years of schooling and on the probability of continuing from one level of school to the next (Fig. 3.3). The data on years of schooling are expressed in tenths of a year of additional education for each year of father's education. The data on continuation rates show the percentage point addition a person received for each year of father's education. Thus, for example, the data show that in the pre-1949 cohort, for each additional year of father's education, a person was 3.2 percentage points more likely to advance from high school to college. This is a large effect. If one's father were a college graduate rather than a high school graduate, a person would be 13 percentage points ($4 \times 3.2 = 12.8$) more likely to advance to college. In the 1940s and 1950s, about 30 percent of high school graduates continued on to college. Thus, relative to the modest average of only 30 percent of high school graduates continuing to college, the 13 percentage point advantage of having a college-educated father was considerable.[8]

---

8. Indeed, our analysis probably understates the influence. For economy of space we report the influence of father's years of education, which includes the years fathers spent in primary, junior, and senior high school. When a child is trying to prepare for college, it is not the years a father spent in these lower level schools but the years he spent in college that is important (details not shown). Nevertheless, the general point about changing influences is sustained in more detailed statistics.

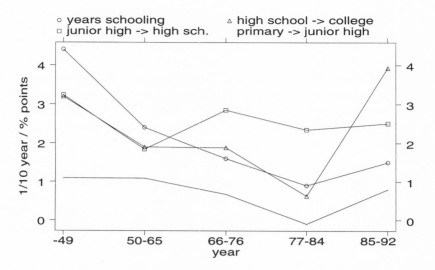

Figure 3.3 Education advantages and father's education. Notes: Results show the additional education from each year of father's education. The advantage in years (expressed in tenths of a year) of education is from a regression equation. The added percentage chance of continuing from one level of education to the next is based on probit analyses. The underlying equations include terms for gender, each of five time periods, and gender by period. Source: 1992 China Urban Survey.

Grouped by when a child turned age fifteen, our data show a U-shaped pattern to parental influence.[9] Parental influence began high before 1949, gradually declined in subsequent decades to a 1977–84 low, and then began a gradual recovery in the late 1980s (Fig. 3.3).[10] The presocialist parental influence of .44 extra years of education for each additional year of father's education is similar to the influence in other societies. Then in the initial fifteen years of socialist rule, parental influence was almost cut in half. In the 1966–76 Cultural Revolution decade, with its

9. With the exception of promotion to high school, all the U-shaped patterns are statistically significant.
10. Here the emphasis is on statistically significant variation across time. If the emphasis were instead on whether the effects of father's education were statistically different from zero, then, with the exception of junior high school continuation after 1977, all coefficients would be statistically significant. Thus, the effect of father's education never disappeared but simply varied in intensity from period to period.

affirmative action for working-class children, parental influence was diminished even more. These are all results that we expected from previous studies.

What is more surprising is that parental influence was dampened even more during the early reform period (1977–84). Several things may have occurred. Exams were not fully restored until the end of the 1970s. Many of the children from administrator and working-class backgrounds were already on advantaged tracks because of Cultural Revolution policies. Thus as children matured into their late teens, their futures may have already been cast by pre-1976 policies. Many of the Cultural Revolution policies for education emphasized class origin, with the children of intellectuals (typically professional and technical workers) discriminated against while the children of cadres, workers, and peasants were advantaged. Unsurprisingly, popular suspicion has always been that the cadres (administrators, managers, etc.) used this system, which emphasized personal recommendations rather than exams, to unfairly advantage their own children. The 1992 urban survey results suggest that the children of intellectuals were most disadvantaged during early reform, while the children of cadres were most advantaged during this period (details not shown). Thus, in cities, it may have taken some time for the full effects of the Cultural Revolution to play out.

In the mature reform period, however, as China returned to more of a credentialist, exam-based system for promotion in school, the natural advantages of children raised in intellectual families began to reappear. Particularly in entry to college, the children of intellectuals were again advantaged over children born in other types of families. In this final period, for each extra year of father's education, a child was 4 percentage points more likely to go on to college. Thus, from the pre-1949, more laissez-faire, exam-based system of educational promotion, to the late 1980s return of a similar system, China went through an extraordinary cycle that first weakened the influence of family origins on education and then began to allow those influences to reemerge.

Simply because basic level education is far more common now than in the past, we do not expect parental level influences to ever return to levels of the past. In market societies as well, the universalization of public education weakens parental influences over educational attainment (e.g., Mare 1979, 1980; Blake 1989; Parish and Willis 1993, table 1). Nevertheless, parental influences in market societies are never as modest as they were for a time in China, and we expect parental influence to continue to increase, particularly at the college level. It is this strengthening influence that we will explore in greater depth in the following section on current patterns.

Current Access to Education

We can examine emergent tendencies with data from the 1988 CHIP urban household survey. The data set contains information on whether high school and college-age youth (aged 16-21) were in school. Because 96 percent of these youth remained at home, we can link parental and city characteristics to the data on current enrollment. About half the sixteen- to twenty-one-year-olds were in either high school or college. For the father, we know characteristics such as income, job, and education that might have shaped decisions about schooling.[11] For each city, we know the rate of economic growth, average income, and whether a family lived in the city itself or in the rural hinterland. Our analysis reports proportional change coefficients (Fig. 3.4).[12] A coefficient such as .08 means that a person is 8 percentage points more likely to be in school. A negative coefficient, of course, means that the person is less likely to be in school.

We focus on gender, occupation, work unit status, and market forces. The occupational categories distinguish professional and technical workers, administrators (including government administrators and party officials in diverse types of work units), managers (in economic enterprises), clerical office workers, entrepreneurs (mostly in small, family-run enterprises), and manual, sales, and service workers. Work unit distinctions are by both function and ownership. The functional distinctions include economic enterprises (stores and factories), public organizations (publicly owned hospitals, schools, broadcasting stations, etc.), and

11. Since mothers retire earlier, we do not have enough data on mothers to do a useful analysis of the mother's influence.
12. The results are proportional change coefficients from a probit analysis of 3,334 youth from families with the father present. The standard errors used to calculate statistical significance are corrected for multiple children from the same household. Unshown determinants in the results include flags for each year of age and for some missing values. Appendix Table A3.1 provides descriptive statistics on the variables in Figure 3.4.

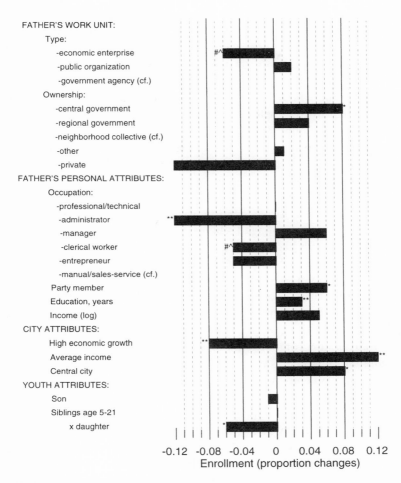

FATHER'S WORK UNIT:
  Type:
    -economic enterprise
    -public organization
    -government agency (cf.)
  Ownership:
    -central government
    -regional government
    -neighborhood collective (cf.)
    -other
    -private
FATHER'S PERSONAL ATTRIBUTES:
  Occupation:
    -professional/technical
    -administrator
    -manager
    -clerical worker
    -entrepreneur
    -manual/sales-service (cf.)
  Party member
  Education, years
  Income (log)
CITY ATTRIBUTES:
  High economic growth
  Average income
  Central city
YOUTH ATTRIBUTES:
  Son
  Siblings age 5-21
    x daughter

-0.12 -0.08 -0.04   0   0.04 0.08 0.12
Enrollment (proportion changes)

Figure 3.4 Determinants of school enrollment, youth aged 16–21, 1988. Notes: Proportional change coefficients from a probit analysis. (cf.) Comparison group; (**) $p < .01$; (*) $p < .05$; (#) $p < .10$; ($\wedge$) $p < .05$ in comparisons involving enterprises/public organizations, centrally owned/neighborhood collective work units, and professionals/administrators; ($\wedge$) $p < .10$ in comparisons involving ownerships of central/regional and regional/neighborhood. Source: 1988 CHIP urban survey, person data.

government agencies. The ownership distinctions include centrally owned state firms, regionally owned state firms, neighborhood licensed collective enterprises, privately owned (both small, self-employed units and larger, privately owned units), and all other types of work units. City attributes include whether the city had a high economic growth rate and whether a family resided in the urban core rather than in a suburban town or village (attributes coded 1 and 0). Youth attributes include the number of school-age siblings aged five to twenty-one and an interaction term for number of siblings if the child was a daughter.

To return to our narrative, gender was important for school enrollment in 1988 (Fig. 3.4). In families with multiple school-aged children, daughters were the ones whose education was sacrificed. About one-fourth of the youth had no school-aged sibling, one-half had a single sibling, and another one-fourth had two or more siblings. Repeating patterns found elsewhere in East Asia, when the family faced budget constraints because of multiple school-aged children, the daughters were the ones pulled out of school (see Parish and Willis 1993). Each extra sibling reduced school attendance by six percentage points. Sons were unaffected.[13] There is a potential hopeful note here. The neutral influence of being a son suggests that sibling competition for family resources was the principal determinant of women's dropping out of school. Thus, as a new generation of post-1980 one-child policy children mature, they will have few or no siblings competing with them for resources, and son/daughter differences will fade.

Father's occupation was also important. In a separate analysis, not controlling for other background characteristics, the children of professional and technical workers were one-fourth more likely to be in school when compared with the children of manual workers. Though lagging behind the children of professionals, the children of administrators, managers, and clerical workers were still more likely than working-class children to remain in school. In the detailed analysis here, of course, the patterns are somewhat more complex (Fig. 3.4). Our explanation of the negative

13. An "interaction term," the "x daughter" term is the number of school-aged siblings if the child is a daughter and zero otherwise. Implicitly, then, the normal "siblings" term above it is for sons. We looked for potential interactions between other background conditions and gender and found none – though females were slightly more likely to drop out of school if their father was in an economic enterprise.

effect of having an administrator father is that the high education of many administrators was via mid-career short-term courses in junior college programs. Thus relative to their father's "on paper" degree, the children are underperformers.[14] Nevertheless, most of the results imply that by the end of the 1980s, many presocialist tendencies were returning. The children of better-educated parents, particularly professional and technical parents, were able to excel in school.

Besides being helped by parental educational and occupational advantages, a child might be helped by having a father in a higher status work unit and in the party. This is Bian's (1994a) hypothesis. In 1988, children were advantaged by eight percentage points when their father worked in a central government work unit rather than in a neighborhood collective unit (Fig. 3.4). They were also advantaged by six points when their father was in the party. These were significant advantages, suggesting that important parts of the old reward system remained; nevertheless, these were not overwhelming advantages. A child whose father was a high school graduate rather than a primary school graduate had an 18 percentage point advantage ($6 \times .03 = .18$), which was three times greater than either of the advantages listed above. Thus, the emphasis on educational merit was to some extent making headway in comparison with the old administratively based advantages.

Before proceeding, however, we should note how the influence of party membership is expressed. It is concentrated on youth not of high school age (16–18) but instead of college and junior college age (19–21). For the former, the additional boost in enrollment is a statistically trivial single percentage point. For college, in contrast, father's party membership boosts enrollment by a full eight percentage points.[15] Moreover, while father's work in a centrally owned work unit had little effect on high school enrollment, it increased college attendance by a statistically significant nine percentage points. This leads to the possible conclusion that parents with party and work unit influence expend that influence not on easily available high school education but instead on highly competitive college education. Scholars who adhere to the bureaucratic bar-

---

14. Also see the Chapter 7 discussion of mid-career training for administrators.
15. Based on the same analysis as Figure 3.4. Most other coefficients in the age differentiated analysis remain similar to those in Figure 3.4. Also, redoing the analysis of father's years of education with separate measures for each level of father's education produces similar results.

gaining position will, of course, draw the conclusion that traditional bargaining persists.

Finally, we were concerned how the spread of the market might cause a race between new income, which would help keep children in school, and the enticement of new employment opportunities, which would pull children out of school. We find evidence of both tendencies. To some extent, central cities, richer cities, and richer parents all keep their children in school (Fig. 3.4). In the long run, these are all tendencies that would be strengthened by growth of the market. In the short run, however, the growing market also promotes opposing tendencies. More rapidly growing cities and fathers who work as entrepreneurs and in economic sectors all tend to pull their children out of school. Our guess is that entrepreneurial fathers need their children in the family business. Fathers in economic enterprises probably see income earning opportunities that other fathers miss. Thus there is, indeed, a race between the short-run centrifugal and long-run centripetal tendencies of a growing market economy.

RESULTS FOR JOB MOBILITY

The task of this section is to examine whether the socialist promise of equal opportunity was realized and whether that opportunity is being significantly reshaped by market transformation. We want to look back to past trends, asking whether China simply repeated the pattern of other socialist states, which typically began with rapid growth in opportunity followed by long-term stagnation in opportunity. We also want to examine whether a return to the market is providing more opportunity and whether that opportunity is heavily shaped by parental status and educational credentials.

Job Recruitment and Meritocracy

Changes in the bases of job recruitment in the 1980s favored both parental status and educational credentials. Bureaucratically controlled employment practices declined. Under China's version of socialism, both firms and individuals had little control over job assignments. In the 1980s, bureaucratic control over assignments began to weaken.

Though our data are only approximate, they suggest that sharp

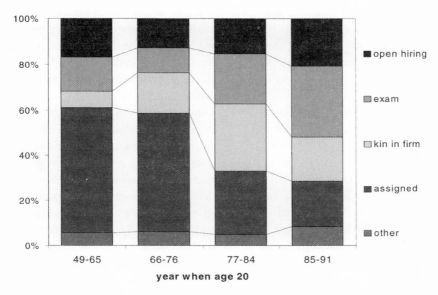

Figure 3.5 Job channel by year. Notes: "Open hiring": applicant applied directly, including with a letter of introduction; "exam": applicant took personnel exam; "kin in firm": recruited because parent took early retirement (*dingti*) or firm was recruiting from employee family members (*neizhao*); "assigned": administrative assignment; "other": other, including applicant given job when farm or house land was requisitioned by firm. Data are only for people in stores and factories and not for those in government agencies or public organizations. Source: 1991 Firm (Enterprise) Survey.

changes occurred (Fig. 3.5). With the start of economic reform, the proportion of new hires chosen through official assignment declined. In the early reform years, the old assignment system was not replaced by impersonal open competition. Instead, for several years in the late 1970s and early 1980s, hiring privileged the children and other kin of people already in the work unit (for details, see Bian 1994a, ch. 3). Since 1985, however, hiring practices favoring kin have receded in importance. In the post-1985, mature reform period, personnel exams and other forms of open hiring have become the most common means of recruiting people into work units. With the turn to exams, people with better educational background have been favored.

This turn to exams has helped move China toward more of a meritocracy, where education is an important determinant of finding desirable jobs. In a simple analysis of initial jobs, the role of education increased sharply since the Cultural Revolution decade. Initial jobs were ranked on a five-point scale – manual, sales/service, entrepreneur, clerical, and upper nonmanual (professional and technical workers, administrators, and managers). Using 1992 urban survey data, we examined the consequence of having an extra three years of education – the equivalent of advancing from primary to junior high school or from junior to senior high school. In the 1950s and early 1960s, an extra three years of education produced four-fifths of a point gain in occupational status. In the Cultural Revolution, this gain declined to two-thirds of a point. In the post-1978 reform period the gain grew to more than a full point advantage in occupational status.[16] This repeats the U-shaped pattern we have already observed in education. In job mobility, this U-shaped curve reached its nadir in the Cultural Revolution decade. Since then, the occupational return to more education parallels the increased return to parental education. This implies, of course, that in the future, much as in market-based societies, educated parents can transmit some of their advantages to their children.[17]

The pattern of increasing returns to education is seen not only in the initial job assignment but also in subsequent job mobility. In the 1992 urban social survey, for example, educated workers were more likely to have changed jobs, even when other personal and occupational conditions were controlled. In the 1991 firm survey, people who had changed jobs were advantaged by three to four percentage points in both income and benefits. Again, this is apart from several other conditions that influenced income and benefits (details not shown). All these tendencies

16. Based on 1,758 observations from the 1992 urban social survey. Other unreported determinants in the analysis included father's education and occupation, urban/rural origin, and gender. Compared with the Cultural Revolution decade, 1980s gains were statistically significant at .01 and 1950s gains were significant at .06. Total $R^2 = .27$.
17. Nevertheless, repeating a pattern common to market societies, the spread of basic education will continue to soften the effect of parental education on the child's job placement (Deng and Treiman 1997). For example, controlling for urban/rural origin and gender, the effect of father's education on initial occupational status remained modest even after 1985. On the scale used above, for each extra year of father's education, a child gained a full .30 points before 1949 and .27 points in 1950–65, but only .09 points in 1966–76, and an insignificantly higher .11 and .12 in 1977–84 and 1985–92.

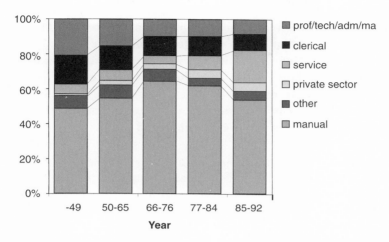

Figure 3.6 Initial job by year. Notes: "Year": year that person turned age 20; "prof/tech/adm/ma": professional and technical workers and administrators and managers; "service": sales and service workers; "private sector": mostly entrepreneurs running small factories and shops; "other": farmers and others; "manual": blue-collar production workers. Source: 1992 China Urban Survey, weighted data.

suggest that by the early 1990s a capitalist-style labor market was beginning to emerge and that in that labor market educated labor was advantaged.

Occupation Trends

As in other societies, larger structural changes in the types of jobs available were the major determinants of opportunities available in China. Radical attempts to right past wrongs, based on affirmative action programs for children of workers and farmers, were doomed to failure when few white-collar jobs were available to anyone. We can illustrate the problem first with data on overall occupational trends and then with separate data on the children of farmers, blue-collar workers, and white collar workers.

We classify people according to when they were age twenty, which is about the time that most people entered the labor force (Fig. 3.6). Just before and after the socialist takeover in 1949, there were many nonmanual, white-collar jobs to be filled. The rebuilding after World War II and then again after the socialist revolution in 1949 provided many new urban jobs for administrators, managers, professionals, technicians, and clerical workers. Nonmanual, white-collar job opportunities grew.

However, because of the emphasis on converting China from a consumer society to a producer society, most of the new jobs became manual, blue-collar jobs. This tendency was exacerbated by the 1966–76 Cultural Revolution policy of diminishing the size of the nonproductive nonmanual sector in favor of the blue-collar productive sector. Because of this policy, administrative and clerical jobs shrank, as did jobs in the already modest service sector. The final consequence of these tendencies was that an extraordinary number of people were forced into manual, blue-collar jobs.

It is only with economic reform in the 1980s that opportunities to escape manual work once again increased. Few of the new opportunities were in upper nonmanual positions, including administrators, managers, and professional and technical workers. However, over time, there was rapid growth in both private sector positions (often in small family-owned firms with fewer than eight employees) and in service occupations (store clerks, waiters, etc.). With these trends, Chinese cities began to be more like cities in other developing market societies (for comparative data, see Whyte and Parish 1984, ch. 3). Thus, as for education, for jobs there was a U-shaped pattern as China moved from market to extreme socialism and then back again. White-collar opportunities were common in the early years, rare in the intervening years, and then common again as China moved toward a market system. As with other Stalinist-style socialist systems, the middle period of socialist rule, with its scarcity of white-collar jobs, provided a difficult structural context when it came to attempts to provide new opportunities for the previously disadvantaged.

Job Opportunities by Social Origin

Though the Cultural Revolution decade narrowed the gap between the children of white- and blue-collar parents, it never completely erased the white-collar advantage. The data show, first, that while there was an explosion of new administrative, managerial, professional, and technical jobs in the first decade of socialist rule, those types of jobs soon shrank in importance (Fig. 3.7, top left). As intended by radical policy makers,

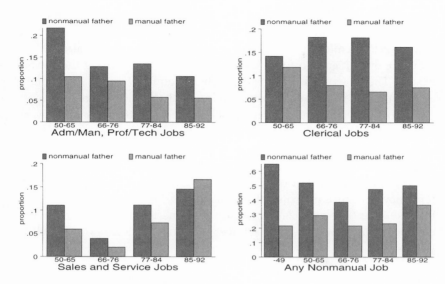

Figure 3.7 Type of job by father's background and year. Notes and source: See Fig. 3.6.

the gap between working-class and white-collar children shrank to its lowest level in the 1966–76 decade. Thus, the radical program to discriminate against the children of old elites while providing affirmative action measures for workers and farmers had some effect. Nevertheless, the gap never disappeared.

For clerical jobs, ironically, there was never a narrowing of opportunity for children from different class backgrounds (Fig. 3.7, top right). It would seem that the Cultural Revolution focus on the highest administrative and managerial jobs left clerical jobs open for children of white-collar families. Finally, though sales and service jobs were initially open more to white-collar children, these types of jobs eventually became a haven for children from working-class backgrounds – many of them female (Fig. 3.7, bottom left).

Data on movement into all types of white-collar jobs help show the net effects of all these tendencies (Fig. 3.7, bottom right). As in earlier statistics, there is a familiar U-shaped pattern, particularly for children from white-collar families. After 1949, opportunities for white-collar children diminished sharply, reaching their lowest point in 1966–76. The low figure in 1966–76 implies that over 60 percent of white-collar children were downwardly mobile, which is an extremely high figure.[18] Though working-class children had somewhat more opportunities after 1949, their opportunities also followed a U-shaped pattern during the socialist era. The draconian attempts to achieve equality never completely erased the blue/white-collar differences. And the near-equality was at great cost, relying as it did on reducing everyone to the same lowest common denominator.[19] Ironically, by the measure of simple blue/white-collar job distinctions, opportunities were more equal in the late reform period than at any other period. Thus, by this measure, instead of creating greater inequality in opportunities, the market caused a surprising tendency toward equalizing of opportunities.[20] As the previous figures have shown, this equalization occurred primarily because the market created many new sales and service jobs that attracted working-class youths.

CONCLUSION

We began this chapter with the question of whether shifts in the social contract made a dramatic difference in people's life chances. The larger question was whether status transmission systems are malleable, and whether life chances improved or worsened as China first moved into a period of idealistic socialism and then as it exited into more of a market regime.

The answer to the question of malleability is that society was malleable. In China, the socialist period made a difference both because of

18. As their economies began to stagnate in the early 1970s, about 45 percent of new hires in Hungary were downwardly mobile from nonmanual to manual occupations. At the same time, only about 30 percent were downwardly mobile in European market societies (Erickson and Goldthorpe 1994, p. 301). Thus, the Chinese downward mobility rates in the Cultural Revolution decade were greater compared not only with European market societies but also with mature European socialist societies. By these comparative standards, Chinese downward mobility rates remained high even in the 1980s.

19. In the 1970s and early 1980s, China's degree of inheritance of manual occupations was similar to that in the Soviet Union in the 1970s (Connor 1991, p. 54). Connor argues that this high degree of inheritance led to considerable discontent.

20. Stronger for females, these tendencies were marginally significant in a multivariate analysis that included gender, nonwhite father, period, and both gender and nonwhite father by period.

tendencies toward mobility stagnation shared with other socialist states and because of China's extreme attempts at producing equality through reducing most people to the lowest common denominator of a blue-collar, manual job. Ironically, during the high tide of socialist idealism, China came to resemble the bleakest of Marx's predictions about capitalism's tendency to reduce everyone to low-status blue-collar jobs. As China moved away from idealistic socialism toward more of a market economy, the distribution of jobs and the uses and distribution of education began to resemble the patterns of market societies.

The distribution and uses of education illustrate the U-shaped pattern to China's entry and then exit from an extreme socialist order. Initially, as in market societies, parental education was very important for a child's education. This parental influence was severely eroded by the new socialist order, and particularly by the more extreme measures of the Cultural Revolution decade and the years immediately following. Then by the late 1980s many old patterns returned, with educated parents again being able to transmit advantages to their children.

While the extreme measures of the prereform period caused parents dismay, these measures did have the advantage of providing a basic junior and senior high school education for virtually everyone. The attempt to equalize education by shifting resources from college to basic education had its intended effect of making basic education widely available. This distinguished China from developing societies following a market model, where parental interest groups typically insist that government concentrate resources on college education. With the turn to reform, China moved ever so slightly toward a market, pluralist society. Though still modest by developing market society standards, Chinese college enrollment increased and educational credentials became more important for securing the best jobs. These tendencies all repeat the theme of a U-shaped pattern as China moved from market to high socialist principles and then back again.

A similar U-shaped curve was repeated for jobs and job mobility. Despite an early fluorescence of good jobs for children of all backgrounds, China's particular pattern of idealistic socialism meant that many kinds of white-collar jobs disappeared. The emphasis on production for production's sake, the bans on marketing and other service activities, and the shrinkage of managerial and administrative jobs reduced opportunities not only for the children of intellectuals and others but also for working-class children. Many white-collar children were downwardly mobile and most working-class children merely repeated their parents' status. It is only with the return of the market that opportunities have once again increased. Though upper-level administrative, managerial, and professional jobs remain scarce, many more white-collar clerical and service jobs are available for children of all class backgrounds.

China's U-shaped changes in opportunity again illustrate how total economic growth and an increasing number of white-collar jobs are essential to increasing opportunity (e.g., Erikson and Goldthorpe 1994). With a failure in growth and white-collar job expansion, all manner of discriminatory policies against old elites and affirmative action programs for working-class children failed to increase working-class opportunities. With the return to a more open market, elite families may more easily pass on advantages to their children. Nevertheless, total opportunity is sufficiently greater as to increase mobility for people from all types of family backgrounds. All these patterns suggest a complex set of social consequences secondary to differing social contracts.

4

Economic Rewards

THIS chapter continues the theme of the multiple consequences the shifting social contract has for individuals' lives. This time our emphasis is on economic rewards, with particular attention to the changes that are expected to occur as one moves from an administered, redistributive economy to a competitive market economy. For both Europe and China there is much debate about the pace and character of changes in the reward systems of former socialist economies. Some see many instances of the lingering advantages of work units and of close proximity to the centers of bureaucratic redistribution. Others see more wholesale changes toward rewards to the education and skills to compete in an open market (see references below).

The debates about former socialist economies are made more complex by the nature of "actually existing" market societies. A simple market perspective leaves the perhaps unintended impression that existing market economies provide a level playing field where people with similar degrees of human capital (education and experience) have similar opportunities to compete for jobs. An alternative structuralist perspective highlights the many "hills and valleys" that channel people into different types of jobs. According to this perspective, oligopolistic positions and other forces segregate labor markets into core and periphery sectors. Even with similar education and skills, people who begin their careers in the competitive periphery sector face a very different future of income and benefits from persons who begin work in large corporations and other core locations (for reviews of this contentious literature, see Smith 1990; Baron 1994; Tilly and Tilly 1994; Kalleberg and Van Buren 1996). Similarly, in many developing market economies a divide exists between formal and informal sector firms. Firms in the formal sector have high wages, generous benefits, and rules regulating labor and management relations. Firms in the informal sector of small firms have few of these rules or rewards (for a literature review, see Portes 1994). Thus, our examination needs to avoid comparison to an idealized market economy and instead to compare actually existing market economies with labor markets segmented on multiple dimensions.

ISSUES

Three views dominate the literature regarding China's pace of change. First, the bureaucratic bargaining view suggests either little change or only highly selective change. Inspired in part by a literature on informal bargaining in Eastern Europe and the Soviet Union, scholars working on Chinese labor call attention to the extensive bargaining between both workers and managers and between managers and the bureaucrats who are supposed to regulate factories.[1] Because of effective bargaining from below, Chinese state-run factories continued to enjoy many soft budget constraints through the early 1990s. Fearing urban turmoil, central and regional governments subsidized factories rather than let them go bankrupt. From below, Chinese workers had several mechanisms that increased their internal solidarity and bargaining power relative to managers, including lifetime employment, shared manager–worker residence, and the hiring of many kin in the same work unit (see Chapter 6 on this theme).

Yanjie Bian (1994) and other scholars note how differential bargaining power among enterprises created segmented labor markets, with differential fringe benefits flowing to units with more bargaining power (see also Lin and Bian 1991; Walder 1992; Logan and Bian 1993). Moreover, in an era of lessened central control, managers and administrators secured more benefits for themselves. Often these additional rewards were not in fixed wages, but in housing and other fringe benefits that were freer from central administrative control (Bian 1994a; Bian and Logan 1996). Thus, consistent with Stark's (1992) emphasis on the path dependence of reform in Eastern Europe, what occurs with reform is not continuous, unimpeded movement toward market equilibrium on a level playing field (see also Parish and Michelson 1996). Instead, the terrain

1. On both pre- and post-1989 Europe, see Sabel and Stark (1982), Burawoy and Krotov (1992), Burawoy and Lukacs (1992), Blanchard et al. (1993), Titma and Tuma (1993), Róna-Tas (1994), and Szelényi and Kostello (1996). On China, see Tidrick and Chen (1987), Walder (1989), Huang (1990), Stepanek (1991), O'Brien (1992); Walder (1992).

remains one of peaks and valleys, with centrally owned state firms, managers, and administrators continuing to control the commanding heights.

In some ways, these patterns parallel the Western market tendency for labor markets to be segregated between small businesses and large corporations. What is different about socialist states, ostensibly, is how advantages in large firms and government units are derived. Core firms in the West tend to be more capital-intensive and to enjoy a more oligopolistic position, which allows them to provide higher wages and benefits. Though large state firms in former socialist states are also more capital-intensive and more oligopolistic, these firms enjoy the additional benefit of being able to lobby the state bureaucracy for continuing subsidies and tax relief even when the firms are minimally productive.[2]

In China, evidence for the bureaucratic bargaining perspective includes modest returns to education, little interfirm mobility, continuing legal barriers to interregional labor migration, continuing high returns to administrators and party members, and continuing high income and in-kind services to firms with greater bargaining power (e.g., Walder 1992; Griffin and Zhao 1993; Bian 1994a; Bian and Logan 1996; Xie and Hannum 1996).

In contrast, the second, market transformation, view is much more optimistic. Róna-Tas (1994) labels this the "structural transformation" view for its insistence that planned and market structures reward entirely different kinds of individuals. The most outspoken scholar on this issue, Victor Nee (1989, 1991, 1992), sees widespread evidence of the liberating effects of market forces. Nee argues that he finds higher returns to education as the market creates more demand for skilled labor. Also, following themes that Ivan Szelényi (1978, 1988) developed for Hungary, Nee finds that direct producers (entrepreneurs, nonagricultural laborers) are reaping larger rewards than simple redistributors (administrators). Even more cautious authors such as Tom Rawski and Gary Jefferson see fundamental transformations since 1985, most rapid in rural enterprises and urban collective firms but gradually accelerating in urban, state-owned firms as well (Jefferson, Rawski, and Zheng 1992a, b; Jefferson and Rawski 1994). The reforms since 1985 increased the link between enterprise profit and personal income. By the late 1980s, half of all

---

2. For hypotheses about the differences of segmenting mechanisms in Chinese and Western firms, see Walder (1992).

income was derived from bonuses and fringe benefits, and only successful firms could pay so much in fringe benefits. Accordingly, workers
began to pressure managers to be more productive in order that bonuses
and fringe benefits increase. Other incidental evidence suggested increasing market responsiveness. Ever more quasilegal migrants from the
countryside took menial jobs in textile mills, construction, transport, and
personal services. The accelerating flow of migrants moved predictably
from less to more affluent areas (e.g., Oshima 1990; Liang and White
1994, 1996). Additionally, 1990s data showed increasing income returns
to education (Maurer-Fazio 1994; Zaks 1994; Bian and Logan 1996;
Zhou, Tuma, and Moen 1996, 1997).

A third, mixed solutions, view suggests an answer to the debates about
marketization in China. The mixed solutions are of two types. One type
of mixed solution is sensitive to timing. In China through the early 1990s,
most firms continued to be publicly owned at the national, regional, or
neighborhood level. Though private firms and collaborative joint ventures with foreign firms were growing rapidly, they remained a small part
of the total economy. Most of the initial private firms were small family-
owned restaurants, stores, and factories that represented an erosion from
below, reminiscent of the pre-1989 second economy in European socialist states. This was quite unlike the post-1989 transition-from-above
pattern that came to dominate East European privatization efforts
(Róna-Tas 1994). Since old bureaucratic elites in both China and Europe
had little interest in small, erosion-from-below enterprises, it is little
wonder that they were little involved in early privatization efforts
(Szelényi and Kostello 1996, p. 1088). Only with an increasing pace of
spontaneous privatization and officially sponsored privatization of large
state firms at the very end of the 1990s did Chinese administrators and
managers get involved in the new private enterprise sector. Meanwhile,
the mixed economy continued to reward bureaucrats in many traditional
ways. Unsurprisingly, many authors suggested that both old bureaucratic
advantages and new market advantages were maintained through the
early 1990s (e.g., Bian and Logan 1996; Zhou, Tuma, and Moen 1996,
1997).

A second mixed solution is that each sector of the bureaucratic elite
benefits (or benefited) differently from new patterns. Scholars working
on Eastern Europe suggest that as private market principles become
more pervasive, old administrators, initially privileged by being close to

centers of redistribution, gradually lost their advantage. However, old technocratic managers, with specialized skills needed for the new economy, continue to be amply rewarded along with new entrepreneurs emerging from society (e.g., Szalai 1990; Róna-Tas 1994; Szelényi and Kostello 1996, table 1). This thesis of technocratic continuity contradicts both the thesis of power continuity (as in Bian and Logan) and the thesis of structural compensation (as in Nee). The technocratic continuity view suggests that the emerging market structure required technocratic skills that were common among the old managerial elite. We explore the possibility of technocratic continuity by paying particular attention to how managers fared compared with administrators.

ANALYSIS STRATEGY

In this section, we examine evidence related to the issues of continuing bureaucratic politics (power continuity), market transformation (structural transformation), and the mixed solution of technocratic continuity. If most jobs continue to be secured through bureaucratic channels, if income returns to education remain modest, if firm ownership remains more important than occupation and education in determining income and benefits, and if redistributing administrators continue to be more highly rewarded than managers and private, self-employed personnel, we will conclude that much of the old, bureaucratic politics regime persists. Conversely, we will conclude that market transformation is progressing if income returns to education are increasing (particularly among new hires), if firm ownership has little effect on rewards, and if managers and the self-employed are more highly rewarded than others.

We plan to proceed in the following way. First, we include fringe benefits along with regular wages. In the analysis of both European socialist economies and China the point is emphasized that fringe benefits, including in-kind housing and other rewards, are often as important as regular wages. For workers at the bottom of society, there is a "social wage" consisting of free or highly subsidized medical care benefits, housing, and the like. Those at the top have access to cars, drivers, special hospital wings, travel, and other perquisites, in ways that greatly increase the elite's income (Matthews 1982). In the analysis of bargaining advantages of elites in China, much attention is given to benefits – including the increasing role of monetary bonuses, special subsidies, housing, and other rewards (e.g., Walder 1992; Bian and Logan 1996; Zhou, Tuma, and Moen 1996). Given less top-down control of these additional sources of income, the greater fluidity of benefits and other nonwage income by type of employee and type of enterprise ostensibly shows the continuing role of bargaining between firms and workers and between firms and the bureaucracies that govern them.

We add two items to the debate over bargaining and benefits. One is to provide a valuation of all benefits, both in cash and in kind. The 1988 CHIP data set imputes a monetary value for housing and other in-kind benefits.[3] We include this in our analysis of both "other income" and "total income." Next, we suggest caution in overgeneralizing from differences in fringe benefits by type of enterprise. In the U.S. economy, for example, benefits are closely related to size and type of enterprise. Much as in China, larger U.S. firms provide more fringe benefits. Moreover, compared with workers in the private sector, U.S. government workers get as much as one-fifth greater fringe benefits (U.S. 1995, p. 435; Kalleberg and Van Buren 1996, p. 58). Thus, American firm size and public/private sector differences roughly parallel those found in China, suggesting that some processes by which benefits are derived can be shared across market and planned economies.

A second preliminary note on the analysis involves the analysis of returns to human capital. In both the structural/market transition views and in the technocratic continuity views, there should be increasing returns to education and experience. We suggest, however, that one should expect change not across the board but primarily among young new hires. Also, in line with patterns elsewhere in East Asia, we expect only modest increases in income returns to education. Though most developed market societies provide 7 to 9 percent extra income for each additional year of formal education, returns of only 4 to 6 percent are common in Japan and Taiwan (Maurer-Fazio 1994; Psacharopoulos 1994). Thus, though we expect rates higher than the 2 percent usually found for China, we expect rates to be only marginally higher. Also, one reason that rates of return to education have been so low is that most income promotion has been based on simple seniority. Thus, one thing

3. The imputed housing subsidy includes housing area, nature of sanitary facilities, and the average cost of construction per square meter in the region, with all of this multiplied by 8 percent to estimate the rental value. Rental value net of actual rent is the housing subsidy. See CHIP codebooks (1998, vol. I, part 13, item UY9).

that we will note is whether increases in income continue to be a linear function of seniority or whether Chinese income patterns are beginning to assume the more parabolic pattern characteristic of most market societies, of rapid rises early in the career followed by a leveling off in income (Mincer 1974).

Finally, the analysis proceeds in two parts, first focusing on income returns to education, where income includes cash and in-kind benefits. Second, we look at returns to authority, by which we mean returns to being an administrator (redistributor) rather than a manager or private entrepreneur (producer).[4]

RETURNS TO EDUCATION

We begin by replicating parts of the Maurer-Fazio (1994) analysis of the 1988 CHIP data set. We are trying to explain the determinants of total income, including all bonuses and fringe benefits. Our primary interest is in the returns to education in the top part of Table 4.1. Let us start, however, with a few notes on the findings shown in the bottom half of the table.

In 1988, returns to work experience initially increased and then leveled off at higher levels of work experience. This parabolic pattern, though beginning to approximate trends in market societies, was still much more linear than in the average market society. Thus, major parts of the old seniority-based system of promotion remained in place through the late 1980s. Men earned about 11 percent more than women, an income difference that was modest when compared with market societies. Unsurprisingly, average city income was closely related to personal income.

Of greater interest is the relationship between income and education. As in other studies of China, the basic link between income and education was modest. However, in the emerging nonstate sector, the relationship was closer. Added to the basic educational effect, the return to

4. For a time, it seemed that worker-producers would gain on managers and administrators, producing greater equality between these two groups (see Walder 1995). However, that moment has passed, with manager–worker income differences now growing (see Chapter 6; Bian and Logan 1996; Szelényi and Kostello 1996). Moreover, because Walder (1995) used monthly bonuses that favor workers rather than year-end bonuses that favor management, he may have overstated the equalizing effects of bonuses.

Table 4.1. *Returns to Education, 1988*

Education (years)	
Basic relationship	.020**
×Nonstate sector	.013**
×Age	
20–29	.015**
30–39	.013**
40–49	.006*
50–54 (cf.)	
Work experience	.043**
Experience^2 /100	−.062**
Nonstate sector	−.262**
Age group:	
20–29	−.215**
30–39	−.141**
40–49	−.092*
50–54 (cf.)	
Male	.111**
Income average of city	.953**
Constant	−.290
R^2	.403
Observations	16,249

Notes: Regression analysis of logged income, including bonuses and fringe benefits. Education coefficients after the basic education relationship are interaction terms between nonstate sector, age, and education. Each of these can be added to the basic relationship. For example, for those in the nonstate sector, the total effect of each extra year of education was .020 + .013 = .033. Probability calculations are adjusted for multiple members of a single household. (cf.) Comparison group; (**) $p < .01$; (*) $p < .05$.

Source: 1988 CHIP urban survey, income earners aged 20–54.

each additional year of education in the nonstate sector was 3.3 percent.[5] This was still modest, but higher than in the traditional state sector. Moreover, returns to education were higher among youth. Added to the basic education effect, younger workers obtained returns to education of more than 3 percent.[6] Again, this suggests an emerging market pattern, which is encouraged partly by the spreading use of entrance exams for entry into the most desirable jobs. The increasing returns are not just the result of credentialism, however, for even in the private sector of small family firms, where degrees are largely ignored, higher education brought higher incomes among young workers (details not shown). In short, though the changes might be glacial in tempo, the greater returns to education in the nonstate sector and among the young suggest gradually emerging market trends.

RETURNS TO AUTHORITY

Next, we explore returns to authority, including returns to being an administrator (e.g., in government or as a party secretary in a factory) or manager (of a factory or store) and returns to being in an administratively high-level work unit. This continues with the analysis of the 1988 CHIP data set, adding this time a distinction between types of rewards. Because jockeying for publicly owned housing space is a common concern in work units and neighborhoods, square meters of housing space deserve a separate treatment. The "base wage," controlled by administrative rules, should be less responsive to market trends. Because "other income" – including bonuses, the imputed rental value of housing space, and other cash and noncash benefits – is less subject to centralized administrative control, it should be more responsive to market trends. In this data set, "other income" was about one-third of "total income."

Our questions include the following: Do people closer to the centers of redistribution receive more rewards? In particular, do more rewards

5. Derived from the basic relationship coefficient of .020 plus the nonstate additional coefficient of .013, for a total effect of .033, or 3.3 percent.
6. Derived from the coefficients of .020 (basic) + .015 (ages 20 – 29) = .035. Of course, the younger workers average less pay than older workers, but within their respective cohorts the marginal return for each extra year of education is greater for younger than for older workers. Our interpretation, though surely debatable, is that much of this higher marginal return to education will persist as these workers mature.

flow to government agencies, centrally and regionally run government work units, administrators, and party members? Or, instead, do more rewards flow to economic enterprises (factories, stores), joint ventures, private enterprises, entrepreneurs, and the educated? If the latter, then, people closer to production and marketing are reaping the greatest benefits from the new economic regime. Let us proceed by considering, in order, work unit type, work unit ownership, occupation, party membership, and the human capital attributes of education and experience (Table 4.2).

Work Unit Type

Though people in government agencies obtained more housing (and other in-kind benefits not shown), housing advantages only partially compensated for lower cash income. In both base wages and in the bonuses and other benefits that make up "other income," government employees got less than other people. Thus, it turns out, the penchant for in-kind benefits was a desperate response to low pay, which through the late 1980s failed fully to compensate for administrators' low salaries. Instead, the big winners in the struggle for rewards were people in factories, stores, and other similar economic enterprises. Though these individuals closer to the market lost in the struggle for housing, they did much better in the struggle for other kinds of benefits. The net result was that in total income, people in economic enterprises were major beneficiaries.

Finally, the anomaly occurs that people in publicly funded hospitals, schools, and other public organizations received rewards that approached those in the money-producing, economic enterprise sector. These people, close to neither redistribution (government administration) nor to production and sales (economic enterprises), did surprisingly well. To this subject we return later.

Ownership

Rewards by ownership appear much like advocates of the bargaining view have found in other studies. Centrally and regionally run state enterprises provided more rewards than collectively run enterprises licensed by urban neighborhoods, either because they were more capital-

Table 4.2. *Returns to Work Unit Attributes and Authority, 1988*

	Housing space	Base wage	Other income	Total income
Work unit attributes				
Type				
Economic enterprise	−.09**	.05**	.08**	.06**
Public organization	−.04**	.03**	.06**	.04**
Government agency (cf.)				
Ownership				
Central government	.05**	.12**	.22**	.14**
Regional government	.03*	.06**	.24**	.10**
Neighborhood collective (cf.)				
Joint venture	.10	.36**	−.48**	.09
Foreign	.26#	−.05	−.87*	−.32
Private	.08	−.02	1.17**	−.07
Personal attributes				
Occupation				
Manager	.15**	.12**∧	.11**	.12**∧
Administrator	.18**	.07**	.09**	.07**
Professional/technical	.06**	.06**	.10**	.06**
Clerical worker	.08**	.03**	.09**	.04**
Entrepreneur	−.05	.05	.30**	.18**
Manual worker (cf.)				
Party member	.02#	.05**	.07**	.06**
Male	−.04**	.10**	.09**	.10**
Education, years	.008**	.03**	.02**	.02**
Experience, years	−.02**	.04**	.05**	.04**
Experience^2/100	.04**	−.05**	−.08**	−.06**
R^2	.24	.44	.28	.46
Observations	17,392	17,361	17,164	17,493

Notes: Regression analyses of logged space and income. Other income includes cash and cash equivalent values of bonuses, subsidies (including imputed rental value of housing space), and other income. All columns include the following unreported determinants: average income of city, an "other" category for ownership and type of work unit, and a constant. Additionally, the housing space column includes the number of family members, distance from city center, and smallness of city, all of which increase size of housing. In calculating statistical significance, we adjusted for multiple members from the same household. (cf.) Comparison group; (**) $p < .01$; (*) $p < .05$; (#) $p < .10$; (∧) $p < .01$ in manager/administrator comparisons.

Source: 1988 CHIP Urban Survey, income earners.

intensive and had more of an oligopolistic position in sales (as in Western, developed country labor markets) or because they were in a better bargaining position vis-à-vis central planners (as in other socialist economies). Just as the bargaining view predicts, the extra rewards were particularly generous when it comes to more flexible "other income," which is not so tightly monitored by external administrators. One does not want to overstate the one-fifth to one-fourth income gains secured by people in higher-level firms. In the United States, gains of one-third are more are common between core and peripheral firms (e.g., Weakliem 1990, p. 581). Nevertheless, the state sector gains in China are still consistent with the view that being near the centers of administrative redistribution was beneficial.

Newer, nonstate ownership forms were beginning to exhibit some alternative patterns of rewards. Nevertheless, as of the late 1980s, these other forms of ownership did not seriously challenge the first types of publicly owned work units. Joint ventures provided ample wages but few other kinds of benefits, so that total rewards were like those in regionally run enterprises. Foreign investors (mostly from Hong Kong and Taiwan) provided modest benefits of all sorts. Family-owned stores, restaurants, and other types of small, private operations provided ample rewards through nonwage channels but little else. Thus, as late as 1988, nonstate firms more squarely in the market did not provide major competition to centrally run state firms. This supports the bargaining view that through the late 1980s change was modest.

Occupation

In the bargaining view, administrators, closer to the centers of redistribution of central government budgets should have reaped greater rewards. Though they do get more housing, this was a hollow victory, since in all other types of rewards, administrators were only marginally ahead of professional and technical workers and severely behind managers of economic enterprises. Enterprise managers were themselves not well paid. A comparable group of managers in Taiwan, for example, would be making a full 45 percent more than manual workers.[7] Never-

---

7. From analysis of raw data in Taiwan's May 1990 Labor Force Survey, with controls for the same background factors as in Table 4.2. The same survey shows that relative to

theless, the marginally higher pay of managers compared with administrators and other laborers suggests that people closer to production were gaining more than simple redistributors.

Party Membership/Education

Party membership can imply little more than a measure of status, in ways that are not picked up by our crude measure of occupation. For example, in each of the separate categories of administrators, managers, and clerical workers – groups among which party membership is concentrated – party members were concentrated in more responsible positions. Party membership could also imply a less benign access to redistributors in ways that led to additional rewards that were unavailable to high-status white-collar workers in other societies. Unfortunately, we cannot separate these benign and not-so-benign influences. Whatever the precise reason, party members reaped additional rewards in 1988.

If the not-so-benign aspect of party membership dominated, the bargaining view would argue for the continuity of the old system, which we can neither prove or disprove. But even assuming less benign advantage, we urge caution in interpreting the size of the effect of party membership. Party members were only marginally advantaged in housing. In total income, their 6 percent advantage was about the same advantage that one could gain from an extra three years of education ($3 \times .02 = .06$). Thus, staying through high school rather than stopping at junior high would have reaped just as many benefits as joining the party. Going back to night school or other programs for mid-career study brought many of the same advantages. These rewards to education were particularly helpful for young people (see Table 4.1). Thus, in at least this one comparison, party membership seemed not to mean as much as it once did.

Not too surprisingly, 1988 was a transitional period. On some dimensions, old bargaining advantages remained – people were more highly

manual workers, professional and technical workers in Taiwan were advantaged by 22 percent and clerical workers by 14 percent. In the United States in the 1990s, income advantages were even greater than those in Taiwan – e.g., uncontrolled for background conditions, among males and in comparison with manual workers the income advantages were 174 percent for administrators and managers, 177 percent for professionals, and 136 percent for technical workers (U.S. 1995, p. 433).

rewarded when they were in centrally run work units and when they were in the party. On other dimensions, change was beginning – people were more highly rewarded when they worked for economic enterprises, when they were managers or entrepreneurs, and when they had more education. Educational rewards were particularly important for new hires in the nonstate sector, suggesting that education would become more important simply from the more rapid growth of the nonstate sector. Moreover, the increasing role of "other income" was strongest for people working in economic enterprises, in the private sector, and as entrepreneurs, groups much closer to the market. As these groups expand, they are causing both an increase in income differentials and a greater responsiveness to market signals. These patterns, then, suggest emerging market trends that will expand in years to come.

RECENT TRENDS

Change has continued at a rapid pace since our data were gathered in the late 1980s and early 1990s. Along with rapid economic growth since 1990 a sharp shift has occurred in the composition of the labor force. The changes are evident in several trends that occurred between 1988 and 1997. The percent of the nonfarm labor force in the service sector grew from 45 to a full 53 percent, continuing a trend that started in the early 1980s (SSB 1998a, p. 28). Employment in nonstate work units grew from 30 percent to a full 45 percent, with much of that growth being in privately owned work units (SSB 1998a, p. 28). Pay levels also increased rapidly in some nonstate work units, making them attractive alternatives to working in state-owned work units (SSB 1996, pp. 120–26). With these changes, inequality increased among urbanites. While the richest 10 percent of all households earned only 3.1 times as much income as the poorest 10 percent in 1988, that ratio rose to 4.2 times as much income by 1997 (SSB 1989, p. 729; 1998a, p. 329). Though the ratio of 4.2 was still modest by international standards, the increasing gap meant that the prize for economic success was greater than in the past (World Bank 1995).

A comparison of surveys completed during early and mature reform suggests that one of the results of increasing income inequality was that both redistributing administrators and producing managers and others had ample opportunities to reap greater rewards (Bian and Logan 1996).

Consistent with a mixed solutions view, then, both redistributors and producers benefited from a wealthier, more unequal system.

New Income Patterns

Nevertheless, even this emendation may be insufficient. Though use of aggregate income figures is difficult, in part, because reporting procedures changed in 1995, many aggregate changes are consistent with other types of evidence about changes in the labor force. We ask how workers in different sectors are faring relative to manufacturing workers. The relative income is expressed as a percentage, with 100 meaning that they are earning the same income as manufacturing workers. We group the results in line with our previous classification of government agencies, public organizations, and economic enterprises.

We begin with economic enterprises grouped at the bottom of Figure 4.1. Taken as a percentage of the average wage in manufacturing, many groups rose in income by 1997. This is exactly what we would we expect for sectors such as finance and other business services, for transport, and social services (including consulting and legal services). Compared with the faltering rustbelt activities of the old state manufacturing sector, it is unsurprising that these newer types of market activities have prospered. It is also unsurprising that people in retail trade and construction have suffered. These are sectors with considerable private sector competition and with considerable competition by immigrants from rural areas.

No matter how economic activities have fared in China since 1985, all the economic activities at the bottom of Figure 4.1 have done better than their U.S. counterparts. Again, this is plausible. Emerging market sectors in China could enjoy much more demand than in the United States. Thus, both the 1985–97 trends in China and the comparisons to the United States are consistent with a market transition perspective.[8]

Supporters of a bargaining perspective will not be disappointed, however. After the official wage reforms of 1993, government workers again rose above the average of manufacturing workers (Fig. 4.1, top bars). The 1997 government income advantage returned government

8. A devotee of the bargaining perspective will note, of course, that some groups such as those in finance were in an interstitial position between plan and market. Thus, some of their return was because these groups could turn public resources to private, market advantage.

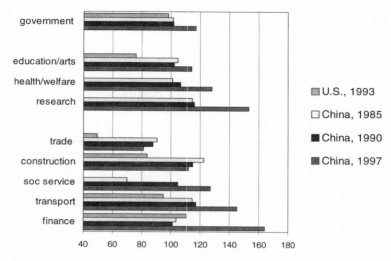

Figure 4.1 Relative income by country and year. Notes: Income is expressed as a percent relative to people working in manufacturing. "Education/arts": education, fine arts, and broadcasting; "health/welfare": health, physical education, and social welfare; "research": scientific research and technical services; "trade": retail trade; "soc service": social services, including consulting; "finance": finance, insurance, and other business services. U.S. data shown with "education/arts" combine health, education, and related services. Source: U.S. (1995, p. 431); SSB (1998a, pp. 160–61).

sector employees to an even better position than they held in 1978 (SSB 1998a, p. 160). It also helped keep them in a much higher relative position than government workers in the United States. These patterns are consistent with a bargaining position.

The redistributors versus producers debate seems too simplistic, however. Between 1985 and 1997, many of the largest income gains were by the middle group of people in public organizations – in publicly funded research institutes, health care, welfare work, education, broadcasting, and the arts. These are people who do not do particularly well in the United States (combined in a single category after education and the arts). Yet they have done particularly well in China, especially after the 1993 wage reform. These are people particularly close neither to production, as we normally understand it, nor to redistribution. One tendency with some of these groups in other societies is that they organize themselves into professional associations that establish licensing procedures that limit access and help raise income. From this pattern elsewhere, one might infer that informal bargaining of doctors in the health care field is responsible for some income gains in China. However, the health care field still lags behind incomes in research institutes. Even in the United States, where groups are free to organize, wages in these types of service activities typically lag behind those of most other sectors. Thus, a story about interest group bargaining appears here that is poorly captured by standard "distributor versus producer" accounts. Certainly bargaining exists, but developing a plausible story of how that bargaining occurs remains a task for more detailed research.

Administrators and Managers

New national-level data on managers and administrators are also available (SSB 1996, pp. 127–30). In 1995, though lagging in housing (39 vs. 42 square meters per household), managers averaged 16 percent more income than administrators. Though the exact size of these relative advantages varied by rank, education, and gender, the directions of the differences were consistent: Administrators excelled in housing benefits while managers excelled in take-home pay. As in earlier data, it appears that the extra housing benefits for administrators failed to compensate for the inequality in take-home pay. Though facing greater uncertainty because of a rising failure rate in economic enterprises, on average, people closer to production remained the ones who were better paid in total rewards.

Private Entrepreneurs

Finally, we also have new national data on private entrepreneurs running enterprises with eight or more employees. A 1995 survey provides data both on who becomes an entrepreneur and who succeeds once the business is opened.[9] The patterns among some 1,600 urban entrepreneurs are

9. Though they have no responsibility for the manner in which the results are presented here, these results are from a joint project with Zhang Houyi, Sociology Institute, Chinese Academy of Social Sciences; Li Yuanzheng; Li Lulu, Sociology Department, Renmin University; and Dai Jianzhong, Sociology Program, Beijing Academy of Social

consistent with several themes. One theme is the expected evolution from an "erosion from below," with many new entrepreneurs coming from the ordinary and sometimes even dispossessed population, to a "transition from above," with many entrepreneurs in larger enterprises coming from the old state sector (Róna-Tas 1994; Szelényi and Kostello 1996). The Chinese data suggest precisely this evolution. Increasingly, as private enterprises were legalized in 1988 and an acceleration of economic reform was signaled in 1992, more entrepreneurs from the old established sectors began to appear. Among firms begun before 1988, only about one-fourth of entrepreneurs had held responsible positions in either state or urban collective work units.[10] However, by 1992–95, almost half of the new urban entrepreneurs had held responsible positions in state or neighborhood work units. "Responsible positions" might include anything from factory head to senior clerical worker. By this definition, more established elites from the old order were shifting into the private sector.

A second theme is that the transition was increasingly one of technocratic continuity. Most people moving out of the old established sector were not government administrators. Former administrators constituted only about one-fifth of the "responsible people" moving from state and neighborhood work units. Instead, the vast majority were from economic enterprises, where they served as high- or low-level managers, engineers, and clerical or sales workers in supervisory positions. Thus, as in Szalai's (1990) and Róna-Tas's (1994) suggestions for the Eastern European transition, it was often a technocratic elite that was switching to the private sector. Old skills in production, marketing, and raw material supply were being redirected to private uses. Consistent with the technocratic continuity, education levels increased among firm owners who began more recently – from a pre-1988 average of 10.5 years education to a post-1991 average of 12 years of education, which was high in comparison with the average population. Education and responsible positions in economic enterprises eased the shift into private entrepre-

Sciences. The analysis here is heavily indebted to work with Li Lulu and with Li Fang. See Li (1997).

10. Of this total, about one-fourth were from neighborhood licensed urban collectives and three-fourths were from state-owned work units. The reference here is to jobs held just before becoming an entrepreneur.

neurship. This is consistent with the technocratic continuity view of economic transition.

The cynic will note that some of the more educated people from economic enterprises were bringing more than their education and experience with them. The daily loss of assets from state-owned firms and the increasing size of initial investments in private investments suggests that, much as in postsocialist Europe, "spontaneous privatization" was occurring (ZGCZNJ 1996, pp. 555, 561, 587). They also brought many network ties that might help them. In other words, these individuals were well endowed not only in human capital but also in financial and social capital. Nevertheless, aside from education, regional prosperity, industry, and year of founding, responsible people from established enterprises had no more initial financial capital than anyone else.[11] This suggests that human and social capital were their major sources of advantage.

 Despite their promising initial advantages, responsible people from established enterprises had only mediocre success in expanding their business. We judged success by total revenue, controlling for city size, transport density, regional per capita income, age, gender, the year of founding, and industry. The remaining factors that were important for success support a technocratic continuity rather than a power transference argument. That is, in urban areas, the entrepreneurs with the highest revenues were neither party members nor responsible people from the established state or neighborhood work units. Party membership provided no boost to current revenue. Prior leadership roles in an established sector helped, but not nearly so much as having had a responsible role in other sectors, including in a joint venture, in a rural collective enterprise, in a combine enterprise, or as a rural administrator.[12] Our

---

11. Statistically, responsible people from established enterprises had no more initial capital than people who had been manual workers.

12. Specifically, among those with any prior work experience, entrepreneurs from professional and technical backgrounds had the lowest revenues. Compared with this less successful group, responsible people from established work units generated somewhat more (logged) revenue ($b = .43, p = .06$), which was about as well as entrepreneurs who had been farmers ($b = .48, p = .09$). Entrepreneurs who had held responsible positions in nonestablished firms or as rural leaders did almost twice as well ($b = .83, p = .002; b = .86, p = .01$). Entrepreneurs who had been only manual workers performed about the same as former professional and technical workers. In a separate analysis, Szelényi's interrupted embourgeoisement argument was not supported. Parental pre-1949 experience in the market did not help 1995 performance.

interpretation is that practical experience in sectors that were already exposed to competitive market pressures provided better preparation for success as an entrepreneur. Experience in a competitive market setting was more important than connections back to the old redistributive sectors of the economy.

Moreover, aside from all these other conditions, education sharply increased chances for success. For each extra year of education, revenue increased 10.3 percent. Thus, with six more years of education – for example, a high school rather than a primary school degree – individual revenue increased by more than 60 percent. This increase was beginning to approach the effect of having had a leadership role in nonestablished enterprises, for which the revenue increase was about 80 percent. Thus, both formal education and experience in more marketized sectors were beginning by 1995 to have a payoff for private entrepreneurs.

CONCLUSION

We began with three potential views of the process of economic transformation and its consequences for economic rewards. These included: the market transition or structural incompatibilty view, predicting a wholesale switch in the types of people rewarded; the bureaucratic bargaining or power transference view, predicting considerable continuity in who is rewarded; and two mixed views, both a partial transition view and a technocratic continuity view.

Our results, we believe, support both of the mixed views. Though unsurprising for a society that was slow to abandon public enterprises, the partial transition results do suggest systematic evolution toward a more market-oriented system. In this evolution, greater inequality allows multiple winners, including both old administrative redistributors and new managerial and entrepreneurial producers, a theme first stated by Bian and Logan (1996). There are several other signs of a gradual evolution, in the way that Szelényi and Kostello (1996) lay out in their "Toward a Synthesis" approach to market transition debates. Gradually, among young, new hires, among new private entrepreneurs, and in the nonstate sector, education is being more highly rewarded. Educational skills have begun to count in China's rapidly changing economic environment. Also, as economic reform has accelerated and private firms have been legitimated, private entrepreneurs appear less in a pattern of "erosion from below" than in a pattern of "transition from above." No longer are entrepreneurs largely from the less educated, sometimes dispossessed, parts of society. Instead, they are increasingly people who have had responsible positions in state and neighborhood enterprises. Thus, even without wholesale privatization of state firms, a gradual evolution is occurring by which people with education and leadership experience leave for the private sector. These tendencies are all consistent with a gradual evolution view of transition.

Our results are consistent in a more fundamental way with the technocratic version of a mixed transformation. Róna-Tas (1994), following Szalai (1990), suggests a technocratic continuity in the pattern of transition. He suggests what in other words might be called "different strokes for different folks." Small family-owned enterprises may be staffed by people with little prior experience in the old redistributive sector. However, as private firms grow in size, individuals with education and technocratic experience in old state-owned firms may be a major source of entrepreneurial talent. We believe that our results are consistent with this viewpoint. Even in an only partially reformed economy, managers were more successful than administrators. This was when they remained in government-owned work units. Similarly, managers and others in leadership roles in enterprises were more likely to leave for the private sector. Former government administrators only rarely left for private employment. Once in the private enterprise sector, entrepreneurs with leadership experience in joint ventures and other units closer to the market were more successful. Party members were no more successful than others. These types of evidence are consistent with arguments about technocratic continuity. People with educational training and practical experience in market-exposed enterprises were more likely to become successful private entrepreneurs.

Our conclusion about partial reform and mixed transitional outcomes suggests that redistributive and market economic rewards can coexist for some time. Bureaucratic bargaining remains important while new sources of market-based advantages emerge simultaneously. Nevertheless, we conclude that China's distinctiveness as a bureaucratic bargaining social system can be overstated. Through the middle 1990s, income differences in China remained modest (World Bank 1995). The Chinese manager and administrator were only slightly advantaged compared with managers and administrators in market societies. Similarly, income differences between centrally owned state enterprises and collectively owned enterprises remained modest when compared with differences between core and periphery work units in market societies (e.g., Weakliem 1990, p. 581). Party members were still advantaged. However, some of their advantage was because they were of higher status, which would lead to higher rewards in market societies as well. Even if party members were advantaged because of special party connections, many of their advantages could be emulated by people who got several more years of education – suggesting that new advantages could increasingly overtake old advantages. Rewards from bonuses, subsidies, and other types of nonwage benefits were greater in administratively advantaged work units, suggesting potentially that high-level work units bargained more effectively with the bureaucracies above them on nonwage items. However, these same work units were also larger, which should have made it easier for them to provide additional benefits, much as it does in market societies (on size effects, see Walder 1992). Government units, close to centers of redistribution, provided more housing and other in-kind benefits. This again repeats a market society pattern where people who are only modestly paid in wages secure alternative kinds of rewards (e.g., Kalleberg and Van Buren 1996).

In short, Bian, Logan, and Lin have done us a great service by noting the considerable segmentation of Chinese labor markets (e.g., Lin and Bian 1991; Bian 1994a; Bian and Logan 1996). The special character of that segmentation, however, rests not on the magnitude of the differences in income and benefits between workers in different segments of the labor force. The size of those differences in China seems modest compared with market societies. In China, what must be distinct are the bargaining mechanisms by which these differences are realized – in the qualitative rather than the quantitative differences between different segments of the labor force. The set of bargaining mechanisms remain poorly understood (Walder 1992).

Of course, not all recent changes have been in the same direction. While people in rapidly growing productive sectors have been major beneficiaries, people in research institutes, health care, and other public organizations have also been major winners when compared with the old rust belt of state manufacturing firms. Government workers also prospered in the post-1993 wage reforms. However, compared with people in emerging economic enterprises and in public organizations, government workers lagged behind. Thus, there is surely bargaining occurring, but the old bimodal contrast between redistributors and producers is inadequate to capture recent changes. We thus need a new political economy of changes in income and benefits.

5

Popular Reactions to the Changing Social Contract

THIS chapter continues many themes of the last chapter, asking whether a sharp shift occurs away from the egalitarian, security, redistributive values of the old social contract toward the inegalitarian, high-risk, producer values of a new market-based social contract.[1] This chapter differs from the former in emphasizing not income but popular attitudes. Do people embrace or recoil from the prospects of a new social contract based on the uncertain promise of more consumer goods and greater chances for individual upward mobility, accompanied by the loss of stable prices and a secure safety net? We capture the changes in popular perception at the very moment that the transition from a socialist to a market-based contract was threatened by rising inflation and falling real incomes. With multiple surveys from the time before and after the student protests of 1989, we examine the personal and regional conditions that affected support or resistance to the changes associated with economic reform. With year-to-year survey data, we examine changes that signaled an increasing acceptance of market reforms among several groups in the population. These data on this critical juncture in Chinese political history provide a rare view of the impact of market reform from the individual level.

ISSUES

A whole range of values and attitudes must change if economic reform is to be welcomed in society. We examine not only total levels of satisfaction with reform but also the demands for speeding or slowing the pace of reform and the levels of dissatisfaction about specific issues. For 1987–91, the specific issues include economic issues (price instability,

---

1. See Tang and Parish (1996) for an early version of this chapter.

102

consumer supplies), government performance (corruption, the rule of law), and democratic participation, which was one demand of student demonstrators in 1989. Shifts in types of dissatisfaction and reform support during the late 1980s and early 1990s say much about the changing acceptability of reform efforts.

For 1992, when China returned to the path of steady economic growth and reform, we examine specific attitudes about hopefulness about one's personal situation, about how reform would affect the respondent, about fairness of pay, about individual economic effectiveness, and about acquisitiveness. The issue of acquisitiveness is particularly significant. Many citizens of former socialist societies in Europe were ambivalent about the growing inequality and the growing focus on earning money for the sake of earning money, which both arise during the market transition. Individuals often longed for the egalitarianism and security of the past, particularly when economic conditions worsened (e.g., Duch 1993; Berliner 1994; Dobson 1994; Millar and Wolchik 1994; Kluegel and Mateju 1995; Mason 1995; Zaslavsky 1995). To some extent, the ambivalence about new, acquisitive behaviors repeats issues of the "great transformation" from traditional communal equalitarianism to market individualism that occurred with industrialization in the West (Polanyi 1944). Following Karl Marx, E. P. Thompson calls this the transition from a "bread nexus" to a "cash nexus" in human relations (Thompson 1971; Tilly 1975).[2]

In this chapter we examine the types of people and locations that appreciated the new "cash nexus" and the accompanying ostentatious display of new wealth. As suggested in the previous chapter, rhetoric and public opinion during the height of socialism emphasized security and redistribution and discouraged flaunting individual achievement and acquisition. These tendencies reached their height in China during the

---

2. Traditionally, agricultural societies, with an image of a zero-sum, finite supply of goods, emphasized egalitarian social contracts. Community members who attempted to rise above their fellow villagers and townsmen were treated with great jealousy. Fearing jealousy and sabotage, economic elites often avoided ostentatious consumption, and redistributed some of their wealth through public invitations to lavish wedding feasts and other similar activities where ordinary people could enjoy the benevolence of elites (e.g., Foster 1965; Scott 1976). Barrington Moore (1966, epilogue) makes this mentality the basis for the communitarian outcomes of peasant based revolutions – a theme that was picked up in Chinese writings in the early 1980s, with the attribution of egalitarian thinking to small peasant mentality.

Cultural Revolution decade when ubiquitous Mao suits in blue and gray helped obscure the social status of their wearers. As already suggested in our discussion of consumerism, the age of blue and gray Mao suits has long past. Chinese cities have rapidly moved into a new consumer age, where ownership of goods is increasingly prized (Chapter 2). We wish to explore whether this consumerism carries over into dramatic changes in underlying attitudes about acquisitiveness.

Determinants

The potential determinants of changes include societal and personal material conditions, expectations, and structural opportunities. Material conditions include both societal and personal material conditions. Societal material conditions can be more important than personal conditions in shaping people's reactions to government policy. In the West, the inflation rate and other macro-level economic conditions often determine whether people vote against the government in power, irrespective of their personal economic situations (e.g., Butler and Stokes 1969; Kinder and Kiewiet 1979, 1981; Lewis-Beck 1988, 1991; MacKuen, Erickson, and Stimson 1992). In the Soviet Union and Eastern and Central Europe sharp downturns in perceived economic conditions helped increase support for former Communists (Przeworski 1991; Duch 1993; Dallin 1995; Zaslavsky 1995; Miller; Reisinger, and Heslie 1996).

Based on these earlier findings, we expect popular support for reform to be closely related to changing national economic conditions, including rates of economic growth and inflation rates. These national conditions, in turn, may relate to the economic conditions of different regions. With the decline in centralized decision-making, regions have become more economically heterogeneous. With the weakening of the former tendency to transfer resources from coastal cities to those in the interior, coastal cities should be much more enthusiastic about reform than those in the interior. With the shift from heavy industry to light industry and to services instead of production, people in cities with less old, state-run, heavy industry should be more optimistic. In particular, the possibility exists that like the United States, China's industrial northeast is seeing the emergence of an old rustbelt dominated by heavy state-run industry. This old rustbelt is being supplanted by a new sunbelt, concentrated in cities along the southern and southeastern coast, especially near Shanghai and Guangzhou.

In addition, there may be a general increase in optimism among residents of large cities. For the first time in several decades cities are now freer to expand, and they therefore attract many more domestic and foreign investment dollars as well as migrants from throughout the country (see Chapter 2), which may lead to a growing sense of optimism at new economic opportunity. If our hunches about these types of influences are correct, satisfaction with reform and optimism about life should be greater in China's emerging sunbelt, in larger cities, and in periods when inflation is low and economic growth rapid.

Personal material conditions, both current and future, will be shaped by one's occupation, age, and party membership. This "class interest" approach asks whether one's satisfaction is based on one's occupation and sector of the economy perceived to be winning or losing in the new transition (see Chapter 4). By the early 1990s, personal "class positions" were shifting. Old-line party work was deemphasized and some parts of the private sector were prospering. Though the rates of pay often remained modest, sales and service sectors were emerging rapidly (Chapter 4). Producing managers appeared to be gaining on redistributing administrators (Chapter 4). The gap between manual workers and white-collar workers was increasing, though the gaps between the two sectors remained modest compared with market societies at similar levels of development. Thus, any predictions about the influence of occupation will be indeterminate. Clearly, people with higher current incomes and in the growing private sector should be pleased with reform. Blue-collar workers may be concerned with their loss of job security, particularly as more of them were forced to sign short-term labor contracts (see Chapter 6). Nevertheless, whether all white-collar workers are pleased with the consequences of reform is uncertain. One reason is that many of the white-collar workers were tied to the old, redistributive system, which emphasized strong internal labor markets for those with seniority and the right political credentials (Finifter and Mickiewicz 1992; Duch 1993). Weakening these internal labor markets might not be welcomed by white-collar workers who might see this as encroaching on their area of privileged access. However, white-collar worker attitudes toward reforms are difficult to determine because this group of workers also has high expectations that would be difficult to meet. These expectations would be fueled in part by education but also in part by increasing contact with neighboring Asian societies, where white-collar workers have much higher incomes. Thus, here as elsewhere, expectations must be considered.

Expectations, shaped by both domestic influences and diffusion from abroad, filter the way material conditions are perceived. Domestic conditions are likely to include both education and natural conditions such as youth and gender. Education will, of course, have mixed effects. With the increased credentialing of good jobs and with higher income returns to education, many educated might be more optimistic and pleased with reform (see Chapter 4). However, while raising human capital that is increasingly valued in today's job market, education also raises expectations in ways that can lead to disappointment and bitterness about perceived government and societal failures (e.g., Inkeles 1959, 1968, 1974; Almond and Verba 1963; Silver 1987; Bahry and Silver 1990; Kohn and Slomczynski 1990; Huntington 1991; Finifter and Mickiewicz 1992; Inglehart 1997). Thus, the exact prediction of satisfaction with reform based on education alone is difficult to determine, as are the effects of youth. In most societies, youth are eager for change. Yet in the late 1980s and early 1990s, Chinese youth had far less job security and pay than older workers in society. As to the effects of gender, one might expect males to be both bolder in their endorsement of change and more likely to be able to withstand the fluctuations in the job market (since women might be the first fired/last hired; see Chapter 10).

One might infer that people are more likely to accept market principles when they have contact with ready examples of successful market societies abroad. Thus, abutting Hong Kong, residents of Guangzhou and the surrounding Guangdong Region, because of their frequent economic and other interactions with Hong Kong, should be more accepting of market principles. Conversely, within the country, people in and around the capital of Beijing should begin with more egalitarian, redistribution norms (see Chapter 4) with less personal contact with successful market societies. We expect the diffusion of attitudes from abroad to be differentiated across different areas of life. Through the late 1980s, though neighboring East Asian societies were beginning to democratize, many authoritarian tendencies remained in places such as Hong Kong, Taiwan, South Korea, and Singapore. Thus, the diffusion from abroad is more likely to have shaped values about economic prosperity and acquisition than values about freedom of expression and popular participation in government policy making.

Structural conditions are also likely to shape whether people rapidly abandon older redistributive norms for new, acquisitive norms. Literature on the West at the time of industrialization suggests that people were more likely to be crassly materialistic and to look out for themselves rather than for others once they gained anonymity in large cities and had weak social ties to their neighbors (Simmel 1903a, b; Fischer 1982; Hummon 1990). Thus, when we examine new values of acquisitiveness, we pay attention to both the influence of city size and the closeness of ties to neighbors. Residence in large cities and weak ties to neighbors should weaken old, redistributive norms.

In sum, we expect societal and personal material conditions to be the primary determinant of a whole range of values related to reform, including general satisfaction with reform, beliefs about whether the pace of reform is too fast, and whether the consequences of reform, including economic opportunity and acquisitiveness, are good or bad. At the societal level, important material conditions will include the rate of economic growth of a city, the inflation rate of the city and the nation, and location not in China's fading industrial rustbelt but in its emerging sunbelt near Hong Kong and other foreign influences. Residence in the largest cities, with the attractiveness to both domestic and international investment, will also induce attitudes positive to reform. At the personal level, we expect location in the emerging private sector and in jobs that earn high incomes to enhance satisfaction with reform. Expectations will moderate these reactions, causing people with more education to be less tolerant and causing people near the orthodox core of Beijing to be less accepting of changes. The anonymity of residence in large cities will accelerate the acceptance of new acquisitive values.

DATA AND MEASURES

We use data from two different sources. One is a national survey, repeated seven times between early 1987 and late 1991. With replies from a cumulative total of 16,450 respondents in 40 cities over five years, this survey focuses on satisfaction with reform and its consequences. Our second survey is again a national survey conducted in June 1992. Covering more than 2,000 respondents in 44 cities, it provides

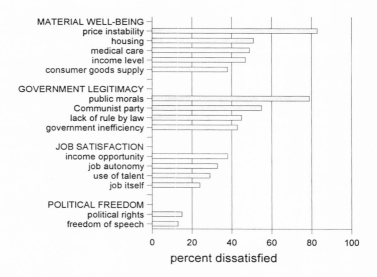

Figure 5.1 Reform dissatisfaction, 1987–91. Source: Combined sample, ESRIC
Semiannual Surveys, 1987–91.

more details on specific responses to reform. From the first survey, we
draw items on satisfaction and the pace of reform. From the 1992 survey
we use items on hope, reform, economic efficacy, fairness of pay, and
acquisitiveness.

Satisfaction with Reform

The 1987–91 surveys include information about satisfaction levels in
fifteen different areas, which we group into four larger domains (Fig. 5.1).
The survey items we use put an emphasis on evaluating the government's
delivery of services or, put another way, on evaluating the government's
"outputs." Averaged over all seven surveys, the government's services or
"outputs" that generated the most dissatisfaction were price increases
and public morality, including bureaucratic corruption. Besides concern
over prices and public morality, urban residents were concerned with
threats to their social security. Half were concerned about losing subsidized medical care and housing. Government credibility suffered almost
as much as welfare and security. With most people resenting bureaucratic

profiteering, the reputation of the Communist party declined rapidly. The decline of government credibility was also related to the lack of the rule of law.

Economic opportunity was perceived as less of a problem than security and government credibility. On average, well under half the respondents were dissatisfied with income opportunity, job mobility, use of talent, and job interest. One possibility, of course, is that the increased opportunities for job mobility under market reform had begun to have an effect. Finally, the responses suggest that freedom of speech and political rights were low on most people's agendas. Though levels of dissatisfaction varied widely, most items tended to be related. People who were dissatisfied on one issue were likely to be dissatisfied on other issues. Accordingly, for the analysis below we sum all fifteen items into a single measure of satisfaction.[3]

Pace of Reform

In the 1987–91 surveys, respondents were also asked about the pace of reform.[4] Potential replies were "too slow," "too fast," and "just right." Over all seven years, about one-fifth replied that reform was too slow, two-fifths said "too fast," and one-third said "just right," though the latter two responses varied widely from year to year (Appendix Table A5.1).

3. For each item, the original coding was (1) satisfied, (2) dissatisfied, and (3) don't know/don't care. We assigned the mean value to "don't know/don't care," and reversed the coding.
4. We use the term "reform" as understood by ordinary Chinese. One component of reform was to improve economic efficiency with programs that included relaxation of central planning, development of market exchange and competition, reduction of egalitarianism in income distribution, separation of power between the Communist party and the state, decentralization of decision making from the central government to the provinces, enterprise autonomy, hardening budget constraints, reducing subsidies at individual and enterprise levels, implementing labor contract and bankruptcy laws, and increased economic opportunities for the nonstate sector. Another aspect of reform was political democratization, including a reduced role of the official socialist ideology and more freedom of belief, the development of a genuine legal framework, the strengthening of government efficiency, the improvement of the Communist party's image in relating to the people, and the curbing of bureaucratic corruption. Because these reform programs were widely discussed in the Chinese media and some had been implemented, the average Chinese urban resident should have had a general idea about the meaning of reform.

Specific Attitudes

In the 1992 survey, we have five different summary scales. Our "hope" scale includes five items that score high when people disagree with such statements as "Life is really meaningless." This scale provides a general indicator of mental well-being and optimism. Our "reform" scale includes five statements that question whether people view life as improving under reform. This scale differs from the satisfaction scale used above because it asks questions less about how well the government is doing and more about how the individual respondent is faring under reform. Our "economic efficacy" scale includes four questions about whether a person can get ahead through his or her own individual efforts without assistance from family or other special social connections. Our "income fair" scale is an affirmative response to the single question of whether respondents agree that their income is reasonable relative to their abilities. Our "acquisitiveness" scale uses seven statements to measure whether one values money and its acquisition highly. It includes statements such as "Work is merely for earning money to get by," "An individual's earning money is always beneficial to society," and "One only needs to have money to gain respect from others." Appendix Table A5.2 provides details on these items.

Explanatory Background

The background factors that should shape satisfaction, beliefs about the pace of reform, and individual reform-related values can be enumerated very briefly. Societal material conditions include the national inflation rate over the last three months, city inflation rate over the current year, city income growth rates, population, location in the sunbelt (Guangzhou City or Guangdong Region,[5] Shanghai, Southeast China, or Yangzi River Delta) as opposed to rustbelt (northeast China), location in one of the three metropolitan centers (Shanghai, Beijing, Tianjin), and proportion of city income generated by light industry and the service sector. Personal material conditions include personal or family per capita income,

---

5. In this analysis, the Guangdong Region encompasses the West River drainage area, or William Skinner's Lingnan Region. The provinces (and cities) are Guangdong (Shantou, Zhaoqing), Hainan (Haikou), and Guangxi (Liuzhou). This captures the capital city of the last two provinces and regional cities from the first province.

work in the private sector, and work in a white-collar job. Expectation factors include education, youth, gender, party membership, and location in the orthodox redistributive core of Beijing. Structural conditions that free people from orthodox, redistributive constraints include residence in large cities and weak ties to neighbors (see Appendix Table A5.1 for descriptive statistics on these measures).

We begin with data on trends between 1987 and 1991. The major influence on these trends is likely to be the sharp increase in inflation that started in 1988 and then was quelled in late 1989 through a sharp contraction of the money supply. Several aspects of economic reform contributed to inflation. Prices were gradually relaxed, as was centralized control of firm and local government budgets. Still enjoying soft budget constraints, local governments and firms fed their investment hunger with loans that could not always be paid back. This contributed to growth in the money supply, causing price inflation of nearly 25 percent in late 1988 and early 1989 (Fig. 5.2). While unexceptional by the standards of many developing market societies, the 25 percent inflation rate was frightening to Chinese on fixed salaries. Part of the old social contract included price stability, and this part of the contract had been honored since 1949. It was honored no more, and for many people, real incomes declined.

The result was a sharp rise in dissatisfaction and in the belief that the pace of reform was too fast (Fig. 5.2). The one-fourth who believed reform was too slow shrank. Even more dramatically, the vast majority of people who began in 1987 by saying the pace of reform was "just right" switched to saying that the pace was "too fast." Specifically, while only 20 percent said reform was too fast in early 1987, almost 60 percent said it was too fast by 1989. Thus, material conditions had a tremendous impact on popular acceptance of the pace of reform. Indeed, had a narrowly circumscribed referendum on reform been held in 1989, the ironic result would have been that reform would have lost.

By late 1989, as the central government reasserted control over the free spending habits of local governments and firms, inflation declined. With this decline, dissatisfaction also declined and resistance to rapid reform softened (Fig. 5.2). Despite this softening, the public never had

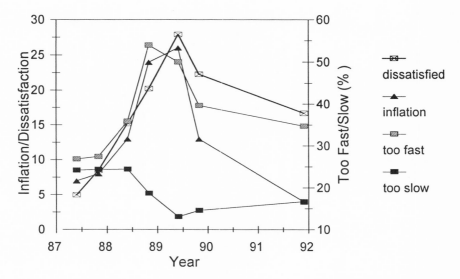

Figure 5.2 Inflation and reform attitudes. Notes: Left axis represents average inflation rate over the previous three months and generalized dissatisfaction with reform (a summary scale). Right axis represents percent of people who say the pace of reform is either too fast or too slow. Source: ESRIC Semiannual Surveys, 1987–91.

the level of trust in government that it did before the onset of rapid inflation. While rising dissatisfaction closely paralleled the rise in inflation, declining dissatisfaction lagged behind the fall in inflation. Though inflation rates returned to their pre-1988 levels, dissatisfaction and distrust of the pace of reform remained high.

The detailed patterns of dissatisfaction with specific items reveal some of the dynamics involved in dissatisfaction (Fig. 5.3). Patterns of dissatisfactions with the economy and with the government increasingly diverged. Economic dissatisfaction rose and fell in concert with the inflation rate and with the increasing supply of consumer goods (see Chapter 2). Indeed, complaints about economic issues were often fewer in 1991 than they had been in the mid-1980s. Specifically, dissatisfaction with prices in 1991 was 60 percent, less than the 80 percent dissatisfaction in 1987. Similarly, consumer good dissatisfaction fell below 1987 levels. In economic realms, then, the population responded positively to

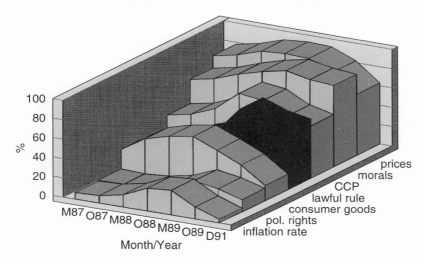

100
80
60
% 40
20
0

prices
morals
CCP
lawful rule
consumer goods
pol. rights
inflation rate

M87 O87 M88 O88 M89 O89 D91

Month/Year

Figure 5.3 Inflation rate and percent dissatisfied by domain and date. Notes: For May and October survey dates in 1987, 1988, and 1989, plus November 1991 survey. Domains are political rights, consumer goods, rule by law, Chinese Communist party, official corruption, and price stability. Weighted percent dissatisfied. Source: ESRIC Semiannual Surveys, 1987–91.

the government's control of inflation and the greater supply of consumer goods that came from the new emphasis on light industry.

In governmental areas, dissatisfactions lingered. Post-Tiananmen coercion, reduced inflation, and increased supplies of consumer goods all had only a marginal effect on complaints against the government. As late as 1991, complaints about public morality, the Communist party, and the failure to sustain a rule of law (as opposed to a rule of arbitrary decisions and personal connections) remained much greater than they had been in 1987 (Fig. 5.3).[6] By 1991, concerns about public morality (including corruption) and the lack of the "rule of law" were the greatest single sources of dissatisfaction. Public morality had deteriorated as the mixed

6. This differentiated set of responses – increasing satisfaction on economic issues and lingering dissatisfaction on government issues – suggests that survey respondents were less than fully intimidated by the coercion surrounding the events at Tiananmen in 1989. If coercion were a major factor, we would expect the pattern of responses to be just reversed – with sudden reports of satisfaction with government and the party and continuing dissatisfaction with economic issues.

market/planned system opened many avenues for official profiteering (see Chapter 7 on corruption). The spillover effect of the increased publicity about these types of offenses was that dissatisfaction with public morals, the rule of law, and the Communist party itself increased and remained considerable in 1991. Thus, in these areas, partial reform led to a set of issues that continued to challenge the legitimacy of the government in the public mind.

Finally, student demands for democratic rule never found much echo in the public. Even at the height of inflation, dissatisfaction with political rights and freedom of speech remained at very modest levels (Fig. 5.3 and statistics not shown).[7]

Sources of Satisfaction

Several aspects other than inflation also helped shape people's levels of satisfaction. We can examine these multiple influences in a multivariate analysis. To examine changes over time, we conducted a separate analysis for each of four years (Fig. 5.4).[8] We group the explanations according to societal and personal material conditions and expectations.

Societal material conditions were quite important. Inflation rates varied from city to city. Satisfaction was lower in high inflation cities. Conversely, high city income, residence in a large city, and residence in the sunbelt (Guangzhou, Shanghai, and, to a lesser extent, southeastern cities) increased satisfaction. Personal material conditions were also important. People were more satisfied when they had more income, worked in the private sector, and worked in sales and service type jobs. People were less satisfied when they were party members or in upper white-collar jobs. Finally, expectations were important. Satisfaction declined when people were more educated, young, and male.

These are all consistent tendencies over the four years surrounding the popular disturbances of 1989, and they largely fit patterns we anticipated

---

7. Even among students, demands to end corruption (71%) outstripped demands for freedom of expression (51%) and free associations (16%) – Calhoun (1994, p. 246).
8. Income was last year's family income, in nine levels: (1) less than 1,000 yuan, (2) 1,000–1,500, (3) 1,500–2,000, (4) 2,000–2,500, (5) 2,500–3,000, (6) 3,000–3,500, (7) 3,500–4,000, (8) 4,000–4,500, and (9) more than 4,500. Education had five levels: (1) illiterate, (2) primary, (3) junior high, (4) senior high, and (5) college and more. Party membership was coded one and nonmembership as zero.

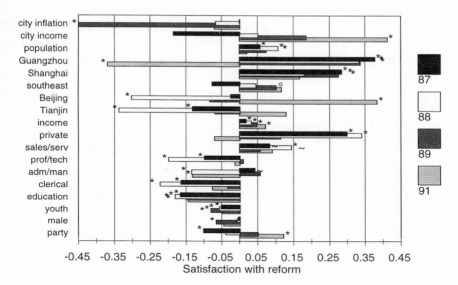

Figure 5.4 Satisfaction with reform by year. Notes: Coefficients from OLS regression. City inflation is ten percentage points, more price inflation compared with previous year. City income and city population are logged. Shown locations are compared with all other locations. Personal income is on a 1 to 9 income scale. "Private" is private sector job. All occupations are compared with manual worker jobs. Education is on a 1 to 4 scale. Youth coefficients show the effect of being ten years younger. Party member is coded 0/1. Coefficients not shown include southwest region, student, retired, unemployed, and "later survey" when there are two surveys in the same year. Truncated bars include 1989 city inflation $(-.55)$. $(*) p < .05$; $(°) p < .10$; $(\sim) p < .05$ when compared with professional and technical workers. Source: ESRIC Quarterly Surveys, 1987–91.

in the introduction. There are some additional patterns that are even more interesting. These include changes in the position of some regional and personal subgroups. We cannot explain all these shifts, such as the Guangzhou shift, which we had not anticipated and of which we are not completely convinced since it fits so little of the other data. Yet several shifts are quite plausible, even if we must now use a post hoc explanation for them.

Several explanations at the societal level present themselves. Over time, city income level became more important. This is consistent with the implicit government policy encouraging people to think more about economic well-being than about other issues; this goes along with a similar shift in the influence of personal income. Income of one's city and one's family became more important over these four years, all of which is consistent with "consumerism" as an increasingly important government output as society moved in a market-oriented direction. If this was intended by government leaders, the intention was achieved.

The southeastern part of the sunbelt (cities in the provinces of Jiangsu, Zhejiang, and Fujian) moved from wariness to acceptance of societal conditions. People in Beijing made an even more dramatic shift, from being significantly displeased to being significantly pleased with current conditions. Also, significant displeasure in Tianjin was dampened and even turned in a slightly positive direction by 1991. Again, these tendencies are consistent with an account that emphasizes increasing market consumerism and the ways that major cities and the southeastern provinces began to have a major role in this market transformation in the early 1990s. Being near the centers of the new, 1990s market transformation heightened people's sense of satisfaction with many aspects of current conditions.

At the personal level, others jumped on the bandwagon as well. Party members were the most notable. They were greatly displeased in 1987 but by 1991 were quite satisfied. For reasons that we explore later, party members made their peace with market reform (see Chapter 7).

Not everyone participated in this delight, however. Through 1991, the private sector continued to suffer from the money supply tightening that began in mid-1989. Many private businesses went bankrupt because of reduced demand and a shortage of capital. The sharp reversal in the attitudes of people in private business is consistent with the reversal of fortunes that persisted through late 1991.

In short, the system was quite dynamic through these years. The changes in position of some regions and social groups suggest that many aspects of market reform were beginning to take hold. People and regions in a position to take advantage of the consequences of that reform were satisfied with how they could participate in the new system. Old, redistributive centers such as Beijing and Shanghai provided some of the best new opportunities. Residents of the new sunbelt were generally the most pleased of all. Though the inflation rates of 1988–89 provided a tremendous shock to many Chinese urbanites, among several groups the trend was toward greater approval of the consequences of market reform even while general dislike of government corruption and inefficiency remained high.

Pace of Reform

When people were dissatisfied, it is not completely clear what they would have proposed as a solution. However, as a starting point, let us make the simple-minded assumption that people respond according to their class interests. If they are already doing well and if further change might endanger that position, they will want to continue the course or even slow reform. If they have education and other skills that might be highly rewarded in a politically and economically more open and competitive system, they will want to accelerate reform. In short, class interests might dominate most opinions.

Much of what is observed fits precisely this predicted pattern. The larger pattern contains three subtypes. The largest subtype includes the dissatisfied who seemed to imagine that they would do better under a highly reformed system. This is clearest for current and potential personal material rewards. Explaining this in figures requires that the reader flip back and forth between the figures for satisfaction with reform and for "increasing the pace" of reform (Figs. 5.4 and 5.5). On average, upper-white-collar workers (professionals, administrators, clerical workers), the educated, the young, and males complained about current conditions (Fig. 5.4). One apparent reason for their complaints was that they believed that they could do much better under a reformed, more openly competitive system. They all saw themselves as doing poorly now, and wanted to increase the pace of reform (Fig. 5.5, bottom half). This subordinate pattern is made up of a group of people who saw themselves as doing poorly now, but who thought they could do much better under a more reformed system. This group included not only those who were in a position to reap an immediate reward but also those who had high expectations of future reward because of their education, youth, and gender.

The second subtype was for residents of locales in which people were already doing well and did not want things to change too much. This included larger cities and cities with higher income per capita. In 1987, it also included the city of Guangzhou, which was prospering and where

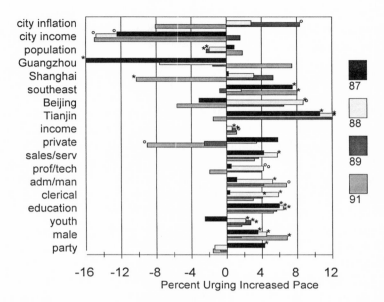

Figure 5.5 Desire for increased pace of reform by year. Notes: Percentage change coefficients from a probit analysis. The possible responses about the pace of reform were "too fast," "just right," or "too slow." This analysis is based on the proportion of people who give the last response, with + values for "too slow" and – values for those who disagree. Truncated bars include 1987 Guangzhou (–22) and 1988/89 Tianjin (19/14). See notes to Fig. 5.3 for definitions of coefficients and for a list of coefficients not shown. (*) $p < .05$; (°) $p < .10$. Source: ESRIC Semiannual Surveys, 1987–91.

people felt the pace of reform was just right. By 1991, it also included party members, who switched sides on the issue of both satisfaction and the pace of reform.

The third, minor subtype includes individuals who were both currently satisfied and also confident that they would do better with accelerated reform. Examples were high-income people and people working in sales and service jobs. They would be helped by a more open economic system.

Other patterns are not so easily explained, though a few are plausible. In the tight money regime that lasted through 1991, formerly optimistic private entrepreneurs who had previously wanted fast reform decided that rapid reform was not such a good idea. It is tempting to continue finding interpretations for particular patterns, but we desist. The more important lesson is the one discussed above. Certain groups felt they would gain under a more highly reformed system; the most prominent were young, male, educated, white-collar workers.

This, at least, was the pattern through 1991 for satisfaction with current conditions and for hopes regarding the pace of reform. Still unsettled are the issues of whether these general responses carried over into more specific values and whether attitudes changed in 1992, when the money supply was relaxed and the political atmosphere became more liberal and open to continuing economic reform. This is the topic to which we now turn.

SPECIFIC REFORM ATTITUDES, 1992

Deng Xiaoping's southern tour in early 1992 was a turning point in China's stagnation after Tiananmen in June 1989. Deng's speech during his southern tour focused on the continuation of market reform. We can see the beginning of public response to this new atmosphere by examining survey results for the summer of that year, several months after Deng's speech.

For attitudes related to optimism, economic conditions, and acquisitiveness, we want to know the consequences of societal and personal material conditions, expectations, and (for acquisitiveness) structural opportunity. Societal material conditions include the city economic growth rates, percent of city income generated by expanding light industry and service sectors (as opposed to old, state-owned, heavy industry), sunbelt location (Guangdong, Shanghai, the Yangzi Delta), and residence in a major metropolitan area (Shanghai, Beijing, Tianjin). These regional locations are compared with the state-owned, heavy-industry rustbelt in the northeast. Figure 5.5 suggests that white-collar workers and those with more income thought that they would be better off if the economy were further reformed. If they were correct in their suppositions, these types of workers should have been much happier in the summer of 1992 when the pace of economic (not political) reform again accelerated. Factors leading to increased expectations include education, youth, and gender. For the analysis of acquisitiveness, structural conditions include weak ties to neighbors and residence in larger cities (see Appendix Table A5.2 for descriptive statistics).

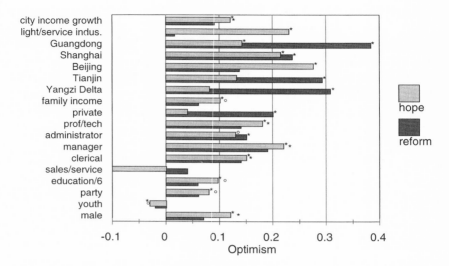

Figure 5.6 Optimism by city and personal characteristics, 1992. Notes: Determinants include city economic growth (1989–91 annual income growth in tenths of a point), light industry and service sector as logged percent of total city income, regions compared with the northeast (Manchuria), logged per capita family income, occupations compared with manual workers, six additional years of education, party membership, and ten years younger. Other coefficients not shown in the OLS regression equations include other regions and never married. Approximate number of observations: 2,143; $R^2 = .07$. (*) $p < .05$; (°) $p < .10$. Source: 1992 China Urban Survey.

Optimism

Our two measures of optimism are for both general views about life and about whether one is likely to succeed during reform. With only a few exceptions, the people who heretofore had wanted the pace of reform to increase were unusually optimistic in 1992 (cf. Figs. 5.5 and 5.6). White-collar workers, the young, the educated, males, high-income people, and residents of fast growth, light industry, sunbelt, and metropolitan cities were all pleased with their life situation and with their chances during reform. Conversely, by comparison, manual workers and people in China's rustbelt were displeased. Thus people with both high personal capital (education, white-collar jobs, income) and "city capital" (access to a city with positive characteristics, including fast economic growth, light industry, service industry, sunbelt, or metropolitan location) were all pleased with their prospects.

Such individuals with high resources and access brought along with them small entrepreneurs in the private sector, who again turned optimistic about reform (cf. Figs. 5.5 and 5.6). The optimistic also included party members, who continued their satisfaction levels from 1991 (cf. Figs. 5.4 and 5.6). It failed to include sales and service workers, who began to look more like manual workers in their attitudes.

Economic Attitudes

Optimism about one's personal situation did not carry over into all attitudes. People in the private sector and in high-growth cities felt that their income was fair and that a person could get ahead by his or her own efforts. But young, educated males and those in professional and technical jobs continued to feel that their expectations were not being met. They continued to complain about poor pay and the inability to get ahead by their own efforts. Thus, much as in the questions about satisfaction and the pace of reform in earlier years, these groups kept wanting more from the economic system. The attitudes measuring optimism suggest partial success, but partial success only in appeasing some of these groups.

Acquisitiveness

Reactions to acquisitive behavior and attitudes provide one of the sharpest demarcations between people linked to the old, redistributive system and the new, rough-and-tumble market system. White-collar workers, party members, educated individuals, and people in Beijing found individual acquisitiveness repulsive. Many of these groups either benefited from orderly, internal labor markets in large firms and bureaus or were close to the orthodox, redistributive center, Beijing.[9] Several other groups took quite an opposite view of acquisition. They found the prospects of individual acquisitiveness and the attendant public display of acquisition much more attractive. These opposing opinion groups

9. Of course, the disdain for acquisitiveness and earning profit may be cultural, with Chinese (and Russian) intellectuals historically looking down on the world of commerce and profit as something beneath them.

included manual workers (the implicit occupational comparison group), sales and service workers, private entrepreneurs, youth, males, and residents of high-growth cities, particularly in the Guangdong Region, abutting Hong Kong. Besides the effect of rapid economic growth and proximity to Hong Kong, there was also the structural effect of residence in large cities and weak ties to neighbors. In the anonymity of large cities, with few close neighbors to frown on one's acquisitive habits, people became less squeamish about abandoning collective equality values for values favoring individual acquisition.[10]

The last set of effects was sizable. On a four-point scale, a person who was half as neighborly (two points down on the scale) was .20 points more accepting of acquisitiveness. Also, compared with a resident of the smallest sample city of 100,000 population, a person in a middle-level city of one million was .08 points more acquisitive and a person in a large city of five million was .14 points more acquisitive. Thus, city size effects heightened acquisitiveness about the same degree as white-collar occupation dampened acquisitiveness. Or, in short, by both type of city and type of individual there was a growing divide between people tied to old and people tied to new economic values.

Thus, in 1992, we could divide urban residents into three basic groupings. The first group included the direct beneficiaries of continuing market reform, such as those in the private sector, major urban centers, cities with rapid growth, and regions abutting Hong Kong. For this group, market reform increased their hope, satisfaction, economic efficacy, feeling of fairness, and acquisitiveness. For the second group, such as party members, Beijing residents, the more educated, and those in the upper occupational subgroups, the story was not that simple. While welcoming continuing market reform in principle, they remained suspicious of the uncertainties and opportunities for themselves. They also eschewed explicit acquisitiveness. The third group consisted of the immediate losers of market reform, particularly those living in the old, rust-belt regions. They did not welcome further reform.

10. Large cities vary greatly in degree of anonymity, with old, inner-city courtyards still maintaining close neighbor ties while new peri-urban high-rise apartments begin to lose those ties. Even in inner-city courtyards, big-city living may create a certain blasé attitude about income differences, much as Simmel (1903a) suggested for an earlier time in the West.

CONCLUSION

In summary, there are two fundamental themes that emerge from our findings. One is that of adaptation and the other is one of class interests. Let us take them up separately.

Adaptation

We began with the issue of whether people could adapt to the new social contract. Could people accept the loss of job and income security that came with the old redistributive social contract, with its restrictions on inequality, consumption, and ostentatious display? Conversely, could they accept the loss of income and job security that came with the new market-based contract, including its high levels of consumption and new acquisitive values? The answer we think is yes. People could adapt though not without considerable tribulation, gradual learning, and significant differences among subgroups in the population.

In the late 1980s and early 1990s, China demonstrated once again the importance of continuous economic growth, modest inflation, rising real incomes, and more consumer goods for the popular acceptance of market reforms. These conditions are, of course, valuable in any society. The initial stable growth patterns of other East Asian societies such as South Korea, Singapore, and Taiwan were based on similar premises. What made these ingredients perhaps even more critical in China were the decades of stable prices. Given that initial stability, Chinese urbanites were shocked by inflation rates in excess of 20 percent. Confronted by this inflation, their level of disapproval of government policy and of economic reform soared. Many switched from approving economic reform to disapproving it, or at least wanting it to slow.

It was only with the control of inflation after 1989, continued economic growth, and an increasing supply of economic goods that people's anger subsided. Though many remained critical of the government, the party, and corrupt bureaucrats, on other dimensions people were much more satisfied by 1992 than in the late 1980s. While inflation again rose to around 20 percent in the mid-1990s, incomes rose apace, so that real incomes always remained at or near the previous year's level. By all signs, discontent never escalated as it had in the late 1980s. With a continuing rise in incomes and consumer goods, the world no longer appeared to be the zero-sum game that it once was. Redistribution could seem less important if incomes were growing for many people.

The findings on the importance of city effects suggest that people paid as much attention to larger societal conditions as they did to their personal fates. This repeats findings for other societies, where the larger social environment is often of as much or more importance as a person's own material conditions. China demonstrates some odd twists, including the fact that people in high-income cities were not eager to accelerate the pace of reform. Generally, however, city income, income growth, low inflation, population, metropolitan status, and sunbelt location all promoted acceptance of reform and of more acquisitive behavior. Weak ties to neighbors, the anonymity of large cities, and proximity to Hong Kong also enhanced the acceptance of acquisitiveness. To the extent that economic growth continues, residential mobility increases, and cities get larger, the trend seems inevitably to lead to more acceptance of reform and the behavioral trait of acquisitiveness. These are all signs of a gradual acclimating of people to the byproduct of the new market-based social contract.

Unsurprisingly, one set of complaints did not rank very high in people's lists of grievances. These were calls for political rights and for freedom of speech. Despite demands for democracy from students in 1989, most people did not rank this concern very high. This is probably not too surprising. Calls for democracy occur more often when competing elites are locked in a stalemate (O'Donnell, Schmitter, and Whitehead 1986; Higley and Gunther 1992). With no private sector to speak of, no elite groups existed that could effectively challenge government and party leaders. Moreover, East Asia through the middle and late 1980s demonstrated very few examples of open democracies. The really successful East Asian models that Chinese might consider emulating – South Korea, Taiwan, Singapore – had only begun to move in a democratic direction, and then only after decades of rapid growth under authoritarian rule. Until the late 1980s, these alternative models provided a model more of successful economic change than of democratic liberalization.

It might be argued that the continuing government control did have some positive consequences. Though governments and firms continued to bargain for soft budget constraints, the continuing authority of the central government allowed tight monetary control to be reimposed in 1989, bringing down the rate of inflation. This contrasts with the initial years of democracy in Russia, where monetary control could not be reasserted. Also, relative immunity from public pressure kept politicians from responding to what in 1989 was the majority public sentiment, that reform should be slowed (Fig. 5.2). No opposition party could use inflation as a rallying cry for bringing in more votes. As Susan Shirk (1993) has noted, much bargaining continued, with local governments always pressing for more financial autonomy from the center. Nevertheless, the centralized control that remained made the Chinese central government less subject to public and enterprise pressure than in some of the former socialist states in Europe. With the ability to impose tight monetary policies, gradual reform could continue.

Class Interests

The other major theme that emerges from our analysis is the considerable importance of class or group interests, where class or group is defined by income, occupation, education, age, and gender. Though some inconsistencies exist, for the most part, societal elites had a common syndrome. This syndrome combined high initial dissatisfaction with a call for accelerating the pace of reform and, by 1992, considerable contentment with how they were surviving during reform (Fig. 5.7). Upper-white-collar workers (professionals, administrators, managers, and clerical workers), educated workers, and males all shared in this syndrome. Though more satisfied with societal conditions in earlier years, high income earners shared many similar traits. They wanted to accelerate reform and they were pleased with reform in 1992. These are the groups of people who were most likely to do well in a more open market economy. As late as 1992, before the 1993 wage reforms, professional and technical workers remained very unhappy with their incomes, as did the more educated (Fig. 5.8). Upper-white-collar workers had disdain for new acquisitive values (Fig. 5.9). Yet on most other dimensions, higher income, upper-white- collar workers embraced reform and its consequences. When they were discontent, it was often only because reform was not moving faster.

When people were discontent, it was often because their occupational groups were hurt by reform policies. Initially optimistic and desirous of

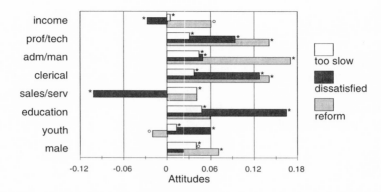

Figure 5.7 Class interests and reform attitudes, 1992. Notes: Based on the same measures and equations as in Figs. 5.4–5.6, only with data for all survey dates combined for the first two measures.

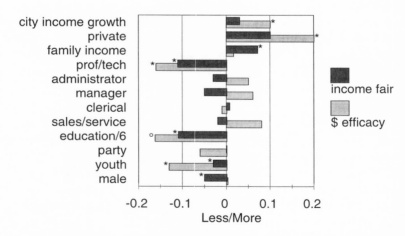

Figure 5.8 Economic attitudes, 1992. Notes: Proportional change coefficients from probit analysis ("income fair") and OLS regression coefficients ("economic efficacy"). (*) $p < .05$; (°) $p < .10$. Also see Fig. 5.6. Source: 1992 China Urban Survey.

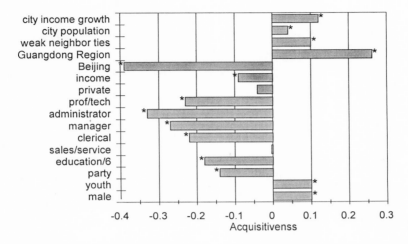

Figure 5.9 Acquisitiveness by city and personal characteristics, 1992. Notes: City income is logged. Guangdong Region and Beijing compared with all other locales. Income is family per capita income. All occupations are compared with manual workers. Education effect is for an additional six years of education. Youth effect is for a ten-year decline in age. OLS regression coefficients, with squared value of age and never married, are additional coefficients not shown. Number of observations: 2,274; $R^2 = .13$. (*) $p < .05$; (°) $p < .10$. Source: 1992 China Urban Survey.

faster reform, private entrepreneurs became pessimistic and turned against rapid reform when the post-1989 tight-money policy dried up supplies of capital and demand, causing many to go bankrupt. By 1992, when monetary policy relaxed and demand increased, this same group became optimistic again.

If one is willing to think of residents of the same city as a class, as a group with a common economic interest, there is also evidence of class interests at this level. People residing in the sunbelt, in major metropolitan centers, and in cities with more light industry and services all tended to greater appreciation of reform. Some residents of these successful locales demurred in the late 1980s, not wanting reform to go any faster, fearing, perhaps, that more rapid changes would kill their "golden goose." Nevertheless, on average, it is surprising how closely group interests, both at the city and individual level, tracked material interests.

6

Labor–Management Relations

T HIS chapter focuses on implications of the new social contract for labor–management relations. The socialist workplace was once riddled with a network of clientalistic ties between supervisors and workers in ways that Andrew Walder has dubbed "Communist neo-traditionalism" (Walder 1986). Here we examine the extent to which these ties have been reshaped by reform and the extent to which both worker satisfaction and bargaining are influenced by this reshaping.

ISSUES

We deal with two major issues in this chapter. The first is the changing nature of bargaining in socialist enterprises, the second is the satisfaction with work and the accompanying tendencies to leave such enterprises.

Bargaining

There are two basic views on the nature of labor–management bargaining in socialist enterprises. One view emphasizes multiple top-down mechanisms that produced dependency and docility among workers. Another view highlights bottom-up forces that allowed workers to pursue their interests even when organized protest was banned. Sometimes the two views are consolidated in an emphasis on mutual dependency between workers and managers in socialist enterprises. As expected, these views have changed considerably over time.

Worker Dependency. The top-down view emphasizes how workers were made docile through multiple dependencies on the firm and supervisors for many of the in-kind goods necessary for everyday survival. The "social contract" between workers and management did not provide a

128

neutral, universally applied set of benefits such as housing, health care, child care, extra rations. Rather, these goods were often distributed in particularistic ways that made workers dependent on immediate supervisors and the official trade union, which administered several in-kind benefits. The results, this literature suggests, are similar to the earlier history of industrialized countries. When workers lived in a company town or received most of their benefits through a specific firm, bargaining was dampened. When the nature of the economy changed and workers were no longer so dependent on owners, open protest increased.[1]

Worker dependency in the socialist firm reached its zenith in China in the 1960s. Increasingly, urban housing and rationed goods were distributed through work units, combined with new limitations on free movement among firms. In his book, *Communist Neo-Traditionalism*, Andrew Walder suggests that this system, which privileged the party faithful and other political activists, led to principled particularism. Individuals dared not offend their superiors, lest housing, promotions, and other rewards be withheld. Those willing to toe the party line, as defined by superiors, received more in-kind benefits.

Similarly, writing about the final years of the Soviet Union, Stephen Fish (1995) suggests that worker dependence helped dampen open political opposition in cities. Single-industry cities, with few alternative employment possibilities, as well as cities centered on military–industrial production and with few consumer goods in the open market, made workers more dependent on supervisors. Multi-industry cities, with many different employment possibilities, and light industry cities, with many consumer goods available in the open market, allowed workers to be less dependent and therefore bolder in opposing supervisors and the government (Fish 1995, pp. 162ff).[2] Stephen Crowley (1994) suggests that worker dependency continued into the post-Soviet period, which helps explain the lingering docility of Russian workers. Housing and other goods continue to be distributed based on an individual's connection to a work unit. Only selected workers were freed from these types of con-

1. McAdam (1982) notes how movement from the countryside to the city freed southern blacks in the United States from landowner control. Also see our Chapter 1 discussion of vertical dependency as a systematic consequence of socialist systems.
2. For additional suggestions that vertical dependency is a systematic consequence of socialist systems, see Chapter 1.

straints – for example, some mine workers who had high salaries but few in-kind benefits – and it was among these groups that strikes first emerged during the final years of Communist rule. Among other groups of workers, such as steel workers for whom salaries were modest but in-kind benefits generous, strikes were rare. While this system of benefits remains and unemployment rates remain high, Crowley suggests, Russian workers will remain docile.[3]

These observations from both China and Russia suggest that in contemporary Chinese data, workers can be expected to be more docile when they work for firms that provide housing and other in-kind benefits and when ties to supervisors are perceived as essential for promotion within the firm. Besides being influenced by these types of indirect controls, workers should also be more docile when they have been coopted by being appointed to factory committees and when they have been induced to buy stock in the firm.

Worker Solidarity. Another set of views attributes much more power to socialist workers. Based on participant observation in a Hungarian factory, Michael Burawoy and Lukacs (1992) note how managers were forced to give considerable autonomy to workers. In a supply-short economy subject to storming at the ends of plan periods and to a host of shop-floor make-do measures needed to achieve assigned targets, workers could not be subjected to tight managerial control. Moreover, managers could be lax with workers because of soft budget constraints that allowed inefficient managers to plead with supervising bureaucracies for more investment funds (Kornai 1992). Workers took advantage of soft budget constraints and lax control to assert their own autonomy over production. Writing on Poland and Hungary, Sabel and Stark (1982), Stark (1986), and Kennedy and Bialecki (1989) note that shortages of skilled labor in East European socialist factories gave workers greater bargaining power. Without extra wages and benefits,

3. With detailed data on post-1991 collective action among Russian workers, Leem (1996) suggests that the consequences of further marketization can be complex. Some previously active groups of workers became passive when their union leaders deserted old workplaces for more lucrative jobs in other sectors of the economy. This suggests a possible curvilinear pattern, with initial marketization increasing collective action among workers because workers have become less dependent on the firm and then later marketization decreasing activism as many of the most capable workers exercise the "exit" option.

skilled workers would leave for more lucrative jobs elsewhere. Thus, management control of worker benefits and work patterns was loosened.

China has been different in many ways. In cities, labor surpluses remained and skilled workers could not move freely from firm to firm. Nevertheless, workers gained many bargaining advantages in the 1970s and early 1980s. In the later chapters of his 1986 book and in a subsequent article, Walder notes that workers began to make more demands on management and that this hindered initial reform efforts by management in the 1980s (Walder 1986, 1987). Lu (1991) observes the high expectations workers had of management and how this slowed reform. Based on studies from the early 1980s, several observers from the World Bank and elsewhere have noted that many gains from the early period of reform were not used to increase factory productivity but were instead captured by blue-collar workers as extra income and benefits (e.g., Tidrick and Chen 1987; Granick 1990). Only Lin (1992) – with data from the late 1980s, when conditions may have changed – questions the degree to which workers were able to bargain successfully for more benefits during the early 1980s.

Several factors increased the bargaining power of workers in the middle 1970s and early 1980s. One factor was the dense network of social ties among workers and between workers and managers. The constraints on interfirm mobility combined with a high proportion of workers and managers living in work-unit quarters meant that both workers and managers had many years of shared work and residence. By the 1980s, much more than in other societies, people in China were more likely to list coworkers among their closest friends (e.g., Bian 1997; Ruan 1997). Dense social networks included not only friends but also kin. In the 1970s and early 1980s, when urban jobs were scarce, work units increasingly hired the children and other relatives of employees (Bian 1994a, pp. 66–69). This tendency meant that by the mid-1980s about one-third of all workers had kin in the same work unit. Considerable anecdotal evidence suggests that dense kin networks emboldened workers in actions against both management and the public. Moreover, many workers and managers lived together in the same work-unit-owned housing compounds. Because of this shared residence, many children of managers and workers went to the same schools. Spouses met each other in line at the market, and in trips through halls and alleyways. Because of this forced familiarity, workers could more easily apply informal social pressure on the administrative staff of work units (e.g., see Chen 1978; Parish 1979).

Initially, managers had few levers with which to resist this kind of informal pressure from below. Under the old social contract, workers could not be fired for suboptimal performance. Promotions were largely lockstep, seniority-based regardless of a worker's skill or effort. When bonuses were reintroduced in the early 1980s, most were distributed evenly to all members of the work group. Thus, in this middle period of Chinese work unit management, managers had few controls over worker behavior.

In other societies as well, the tendency is for workers to have more informal control when they have dense social networks. Though evidence of the effects is mixed, many authors suggest that workers are more likely to engage in strikes and other forms of collective action when they have dense social networks among themselves and when they are separated from competing ties to neighbors and other outside social groups. Kerr and Siegel (1954), for example, propose that the greater strike propensity of miners is a result of the clustering of miners in remote, socially homogenous communities (see Tilly 1978, pp. 65–68, for a critical evaluation of the evidence of these types of effects). Similarly, in an analysis of the International Typesetters Union in New York in the 1950s , Lipset, Trow, and Coleman (1956) found that workers with denser, more exclusive ties to fellow typesetters were more active in union politics. Writing about steel mill neighborhoods on the south side of Chicago, Kornblum (1974) noted how shared work and residence facilitated unionization, politicization, and collective action.

In one sense, Chinese work-unit life recreated the ideal conditions for the mobilization of informal pressure of workers against management. Combining isolation in work-unit-owned housing, long years of shared work and residence, and an increasing number of kin in the same work unit, Chinese workers were ideally positioned to engage in extensive informal bargaining with management, including foot dragging, gossip against managers and their families, and direct contact of managers and supervisors. To the extent that these tendencies remain, we expect that several types of workers will be bolder in the types of demands they make on management. Those with kin in the same work unit or who have lifetime tenure rather than short-term employment contracts should be more willing to engage in work slowdowns and other actions against management.

Historical Periods. In China, part of the reconciliation between the top-down versus bottom-up view of labor–management relations is to note that these relations varied by period. In the late 1950s to middle 1960s, top-down control seems to have been dominant. Managers had many levers for controlling workers, and workers may have been highly dependent on their managers and immediate supervisors.

However, with the Cultural Revolution, when managerial authority was attacked by radicals, bonuses and other material incentives were eliminated, and interworker solidarity was increased, informal, bottom-up bargaining processes increasingly came into play. Even without open protest, workers could get much of what they wanted from management. Though the precise mechanisms differed, Chinese workers began to take on many characteristics of European socialist workers, with successful bargaining becoming increasingly prevalent.

Since 1985, however, Chinese labor–management relations have begun to enter what may be characterized as a third stage. Alarmed by disappointing results in the early years of reform, the central government endorsed a series of reforms that gave factory managers more authority. The subsequent changes in managerial authority involved both direct and indirect mechanisms. Directly, managers were instructed to make more decisions on their own, to impose more penalties for worker underperformance, and to expect that outside bureaucracies would support managers in these efforts. Indirectly, the closer linkage between rewards and profit (hardening the budget constraint) ensured more attention to efficiency and profit between both managers and workers. By the end of the 1980s half of all take-home pay consisted of bonuses and subsidies. No profit meant no bonus or subsidy. Based on a succession of annual surveys, Gary Jefferson and Tom Rawski found that these measures had distinct results. Levels of income were increasingly linked to the profitability of the enterprise. Among both workers and managers, profitability was increasingly mentioned as the primary problem of the factory (Jefferson, Rawski, and Zheng 1992a, b; Rawski 1992). These pressures intensified in the 1990s, when state enterprises increasingly succumbed to competitive pressures. By 1996, a full 12 percent of state-based workers had been downsized (*xiagang*) out of a job, receiving only a type of subsistence wage unemployment insurance from their former work unit (SSB 1997b, p. 31).[4]

Thus by the early 1990s, a mixed situation existed in most work units, with middle-period worker bargaining combined with a new emphasis on the pursuit of profit and renewed managerial authority, reinforced by new threats of unemployment and low income. We explore the consequences of both types of mechanisms.

Types of Bargaining. The major consequence we explore is whether workers anticipate remaining docile or bargaining when problems arise and, if they would bargain, the type of bargaining they would chose. To the extent that socialist regimes accept bargaining, it is expected to occur through formalized institutional channels. These formal mechanisms include direct contact with superiors, contact with the official trade union, and membership on worker committees. For Russian society, Hough (1976, 1977) has referred to this institutional contacting as "institutional pluralism." Chirot (1972), writing about Romania, labels it "corporatism." Based on interviews of Soviet emigres, DiFranceisco and Gitelman (1984) suggest that individual contacting was the primary basis of interest articulation in Soviet society.

Our initial hypothesis is that workers will be more docile where manager and supervisor authority has been reasserted, where workers are dependent on a wide array of work-unit-supplied in-kind benefits, among those workers coopted by appointment to committees, and for workers in the party, of high rank, or with ample incomes. To the extent that these types of workers are active, they will be active not through subversive slowdowns or foot dragging but by institutional contacting through established channels. We also anticipate a potential emerging bifurcation among workers, where older, more established workers would use institutional contacting while younger, more educated

---

4. Based on SSB (1997b, pp. 28, 31), our percent calculation is for employees in state-owned economic enterprises (*qiye*). People are more likely to be downsized if they are in manufacturing rather than in public utilities, postal services, agriculture, and other activities, which are still included in our percentage calculation. Were it primarily manufacturing firms that downsized workers, then the percent downsized in manufacturing could approach one-fifth. The percent simply unemployed and without benefits from a previous place of work also gradually increased to a high of 3 percent by 1996, with not quite half of these being people who were once employed and just over half being young new entrants to the job market.

workers, who feel left out, might using foot dragging and other less conventional forms for pursuing their interests.

Satisfaction and Exit Tendencies

Chinese workers' level of satisfaction and desires to remain at their current place of work can be expected to have waxed and waned along with shifts in managerial power. When managers wielded great power and workers were dependent on supervisors, worker satisfaction should have diminished. In other societies, when economic growth first accelerates and factories grow in size, workers resent being dependent on intermediate supervisors, particularly on supervisors who are free to exercise power arbitrarily, unconstrained by work rules and other checks on authority.

In the United States in the late nineteenth century, workers deplored life in large factories. As forcefully described in Richard Edwards's book, *Contested Terrain* (1979), most intolerable to the workers was the fact that they were newly beholden to foremen and supervisors who governed arbitrarily. Gone were the personalistic ties to the owner that had removed some of the "edge" from the difficult work conditions of small, family-owned enterprises. Now intermediate supervisors substituted for the owner. These supervisors often had personal agendas that ran counter to the interests of both workers and owners. The result among workers was increasing turmoil.

Owners in the United States tried several responses. One failed attempt was to gain worker loyalty through increasing welfare benefits tied to the firm (the in-kind benefit dependency approach). The solution, supported by both union pressure and manager interests, was to establish a system of formalized bureaucratic control. Intermediate supervisors would no longer be allowed to exercise informal control. Instead a formalized set of rules about work duties and promotion criteria would control the nature of the workplace. With this formalization and the removal of supervisor discretion, workplace turmoil began to subside. These formalization tendencies continued to be implemented in many factories after World War II (Burawoy 1979, p. 62).[5]

5. On the struggle in French work settings to resist arbitrary control and to carve out an area of "uncertainty," over which only the worker had autonomous control, see Crozier (1964).

One suspects that Chinese workers also reacted negatively to the increasing role of supervisors in large factories during the initial decades of socialist rule. Given the proclivity of all socialist central planners to invest in large factories, and the natural investment hunger of socialist firms, Chinese firms rapidly became much larger than normal for a society at China's level of development.[6] Besides the natural clash between workers and supervisors in any large firm, Chinese workers may have particularly clashed with their supervisors. Except for Singapore, the natural tendency in Chinese-run firms in market environments (such as Taiwan or Hong Kong) is to be very small (Hamilton and Biggart 1988; Hamilton 1991). Chinese workers in these environments often prefer to run their own business rather than to work for someone else. The socialization of firms in Chinese cities in the 1950s reversed this tendency. Instead of working for themselves or in small firms where they were in direct personal contact with the owner, Chinese urban workers were thrown into hypersized socialist firms where the owner was the distant impersonal state. The workers' resentment of this situation is suggested by the many attacks on supervisors and managers during the 1966–68 Cultural Revolution era (Richman 1967; Laaksonen 1988; Tang 1996a).[7]

Some of these tendencies softened in the 1970s and early 1980s, as workers gained more leverage relative to managers and supervisors. However, with the return of the emphasis on productivity and managerial authority, we expect some of the old resentments to return. Thus, part of our task is to examine how supervisor authority influences work satisfaction and desires to leave the firm.

DATA AND RECENT TRENDS

We rely primarily on a survey of enterprise employees conducted by the Labor Institute of China and the Institute of Sociology at the Chinese Academy of Social Sciences in late 1991 and early 1992. The study is based on a self-administered questionnaire from a sample of 8,071 employees in 100 economic enterprises in seven widely dispersed

6. On the size distribution of Chinese firms, see Lim and Wood (1985, p. 28). On investment hunger in socialist firms anywhere, see Kornai (1992, p. 160).

7. On the theme that large socialist firms in European socialist states created the very "alienation" that socialism was supposed to avoid, see Wiles (1977, pp. 583–86).

provinces at very different levels of economic development (see Appendix B for further description of the survey). The survey includes both white- and blue-collar workers, and because the results are largely similar for both types of workers we analyze both types together. The employees are distributed across state-run (68%), urban collective (22%), and joint ventures (10%). For ease of reference, we refer to this sample as the 1991 Firm Survey.

Besides this primary data set, we also refer to a similar data set from late 1992. Based on a sample of state, urban collective, and joint venture enterprises in twelve economically diverse provinces, the survey provides detailed economic data on 422 firms and 9,397 blue- and white-collar employees.[8] This data set, which we refer to as the 1992 Firm Survey, helps validate findings from the 1991 survey.

Combined with anecdotal materials, both surveys provide a stronger sense of recent trends in managerial authority. There have been several explicit measures taken to restore managerial authority. By the mid-1980s, most state enterprise workers had to take a competitive exam to get their job and then sign a five-year labor contract once recruited.[9] Once on the job, workers often encountered a new set of disciplinary measures designed to speed the pace of factory work. Much as in Edwards's account of early American factories, these measures also implied increased supervisor and manager discretion in the kinds of methods that could be used to control workers.

An internal investigation report by the All-China Federation of Labor Unions (1986) discusses some of these early measures. A study of the Zhengzhou Railway Northern Station provides one example. Supervisory personnel were required to report a certain number of violations of firm policies each month. Supervisors' bonuses were directly related to the number of violations they reported. In 1985, 1,492 fines were collected from 711 employees in this work unit. Within thirty days of bonus payment, the bonus could be taken back if a violation occurred. If one employee committed a violation, all members of the work group were

---

8. The survey was conducted under the leadership of Mr. Xia Jizhi, Labor Science Institute, the Ministry of Labor. Parts of the data preparation were handled by Zhu Jianfeng, Institute of Economics, Chinese Academy of Social Sciences, and Elizabeth Li, Miami University, Ohio. We are grateful to the people who have supplied these data.

9. In state-owned work units, contracted workers increased from 2 to 52 percent between 1984 and 1997 (SSB 1998a, p. 150).

fined. The net result of all these measures was that by year's end, fines taken in were five times larger than bonuses handed out.

In ways that are reminiscent of nineteenth-century American practice, rules were sometimes set arbitrarily. For example, a young male employee was fined when he unbuttoned his shirt at lunch time, and workers were not allowed to go to the washroom within the first two hours of their shift. Humiliation was used as another form of punishment. Those with serious violations had photographs taken, which were publicly displayed. The violator was required to make a public confession and family members were supposed to be present to criticize and educate the violator. Forty-five such cases occurred in 1985.[10]

The same report also contained many other examples of new disciplinary proceedings. A female worker in the city of Dandong could not finish her work assignment due to illness. She was fined five yuan by the foreman. In her conversation with the director of the work shop, she protested about how she had been treated. This led to a second fine of five yuan. Since her conversation with the director took place at work, she was fined another five yuan for absenteeism. One foreman in the same firm in Dandong said he had fined all of the seventy-one employees under his supervision. Supervisors often received commissions from the fines they collected. In an enterprise in Heilongjiang, supervisors who reported a violation kept 40 percent of fines and the remainder was turned over to the security office, which kept another 30 percent. In Zhengzhou Railway Northern Station, some supervisors refused to issue receipts for the fines they collected. When workers asked for a receipt, the supervisors responded, "What do we get out of this if I give you a receipt?"

Increasingly, of course, simple financial incentives surrounding bonuses and subsidies began to play a large role in disciplining workers. Sometimes this incentive was more at the group level, since as late as 1992 almost half of all bonuses in state enterprises were distributed equally to everyone in the same group (1992 Firm Survey). Nevertheless, in state enterprises in 1992, the discipline of workers was secured most often by using financial reprimands such as cutting wages and

10. A 1996 visit to the Shenyang Machinery Factory found a continuing use of humiliation as a method of punishment. Public humiliation is a method long used in both the Chinese and Soviet socialist revolutions (e.g., Fitzpatrick 1994).

bonuses (75%), by publicly criticizing the worker (52%), and by reassigning the worker within the enterprise (25%). Dismissing workers (5%) and excluding workers from housing and training opportunities (2%) were rarely used as punishment. Thus, though public humiliation had receded in importance by 1992, it was still often used in half of all state factories, often in conjunction with other measures.

These methods were, of course, not always effective. As late as 1992, employees often judged that their enterprises had unpunished laggards, people who did not work very hard. Ownership made a difference in the extent of this laggard behavior. It was judged most common in state firms (29%), somewhat common in urban collective firms (25%), and not quite so common in joint-venture firms (17%). Thus, even with the rise of new disciplinary measures, state-owned firms and collective firms found it difficult to erase laggard behavior.

Despite the exact disciplinary method or the pervasiveness of intimidation, the new procedures soon provoked negative reactions from workers. After being fined, one worker in the Zhenghzhou Railway Northern Station protested by attempting suicide. Others protested by leaving urine and manure in their workshop director's office (All-China Federation of Labor Unions 1986, p. 167). Workers demanded that the government intervene to reduce the power of management (Tang 1992, 1996a).

Besides appearing in anecdotal accounts, systematic evidence of workers' negative responses also exists in statistical accounts. In a 1986 survey of 640,000 workers in 519 Chinese enterprises conducted by the Federation of Labor Unions 56 percent of workers said that their status had declined since reform. Worker complaints focused on the following four issues. First, political status had declined. Recruitment for party membership favored intellectuals, not workers. Second, income and welfare policy did not favor workers. Workers' wages were too low compared with other sectors. Special benefit policies existed for intellectuals, cadres, veterans, and peasants, but there were none for workers. Third, discipline against workers was too harsh. Under the old system, workers were the "masters," and managers and bureaucrats were to be the "servants" of the socialist firm. Workers complained that during reform the "servants" were penalizing the "masters." Finally, workers had no say in enterprise decision making. Democracy at the workplace existed in name only (All-China Federation of Labor Unions 1986, p. 15).

Many of these complaints were repeated in the 1991 Firm Survey. In this survey, 57 percent complained that their social status had declined.[11] A full 45 percent complained that the relationship between workers and managers had deteriorated since 1988. Only 18 percent felt that the relationship had improved. Relations with managers had deteriorated much more than relations with technical staff and with fellow workers, which suggests it was something that the managerial staff did that was perceived negatively.

Other evidence from the 1991 Firm Survey demonstrates consistent loss of worker decision-making power. Respondents were asked how decisions were made in several domains. They reported whether these decisions were primarily by leaders at the firm, workshop, or work group level, or whether workers or others (including government agencies) made these decisions. The overwhelming majority of decisions were made at the firm and workshop levels, far from the direct control of workers (see Fig. 6.1).[12] This upward bias in decision making is consistent with a sharp increase in managerial and supervisor authority since the mid-1980s.

MEASURED CHARACTERISTICS

The 1991 firm survey provides multiple indices of employee, firm, and city characteristics. We will use a common set of these characteristics to analyze both bargaining and work satisfaction (Table 6.1).

Bargaining Leverage Mechanisms

In the analysis of bargaining, we predict that workers with kin in the same work unit will be bolder in their tendencies toward collective action. Among respondents, 28 percent have kin at the same level as themselves and 13 percent have kin in a higher level position in the work

11. If the education levels in the 1986 sample were adjusted downward to make the sample more representative of the enterprise population in 1986, the 1986–92 comparison might well show a slight increase in dissatisfaction between the two dates. Regardless, dissatisfaction had not dramatically declined between the two dates.
12. Since managers had more knowledge of the decision-making process and were more likely to provide accurate answers, Fig. 6.1 shows only the responses by managerial personnel in the 1991 firm survey. For a similar pattern of firm decision making in China's local collective industries, see Tang (1996a).

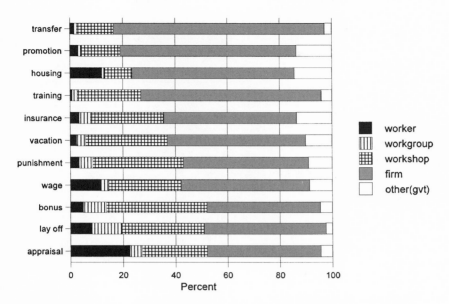

Figure 6.1 Firm decision making, 1991. Source: 1991 Firm Survey.

unit. Respondents with kin at the same level should be more likely to contemplate collective actions such as slowdowns at work. Respondents with kin at higher levels should be more likely to contemplate working through contacts with superiors to get things done. We also predict that workers with lifetime employment contracts will be bolder than those with term contracts and temporary work arrangements. Later, in the analysis of satisfaction we expect that temporary workers from the countryside will be more satisfied, because their comparison is with the less desirable alternative of remaining in agriculture.

Authority

Next in the analysis come measures of managerial authority levels, the degree of dependence on supervisors, and relations with one's supervisor. "Managerial authority" is the average (mean) level at which decisions are made in the firm (see Fig. 6.1 for the list of decision domains). To measure firm characteristics, the measure is averaged

Table 6.1. *Work-Related Statistics, 1991*

	Mean	Standard deviation	Minimum	Maximum
Bargaining leverage				
Kinship				
Family member in same firm	.28	.45	0	1
Family member in management	.13	.33	0	1
No family member in firm (cf.)	.59	.49	0	1
Employment status				
Lifetime tenure	.81	.39	0	1
Term contract	.13	.34	0	1
Temporary (urban)	.01	.11	0	1
Temporary (rural) (cf.)	.01	.11	0	1
Authority				
Managerial authority (firm average)	3.39	.15	3.06	3.88
Supervisor relations bad	2.43	.73	1.00	4.00
Promotion in firm based on (firm avg.)				
Ties to supervisor	.43	.11	0	.69
Family background	.09	.06	0	.32
Seniority	.05	.05	0	.42
Performance, education (cf.)	.43	.50	0	.72
Cooptation				
Committee member	.25	.43	0	1
Stock owner	.19	.39	0	1
In-kind benefits (firm proportion)	.43	.22	0	.95
Firm housing (respondent)	.39	.49	0	1
Firm housing (firm proportion)	.39	.23	0.01	1
Rewards				
Income (logged)	7.80	.40	6.05	9.21
Party member	.24	.43	0	1
Rank	2.07	1.73	1	7
Profitable firm	.69	.46	0	1

Table 6.1. *(cont.)*

	Mean	Standard deviation	Minimum	Maximum
Expectations				
Independent-minded, proactive	1.08	.25	.62	1.50
Education	2.73	.78	1	4
Male	.52	.50	0	1
Youth	4.68	.94	1.70	6.50
Firm characteristics				
Industry				
Transport	.10	.31	0	1
Textiles	.14	.35	0	1
Heavy industry	.22	.41	0	1
Light industry	.30	.46	0	1
Construction	.09	.29	0	1
Commerce, service (cf.)	.15	.36	0	1
Ownership				
State	.69	.46	0	1
Collective (urban)	.21	.41	0	1
Joint venture (cf.)	.10	.30	0	1
Persons (logged)	7.28	1.14	4.44	10.04
City characteristics				
Salary level (logged)	7.95	.21	7.75	8.56
Economic growth rate (1991)	1.12	.09	0.97	1.29
Dependent variables				
Dissatisfaction	0	.85	−2.58	2.48
Wants to leave firm	.24	.43	0	1

Notes: For nonrural firms. Sample size for most variables is 7,632.
Source: 1991 Firm Survey.

across all respondents in the same firm. On a scale from a low of one (all decisions at the worker level) to a high of four (all decisions by firm management), the observed high level of 3.39 indicates that most decisions are now made at a high level.[13] Despite decisions being made

13. The small minority of decisions by others is coded at the mean for each type of decision.

at a high level on average in most firms, significant variation across firms exists.[14]

One measure of worker dependency on supervisors is whether promotion in the firm is based primarily on personal ties to one's superior. Respondents could indicate that promotion in their firm was based primarily on personal ties to superiors, on family background or on family ties, on seniority (which for a time was a major basis of promotion), or on other more universalistic criteria such as work performance, contribution to the firm, or education. Again, we average responses across all respondents in the same firm to give a firm average. The results show that while seniority alone may have dwindled in importance, ties to superiors remain an important basis for promotion.[15] In the analysis of satisfaction, our prediction is that workers will be more dissatisfied and more likely to want to leave when promotion is based on personalistic ties to superiors.[16] In the analysis of bargaining, our prediction is that workers will be more docile and more likely to use institutional channels when a personalistic tie to superiors is the major basis of promotion.

Finally, we consider whether a person has bad relations with one's superior, rated on a scale of one (very good) to four (very bad). The obvious predictions include those that when a person has bad ties to a superior that person will be more dissatisfied, more likely to leave the work unit, and less likely to use institutional channels to express grievances.

Cooptation Mechanisms

Several mechanisms might secure worker loyalty and quiescence, either by coopting the worker with "buy out" devices or by making the worker more dependent on the enterprise for in-kind benefits. "Buy out" devices

14. See Tang (1993, 1996a) for an attempt to categorize enterprise decision making.
15. Responses are influenced by question wording, response alternatives, and question placement in the larger questionnaire. In our second, 1992 firm survey, which asked about criteria for promotion, the state sector responses were performance and education (61%), ties to superior (28%), seniority (10%), and other (6%). Despite somewhat different percentages, the point about the important role of personal ties to supervisors remains.
16. Ties to supervisors are most important in firms with more than 500 workers, in state and collective firms as opposed to joint ventures, in heavy industry, and in most cities other than economically successful Guangzhou (details not shown).

include having workers purchase stock in the firm or appointing them to a firm committee, where they would ostensibly have more say in firm decision making. Since the stock purchases were frequently nonvoluntary and since the value of firm stock might be dubious when the firm was on the brink of failure, the positive effects of stock ownership could be questionable. Worker committees include separate committees responsible for firm management, cadre evaluation, housing assignment, welfare and labor protection, and the enterprise employee's congress. These committees provide a framework for formal corporatist workplace participation, with the final employee's congress being the most common form of participation.[17] Some employees considered these forms of participation to be more than just ritualistic. Respondents of the 1991 survey were asked whether committees played any effective role, with the potential responses being 0 (very little), 1 (average), and 2 (great). The committee efficacy rating increased steadily as committee participation increased – from a low of .83 for those with no committee participation to .93 with participation in one to three committees and 1.12 with participation in more than three committees. Thus, committee participation increased one's sense of efficacy, suggesting perhaps that committees might perform an effective cooptation role for the more activist workers.[18]

In-kind benefits were likely to have a much greater effect, both on satisfaction and on muting overt bargaining with the firm. These are the dependency-inducing mechanisms frequently mentioned for socialist work settings (Walder 1986; Crowley 1994; Fish 1995). Excluding housing, 43 percent of employees in firms received in-kind benefits. Firm scores ranged from a low of zero, for no in-kind benefits provided to any employees, to a high of .95, for firms in which in-kind benefits are provided to 95 percent of employees. Housing benefits have a similar distribution. In 1991, 39 percent of workers lived in work-unit housing.

---

17. Unsurprisingly, committee participation was higher among higher rank personnel, with the following distribution by position: firm administrators (64%), firm managers (55%), low-level administrators (50%), firm technical supervisors (49%), white-collar workers (27%), low-level technicians (21%), and workers (20%). Despite the uneven proportional representation, given their large absolute numbers in an enterprise, workers were the majority on some committees.
18. The correlation coefficient between participation and feelings of effectiveness was .08 ($p < .001$). This positive relationship remained when job type and other background variables were controlled.

Some firms had no housing, while other firms provided housing to almost everyone. The prediction, of course, is that those firms with more in-kind benefits, including housing, will have more satisfied and hence docile workers.

Rewards

Of course, given the natural propensity to report material rewards and status as a major source of satisfaction and dissatisfaction, we expect these types of rewards to rank high in any analysis of the multiple determinants of job satisfaction. Also, in bargaining persons with higher rewards would be more likely to use institutional channels when bargaining over grievances. The 1991 survey contains data on annual income (logged), party membership, administrative rank, and profitability of the firm. Administrative rank is listed in a seven-step scale with manual workers at the bottom and rising through low technical, low managerial, low administrative, high technical, high managerial, and high administrative personnel.

Expectations

Some employees are more difficult to satisfy and more obstinate in bargaining over interests simply because they have higher expectations than the average worker. We have both subjective and objective indicators of probable expectations. The objective measures include education, youth, and gender.[19] Our subjective measure is for "independent-minded" people. This index uses a factor analysis to combine responses to items concerned with whether one supports reform values and is individually assertive.[20]

19. Education is on a four-point scale. "Youth" is the inverse of age, divided by 10.
20. The items are as follows: "Should one work for one's own income or to contribute to the collective interest?" "Should pay be related to effort?" "Should the structural problems of central planning be solved even if this brings instability?" "I will reason with factory leaders when necessary, not simply obey leaders." "I will create my own democratic rights, not simply accept the given rights." "I know how to solve the enterprises' problems." "I will fight for the opportunity for promotion, not wait or yield to others." "I will fight back when unfairly treated, rather than yield and tolerate." One might complain that in explaining bargaining procedures, this measure of individual assertiveness overlaps too much with the type of bargaining behavior we are trying to explain.

Firm Characteristics

Next we include a variety of firm characteristics that should influence people's perceptions and behavior. Though we have only marginal interest in these characteristics, they are important enough to be included as control variables in the analysis. These factors include the distinction between heavy and light industry, type of ownership, and firm size. Urbanites dislike work in noisy, lint-ridden textile factories, and many of these jobs are now being taken by rural women. Heavy industry, often with low profit margins, may be much less popular than rapid growth, high-profit light industry jobs. Anecdotal accounts suggest that the rapid growth service jobs in shops, hotels, and elsewhere are losing their previously despised status. Even controlling for all the other characteristics of enterprises, the level of ownership may still be important. In many accounts, work in joint ventures is often seen as desirable. Work in urban collective enterprises licensed by neighborhoods is often seen as less desirable than work either in joint ventures or in traditional state enterprises. In the 1991 Firm Survey, when respondents were asked where they would wish to transfer if they changed jobs, one-third listed a noneconomic, public organization and one-fifth a joint venture.[21] Only about one-fifth indicated a desire to transfer to an urban collective enterprise. Finally, the size of a firm, measured in total number of employees, could still be important even when all the other characteristics of a firm are included in the analysis.

City Characteristics

City characteristics of potential importance include average salary levels in the city and the economic growth rate of the city in 1991. These two

However, leaving this set of attitude items out of the equation leaves the other results largely unchanged.

21. The preference for noncompetitive public organizations (schools, hospitals, etc.) is consistent with Lin's (1992) suggestion that at least by the end of the 1980s, and probably earlier, state-owned economic enterprises (factories, stores) faced such competitive pressures that they could not give into worker demands for more housing and other fringe benefits. Nonprofit, noncompetitive, public organizations, in contrast, could give in to these demands and increasingly did so by the late 1980s, making these agencies increasingly popular places to work. Also see Chapter 4 on the theme that recent changes have favored employees in public organizations.

factors could have contradictory effects. In the short run, rapid growth and increasing consumption by friends and neighbors could increase satisfaction among workers. In the long run, however, a high average wage in the city might make workers less satisfied with their own income and benefits package. Accordingly, we include both short-term growth and average wage in our analysis.

BARGAINING OVER GRIEVANCES

In this section we deal with continuities and discontinuities in bargaining over personal interests and grievances. The issue is whether the reassertion of managerial authority has dampened worker bargaining, and whether bargaining is now channeled mostly through institutional channels. The contrast is among contacting through institutional channels, slowing down at work, or simply remaining quiescent in the face of grievances.

Grievance Responses

Employees were asked how they would respond if unfairly treated by management on specific issues including injury at work, coworker dismissal, wage adjustment, housing assignment, and the promotion of managers and administrators. Potential responses included going to a government bureau above the firm, going to a supervisor or other firm leader, going to a labor union leader, intentionally slowing down at work, discussing the solution with coworkers, or simply ignoring the problem. Going to government, supervisor, or labor union is a form of institutional contacting that often implies using old particularistic networks remaining from the past. Slowing down at work, particularly in this era of concern with higher productivity, implies a willingness to engage in covert bargaining with management. Merely discussing the problem with coworkers falls somewhere between a feeling of powerlessness and a willingness to mobilize others to resist management. Ignoring the problem suggests either apathy or a sense of futility in the face of new managerial authority.

Let us begin with more detail on the pattern of responses for which we have two initial observations (Fig. 6.2). One observation is that workers are more proactive when personal interests are at stake (injury,

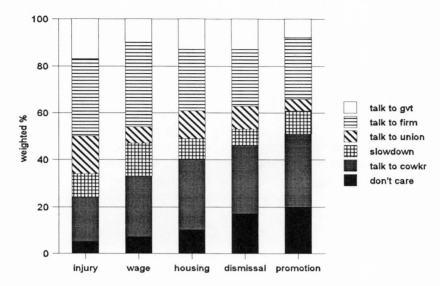

Figure 6.2 Grievance responses, 1991. Source: 1991 Firm Survey.

wages, housing). Workers take more passive avenues of talking to coworkers or saying that they do not care when the injustice involves someone else (an unjust dismissal, wrong person promoted). Because this pattern is not surprising, it suggests that people are giving realistic responses to these hypothetical situations.

The second observation is that institutional contacting remained the dominant mode of dealing with grievances. Use of the official union remained rare – somewhat more common for welfare-related injury issues but still rare even there. Through the early 1990s, the official labor union remained a largely top-down organization that workers found of little use in settling their own grievances. Contacting government officials also remained rare. Bargaining through slowdowns at work was also rare, reflecting perhaps the increased pressure to keep one's job and bonuses. Instead, much as of old – and as described in part in Walder's earlier work on factories – the dominant mode of dealing with personal problems was to speak directly with supervisors at work. The early 1990s factory regime, then, resembled the former factory regime, with the institutional contacting of superiors emphasized over direct action by workers. As workers imagined what they might do in the face of personal difficulties at work, their first thought was to turn to supervisors with whom they had established relationships.

That said, most workers were not passive, at least as they contemplated possible action. Though they had less bargaining leverage than before the mid-1980s – fewer opportunities to relax on the job or to involve themselves in bargaining through slowdowns at work – they still claimed that other avenues were open to them for dealing with personal work problems. For personal problems (injury, wage, and housing) the majority of workers would do something to get their problem solved. Few would simply talk to a coworker or do nothing at all. Thus, while the worker's flexibility of action had been constrained, few saw themselves as paralyzed in the face of difficulty.

Response Determinants

The remaining question is whether responses to grievances varied systematically by type of worker and by type of work situation. For this analysis we group the potential responses into three large groups – institutional contacting (talk to leaders of firm, union, or government bureau), work slowdown, or no action (talk to coworkers, no response). Our predictions about determinants have been largely anticipated above. First, we predict that workers with strong kin ties and secure employment contracts will be more proactive in pursuing their interests, particularly through nonapproved work slowdowns. Second, we predict more docility (absence of any action) in firms with higher levels of managerial authority, with greater reliance on ties to superiors for promotion, and firms where workers have been dependent on many in-kind benefits. If such workers take any type of action, we expect it to be mostly through established institutional channels.

Our analysis is based on responses to each of the five grievances. Thus our unit of analysis is both the worker and his or her response to each grievance. First, both contacting and slowing down at work are contrasted with taking no action. Then, no action is contrasted with taking any action (Table 6.2). Compared with our initial predictions, some findings fit our initial predictions while others did not.

Several findings are consistent with what we expected before beginning the analysis. Authority and dependency produce docility. When most

Table 6.2. *Responses to Grievances at Work, 1991*

	Institutional contact	Work slowdown	No action
Bargaining leverage			
Kinship			
Family member in same firm	.03	.09	−.04
Family member in management	.03	.04	−.03
No family member in firm (cf.)			
Employment status			
Lifetime tenure	−.93**	.37*	.76**
Term contract	−.74**	.55**	.57**
Temporary (urban)	−.78**	.19	.66**
Temporary (rural) (cf.)			
Authority			
Managerial authority	−.45*	−.85**	.51**
Supervisor relations bad	−.42**	.12**	.30**
Promotion in firm based on			
Ties to supervisor	−1.44**	−.05	1.19**
Family background	−.68	1.12*	.28
Seniority	−.21	−.87	.34
Performance, education (cf.)			
Cooptation			
Committee member	.35**	.04	−.29**
Stock owner	.10#	−.08	−.06
In-kind benefits (firm proportion)	.28*	−.14	−.20#
Firm housing (respondent)	.12*	.07	−.11*
Firm housing (firm proportion)	.06	−.10	−.02
Rewards			
Income (logged)	−.06	−.16#	.09
Party member	.35**	.13	−.31**
Rank	.13**	−.00	−.10**
Profitable firm	−.02	−.02	.02
Expectations			
Independent-minded, proactive	−.27**	.24#	.17*
Education	−.20**	.10*	.14**
Male	.04	.16**	−.07#
Youth	−.00	.23**	−.03

Table 6.2. *(cont.)*

	Institutional contact	Work slowdown	No action
Firm characteristics			
Industry			
Transport	−.21*	.17	.15
Textiles	−.17#	.26#	.09
Heavy industry	−.20*	.25*	.12
Light industry	−.17*	.32**	.08
Construction	−.04	.10	.02
Commerce, service (cf.)			
Ownership			
State	.04	.03	−.05
Collective (urban)	.15	−.04	−.12
Joint venture (cf.)			
Persons (logged)	−.05*	.03	.03
City characteristics			
Salary level (logged)	−.20	−.41#	.23
Economic growth rate (1991)	1.62**	.57	−1.38**
Constant			−4.77**
Pseudo R^2		.07	.06
Observations		33,361	33,361
Base %	51	11	38

Notes: The first two columns show coefficients from a single multinomial logit analysis. The last column contains proportional change coefficients from a binary probit analysis. In the first two columns, both actions are compared with "no action." In the last column, "no action" is compared with "any action." Coefficients not shown include missing value flags for education, employment status, male, bad supervisor relations, and a flag for each of five different grievances. In all columns, standard errors are corrected for multiple reports of grievances from the same respondent. (cf.) Comparison group; (**) $p < .01$; (*) $p < .05$; (#) $p < .10$.
Source: 1991 Firm Survey (with multiple observations for different grievances)

firm decisions are made at a high level and when ties to superiors are the major basis for promotion, people avoid contacts through established channels and choose to be passive instead. Conversely, when there are ample rewards and cooptation mechanisms, workers pursue solutions to their grievances through institutional contacting. These mechanisms do not induce docility – which might be one prediction – but instead move people's expression of grievance into institutional channels.

Other findings are less consistent with what we expected at the outset. In particular, bargaining fails to intensify when kin are in the same work unit – though persons with family members at their same work level may be somewhat more likely to slow down at work. Also, people with more secure employment statuses are not more likely to bargain for their interests. Except for rural temporary workers (the comparison group), who are more likely to seek their interests through established channels, among urban workers there is much less pattern in how people respond to grievances. Among urban-origin workers, the responses are much the same regardless of type of employment. Thus, by the early 1990s, the touted role of informal networks and lifetime job security was quite weak.

Other findings are much more consistent with our predictions. With one exception, managerial authority, bad supervisor relations, and dependency on superiors for promotion all induce quiescence. The only exception is that a subset of workers having bad relations with their supervisor contemplated slowing down at work. This, however, is but a minor deviation in the much more significant trend of increasing managerial authority dampening bargaining at work.

Many measures inducing cooptation or dependency have much of their intended effect – though more often by directing grievance expression into institutional channels. Workers who are on committees, who have stock, who live in firm housing, or work in firms with many in-kind benefits are not passive. Yet the move from passivity to action is expressed through institutional channels and not through slowing down at work. Similar patterns occur for people who are in the party and are of high rank in the firm. Much like the committee members, these people must have ready access to higher leaders in the firm, and thus find expression of grievances to higher leaders to be quite easy and of little cost to themselves.

It is quite different among younger, educated males who are more "independent-minded." Though some of these people are passive, contemplating no action at all, many consider foot dragging or slowing down as a means of expressing grievances. This is the possible bifurcation we had expected between different groups of workers. Among older workers, with more seniority, status, and benefits, there seems to be a tendency to go along with established channels for expressing their interests. Among younger workers with lower status, fewer benefits, and less easy access to firm leaders, new disapproved modes of interest expression are more often contemplated.

Only a few other findings in the table require comment. Unsurprisingly, working through institutional channels is more difficult in large firms. Also, foot dragging is more often contemplated in manufacturing (textiles, heavy, and light industry) than in other sectors of the economy. Manufacturing most likely involves larger work groups, where individual shirking is less obvious to supervisors than in smaller stores and other work settings.

The final observation we should make about empirical results is that bargaining through slowing down is uncommon (see the final row of Table 6.2). Though we cannot prove it, we suspect that the 11 percent of workers who say they would respond to grievances by slowing down is much smaller than it would have been a decade ago. If so, then, the attempts to reassert shop-floor discipline and to increase a sense of urgency about profit have been partially successful.

DISSATISFACTION

Next we want to examine when workers are dissatisfied and when they would like to leave their current firm. "Dissatisfaction" is a summary scale that combines responses to each of the following three items (see Table 6.1 for summary statistics):

- "Are you currently considering leaving this enterprise?"
- "Most of the time when you go to work are you happy, unaffected, or fed up?"
- "At work, do you usually feel that time goes by very fast, relatively fast, slowly, or very slowly?"

Workers were then asked about their degree of satisfaction with income, job responsibilities, job position, and promotion opportunities. Using factor analysis, these seven highly correlated items were combined into a single index of dissatisfaction. In addition, simply because it provides a more intuitive sense of workers' moods, we examine desire to leave the firm as a separate item. About one-fourth of the respondents were thinking of leaving their current firm.

Supervisor relations emerge as a major determinant of worker attitudes (Table 6.3). One example is provided by comparisons to firms where there are no reports of promotion based on ties to supervisor. In comparison, if 50 percent of the people in a firm report that ties to a supervisor are the primary basis of promotion in a firm, then 30 percent more people in that firm want to leave the firm ($.50 \times .61 = .30$). Similarly, on a four-point scale, if a person is one point more dissatisfied in relations with his or her supervisor, that person is ten percentage points more likely to want to leave the firm. These all imply that personalistic ties to supervisors are important determinants of dissatisfaction and exit tendencies in Chinese enterprises.[22]

Cooptation and dependency-inducing mechanisms have some effect, though more through in-kind benefits than through stock ownership or appointment to committees. Benefits vary widely among firms, from no benefits to anyone to benefits for everyone (see minimum and maximum in Table 6.1). In comparison with firms with no benefits, workers are 16 percentage points less likely to contemplate leaving when their firm provides in-kind benefits for everyone. Similarly, workers are 12 percentage points less likely to contemplate leaving when their firm provides housing for everyone. Given that the average propensity to leave is 24 percent, these are large effects. Housing and in-kind benefits help dampen dissatisfaction and tie workers to the firm.

Unsurprisingly, increased cash and status rewards also tie workers to the firm and help dampen dissatisfaction. Conversely, high expectations exacerbate dissatisfaction and promote tendencies to leave the firm, as does work in the types of sectors now disfavored by urbanites. Even aside from these conditions, people would like to flee the state sector and

---

22. Statistically, these coefficients have the largest t-scores in the equation. One might surmise that well-connected workers with close ties to supervisors might treasure rather than abhor supervisor discretion in promotions. However, an interaction term for "promotions dependent on supervisor ties" and "respondent has good relations with supervisor(s)" exacerbated rather than dampened dissatisfaction (details not shown).

Table 6.3. *Determinants of Job Dissatisfaction and Exit Tendencies, 1991*

	Dissatisfied	Wants to leave firm
Authority		
Managerial authority	.10	.04
Supervisor relations bad		.10**
Promotion in firm based on		
Ties to supervisor	1.88**	.61**
Family background	.74**	−.11
Seniority	.52*	.42**
Performance, education (cf.)		
Cooptation		
Committee member	−.03	.02
Stock owner	.04#	.02
In-kind benefits (firm proportion)	−.21**	−.16**
Firm housing (respondent)	−.06**	−.03*
Firm housing (firm proportion)	−.08	−.12**
Rewards		
Income (logged)	−.25**	−.04*
Party member	−.10**	−.00
Rank	−.05**	−.00
Profitable firm	−.01	−.01
Expectations		
Independent-minded, proactive	.29**	.03
Education	.05**	.07**
Male	.07**	.05**
Youth	.05**	.03**
Employment status		
Lifetime tenure	.28**	.07
Term contract	.23**	.10
Temporary (urban)	.27*	.20*
Temporary (rural)		
Firm characteristics		
Industry		
Transport	.21**	.18**
Textiles	.15**	.12**
Heavy industry	.10**	.07**

Table 6.3. *(cont.)*

	Dissatisfied	Wants to leave firm
Light industry	.07*	.03
Construction	.05	.00
Commerce, service (cf.)		
Ownership		
State	−.02	.06**
Collective (urban)	−.03	.05*
Joint venture (cf.)		
Persons (logged)	−.02	−.00
City characteristics		
Salary level (logged)	.32**	.14**
Economic growth rate (1991)	−.60**	−.29**
Constant	−1.96**	
Adjusted R^2/pseudo R^2	.13	.10
Observations	7,632	6,172

Notes: Metric (unstandardized) regression coefficients from OLS regression in column one and proportional change coefficients from binary probit in column two. Coefficients not shown include missing value flags for education, employment status, and male. (cf.) Comparison group; (**) $p < .01$; (*) $p < .05$; (#) $p < .10$.
Source: 1991 Firm Survey.

urban collective sector for work in other firms – particularly for work in joint ventures. City characteristics also have some effect. There appears to be a comparison effect, with people in high-income cities comparing themselves unfavorably with those around them. High economic growth rates, in contrast, tend to dampen dissatisfaction.

Thus the results for dissatisfaction are much as we expected. Rewards and other conditions shape attitudes and behavior in intuitively obvious ways. Personalistic dependence on supervisors exacerbates dissatisfaction while dependence on in-kind benefits distributed by firms helps dampen dissatisfaction.

The significant role of personal ties to supervisors is also found in a set of additional statistical analyses on the 1991 Firm Survey that we only summarize here. These analyses show that when firms emphasize personal ties to supervisors in promotion, workers are more likely to say that relations with managers are worse than in the 1980s, that managers are overpaid, and that reducing the number of managers and supervisors is one of the first things that should be done to improve efficiency. They are also more likely to say that workers are underpaid. These patterns hold up under an extensive set of controls, suggesting that dependency on potentially arbitrary supervisors has a series of negative spillover effects on how workers view their firms.

STRIKES AND COLLECTIVE BARGAINING

One sign of the negative spillover effects of the current economic regime is the increasing number of strikes and individual worker complaints. Several factors contribute to this recent increase. Despite the reassertion of managerial authority, the use of raw coercion and the fear of it is probably less common today than in the past. Thus, the repercussions of complaints outside institutional channels are less serious than before. Because of partial relaxation of control over the media, information about the situation of other workers in similar situations flows more freely these days than in the past. Although we have no evidence for this, local union leaders may occasionally find it in their interest to help workers express their grievances. More important, as suggested above, there are more young, educated workers who feel they cannot express their grievances in standard channels and who have some of the verbal and organizational skills to mobilize other workers. With rapid changes in compensation levels and increased attempts at instilling worker discipline, there are many grievances around which workers might mobilize.

For these types of reasons, labor disputes proliferated in the early 1990s. In response, labor bureaus in each city strengthened the role of their regional arbitration committees. The subset of disputes appearing before these committees grew by a factor of six between 1992 and 1996.[23] Though many disputes consisted of single individuals coming before the arbitration committee to press a complaint, there was also a rapid growth in groups of individuals complaining together. Between 1992 and 1996, group-based or collective complaints, with an average of thirty workers

23. Disputes coming before arbitration committees may have represented as few as a tenth of all disputes (All China Federation of Labor Unions 1993, pp. 346–51).

complaining at a time, increased by a factor of eight. The result was that by 1997, complainants in groups came to constitute 57 percent of the people appearing in arbitration committee hearings (SSB 1998a, p. 782). These groups were not permanently organized but were often wildcat strike groups protesting against cancellation of contracts, violation of terms of contracts, and other problems induced by managers trying to assert control in an increasingly competitive environment. Though the total volume seems modest in comparison with developed industrial countries, the disputes were often frightening to leaders of society.[24] The fear of disputes was exacerbated by the fact that China was unused to wildcat strikes and other types of noninstitutional collective protest actions. China had yet to develop the kinds of institutional accommodations to worker protests that Dahrendorf (1959) suggests eventually brought labor peace to the industrialized West.

To the extent that protests were being accommodated in an institutional way through arbitration committees, managers might often be unhappy with the results. Of all cases accepted by arbitration committees in 1997, 56 percent of the cases were won by workers and a little more than one-fourth resulted in compromises between workers and managers. Only 16 percent of the cases were won by management (SSB 1998a, p. 782). Thus, at least for the portion of cases that made their way to arbitration committees, managers were disadvantaged.

Because of the growing concern about the potential for out-of-control disputes, the government has taken several steps to help institutionalize conflict. In 1994 China passed a comprehensive labor law and seventeen other related regulations (Ministry of Labor 1995). With thirteen chapters and 107 articles, the law includes regulations on equal access to employment, labor contracts, work time, minimum wages, work conditions, female worker benefits, training, social security, welfare, labor dispute resolution, supervision, and the legal responsibility of the

24. Group-based complainants constituted only 0.1 percent of the urban labor force in 1996. This is a figure closer to France in the late nineteenth century than to France in the 1950s, when strikers were 6.9 percent of the labor force, or to the United States in the 1970s, when strikers averaged about 4 percent of the formal labor force (U.S. 1976, p. 373; Tilly 1978, p. 163). In China, as a percent of the work force, collective complaints were more common in joint ventures (.9%) and overseas Chinese firms (1.1%) and less common in state (.02%) and urban collective firms (.04%) – which illustrates how more marketized sectors of the economy invite more open protest (SSB 1997a, pp. 93, 744–45).

employer (NPC 1994). These new laws and regulations are intended to provide more protection for employees. Another step is the achievement of collective bargaining. Since the late 1980s, China has been experimenting with a form of collective contract negotiated between labor unions and enterprises. Between 1989 and 1991, the number of work units under collective contract increased 23 percent, to 82,862 (All-China Federation of Labor Unions 1992, p. 120). In 1994, the Ministry of Labor issued a document encouraging further negotiations between firms and labor unions.[25] The state is supposed to play a mediating role. Collective contracts are to include remuneration, work time, vacation, safety, insurance, and welfare. The document states that China should emulate the convention of collective bargaining from market societies. Similar to the development of labor unions in postsocialist Russia (Connor 1996), this policy will increase the independence of official labor unions.

On paper, at least, China's unionization rates in all types of firms are high. In the early 1990s, most workers were in the officially sponsored union, from 93 percent of employees in state firms to a still high 57 percent in foreign-owned firms (All-China Federation of Labor Unions 1992, p. 85). Thus, if these measures were indeed effective, and China's unions became more autonomous, they could become a significant actor in labor–management relations. As Tilly (1978, p. 163) notes in describing the pattern of strikes in the West, the number of strikes would continue to increase as would the number of workers involved in strikes. But with standard institutional paths for resolution of issues separating labor and management, the number of days of work stoppage and potential violence would drop sharply.

CONCLUSION

Several major findings of this chapter are related to both bargaining and satisfaction. First, with regard to bargaining, it appears that dense social networks no longer support bargaining in ways that they might once have in the 1970s and early 1980s. Workers with kin in the same work unit are not more likely to pursue their interests either through institutional contacting or through slowing down at work than others. A few workers with longer-term employment contracts are more likely to con-

---

25. Ministry of Labor, document 486 (1994), see *Laodong Neican*, March 1995.

template slowing down, but most workers with long-term employment contracts are more likely to be docile in the face of grievances. These findings are consistent with an account that emphasizes how the late 1980s enterprise reforms shifted the balance of power toward managers and supervisors.

Second, worker dependency has many of its anticipated effects. Workers are more docile when promotion is highly dependent on ties to supervisors. They are not completely docile when the firm distributes housing and other in-kind benefits, but they keep their bargaining to institutional channels. Thus, while in-kind benefits are distributed through enterprises and promotion relies heavily on personal ties to superiors, open protest will be dampened through manipulating these benefits.

The current tendency is for firms to divest themselves of in-kind obligations, however. With such a heavy burden of in-kind benefits, state firms cannot compete with the emerging nonstate sector. With so many workers dependent on the firm for benefits, a flexible labor market with workers moving freely from firm to firm cannot emerge. Current policy is to shift many of the benefit programs to either the market or the government sector. To the extent that this policy is successful, workers will be less dependent on their firm and supervisor, and open worker activism will increase.

The third finding about bargaining is that there is an emerging bifurcation among different types of workers. Older, more established workers tend to rely on contacting through institutional channels. These are the same workers who are more likely to be in the party, on factory committees, and to receive housing and in-kind benefits. Younger, more educated workers, with few of these status and material rewards, in contrast, are more likely to think of direct action such as slowing down. These young workers then could be the leading edge of a more belligerent labor force that demands action outside current institutional channels. With higher expectations, greater organizational skills, and a feeling that they lack ready access to established channels of influence, young workers could help spur a sudden increase in strikes.

Our major finding with regard to satisfaction is that unregulated dependency on supervisors has negative consequences. While in the short run, dependency on supervisors may dampen open protest, it also increases dissatisfaction, much as in the early industrial revolution in the

West. In firms with higher levels of dependency on supervisors for promotion, workers are more dissatisfied and more likely to contemplate leaving the firm. With increasing education levels among workers and a declining dependency on the firm for in-kind benefits, these levels of dissatisfaction could easily help further accelerate the pace of wildcat strikes against management.

One suspects that much as in the West, Chinese firms over the next few years will be required to move toward more "rule of law" in the workplace. External arbitration committees, which already rule heavily in favor of the worker, are steps in this direction, as are new labor laws that specify some worker rights. We suspect that there will need to be several additional steps, one of which will be further regulations that govern supervisor behavior, new promotion procedures that limit supervisor authority, and new grievance committees that help resolve disputes. These are the sorts of steps that Richard Edwards describes as having limited workplace conflict in the West. A second difficult step will be the creation of a new independent union structure that regularizes conflict and avoids the wildcat strike pattern that is becoming increasingly common. This second step provides the kind of institutional regulation of conflict that Ralf Dahrendorf suggests was necessary to purchase labor peace in the West.

The socialist social contract once promised in-kind benefits and lifetime employment in exchange for workers' docility and dependence. Under the new social contract, security of employment and in-kind benefits are disappearing. Instead, workers now have more freedom to protest, to increase their income, and to move between jobs. The changing social contract has transformed labor–management relations.

7

Civil Servants and Bureaucratic Behavior

THE impact of the switch from socialist to market social contract can be just as great for those at the commanding heights of society as it is for the workers who we examined in the last chapter. The existing literature disagrees on whether the old bureaucratic elites can survive, and on whether these bureaucrats can be reborn as effective technocrats. We visited this issue in Chapter 4, where we reviewed the debates among bargaining, market transformation, and technocratic continuity schools of thought. We concluded by suggesting that the debate was undertheorized, with the binary opposition of producers (managers, entrepreneurs) and redistributors (administrators) being too simplistic.

This chapter adds to the indictment of existing accounts being too simplistic by suggesting additional issues. First, among elites on the bureaucratic pay scale, there is not only a two-way grouping of government administrators and enterprise managers but also a third grouping of party and political operatives scattered throughout all types of organizations. For many people in China, the focus was not so much on reducing the power of ordinary administrators as it was on reducing the number and power of this third group of political operatives. If reform were successful, one indicator would not be the changing income of administrators but the personal fates of political operatives. This was part of China's move away from a virtuocracy, where the political operatives were all-important, to a technocracy, with people promoted based on technical expertise. We examine whether the fates of the political operatives were reversed in the late 1980s and early 1990s.

Closely related is the changing nature of bureaucrats who remained in power. Through compulsory retirement programs and requirements for initial educational credentials and continuous in-service training, the transition from virtuocracy to a meritocractic technocracy was purportedly accelerated hothouse-fashion. Chapter 3 on life chances has already suggested progress on this front. We revisit the technocratic transition in this chapter, asking in addition whether the transition is associated with changes in the types of values that administrators hold. If there is, indeed, a transition in values, we conclude that we can extend Róna-Tas's (1994) argument about technocratic continuity. The transition need not involve just continuity, with technically skilled administrators and managers moving out of the bureaucracy into private enterprises. The transition could involve administrators becoming technically more skilled – including administrators receiving more education and political operatives retreating from public organizations and enterprises.

Before concluding, this chapter considers the potential pitfalls of the market/technocratic transition. In earlier decades, bureaucratic control mechanisms focused on both principled particularism and normative control. The "principled particularism" included a set of selective incentives – housing, income, and so on – for party members and others destined for leadership (Walder 1986). The normative control mechanisms included an emphasis on Rousseau-like virtue, guaranteed by small group study, criticism and self-criticism, and the insinuations of political operatives into every organization. When this worked well in the early years of socialism, it helped provide social control "on the cheap" (Skinner and Winkler 1969; Whyte 1974). The early socialist enthusiasm faded, and the operatives became despised in many quarters. Yet the operatives continued to provide some measure of top-down control. Now, with the role of operatives and normative control disappearing, and with the growing temptations of income outside established bureaucratic channels in the more open market economy, the temptations to "cheat" – to take bribes and other side payments – have increased (Walder 1995). We visit this issue in passing, noting again that the search for the size of redistributor/producer incomes in standard market transition debates misses the much more serious problem that if redistributors (administrator) incomes are not high enough to prevent temptations from bribes from people in the private market economy, the market system will be endangered.[1]

---

1. Leff (1964), Rueschemeyer and Evans (1985), Jagannathan (1986), Sandbrook (1986).

Figure 1 Anxious parents wait while their children take college entrance exams in Beijing, July 1996. Currently, less than 2 percent of China's labor force is college educated. China Photo Archives.

Figure 2 Elections for urban district people's deputies, Haidan district, Beijing, May 1987, just before the 1987 Political Participation Survey (see Chapter 8). China Photo Archives.

Figure 3 Advertisement for five deputy director-level cadres and high-level managers in Beijing, January 1996. This was the first time Beijing was to choose high-level cadres through a combination of personal application and examination. China Photo Archives.

Figure 4 Some of the 500 undergraduate and graduate students at Qinghua University who were sworn into the Communist party, June 1996. China Photo Archives.

Figure 5 Patients wait outside the Beijing Tongren Ophthalmology Hospital, July 1996. Specialization combined with government-regulated low prices created a high demand for service.

Figure 6 "This hospital does not accept bribes" reads the center sign of Hefei First People's Hospital in Anhui Province, May 1996. China Photo Archives.

Figure 7 Laid-off workers being interviewed for jobs at the residential committees in Nanjing, August 1997. China Photo Archives.

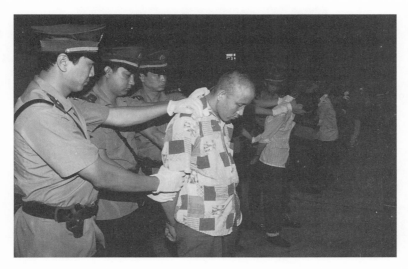

Figure 8 A public sentencing ceremony of twenty-one drug traffickers in Beijing, June 1996. Five received the death penalty. China Photo Archives.

Figure 9 A newly completed residential housing area in Hubeikou, Beijing, May 1997. China Photo Archives.

Figure 10 Women's tea gathering in Beijing, July 1996. Organized by Shi Jianping, a divorced woman, most visitors were divorced middle-aged women without much education. A lawyer (second from right) is providing free legal advice. China Photo Archives.

Figure 11 A newsstand in Beijing, January 1998. Photo by Wenfang Tang.

Figure 12 An example of China's "sex reform": a store in Beijing's Wangfujing shopping area, January 1998. Products include erotic condoms, vibrators, and breast-expanding machine. Photo by Wenfang Tang.

BUREAUCRACY UNDER STATE SOCIALISM
AND AFTER REFORM

Redistributive Virtuocracy to Technocratic Meritocracy

Scholars disagree on whether socialist bureaucracies can evolve into efficient technocracies without abandoning public ownership. A pessimistic view sees few prospects for change in socialist bureaucracies. According to Kornai (1992), under state socialism, the absence of an exit option and the close administrative supervision have unfortunate effects on civil servants. They learn the "six don'ts" – don't criticize one's superiors, express opinions, produce innovative ideas, or take initiatives, risks, and responsibilities. Lucian Pye (1988) is equally pessimistic about China's bureaucracy, with Third World backwardness, Confucianism, and the Leninist party principles all causing problems (Pye 1988, ch. 5).[2] Through their Confucian socialization and work experience for the party, he argues, bureaucrats learn to be obedient conformists. In contrast to Pye's position, others argue that the problems of the bureaucratic system originate not in China's culture but in the systemic features of socialism and the neglect of China's well-developed civil service tradition (Li 1993; Williams 1993).

Market economies must cope with many parallel issues in public bureaucracies, and the success of bureaucratic management in East Asian market states suggests an alternative path.[3] With little emphasis on ideology and (until recently) limited pluralism and considerable political apathy combined with bureaucratic dominance, the economically successful examples of Taiwan, South Korea, and other East Asian countries provide potential models for China to follow.[4] Sharing a cultural tradition that esteems education, these societies early completed a technocratic transformation of their state bureaucracy, including a strict civil service examination system for the selection of skilled bureaucrats.

2. For another creative attempt to link China's contemporary problems with bureaucracy to earlier authoritarian traditions, see Fu (1993).
3. For the literature on successful civil service reform in developing countries, see Nunberg (1995). On the problems of bureaucracy in developed market economies, see Block (1987).
4. For a similar model of bureaucratic authoritarianism in South America, see O'Donnell (1979, p. 91; 1988, pp. 31–32).

Educational credentials in selection of bureaucrats and an emphasis on rational promotion procedures are no guarantee of success in bureaucratic management, of course. Barrington Moore (1958) and Jerry Hough (1969, 1977) argue that the Soviet bureaucracy was staffed by technocrats who made their decisions based on technical and rational criteria. Nearly all significant Soviet officials were college graduates. Promotion seemed based primarily on performance, and, except for those at the highest political levels, honest officials were usually assured tenure with good performance. Nevertheless, when combined with other efficiency-inducing measures, an increased emphasis on technical proficiency and rational promotion procedures might help.

Already by the early 1980s, China's bureaucracy had begun to change. The early years of the regime emphasized normative and coercive control of the bureaucracy, often organized through an active program of political study, small group criticism and self-criticism, and episodic political campaigns. Service in the pre-1949 revolution, party seniority, and political loyalty became important bases for promotion. Initially, centralization was possible because of the relatively simple task of economic coordination at China's early stage of economic development. However, in time, bureaucrats became inured to continual ideological appeals and skilled in dissimulating in small group and political campaign settings (Whyte 1974). As society stabilized and the economy became more complex and the division of labor more elaborate, centralized control became more difficult. Bureaucratic agencies proliferated and hierarchies flattened. Decision making became less arbitrary and bureaucratic bargaining increased.[5]

Civil Services Reform and Potential Pitfalls

As a part of China's effort to modernize the economy, the post-Mao leaders decided to modernize its bureaucracy (Deng 1988, pp. 19–21). The programs began with a massive mandatory retirement program in the early 1980s (Harding 1987; Lee 1991; Manion 1993; Lieberthal 1995).

---

5. For a discussion of fragmented authoritarianism, see Lieberthal and Oksenberg (1988, ch. 8), Lieberthal and Lampton, ed. (1992, introduction), and Lieberthal (1995, ch. 6). Even during the radical period of the Great Leap Forward, bureaucratic interests and coalitional politics were dominant and Mao was never the only unquestionable decision maker (Bachman 1991, p. 219).

Another effort was retraining mid-career bureaucrats (Harding 1987; Chi 1991). A third program was modernization and streamlining. Various measures of cadre evaluation, job rotation, and demotion were attempted (Burns 1989, p. 743). At its fifteenth congress in 1997, the party called for continuing improvement of bureaucratic efficiency by streamlining organizations and personnel and by separating the functions of the party and the state. The fourth program was decentralization of political power from the center to local levels and to nongovernment sectors (Shirk 1993; Jia and Lin 1994; Wang 1994; Lieberthal 1995). The fifth program was the separation of the party from the state (Lee 1991). In 1993, after nearly ten years of experiment and numerous drafts, China passed tentative civil service regulations (*guojia gongwuyuan zanxing tiaoli*). Despite continuing party influence (Xu and Hou 1993), technical expertise in recruitment was emphasized.

Though Chinese bureaucrats have become more technocratic since 1978, several authors remain dubious about the success of new trends. First, some of the rapid increases in education were the product of two-year junior colleges and night schools (Chi 1991). Thus, one has to be cautious about assumptions of the quality of the newly improved bureaucracy. A second problem was the declining capacity for the central bureaucracy to control. Under the old system, bureaucracy had effective control over career opportunity and reward (Walder 1986). Economic reform created more alternatives for career opportunity and for personal sources of income (Walder 1995). Third, political decentralization and the decline of morale, combined with the relative decline of income compared with the private sector, created opportunities for local bureaucrats' profiteering (Chi 1991). Local officials were captured by local interest groups and the center's monitoring capacity declined (Rueschemeyer and Evans 1985, p. 56). As a result, bureaucratic corruption increased during reform (Yang 1994). The question, then, is whether China can become a smoothly functioning bureaucratic authoritarian state or whether it will come apart as a petty patronalistic and highly corrupt state.

We examine these types of issues with survey data on attitudes in 1987, with survey and other data on objective and subjective changes between the 1980s and 1990s, and, finally, with secondary and primary data on corruption. The 1987 data are from a survey of bureaucrats, including enterprise managers (*qiye ganbu*), administrators (*zhengfu ganbu*), public organization (schools, hospitals, broadcast stations, etc.) administrators (*shiye danwei ganbu*), and party, political, and mass organization (unions, women's associations) operatives (*dangqun zhuzhi fuzeren*). The range of the group surveyed is defined primarily by whether they were on the bureaucratic (civil service) pay scale – one of three pay scales, with the other two being for workers and professional/technical workers.[6]

HOPES AND FEARS, 1987

Change was well under way by 1987. By carrot and stick – or, more precisely, by golden handshake and compulsory retirement laws – many older bureaucrats were induced into retirement. New credentialing requirements provided a big carrot to get additional training either before entering the bureaucracy or once on the job for those who wanted to advance. There were increasing motions toward separating the party and political operatives from economic enterprises and public organizations (schools, hospitals, etc.). If these efforts were indeed successful, there should have been an immediate change in the perceptions of different types of bureaucrats. Leading by many years the changes in income that scholars often use to index market transformation, changed perceptions should provide an index of realized, or soon-to-be-realized, change. Bureaucrats with more education and in technical and managerial positions should be optimistic about the future and eager for civil service reform. Bureaucrats with less education and in political operative positions should be far more pessimistic about civil service reform and resistant to civil service reform. Some of the same resistance and pessimism should apply to the elderly, who were about to be mustered out of the bureaucratic service. In short, much as we suggested for popular attitudes toward reform, group interests should dominate peoples' attitudes about technocratic transformation of the bureaucracy (see Chapter 5).

6. For the distribution of managers, administrators, and clerical workers across different types of enterprises, see Appendix Table A1.2 and the summary descriptive table for the 1987 survey in Appendix Table A6.1. For an earlier analysis of this data set, see Zhou (1995).

Reform Attitudes

For 1987, we know peoples' attitudes on two issues. One is the issue of "separating politics and economics," with the three responses of disapproval, uncertainty, and approval to the specific question of whether party and political operatives should abandon economic enterprises. The second issue is whether these same operatives should then "go into business." The analysis of the responses shows strong group interests (Fig. 7.1). Subgroups of bureaucrats are compared with party and political operatives in economic enterprises (18% of the total) and public organizations (2% of the total).

Unsurprisingly, when asked whether they wanted to vote themselves out of a job, the political operatives in enterprises (and public organizations) were not very enthusiastic. Most of the other bureaucrats were, however. In raw numbers, about one-fourth of the political operatives in enterprises were ready to vote themselves out of a job. Twice as many bureaucrats in enterprises were ready to show political operatives the door. Or, on the scale in Figure 7.1 (maximum value of 3 in either direction, not shown) the top three groups of bureaucrats were .3 to .4 points more likely to want to rid themselves of the political operatives. Clerical workers in government held similar opinions, and even the lower-level party operatives in government offices failed to support their "comrades" in the enterprise sector.[7] Though we have no direct data on the subject, the tendency of lower-level bureaucrats in all lines of work to want the expulsion of "extra" political operatives is consistent with a revulsion against dependency on others at one's place of work. This is a theme that we began in Chapter 6. The evidence here is consistent with an argument that the revulsion against additional supervisory personnel at one's place of work extends far beyond the level of blue-collar workers. Clerical workers also abhorred extra levels of supervisory personnel at their places of work.

When it came to the issue of where the dispossessed political operatives should go, people agreed on only one thing, which was, "NIMBY!"

---

7. Statistically, responses by technical specialists were higher than those by political operatives in government ($p = .054$). Responses by enterprise clerical workers were greater than by either government clerical workers ($p < .10$) or high-ranking government political operatives ($p < .05$).

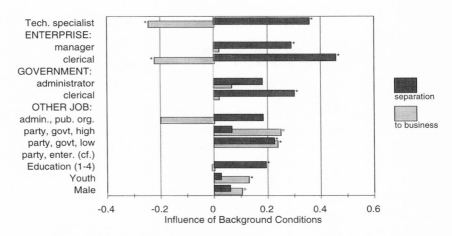

Figure 7.1 Attitudes about civil service reform among bureaucrats, late 1987. Notes: Determinants of approval of the ideas of "separating politics and economics" by getting party and political operatives out of economic enterprises and of letting these same operatives go "into business." OLS regression coefficients. "Party" work includes "party and political functionaries, with the final comparison group (cf.) including functionaries in both economic enterprises (stores, factories) and public organizations (schools, hospitals, etc.). "Clerical" workers includes all lower-rank bureaucrats in enterprises and government. Education is on a four-point scale, from primary through college. Youth is the inverse of age divided by 10. The underlying equations also include coefficients not shown for each city. (*) $p < .05$; (°) $p < .10$. Source: 1987 Civil Service Survey.

(not in my backyard). One logical solution would have been to move the political operatives into closely allied work in government administrative offices. However, the government operatives were unanimous in endorsing the idea that the enterprise operatives go into business – by implication, then, not hanging around the office hot-water kettle with everyone else. Conversely, enterprise clerical workers and technical specialists did not want the former operatives anywhere near their territory. Enough was enough, it seems – particularly for lower-level workers who suffered the greatest brunt of operative intervention in earlier years and who could suffer from unfair economic competition if former political operatives used their personal connections to succeed in business. If the people who answered this survey had their way, then, the former operatives would be people without a workplace to call home.

Work Attitudes

The 1987 bureaucrats were internally differentiated on several other issues as well. The survey asked them whether they were satisfied with their job, whether they felt that their job would be secure during reform, and whether on balance they would gain or lose from reform (see Appendix A6 for specific items). The educated, young, and males illustrate a pattern that we have already seen in popular responses to other types of reform issues (Fig. 7.2). Though this group was dissatisfied with current work conditions, it thought that it could either hold on to its job or make additional gains as reform progressed (cf. Chapter 5).[8] Among different bureaucratic positions, people closer to technocratic, production work were the most optimistic. The tendency was strongest for technical specialists, who in 1987 were already more satisfied than political operatives in enterprises. The specialists were also more convinced that they could keep their jobs and that they would make additional gains.[9] The rest of the bureaucrats trailed in a similar order. Managers and clerical workers in enterprises were the second most optimistic, and party/political operatives in government and other similar groups were the third most optimistic. The comparison group of political operatives in enterprises was, of course, the laggard in the fourth group of bureaucrats.

All this suggests that by 1987, the bureaucracy was becoming more differentiated. With skills that could be used in production, technical specialists stood out in level of optimism about the future. This, we suggest, does more to document an increasing bifurcation between "producers" and "redistributors" than the income statistics that are typically used to examine this type of issue. Moreover, the group that anticipated losing most was not the government administrators but the political operatives,

8. The overall level of bureaucratic job satisfaction in the sample was 65 percent (weighted). To use a rough comparison, among U.S. federal employees, job satisfaction is about 75 percent among both political appointees and career bureaucrats (Aberbach and Rockman 1994, table 1). For China, when only political and administrative officials in the government were included, the results were very similar: 70 percent of party officials and 77 percent of administrators were satisfied. Thus, by 1987, party and administrative officials were not too unhappy.
9. Compared with technical specialists, the following felt significantly ($p < .05$) less secure about their jobs: clerical workers (enterprise and government) and high-ranking political operatives in government.

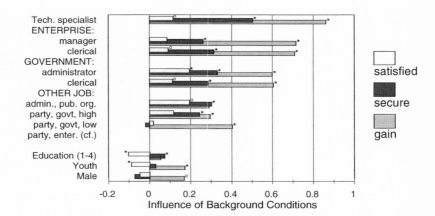

Figure 7.2 Attitudes about work among bureaucrats, late 1987. Notes: Coefficients for "satisfied with job" or proportional change coefficients from a probit analysis. Coefficients for "expect job to be secure during reform" and "anticipate gaining from reform" are from an OLS regression. "Party" work includes party and political functionaries, with the final comparison group (cf.) including functionaries in both economic enterprises (stores, factories) and public organizations (schools, hospitals, etc.). "Clerical" workers includes all lower-rank bureaucrats in enterprises and government. Education is on a four-point scale, from primary through college. Youth is the inverse of age divided by 10. The underlying equations also include coefficients not shown for each city. (*) $p < .05$; (°) $p < .10$. Source: 1987 Civil Service Survey.

who were previously responsible for the "virtuocratic" emphasis in the bureaucracy. It is this transformation from virtuocracy to technocracy – the technocratic transformation – that is in many ways just as important as market transformation. Both technocratic and market transitions privilege managers and specialists close to production.

CHANGES, 1980s TO 1990s

The 1987 data on hopes and fears suggest important initial changes and the possibility of much more significant changes after that date. However, the worst fears of the virtuocrats and the fondest hopes of the technocrats need not have been realized in the subsequent decade. Though the time period is short, we can begin to get some appreciation of the actual changes – both by examining objective changes in the qualifications and numbers of bureaucrats and by examining subjective attitudes in the 1990s as compared with the 1980s.

Objective Indicators

Judging from perceptions in late 1987, China's bureaucracy was beginning a massive transformation from a virtuocracy to meritocracy, with an emphasis on the separation of political and economic functions and the recruitment and retraining of technocrats who could better adapt to the needs of a complex economy.

Quality of Bureaucrats, 1987. The 1988 CHIP survey provides an early benchmark of the transformation. In that year, the technocratic transformation of the party itself – and, in turn, the higher ranks of the bureaucracy, since 80 percent of all administrators and managers are party members – was well under way (Fig. 7.3). Party recruitment begins seriously only when people are in their thirties. By their late thirties, two-thirds of all junior and regular college-educated (14–16 years of education) were in the party. For those with only primary through high school education (6–12 years), one required much more seniority to approach this level of party membership. This pattern was based on the experience of older cohorts. Among the younger cohorts, even seniority may not help individuals overcome modest education and be recruited into the party. Thus, the party itself is becoming more educated.[10]

Quality of Bureaucrats, 1994. Statistics for 1994 suggest that the 1980s technocratic tendencies continued into the 1990s. In the 1994 State Statistical Bureau Survey of administrators and managers, government administrators were better educated than managers (Table 7.1). Though much of their postsecondary education was midcareer training at junior colleges, both were better educated in 1994 than they had been a decade earlier (CHIP 1988; Census Office 1985, p. 464). This is consistent with

---

10. Of course, the government was giving into the lobbying of educated interest groups who wanted education credentials made a central criterion for appointment and promotion (see literature in Chapter 3).

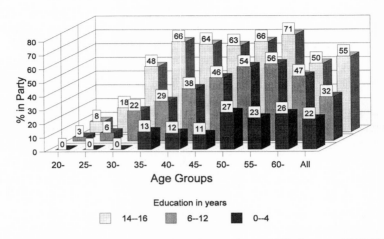

Figure 7.3 Party membership by education and age, 1988. Source: 1988 Urban CHIP Survey.

Table 7.1. *Administrators and Managers, 1994*

	Administrators	Managers
Education (years)	11.8	11.2
College degree (%)	10	9
Junior college degree (%)	35	26
Income, annual (RMB$)	$6,020	$6,769
Housing space, sq. meters	42	39
Age (years)	42	44
Length of time as a party member (years)	16	11.8
Seniority (years at work)	20	22
Tenure (years at current job)	5	7
Observations	55,509	65,912

Notes: State Statistical Bureau survey, including managers and administrators through clerical workers in government organizations and economic enterprises. *Source*: SSB (1996, p. 130).

the story of increasing education credentials for China's administrative and managerial elite.

In addition, in Table 7.1 we see a pattern from Chapter 4 repeated. Managers got most of their additional material rewards in take-home pay. Lower paid, administrators tried to compensate for their inferior pay through higher in kind benefits – this time in housing. This repeats both the pattern we saw for 1988 and the pattern found in the United States.

Finally, administrator and manager ages are not all that high. This is consistent with the emphasis on getting older leaders to retire, allowing more young leaders to be recruited. Between the 1982 and 1995 census, the percentage of administrators and managers age fifty-five and above fell from 14 to 10 percent while the percentage below age thirty-five grew from 14 to 22 percent.[11] There was a significant shift in the intended direction of creating a younger bureaucracy. Moreover, mobility among bureaucratic positions was considerable, with the average administrator serving in the current post only five years – which is even less than among managers who have served an average of seven years (Table 7.1). Thus, by the mid-1990s, administrators, in particular, were no longer a group who were old or who had stagnated in the same post after many years of service. This pattern is consistent with an increased emphasis on technocracy and the provision of new mobility opportunities that might motivate administrators to better service.

Quantity of Civil Servants, 1982–95. One would be even more impressed if the number of administrators declined while their quality was increasing. By this measure, the results are more mixed. While the number of very top national administrators declined, lower-level administrators continued to increase in many areas. If we count bureaucrats as "persons responsible in government, party, mass organizations, public agencies and economic enterprises" (*guojia jiguan, dangqun zhuzhi, qishiye danwei fuzeren*), their total number increased from 8.1 million in 1982 to 14.1 million in 1995 (Census Office 1985, 1997). To discount the effect of the increasing size of the total labor force, one can examine the change in percentage of state bureaucrats in total number of employees in nonfarm sectors. By that standard, bureaucrats increased from 5.6

11. Census Office (1985, table 62; 1997, tables 3 and 4).

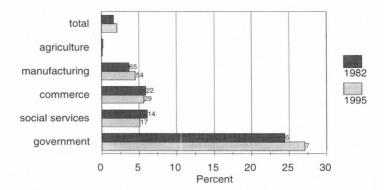

Figure 7.4 Administrators and managers, 1982–95. Notes: Percent of administrators and managers in agriculture, manufacturing (including mining, construction, public utilities), commerce (including transport, communication, finance,
insurance, real estate), social services (including health, education, research,
culture), and government. Numerals at ends of bars indicate the percent each
sector was of total nonagricultural labor in 1982 and 1995. Based on census data
tabulation of industry and occupation. Sources: SSB (1985, table 60); Census
Office (1997, table 3-5).

percent in 1982 to 6.6 percent in 1995. This represents a modest increase
of bureaucrats.

Despite the overall increase, some sectors declined in the proportion
of administrators and managers, and those declines were much as one
might anticipate from trends during the early reform period (Fig. 7.4).
Agriculture had few administrators and managers initially, and by 1995
it had proportionally even less. Manufacturing gained in administrators
and, one suspects, even more in managers. Government also gained.
However, both commerce (stores, restaurants, financial services, etc.) and
social services (health, education, culture, etc.) saw declines in the proportion of administrators and managers. Thus, some of the groups who
wanted to rid themselves of administrators appear to have done so by
1995. This shedding (or at least slowed growth) of administrators and
managers was greatest in the sectors that were growing rapidly – for
example, commerce, which grew from 22 to 29 percent of the nonfarm
labor force, and social services, which grew from 14 to 17 percent of the
labor force (numerals at ends of bars in Fig. 7.4). Manufacturing shrank

in relative size, while gaining in proportion of administrators, suggesting that in this sector manual workers were shed more quickly than managers. More generally, the pattern of results suggests that rapid economic growth in a sector is associated with a declining load of administrators and managers. All this suggests that in the rapidly growing portions of the economy, marketization was having the anticipated effect of reducing the role of administrators and managers.

Subjective Indicators, 1987–92

After 1987, although explicit civil service reform moved slowly, many other reform programs were implemented. In 1992 the fourteenth party congress again proposed civil service reform, providing us yet another chance to examine bureaucratic responses to reform efforts. We can compare the change of attitudes in both the 1987 civil service survey and the 1992 urban social survey. One question was on the dependence of the respondent on the government for jobs: "If your work unit has to reduce the number of employees and if you have to be cut, would you wait for the government to allocate you another job?"

We had to use crude categories of bureaucrats for this comparison. The 1992 survey has only three subgroups of bureaucrats: (1) clerical workers: low-level bureaucrats (*yiban ganbu*), the market equivalent of low-level white-collar employees; (2) administrators above the section chief (*ke*) level in government and public agencies; and (3) managers above the section chief level in enterprises.[12]

The results reveal some important changes of attitudes from 1987 to 1992, particularly among administrators and managers (Fig. 7.5). The increasing belief in the role of self-effort is particularly evident in responses to the question about what one should do if laid off. The sharp decline in reliance on the government to assign jobs provides striking evidence that the market was making inroads among administrators,

---

12. We combine the smaller subgroups in the 1987 survey to match these three groups. The first group (clerical workers) includes low-level political, administrative, and managerial bureaucrats in enterprises, government, and public organizations. The second group (middle- and high-level in government and public organizations) combines those middle- and high-level party leaders and administrators in government and public organizations. The third group includes enterprise party officials and managers. Technical specialists were not compared, since the 1992 survey did not demarcate this group in the 1992 survey.

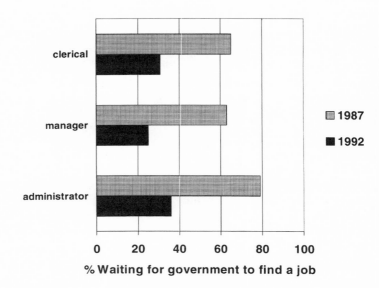

Figure 7.5 Percent responding yes to the question "Would you wait for the government to find you a job if laid off?" All 1987–92 differences are statistically significant at .01. Because of coarser categories in the 1992 data, for both survey years, party and political workers are merged with other administrators and managers. Sources: 1987 Civil Service Survey and 1992 China Urban Survey.

managers, and clerical workers. In a short five years, the majority of top bureaucrats went from expecting that the government would take care of them to expecting just the opposite. On the personal career dimension, then, there were very sharp changes in a brief five years.

CORRUPTION

The process of technocratic and market transition posed severe threats to bureaucratic stability, with bureaucratic corruption leading the list of problems – both because it can reduce government efficiency and because it induces a popular backlash (Chapter 5). The threats came both from the mixed economy, with the bureaucracy continuing to act as a

redistributor of scarce, underpriced goods, and from the incomplete vir-
tuocracy/meritocracy, normative/remunerative transition in bureaucratic
command and control mechanisms.[13]

China today provides a fertile environment for corruption. Reform
legitimized individual interest. One no longer has to work for society and
the collective interest. Greed is not necessarily a bad thing. The rapid
transition from the centrally planned system also created many gray
areas where bureaucrats had no rules to follow. Legal loopholes created
by contradictions between the rules from the old and rules from the new,
reform system exacerbated the situation. The result of all these factors
was an increase of arbitrary power by bureaucrats. As we mentioned in
the beginning of this chapter, political decentralization further weakened
the monitoring power of the center (Rueschemeyer and Evans 1985, p.
56; Wang 1995b). Local officials gained more authority to promote local
interests, even if this required illegal means. Yet another reason for a
favorable environment for corruption was the declining status of bureaucrats during reform. As we showed in Chapter 4, although administrators enjoyed better housing, their income was falling behind that of
managers, the self-employed, and workers in joint-venture firms. Even
where administrator income was higher than that of other groups, the
gap was quite narrow compared with market societies. The contrast
between too little pay and too much power created a strong temptation
for bureaucrats to convert power into profit. Finally, the rapid development of the private sector during reform provided resources outside the
bureaucratically controlled distribution system. These new resources
were often used to pay off officials and to get favorable regulations (Yang
1994; Wank 1995; Yan 1995).

Under such conditions, corruption became a serious problem. In the
first eleven months of 1994, for example, 24,990 corruption cases were
investigated, a 35 percent increase from the same period in 1993. Among
these cases, 1,833 involved middle-level (county and department head)
and high-ranking (bureau chief and above) officials, an 86 percent
increase from the previous year (Wen 1995).

These and other bureaucratic corruption cases caused widespread

13. See Harris (1986) and Gong (1994). Also see Lee (1990) for a discussion of the similarities of corruption in China and Soviet Union.

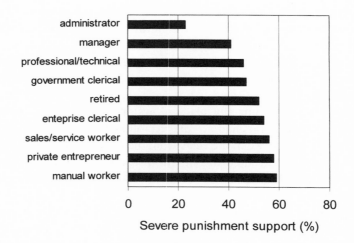

Figure 7.6 Support for severe punishment of corruption, 1987. Source: 1987 Political Participation Survey.

public resentment. This resentment was one of the main reasons that triggered the 1989 urban protests (see Chapter 5). In the 1987 Political Participation survey, there was a question about the punishment of corruption: "In order to improve the communist party's work style, do you think it is important to severely punish corrupt officials?" The most noticeable distinction is between administrators and others (Fig. 7.6). A much smaller percentage of administrators thought corrupt officials should be severely punished. Or resentment of corruption increased in inverse proportion to the occupation hierarchy, with workers being the most resentful. This pattern suggests a tendency for bureaucratic officials to use power and influence to gain profit, and for those without that influence to resent its use in this way.[14]

The government has taken several measures to combat corruption. In 1984 and 1986, the government issued two documents banning party and

14. The difference between administrators and managers is not statistically significant. Differences between administrators and all other groups are statistically significant at .01. The difference between managers and manual workers is statistically significant at .01.

state organizations from making a profit. Party and state organizations are not allowed to own businesses; bureaucrats and their family members are not allowed to be employed by private companies (ZGFLNJ 1993, pp. 290–92). In 1989, during the peak of popular dissatisfaction with corruption, the Supreme People's Court issued regulations on criminal charges against illegal profiteering. A "serious" case is defined as making an illegal profit of more than 100,000 yuan by a company, and the illegal use of more than 50,000 yuan public funds by an individual (ZGFLNJ 1990, pp. 667, 680). In 1993, the party central committee and the state council jointly issued another document, specifically banning bureaucrats at the county (and department head) level and above from doing business, being employed by companies, buying and selling stocks, accepting work-related gifts, or using public funds for club membership (ZGFLNJ 1994, p. 574). Anticorruption legislation was accompanied by increased deterrence. A "serious" case usually means a life sentence or death penalty. In 1993, 32 percent of the 21,214 sentences of economic crimes were for five years in prison or longer (including life in prison and a death penalty), a 7 percent increase from 1992 (ZGFLNJ 1994, p. 96). The post-Deng leaders called for a continued anticorruption campaign in the fifteenth party congress in 1997.

A carrot accompanies this stick. As mentioned earlier, one source of corruption is the problem of "too little pay and too much power." In 1993, the government adjusted wages for bureaucrats in party and state organizations. For a middle-level cadre (county or division chief), the newly adjusted scale increased income by 34 percent. Another purpose of the 1993 wage adjustment was to widen the income gap and eliminate egalitarianism, so that high-ranking officials would not feel underpaid. This was achieved by increasing the relative weight of basic wages distributed by rank, while reducing subsidies equally distributed to everyone, regardless of rank. Before 1993, the basic wage was only 45 percent of an individual's paycheck, with the remaining 55 percent consisting of subsidies. In the post-1993 paycheck, the basic wage accounted for more than 80 percent of individual monthly income, while subsidies were reduced to only about 20 percent (State Council 1993). Therefore, the 1993 wage adjustment was designed not only to move away from the traditional social contract based on dependency-inducing in-kind payments, but also to make high-ranking officials feel an improvement in their income in both absolute and relative terms.

DISCUSSION AND CONCLUSION

Let us return to the issues raised at the beginning of this chapter. We suggested there that the typical analysis of administrators and their fate during reform was too simplistic. Simply picturing them as redistributors who must fall behind in income and rewards, if market transformation is to be complete, fails to note several issues. We suggest, in contrast, that if market transition is to be complete, several other changes must occur – including more (not less) pay for administrators and better-quality administrators, with an emphasis on technocratic qualifications. For the administrative side of the social system, the issue is not market transformation alone but the equally important issue of technocratic and incentive transformation of the government bureaucracy.

Technocratic transformation was well under way by the late 1980s and it continued into the 1990s. By 1995, administrators were far more educated than they were at the beginning of the 1980s. They were younger than managers, and their shorter tenure in office compared with managers suggests that they were moving from job to job or from position to position in ways that implies a new responsiveness to promotion and other kinds of opportunities. The attitudes of subgroups of administrators is consistent with these trends. By 1987, technical specialists, enterprise clerical workers, and others close to economic production were optimistic about the future, foreseeing major gains as reform progressed. Between 1987 and 1992, administrators became more independent-minded, being less willing to listen to orders from on high and being more willing to take control of their own fates.

Incentive transformation was occurring, though at slower than an ideal pace. If the transition from virtuocracy to meritocracy was to be complete, the structure of incentives had to change. The pre-1978 virtuocracy emphasized normative appeals, combined with selective material incentives for a chosen party and political activist elite (Skinner and Winckler 1969; Walder 1986, 1995). Using political study, small group criticism, and class struggle in political movements, the system sanctioned those who didn't comply with orders from on high (Whyte 1974). With these types of top-down and peer group controls and with few competing material incentives outside established bureaucratic structures, bureaucrats needed only modest payment to comply with guidelines within their bureaucratic chain of command. In the jargon of social science, principal–agent problems were unimportant – even while problems with creative thinking, initiative, and work for the societal good rather than the interests of one's bureaucratic subunit became increasingly severe.

If the combined market transition of society and the technocratic transformation of the bureaucracy are to succeed, the old incentive structure must be replaced by a new incentive structure that emphasizes remunerative in place of normative and coercive incentives. With the wiles of the market attracting underpaid bureaucrats, who continue to have many redistributive powers, corruption is inevitable. This is where the "market transition" attention to the relative pay of producers and redistributors can lead us astray. If pay to administrators does not rise in pace with the increasing pay to those in production, not only will the most energetic and creative administrators leave for work in the private sector, but those who remain will be "bought off" by private sector and state sector managers who will pay to remove administrative bottlenecks and to seek monopoly positions that guarantee higher profits. Thus, besides reducing redistributive powers by freeing the economy of administrative controls, the government needs to pay administrators more. The 1993 income reforms move in this direction. As private sector incomes continue to rise, administrator (redistributor) incomes will need to be raised to avoid increases in corruption and inefficiency. Since the relative incomes of administrators in other East Asian societies are already much higher than those in China, it seems probable that over the next two decades increases in Chinese administrator (and manager) incomes will be rapid (see Chapters 4 and 11).

8

Political Participation and Interest Articulation

THIS chapter returns to the issue of market transformation, with a focus both on forms of political participation and on the expression of group or class interests. Both dimensions should change as China moves from a communal, egalitarian social contract to an individualistic, market-based social contract. For the late 1980s and early 1990s, we expect these changes to be only incipient. Nevertheless, even at such an early date, it might be possible to catch some hint of the changes, if not the nose of the camel under the tent, at least the camel's breath.

The change in forms of political participation should involve a change from corporatist to individualistic interest seeking – from working through institutional chains of command to pursuing interests independently of those commands, on one's own volition, rather than on orders from on high. In our study of workers, we have already seen a bifurcation between groups that worked through established channels, including workers coopted by being appointed to advisory committees, and groups that pursued interests on their own (Chapter 6). In this chapter, we want to see if this bifurcation is spreading to issues beyond the workplace.

The change in group interest articulation asks whether interest groups are differentially served by planned, redistributive socialist and producer-driven market systems. In many ways, this inquiry repeats our Chapter 4 examination of the fate of redistributors (administrators) versus producers (entrepreneurs, managers). Only this time, we examine not the final "output" of more income but the "inputs" of contacting, voting, and other actions in pursuit of one's interests. If our ideas about market transition are correct, then one of the ways that producers and others such as professional and technical workers should become more highly rewarded includes not just more efficient behavior in the market but also more effective bargaining for advantages from the political system. Or this repeats our theme that market transition is not a purely economic process but one that involves interest group lobbying in an increasingly porous political system (Chapter 3).

ISSUES

State Socialism

Before elaborating the research issues, we should review some of the voluminous writings on the politics of state socialist societies. The writings divide into two broad groups: one emphasizing top-down processes and the other emphasizing bottom-up processes. Broadly speaking, the two approaches can be labeled corporatist and bargaining.

Corporatist. The top-down mobilization of participation included both mobilized participation and institutional channels for interest articulation. The emphasis on top-down participation and control can be overstated, as occurred in earlier emphases on the totalitarian nature of socialist societies (e.g., Arendt 1951; Kornhauser 1959; Friedrich and Brzezinski 1966). The totalitarian models now seem inadequate, both because these simple models obscure many of the detailed bargaining processes that occur in any large state organization and because they fail to take into account the softening of top-down control that occurred as socialist states became larger and more complex (e.g., Hough 1977; Lieberthal and Oksenberg 1988). Nevertheless, even with softening, socialist states emphasized mobilized participation, including mandatory voter turnouts and omnipresent political exhortation from above. By implication, then, one of the indicators of change that we will be looking for in China is whether mandatory participation is in decline.

Another indicator will be whether interests continue to be pursued through institutional channels. In the 1970s, several students of East European and Soviet politics proposed a set of models emphasizing how different chains of command within the state bureaucracy competed against one another in representing the interests of their respective constituencies. The attempt to capture this type of "feedback" mechanism went variously under the label of institutional pluralism, corporatism, or interest group politics (e.g., Skilling 1971; Chirot 1972; Hough 1977).[1] To obtain adequate information, the Soviet leadership had to loosen top-down control and allow the upward stream of influence to flow freely (Daniels 1971). Similarly for China, Lieberthal and Oksenberg argue that "the mature Soviet type system . . . is a bureaucratically dominant but fragmented system with a protracted, disjointed policy process characterized by bargaining and consensus building" (Lieberthal and Oksenberg 1988).

In the institutional pluralism/corporatism models, those who want to affect policy outcomes must work within the official framework. Failing to do so runs the danger of severe punishment, especially if the foundations of the system are challenged. Although any citizen can make appeals or suggestions through official channels, the leading political participants are "establishment" figures – usually civil servants and political figures. The model also includes bureaucratic officials who represent the diverse interests of their clientele and low-level subordinates, as well as politicians who take the danger of popular unrest into account as they mediate conflicts among the political participants. The wide use of letters to the editor and other similar avenues of collecting public opinions gives some credence to this view of institutionalized feedback mechanisms in mature Soviet-type polities (e.g., Nathan 1985). If change is occurring, then, standard institutional channels will be supplanted by more ad hoc means of participation.

Individualistic Bargaining. Some authors suggest that the above models err by implicitly assuming an all-seeing state that uses its unclouded crystal ball to organize the way interests are channeled. Another set of models emphasizes a messier process of bottom-up bargaining. Many of

1. Drawing on the Soviet experience, Schmitter developed a "monist" model of corporatism. According to this model, society is organized into a fixed number of constituent units that represent various interests. These units are "singular, ideologically selective, noncompetitive, functionally differentiated and hierarchically ordered categories, created, subsidized, and licensed by a single party and granted a representational role within that party and vis-à-vis the state in exchange for observing articulation of demands and mobilization of support." In a corporate state, elections are nonexistent or plebiscitary, party systems are dominated or monopolized by a weak single party, executive authorities are ideologically exclusive and more narrowly recruited, and political subcultures based on class, ethnicity, language, or regionalism are repressed (Schmitter 1974, p. 97; Lehmbruch and Schmitter 1982, pp. 5–6).

the same influence channels get used, but with less state "prescience" than implied in the above models. In Eastern Europe and the Soviet Union, there was tacit bargaining that gave increasing rewards to workers with scarce skills in vital industries (see Chapter 6). Studies of Soviet émigrés note that when asked how they would solve problems of housing, school admissions, and the like, they placed great emphasis on particularized contacting. Those with better contacts got better benefits, all of which helped fuel petty corruption and increasing cynicism about regime behavior (Eisenstadt and Roniger 1981, 1984; Jowitt 1983; DiFranceisco and Gitelman 1984). Similarly, in a study of Beijing residents, Shi (1997) suggests that political participation occurs during policy implementation and through individual resistance and personal connections.

In Chapter 6, we found that although the dense network of personal ties within work units and the close residence of managers and workers in work unit housing had little influence, employment security did increase workers' bargaining power at work. In this chapter, we examine whether these and other factors contribute to individual bargaining power. Other signs of individualized bargaining include frequent anecdotal accounts of how connections are necessary to get goods, services, and advantages that are not easily acquired through standard bureaucratic channels. With the partial relaxation of political controls and the emergence of a half-market, half-planned economy, this tendency to use connections not only helped fuel insidious bureaucratic corruption (Chapter 7), but also provided new opportunities for using connections as resources in individual bargaining. If this model is correct, then, among the young, the more educated, and in more rapidly growing cities with less reliance on the state sector, individualistic contacting should be more important.

Research Questions

Drawing from the existing literature, we examine, first, whether participation is beginning to shift ever so slightly from corporatist to individualist forms and, then, whether market-oriented social groups are better able to take advantage of these shifts (see Table 8.1). If the first shift is beginning to occur, then between the late 1980s and early 1990s, people should be less eager to pursue their interests through institutional channels. Also, at both dates, when people are less dependent on state insti-

Table 8.1. *Old and New Forms of Political Participation*

	Old (socialist corporatist)	New (market individualistic)
Form of participation (How are inputs mobilized and channeled?)		
Channel	Corporatist, through approved vertical chains of command, particularly through supervisors at work. High participation.	Individualist, through ad hoc channels outside standard lines of authority. Modest participation.
Voting	Mobilized, involuntary. High participation.	Voluntary. Modest participation.
Interest groups (Who has inputs?)	High traditional status, redistributors (administrators, managers, government clerical workers, party members, high seniority workers).	Low/modest traditional status, producers (private entrepreneurs, professional/technical workers, the educated, low seniority workers)
	People dependent on government for services.	Not dependent on government for services.
	Low-growth cities with mostly heavy state industry.	High-growth, nonstate, light industry/service cities.

tutions for consumer goods, housing, and other items, then they should turn less to institutionalized channels of participation (for additional literature on the dependency theme, see Chapter 6). Specifically, people in the private sector and people in rapidly growing cities with many consumer goods on the open market should be less likely to use institutional channels.

Our search for shifts will include a study of 1987 patterns of voicing particularistic complaints, 1987 district voting patterns, 1989–92 changes in use of grievance channels, and 1992 patterns in grievance channels.

Except for the voting, much of the data is about particularistic complaints. Thus, we should say a bit more about this type of political "participation." Pursuit of interest in socialist societies is often primarily preoccupied with narrow parochial issues, related to one's own work, family, or to other personal interests. This is because the government controls resource allocation and provides extensive social services in urban areas, such as employment, income, housing, education, and health care. In a market society, people have other economic and legal means to solve their individual problems. This lack of alternatives in China and other socialist societies forces people to engage in particularized contacting. It also explains why things considered nonpolitical (getting an apartment, fixing a water pipe, etc.) in a market society often become political in China, since the individual attempts to influence governmental allocation decision through personalistic contacting. Verba (1978, p. 26) suggests that when the government produces services, people learn to expect more services, especially if the population is nonaffluent. In less-developed societies, high expectations and excessive demand lead to poor service and dissatisfaction, which, Verba argues, heightens awareness of government potential and particularistic contacting. From precisely these kinds of dynamics, one would expect parochial participation to be common among Chinese urban residents.[2] People familiar with old-style Chicago machine politics will find all of this quite familiar, of course (Banfield 1963). The difference is one of degree. As we have already suggested, with declining dependency on state institutions for goods and services, this particularistic contacting should decline in importance, much as it did after a long delay in Chicago and other machine-based cities in the West.

Besides searching for incipient change in the use of institutionalized channels to pursue one's interests, we examine whether new social groups are beginning to have more input into politics (Table 8.1). More broadly, this inquiry asks whether socialist institutions were biased toward elite groups, which is frequently alleged, and whether the composition of those elite groups is beginning to move away from redistributors (administrators, party members) to producers (private

---

2. Existing writings are divided over whether particularized contacting can lead to broader political participation, with Verba (1978, p. 2) and DiFranceisco and Gitelman (1984) suggesting not and Bahry and Silver (1990) suggesting possibly in a postsocialist environment.

entrepreneurs, managers). In addition, we can note that seniority was a very important basis for promotion in China. This should be more characteristic of older people, with more shared time on the job and denser networks of social contact, than the young who do not yet have those channels. In short, we expect a bifurcation between older, established and young, unestablished individuals that parallels the bifurcation among workers (Chapter 6).

Existing evidence suggests that even before their late 1980s demise, European socialist states had an upper-class bias in their patterns of political participation (see Bahry and Silver 1990; Finifter and Mickiewicz 1992). In China in the late 1980s and early 1990s, party intellectuals expressed more political activism than both nonparty intellectuals and non-intellectuals (Tang 1999a). This repeats the frequent finding of strong upper-class bias in participation in market societies.[3] Thus, if there is a change that accompanies marketization, it will probably be not in the elite bias of political inputs and outputs, but in the specific elite that has inputs into the political system.

The variations by age and gender are also likely to replicate many market society patterns. Around the world, the middle-aged and old typically participate more in routine politics than the young. The young are too concerned with getting a job, finding a spouse, and beginning to establish a family to be greatly concerned with politics, though they participate more in radical and extra-system politics such as rallies and protests. It is not obvious that China should differ greatly on this dimension. By the mid-1980s, some of the job security of earlier decades had begun to fade. Many young adults began work in temporary jobs in inferior neighborhood enterprises rather than in the old, established state sector. Marriage was often delayed until a person's mid- to late twenties. Thus, many of the dynamics inhibiting political participation for the young in other societies should have begun to intensify in China.

Elsewhere, males typically participate more than females (e.g., Jennings 1983; Shapiro and Mahajan 1986). The sexist explanation is that concerns with home and child rearing displace concerns with politics,

---

3. E.g., Lipset (1961, pp. 39, 61, and 189), Barnes and Kaase (1979, pp. 15 and 133), Verba, Nie, and Kim (1978, p. 258), Dahl (1985, p. 64), Dalton (1988, ch. 2), Almond and Verba (1989, p. 134), Marsh (1990, p. 33), and Conway (1991, ch. 2).

though increasing living standards, education, and occupational status narrow the male–female participation gap. To the extent that these factors are important, one might expect the participation gap to be narrower in China than in most cities of the developing world. Virtually all adult women are at work in Chinese cities, and the male–female education gap has narrowed rapidly (Chapter 9). Nevertheless, work on other socialist societies shows that the gender gap in political participation remained (e.g., Carnaghan and Bahry 1990). Thus, the exact prediction for China is indeterminate.

VOICING COMPLAINTS, 1987

In 1987, respondents were asked about dissatisfaction with problems at work (such as wage increase, promotion, housing assignment, job assignment, and leadership style) and outside of work (price policy, transportation, environment, and public facilities), whether the dissatisfaction was voiced, reasons for not voicing their dissatisfaction, and the official response to reported dissatisfaction (see Appendix A7). Understandably, most people were dissatisfied with some issue either at or outside work (Fig. 8.1). It was more common to voice complaints at work than outside work, suggesting that it remained easier to pursue one's interests through older work unit channels. Once a complaint had been voiced, both work- and nonwork-related issues had broadly similar response rates and similar rates of favorable solution. For those who voiced a nonwork complaint, one-third got a response. And among those responses, one-fourth solved the original nonwork problem. Or, to state the results somewhat differently, among those who voiced nonwork complaints, the problem was solved for 7 percent ($.31 \times .24$) of all complainants.

These results can be compared with Verba's (1978) six-nation study of parochial participation on issues related to job, income, housing, education, and health care. In his study, an average of 61 percent of the respondents had a complaint, with Nigerian (74%) and U.S. (71%) respondents being the most dissatisfied, and Japanese (34%) and Dutch (39%) respondents being the least dissatisfied. These responses suggest potentially more discontent in China than elsewhere.

In China, absence of participation was largely unrelated to fear of authority. When asked why some complaints went unvoiced, the most

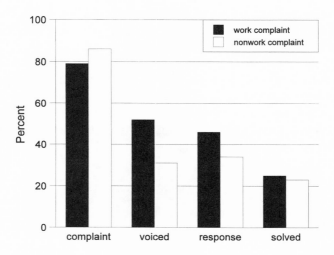

Figure 8.1 Complaints and solutions, 1987. Notes: Each percent is relative to the prior action – e.g., "response" is a percent of those who "voiced" a complaint. Source: 1987 Political Participation Survey.

common reason was lacking the feeling of efficacy ("no use" or "too much dissatisfaction," 80 and 75%).[4] Though fear of retribution was more of a concern at work (7%) than outside work (1%), it was a minor factor for both locations. As one would expect, not knowing where to voice one's complaint was more of a problem for issues outside work (18%) than at work (5%). Others answered "didn't concern own interest" (7% at work and 5% outside work).[5] Thus, when it came to parochial concerns, people largely seemed to know where to voice complaints and not to fear retribution in this highly bureaucratized system.

Available Channels

The Political Participation Survey includes information on the channels that urban residents used to pursue their interests (see Appendix A7 and

4. We combined "no use" and "too much dissatisfaction" into a single item. Essentially, these two reasons for not voicing are the same, as shown by II.B.c.2 and II.B.c.4 in Appendix A7.
5. The total number of observations is 603 for work issues and 877 for nonwork issues.

Table A7.1). These channels ranged from the more traditional, institutionally oriented channels originating in work units to newer, more individualistic, autonomous forms.[6]

Work Units. In China, work units have heretofore assumed responsibility for much of people's lives, including for many people not only lifetime employment but also housing, medical insurance, and other fringe benefits. The supervisor is a linchpin in the dispersal of these benefits and for many other issues, including dispute settlement, marriage permissions, divorce permissions, and birth control. Long periods of shared work help promote partly paternalistic, partly mutually dependent relationships between workers and supervisors (Chapter 6).

Government Bureaus/Mass Organizations. Individuals can also voice their opinions and express their dissatisfaction by writing to or visiting government bureaus to speak with officially appointed ombudsmen (*shangfang*). There are specific ombudsmen offices to deal with letters and visitors. These offices are intended to help the individual without revealing a complainant's identity to his or her workplace or immediate supervising organization. Another officially approved channel of participation is mass organizations, including workers' unions and women, youth, writers and artists, and other professional associations. All are supposed to serve as channels of interest articulation.

Media. Another reinvigorated channel of participation is the media, where one can write a letter to the editor of a newspaper or call a local television station. With some widely touted success stories in the 1980s,

---

6. The most explicit forms of expressing dissatisfaction are protest, demonstration, and petition – all highly risky activities that may mean loss of one's political life and imprisonment. One may expect rare occurrence of such activities under state socialism. Yet they repeatedly took place in post-Mao China, including the 1976 and 1979 protests against the Gang of Four and other radical Cultural Revolution leaders, demonstrations in 1984 and 1987 by college students demanding more democracy, and in 1989 by people from all walks of life against inflation, corruption, and authoritarian control. In the 1980s and 1990s, there was also ethnic unrest in Tibet and Xinjiang, and strikes held by workers in cities. Although an important topic, this chapter does not include protest activities, because participation is highly situational and rare in the general population. In both the 1987 Political Participation Survey and a 1988 survey of 750 Beijing residents (Shi 1997), 1 percent said they would resort to protest when dissatisfied.

this increasingly popular type of media publicity serves two functions. It forces the defendant to change through moral pressure, since administrative pressure is often ineffective in this kind of situation. By putting both sides in the public eye, media publicity also prevents the defendant from retribution. In issues related to consumer affairs, public facilities, and sometimes government corruption, this channel can achieve results (Nathan 1985).

Connections. Another channel of participation is personal connections (*guanxi*). One reason for contacting through connections in China is the emphasis on consensus building and the tendency to avoid direct conflict in policy making. Informal opinion-seeking (*zhengqiu yijian*) conversations are common practice before finalizing a decision, thereby giving individuals an opportunity to express their opinions and dissatisfaction. Many Chinese, and scholars abroad, believe that a network of personal ties is the key to interest articulation and career success (e.g., Bian 1994b; Yang 1994).

Voting and Contacting Elected Deputies. Voting and elected deputy contacting are influenced by electoral reform. The 1979 and subsequent 1982 and 1986 revisions of the electoral law extended the direct election of deputies upward to include the 2,757 people's congresses at the rural county and urban district levels (see Zhang 1992a, p. 280). In cities, electoral districts are subdivided by work unit (for those in large work units) and by neighborhood (for the nonworking and those in small work units). Proportional to size, each electoral district has a quota of deputies to be elected.[7] Voters, then, elect deputies from their own work unit or neighborhood. This emphasis on work units and neighborhoods greatly increases the chances that an urban voter will know his or her potential deputy.

In the revised electoral law, the policy of one candidate for one seat was replaced by a policy allowing up to twice the number of candidates as there are seats to be won in a direct election.[8] Candidates can be

7. The quota system explicitly favors urban population. The rural population for each deputy must be four times larger than the urban population.
8. Above the local level, there can be up to 50 percent more candidates than seats to be won. In practice, this has led to the nomination of up to 50 percent more candidates not officially endorsed by the government.

Table 8.2. *Channels for Expressing Nonwork Problems, 1987*

	Perceived most effective	Actually used	Success rates when used (%)	
			Response	Solved
Expression channel				
Work unit leader	17	42	34	11
Government bureau	18	21	36	19
Mass organization	6	13	28	1
Personal connection	12	3	17	14
Media	30	8	44	13
Local representative	11	11	34	15
Other	6	2	40	19
Total (%)	100	100	34	13
Observations	(416)	(592)	(592)	(592)

Notes: First two columns are percentaged vertically. Last two columns are percentaged horizontally, showing the percent of those using each channel who achieved success with their voiced complaint.
Source: 1987 Political Participation Survey.

nominated by any organization of ten or more individuals. The secret ballot became mandatory and campaigning on behalf of a candidate was legitimized. Provincial and national people's congress deputies are elected indirectly by the elected local deputies according to similar rules. Government officials at each level are also elected indirectly by the elected people's deputies at that level. Since the early 1980s, China has been experimenting with direct village and even township elections. Currently, more than half of the council chairs in China's 740,000 village committees are directly elected (Tang 1999b).

Effective Channels

People were also asked which channel for voicing complaints would be most effective and about the channel they actually used to voice their complaints. There were significant differences between the channels perceived to be most effective and the channels actually used (Table 8.2).

Some reputedly effective channels were in fact rarely used. There is a perennial belief in China that personal connections are the most effective way to get things done. But though one-tenth said this would be the most effective way, very few actually used this channel. Also, in the 1980s, there were many high-profile cases of letters to the editor or calls to television stations leading to bureaucratic malfeasance being exposed and personal problems being solved. It is not surprising that many in the sample said media contacts would be effective. However, while 30 percent said that media reports would be the most effective, only 8 percent used this channel to try to solve their own nonwork issues. In reality, for nonwork issues, appeals through one's work unit remained the dominant mode of trying to settle issues. Contact with a government bureau (21%) was also important, and contact with a people's deputy accounted for 11 percent of all contacts. Thus, in nonwork issues, there was a slight movement away from the traditional institutional interest articulation channels of the work unit, government bureau, and mass organization. The movement was slight, however, with people's representatives and media channels still representing a total of only about one-fifth of all actual usage in attempts to solve nonwork issues. Most actual interest articulation remained within old, established channels, namely, work units, government bureaus, and mass organizations (unions, youth leagues, and women's associations).[9]

The effectiveness of different channels did not vary as much or in the directions that one might have predicted (Table 8.2, last two columns). True to popular perception in China, mass organization-directed complaints led to few solutions. But contrary to these same beliefs, personal connections were not better in getting responses or solutions. The other channels were more or less similar in rates of response and solution to voiced problems.

Occupation and Complaints

The variation in complaint voicing by occupation should reveal something about tendencies toward new patterns of participation. At the

9. The pattern is similar and even more extreme for work-related issues (details not shown). For work-related complaints, media contacts and personal connections accounted for a very high 26 and 22 percent of all contacts perceived as effective. In actual practice, 72 percent of all work-related issues continued to be voiced through work unit channels.

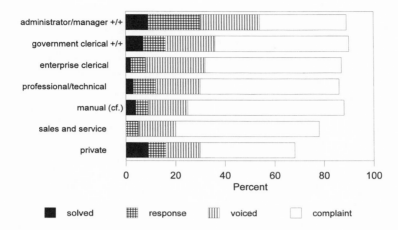

Figure 8.2 Voicing complaints by occupation, 1987. Notes: (+/+) solved/voiced complaints greater than for manual at $p < .05$ in a multivariate equation (see Appendix Table A7.2). (cf.) comparison group. Source: 1987 Political Participation Survey.

beginning of the chapter, we predicted several new trends. People less dependent on large organizations for services and closer to the market would have fewer particularistic complaints. At the same time, because they are less dependent on supervisors these people should have greater freedom to voice their complaints. This suggests that private entrepreneurs will have fewer complaints. Sales and service workers, closer to the stream of consumer goods, might also have fewer complaints. Also, much as in market societies, people with more education and monetary resources should know where to complain and have the means to successfully influence decision makers, giving proper gifts and the proper invitations to meals. These fall under "new" types of participation. "Old" types of participation should persist, as well, with adminstrators, managers, government clerical workers, and party members having easier access to and responses from decision makers.

We begin with a visual display of variation by occupation (Fig. 8.2). In this display, the bars are cumulative. That is, each segment of the bar is understood to include all the segments below it. Thus, at the top, among administrators and managers, 89 percent had a nonwork complaint, 54 percent voiced that complaint, 30 percent got a response, and 9 percent solved their complaint.

Some of the occupational groups have special characteristics that should be kept in mind. Most of the named occupations are in the state sector, and on occasion below we refer to them collectively as the state sector. Virtually all administrators and managers are party members – so much so that we have left "party membership" out of much of the analysis to avoid obscuring underlying dynamics (see Appendix Table A1.3).

The data show both old and new patterns of participation. The old patterns are threefold. First, virtually everyone in the public sector – administrator through laborer – has a complaint. These are the people who are highly dependent on public services and who, it would seem, were accustomed in 1988 to complaining to authorities to get particular problems solved. Over four-fifths of all these groups had a complaint in 1988. Second, the frequency of acting on and of getting a successful response to complaints pretty much follows the status order. Even on nonwork complaints, administrators and managers are the most likely to voice their complaints and to get a response and successful solution to the complaint. Others more or less follow in order. Third, those closest to the government chain of command – what we have heretofore called the center of redistribution – are the most successful in solving their complaints. One of the most telling comparisons is between clerical workers in government and in the enterprise sector. The government clerical workers are the more successful of the two. Professional and technical workers, distant from the centers of both production and redistribution, were much less successful in solving their complaints than one might otherwise expect. These are the old patterns.

The new patterns were twofold. First, private entrepreneurs and sales and service workers had fewer complaints. Second, when they did have a complaint, private entrepreneurs were more likely to successfully resolve their complaints.

This bifurcation between old and new patterns persisted in a multivariate analysis that we will only summarize here. On the new side, the more educated had more complaints. Those with more income were more successful in solving their problems. And the pattern of fewer complaints observed above in the descriptive results persisted when education, income, and gender were controlled. On the old side, high-seniority people, administrators, managers, and government workers were much more successful in solving their complaints (Appendix Table A7.2).[10] Thus, regardless of the mode of analysis, there is a bifurcation between new and old patterns. Both may continue to exist for some time, with the new, more market-like patterns increasingly spreading throughout the population.

VOTING, 1987

Voting could also exhibit the bimodal pattern, including a new withdrawal from mobilized voting by those less dependent on state organizations (the private sector) and more independent of mind (the educated). Urbanites were asked whether they voted in the 1987 county/district-level people's congress election. A full 86 percent did, which is similar to the 89 percent voting turnout in Brezhnev's Soviet Union (Bahry and Silver 1990). The respondents were then asked whether their vote was voluntary, required by authorities, or whether they just followed the crowd.

Again, there are both old and new patterns (Fig. 8.3). Consistent with old patterns, most people voted and much of that voting was required. Consistent with new patterns, private entrepreneurs were less likely to vote, and when they did vote it was mostly voluntary. Private entrepreneurs were most similar to retired workers, who also were freer of organizational dependency. Also consistent with the new pattern, a multivariate analysis found that the educated were not as likely to vote and even less likely to "know the candidates" or even vote voluntarily – a pattern that is not consistent with Western market societies but which is consistent with an early postsocialist tendency to boycott "meaningless" elections (Appendix Table A7.3).[11]

10. When we included channels in the multivariate analysis, all the formal channels (work unit, government bureau, media, and people's deputies) were more effective in getting a response than going through personal connections. This is quite different from the popular impression that personal connections are the way to get things done in China.
11. When party membership is included in this and the preceding multivariate analysis, the results are mixed. When included in the preceding analysis, though party members often had complaints (odds ratio = 1.69*) and commonly voiced these complaints (odds ratio = 1.30*), they were no more effective than anyone else in getting a response (odds ratio = 1.11, not significant) and solving their problem (odds ratio = .95, not significant). When included in the voting analysis, party members reported that they were about

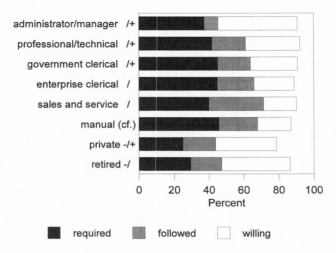

Figure 8.3 Voting, 1987. Notes: (cf.) comparison group; (–/+) significantly less or more total/willing voting when compared with manual workers in a multivariate analysis at $p < .05$ (see Table A7.3). Source: 1987 Political Participation Survey.

The bifurcation between old and new suggests several possible patterns for the future. As state control over work organizations recedes, voting should decline among all groups. However, the voting that remains should be heavily biased toward upper-status groups. Among administrators, managers, professionals, government clerical workers, and private entrepreneurs, voluntary voting was common. As manual workers retreat from elections, local politicians will increasingly find it in their interests to appeal to upper white-collar workers and private entrepreneurs. The votes (and campaign contributions) of these groups will help decide local elections. And, in a pattern reminiscent of market societies, political decisions should be slanted toward upper-status groups.

half again more likely to know their people's deputy (odds ratio = 1.57*) and vote voluntarily (odds ratio = 1.47*). Other analyses show that party members effectively pursued their interests at work. However, outside work, though party members were quite vocal, they were not particularly effective in getting results for their personal concerns.

We have several types of data on changes in participation, including information on sense of participation channel, political efficacy, and political action. Participation channel was tapped by the same question in both the May 1989 semiannual survey and the 1992 urban survey. The responses about who one would see or what one would do about a problem can be grouped into corporatist (government official, media), individualistic (public protest, illegal channel, and own methods), and passive (complain, do nothing). Political efficacy combines the answers to the following two statements into a single scale: "If one always raises opinions, [even] people like us can influence society's development." "Ordinary citizens can also influence government policy." A political action scale asked whether people would or did raise issues and make suggestions in society and at work. (See Appendix A7 for specific wording.)

Changes over Time

The 1989 and the 1992 surveys are similiar. They were both conducted in the same cities with the same sampling frame. The wording of the question concerning political action was exactly the same in both surveys. Both surveys were conducted during a more relaxed political atmosphere. The 1989 survey was conducted in May, before the June 4 crackdown of urban protests. This was a time when freedom of expression was temporarily allowed. The 1992 survey was conducted after Deng Xiaoping's southern tour symbolizing the continuing support for market reform. After three years of tight political control after the Tiananmen incident, Deng's speech during his tour of southern China lit a green light for further market reform. Therefore, both surveys were conducted when people felt relatively optimistic, although the memory of the 1989 crackdown did not completely disappear in 1992. The issues we are concerned with are whether spreading market tendencies caused people to retreat from politics and particularistic contacting, and whether these tendencies were class-differentiated.

The comparison of 1989 and 1992 patterns (Fig. 8.4) suggests three conclusions. First, except for private sector workers, everyone became less active in the years after 1989. Whether because they were intimi-

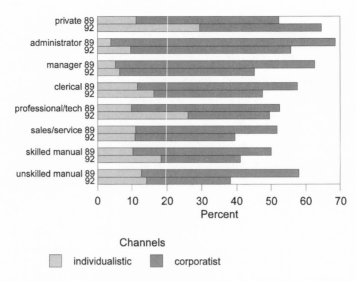

Figure 8.4 Grievance actions by occupation, 1989–92. Notes: "No action" is the implicit category that causes the responses to add to 100 percent. Sources: ESRIC Surveys: May 1989 Semiannual Survey and June 1992 China Urban Survey.

dated by the government clamp-down on students in 1989 (as in the Chinese idiomatic expression of "killing a chicken to scare the monkeys"), distracted by the prospects of earning money in a blossoming market economy, or discouraged by something else, total participation – combining institutional and personal channels – was much lower in 1992. Second, the forms of participation changed significantly. People increasingly turned from old, institutional channels to new, more individualistic channels.[12] Though this shift was most obvious among professionals and private sector workers, it occurred to some extent among other groups as well.[13] Third, the groups participating changed. While

12. In a multivariate analysis including age, gender, education, and occupation, respondents were less likely to use official channels and more likely to use self-initiated channels in 1992 than in 1989.
13. For self-initiated action, all differences between 1989 and 1992 are statistically significant except for managers and sales/service employees. Differences for using official channels are statistically significant except for the private sector. Differences for no action are statistically significant except for professionals, private sector workers ($p = .16$), and skilled workers ($p = .17$).

those in the private sector and professionals became newly assertive, all other groups declined in total participation. As expected, by the early 1990s, workers had the lowest level of overall participation, a likely result of increasing managerial authority in enterprises (see Chapter 6). Thus, the assertiveness of different groups appeared to be shifting in precisely the direction one would expect in a more marketized environment. The sample sizes for the private sector changes are small – roughly sixty in both surveys. But they are sufficiently consistent with what we know about changes in the larger environment to suggest that much of the anticipated change in the bargaining position of different groups was beginning to happen by the early 1990s.[14]

1992 Patterns

Some of these same themes were repeated in a multivariate analysis of 1992 participation patterns (Fig. 8.5). Respondents tended to be more proactive and to have a greater sense of political efficacy when they were in the private sector and when they lived in high economic growth cities. Moreover, people in the private sector used not only corporatist channels but also personal connections and other channels of influence outside corporatist channels. These tendencies suggest newly emerging market trends. There were other trends implying a sharp bifurcation in participation patterns. Some of the old political influences for high-status people persisted. With some exceptions, party members, administrators, managers, and clerical workers were more proactive in pursuing their interests through corporatist channels. This seems very much like the old socialist pattern. This is a pattern which, in addition, favored people with more seniority. Older people had a greater sense of political efficacy and raised more issues, and did this not through individualistic but through corporatist channels.

Finally, one group that did not fit so neatly in the old (party, higher status) versus new (private, high-income city) categories were the professional and technical workers. This group felt particularly disenfran-

---

14. In a multivariate analysis including occupation, establishment and nonestablishment intellectuals, age, gender, and income, private sector workers continued to show high levels of political efficacy (similar to the establishment elite) and willingness to use both official channels (as high as the establishment elite) and self-initiated channels (similar to nonestablishment intellectuals) for problem solving.

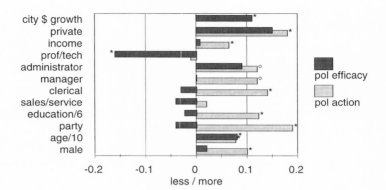

Figure 8.5 Political attitudes, 1992. Notes: Political efficacy and political action coefficients from a regression analysis. (*) $p < .05$; (°) $p < .10$. Source: 1992 China Urban Survey.

chised – with a low sense of political efficacy. When they contemplated political action, this action was more likely to be through individualistic channels. For them, the sense of being left out remained strong, though as we saw above, the possibilities of autonomous, noninstitutional action seemed stronger than in the beginning years of reform.

CONCLUSION

We began the chapter in search of incipient changes in patterns of political participation. Signs of those changes would include an increasing bifurcation between groups that were involved in old, corporatist modes and groups that were involved in new, individualistic modes of participation. We believe that we have found evidence of these types of changes, including changes in both forms of participation and the types of interest groups involved. Both types of changes suggest the influence of increased marketization and a softening of the socialist state (compare observed patterns and the ones suggested in Table 8.1).

Forms of Participation

We suggested in the beginning of the chapter that parochial interest articulation should be quite common. Based on patterns in market societies, we expected that in less-developed societies with high levels of government services, citizens would have a strong incentive to contact the government to fulfill their everyday needs. Also, based on studies of European socialist societies, we expected in a mature socialist system that people would have long figured out what set of institutional levers to pull to seek their interests. That original set of expectations has been confirmed. In the late 1980s, the corporatist/clientalist forms of participation were commonly practiced in urban China.

Nevertheless, this traditional pattern of political participation was changing. By the early 1990s, two new trends had emerged. The first was a significant decline of interest in political participation. People seemed distracted by the increasing opportunities of making money in a blossoming market economy. This sense of futility fits the description of a bureaucratic authoritarian society which is characterized, among other things, by popular political apathy and rapid economic growth. The second new trend was the decline of the traditional corporatist channels of participation and the increase of other, informal channels. Unsurprisingly, with the retreat of the state from redistributing wealth, there was less need for people to go through official channels to acquire wealth. Currently, although traditional forms of participation remained dominant, with further marketization and retreat of the state, the new trends will continue.

A subtheme that emerged in our inquiry was the role of personal contacting (contacting someone personally known rather than approaching superiors or the bureaucracy directly). This issue is of particular interest in China because of the pervasive belief there that this is one of the most effective ways to get things done. Among our respondents, though contacting someone in one's personal network was, in the abstract, perceived as one of the more effective methods, this method in reality was practiced much less often. Moreover, when practiced, it was less effective in getting a response. All this contradicts popular impressions.

The major theme that emerged was the signs of change in voting and in the channels used for articulating interests. Between 1989 and 1992, most groups became less involved in corporatist contacting. Everyone became more self-reliant, emphasizing individualistic rather than corporatist solutions to their problems. Private entrepreneurs and others free of dependency on large state organizations for supplies and services increasingly refused to participate in mobilized voting, and contemplated individualistic rather than corporatist solutions to their problems. All this, as early as it may be, suggests the potential for considerable change in the future.

Interest Groups

The next issue we raised concerned the impact of market reform on political participation for different interest groups. Those outside traditional bureaucratic organizations are using more nontraditional channels for problem solving, avoiding traditional mobilized voting and feeling somewhat freer to voice a wider array of complaints. Private entrepreneurs had fewer complaints, but what complaints they had were actively expressed; once expressed, their complaints were often acted on. In the early 1990s, this sector had begun to compete with the traditionally influential groups (administrators, party members) in getting its voice heard. So, with economic reform, and the growth of a significant sector outside traditional bureaucratic channels, there is more freedom of expression. This spread of activism beyond traditional, corporatist domains was spreading more generally to people in cities with rapid economic growth. In these cities, there was increasing optimism about shaping political decisions and an increased use of official channels. In the new patterns, as mandatory, mobilized voting declines, manual workers will be left behind. Upper white-collar groups and private entrepreneurs, who are more likely to vote voluntarily, will begin to have more influence over local elections and subsequent decision making. Thus, in the activity and influence of different interest groups, there are signs of the emergence of a pattern that is more common to market societies.

Part III

GENDER

9

Gender and Work

WILLIAM L. PARISH AND SARAH BUSSE

S OCIALISM promised women rapid improvement in their health, education, income, work, and family relations. While not all of these promises were met, the classical period of socialism lasted long enough to have a dramatic impact on the social conditions for women. China displays patterns common to other socialist nations, including distinctively high levels of primary and secondary education for women and female employment. A key question is whether and how the socialist contract for women is being rearranged under market reform. This chapter focuses on changes in employment and income, while the following chapter explores consequences for family life, household chores, and husband–wife relations. We begin this chapter with a brief comparison of women's work in China with other socialist nations, followed by an explanation of the specific issues regarding employment that this chapter addresses.

HISTORICAL COMPARISONS

Socialist Ideals

Socialist states long employed the rhetoric of the emancipation of women. Early socialists, including Marx, argued that the capitalist system was oppressive to women by requiring them to be chained to child-care and household responsibilities. As part of the social upheaval that was the Russian Revolution, women were encouraged to enter the work force to show their liberation from the tsarist and capitalist regimes. In the early years of the Soviet Union, women were encouraged to move into nontraditional occupations: construction, tractor driving, engineering. Some of this role reversal led to the feminization of occupations seen in Western societies as typically male, which then paid less than occupations in which men dominated (Zdravomyslova 1995, p. 191). For example, in the Soviet Union, besides their strong representation in heavy industry, women made up most of the doctors and engineers, although as this shift occurred, the prestige and average salary of these professions declined correspondingly. In Eastern Europe, women formed a high proportion of workers in heavy industry, construction, and mining, although they were often employed in clerical and administrative positions (Einhorn 1993, pp. 121–22). In the Soviet Union and Eastern Europe, women were encouraged to work as a means of demonstrating their selfhood, as the "right to work" was extended to all citizens, regardless of gender.

What began as a right to work eventually was transformed, even at the rhetorical level, by combining it with the simultaneous "obligation" to work. European socialist states considered it the duty of all adult citizens to be gainfully employed. This rhetoric was matched by practical measures that made individuals eligible for social benefits based on their status as employed members of society, not simply as citizens. In the Soviet Union and in Eastern Europe, people not in paid employment, including women with small children, were seen as parasites on society (du Plessix Gray 1990). While the Soviet Union and East European socialist nations may have needed women to work for pragmatic reasons, to raise the level of industry and because of the chronic labor shortage of the European socialist economies, official rhetoric exhorting women to work used the dual language of a woman's right and duty to be employed.[1] After forty or seventy years of state socialism, such ideology continues to affect women's notions of employment and what it means to be employed in Eastern Europe and the former Soviet Union.

In China as well, there was an official rhetoric encouraging women to work. "Women hold up half the sky" was one of Mao Zedong's many slogans encouraging women to be respected and to respect themselves. In cities, the backyard steel furnaces and neighborhood enterprises of the late 1950s Great Leap Forward pulled most women into the labor force, and this is where they remained. By the 1970s, women's work was so accepted that women had a hard time saying why they worked, and thought it odd that a foreigner would ask (Whyte and Parish 1984). Of

---

1. See Kornai (1992) on the tendency to hoard labor and supplies and how this causes shortages of both labor and supplies.

course, the switch from rhetoric to accepted practice was encouraged by the freezing of wages in ways that made it increasingly difficult for single-income families to keep up with accepted consumption standards.

Socialist Reality

The record of socialist states with regard to women and the family is mixed. On the one hand, compared with other societies, women in social-ist states have made great gains in health, education, work, and income attainment (e.g., Jancar 1978; Lapidus 1978; Whyte and Parish 1984; Einhorn 1993; Sorenson and Trappe 1995). On the other hand, the rapid gains in these types of material conditions have been slow to translate into other advantages. Women in socialist states typically continued to suffer from the double bind of work and home responsibilities, despite the socialist rhetoric of female emancipation.

One result was that while they began their careers with incomes close to those of men, they soon fell behind men in occupation and income achievements. As in other societies, they dominated the caring profes-sions. Though they obtained more political, administrative, and manage-rial positions than in comparable market societies, these were often nominal positions mandated for women which got little respect from the general population. Thus, for many observers, the final achievements of women fell short of what was hoped for (e.g., Stacey 1983; Wolf 1985; du Plessix Gray 1990; Einhorn 1993; Braun, Scott, and Alwin 1994; Gilmartin et al. 1994).

There are multiple explanations of this shortfall. The pressure to go to work came often not from an internal drive to achieve or find fulfillment, but from external forces, either economic or ideological. Ideological pressures include the rhetoric of right and duty as discussed above. Eco-nomic pressures resulted from the effects of Stalinist-style emphases on extensive economic growth based on forced savings and lower wages which made two incomes in a family necessary to survive.[2] Many women thus entered the labor force to help maintain family budgets and pay for basic necessities.

These tendencies created considerable ambivalence among women

---

2. See Nove (1983) and Kornai (1992) on the inevitability of investment hunger in social-ist systems, which thereby drives down current consumption.

about work in the post-1989 period. Some women in Eastern Europe and
Russia fantasized about fleeing work for more traditional family roles
(Buckley 1992; Einhorn 1993; Kligman 1994). Despite the fantasy and
some managers using the new freedom to lay off workers, most women
continued to work – both because they wanted to and because economic
downturns made it necessary to keep working to sustain family living
standards (e.g., Pilkington 1996; Ashwin and Bowers 1997). In China, the
fantasy of retreat to the home seems less pervasive, though the tendency
for managers to discriminate against women seems common across postsocialist states (Robinson 1985; Honig and Hershatter 1988; Jacka 1990;
Tan 1994; Chang 1995). Thus, either from the manager's or the woman's
side, one of the short-term consequences of reform seems to be a backlash in which women either voluntarily considered withdrawing or were
forced to withdraw from full involvement in the world of work.

SOCIAL CONTRACT AND WOMEN'S WORK

The task of this chapter is to examine whether changes in the social contract increase or decrease the number of jobs women secure and their
relative wages. There are potential arguments for both optimistic and
pessimistic projections, which depend on a combination of demand- and
supply-side changes in the labor market. Demand-side changes include
both new types of jobs that might employ women and new freedom for
employers to discriminate against married women now that central labor
bureau control over job assignments has been relaxed (see Chapter 3).
Supply-side factors include conditions of women and their families,
including increased education, low birth rates, and new freedom to
choose between family and work.

Demand-Side Changes

Several changes favor women's continued role in market labor. These
include a shift away from blue-collar jobs in heavy industry. The new jobs
replacing the old, heavy-industry jobs include work in textiles and other
types of light industry that typically employ females in other countries
(e.g., Tilly and Scott 1978). New opportunities include white-collar jobs
in clerical, sales, and service jobs, the typical pink-collar jobs that
absorbed so many U.S. females after World War II (e.g., Oppenheimer

1970; Goldin 1990). Eventually, these new jobs may produce a set of light industry and pink-collar "ghettos," predominantly female fields in which wages are lower than in other fields because they are characterized as women's work (Jacobsen 1994). However, in the short run, the high levels of demand may sustain female participation and provide more well-paid white-collar jobs (e.g., see Brinton, Lee, and Parish 1995). Moreover, in China, the rapid rate of economic growth in most cities should maintain demand for female labor, and hence encourage women's continued participation in the labor market. If such demand factors are important, we should find higher levels of participation in rapid-growth cities. We should also find women moving from blue- to white-collar jobs in clerical, sales, and service work.

Several other changes on the demand side are less supportive of women's continued role in market work. This is particularly true for married women. Freed from labor bureau control, employers are freer to discriminate. Fearing the additional health care costs and lost time of women with young children and pressed by market competition to cut costs, employers might be less inclined hire married women. Of greater threat in the long run is the rapid growth of nonfarm jobs in small towns and villages. In cities, one suspects, married women were drawn into the labor force by artificially high levels of labor demand. With rural migrants frozen out of cities for three decades, employers had to turn to married women even if the labor bureau had not ordered them to do so. In the countryside, there is a huge labor surplus, and employers can be more cautious about hiring married women. In most locales there is an ample supply of men and young, unmarried women to take married women's place (see Perkins 1990; Census Office, various years). This suggests that while married women might continue to work at high levels in cities they will not do so in more rural areas.

Supply-Side Changes

Supply-side changes also have both positive and negative consequences for women, with the changes again being most ambiguous for married women. Four supply-side factors could continue to support female labor force participation. First, women's increasing equality with men in education helps young women qualify for good jobs (see Chapter 3). Second, child-care burdens have declined. While the one-child policy means that parents lavish huge amounts of time on their single child, once that child enters school, total time spent on the child drops. Even during the child's early years, the early retirement policy means that more middle-aged grandmothers are available to help with child care. All of this should make it easier for young mothers to remain in the labor force. Third, the growing consumer revolution makes it harder to keep up with neighbors in consumer consumption levels unless both husband and wife work (see Chapter 2). Fourth, generations of socialist ideology extolling the virtue and civic obligation of employment induced a social norm that women should work in order to be good citizens, a sentiment which may be slow to erode. Such supply-side factors should help keep women in paid employment.

The list of supply-side conditions that could cause women to withdraw from market work include an increased possibility for young mothers to remain home with their children. Western, Hong Kong, and Taiwan models of the proper role for women provide new examples of alternative, nonwork-based models for women (see Chapter 10). Should these increasingly prevalent models find acceptance, there would be less social pressure on women to remain in the labor force and alternatives would increase. Heretofore, women's labor force participation has taken the shape of an inverted U, remaining high for women aged twenty through forty-four. Should young mothers begin to withdraw from the labor force, for either employer- or family-related reasons, Chinese women's labor force participation could begin to approximate the M-shaped pattern of some other East Asian societies. In this M-shaped pattern, employment would rise sharply for young single women, decline for young married women, rise again for women whose children had gone on to school, and then decline as women reached retirement age (on the pattern in Japan, see Brinton 1993).

Experience

There is anecdotal evidence that by the early 1990s urban women had difficulty getting the better jobs (Rosen 1993; Tan 1994; Chang 1995). These anecdotal accounts include revealing examples of state-owned firms setting job entrance exam score requirements higher for females than males (e.g., Honig and Hershatter 1988, p. 245). There are examples of employers forcing women out of the labor force at age forty-five or age forty-two, when the official retirement ages for women are officially fifty for women in manual work and fifty-five for women in nonmanual work (Liu 1995b). There are examples of employers either refusing to hire women or encouraging women to retire at marriage or pregnancy in order to avoid increasingly strict regulations about protecting women's health (Woo 1994). There are also stories of women and men taking early retirement in order to guarantee their children a job in the parent's work unit (see Chapter 3). Reputedly, women were more likely to take early retirement than men (Bauer et al. 1992, p. 353).

Local variation in labor markets also shapes women's opportunities, as does the set of skills they bring to the labor market. One of the major consequences of economic reform may have been to create more differentiation among local labor markets. Demand for women's labor will be greater in high-growth cities and in cities with an emphasis on light industry (for rural patterns that support this generalization, see Parish and Zhe 1995; Michelson and Parish 2000). Demand for women's labor may remain high in large cities, since in these cities restraints on inmigration continue to cause a shortage of skilled labor (see Chapter 2; Perkins 1990). In smaller towns and villages, with fewer restraints on labor mobility, less investment, and lower labor demand, fewer women may be in the labor market. Thus city size and rural–urban differences may remain considerable.

This chapter relies on both survey and census data. The survey data are from a 1991 study of 4,509 married couples in six provinces (see Appendix B). The census data are from the 1982, 1990, and 1995 censuses. From these data sets, we consider both the quantity and quality of paid work available to women.

QUANTITY OF WORK

By "quantity of work" we mean simply whether women were likely to be in paid employment. We have subjective measures of whether securing paid employment was easy or difficult and whether the work secured was satisfying. We also have objective measures of whether women are continuing to work in the formal labor force or whether they are retreating from the labor force for either demand (e.g., employer discrimination) or supply (e.g., staying home to take care of children) reasons.

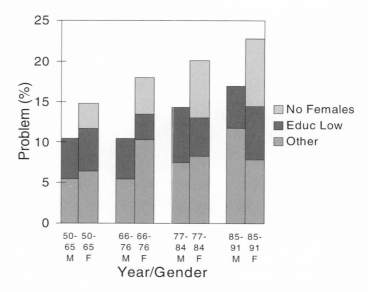

Figure 9.1 Difficulties finding initial job by year. Notes: "No females": employers were not hiring females; "education low": had too little education to get a good job; "other": other difficulties, including a small percent who list poor health as a difficulty. Source: 1991 Women's Study, urban women only.

Subjective Measures

Perceived Discrimination. In the 1991 survey data, women perceived that it was increasingly difficult for them to get a job, in part because employers were discriminating against them. Following a question about the timing of their first job, the 1991 women's status survey asked whether the respondent felt that she had difficulty getting a job. The data are grouped according to the year a person turned age twenty, about the time most people would begin their first job (Fig. 9.1). Although the results show a steady increase in reported perception of difficulty in obtaining work since 1950 for both men and women, it is important to note that increasing marketization (since 1978) did not made finding work easier for men or women, but rather exacerbated the previous trend toward increasing difficulty. The respondents reported whether the difficulty finding work was related to their own low education, to the employer's not hiring women, or to other reasons. While both men and women report increased difficulties, women had the added possibility that employers were not hiring them. After 1978, there was a large increase in the perception that job search difficulties were due to employers not hiring them. This is consistent with increasing anecdotal reports of women having more difficulty in the job market.

The perception of increasing difficulties could be simply an artifact of fading memories and reduced expectations among older workers, who acquired their jobs many years ago. Several features suggest that this was not the case. First, patterns of difficulty varied systematically by education. In the early years of socialist rule, when many white-collar jobs had to be filled and college graduates were mostly assigned jobs through formal channels, with little room for student initiative, college graduates reported very few difficulties getting a job. However, by the early 1990s, with the abandonment of the formal assignment of college graduates to jobs, search difficulties among college graduates approached that of people with less education (details not shown).

At the same time, senior high school graduates continued to experience only moderate levels of difficulty in finding a job, while junior high and primary school graduates are experiencing increasing difficulty. This pattern is consistent with a tendency to increasingly emphasize exams and the senior high school degree itself as necessary credentials for employment (see Chapter 3). Thus, there is reason to think that the reported changes are real.

Several other indicators reinforce the view that the increasing difficulties in getting a job has basis in fact. First, among women, current income was 5 to 9 percent lower for women who reported difficulties in finding a job.[3] This lower pay is consistent with objective difficulties. Second, women with less education reported more job difficulties associated with inadequate education. Thus, the formal credentials a woman brought to the labor market shaped her reception in the job market and hence her reports of job search problems. Third, the regional concentration of difficulties were in inland, Muslim provinces, especially in Ningxia Province. Reports of problems associated with employers rejecting females therefore were consistent with known cultural and economic differences among regions. These patterns suggest that women's anecdotal

---

3. This is based on a regression analysis of logged income of urban women in the 1991 women's data set. Other items in the equation were the income-enhancing features of urban origin, education, age, and provincial locations such as Guangdong.

accounts have been responding to objective conditions, that is, the skills that they bring to the labor market and to the pattern of discrimination they find in that market.

Job Satisfaction. We can continue the theme of changing objective difficulties on the demand side of the labor market by adding material on satisfaction with work. In addition, we consider the possible effects of supply-side conditions that reduce women's paid work, including the desire to spend more time with young children. When increased autonomy joins with heightened concerns about taking care of young children, the result could be that more women with young children would abandon paid employment.

In 1991, women's levels of job satisfaction were high. When asked a simple yes/no question to whether they were satisfied with their job, three-fourths said they were satisfied. When asked whether they would continue working if their husbands had enough income to support the family, fully 84 percent of wives said they would continue working. When asked why they would continue, most said it was because work was important for self-actualization or because the work was interesting. These percentages are consistent with many anecdotal accounts, including reports from taxi drivers who say that their wives refused to quit work because life would be too boring, even when the wife's income added little compared with the husband's much higher earnings.

The percentage of women who would continue working is higher than in other societies. In the United States in 1989, a smaller 63 percent of women said they would continue working even if they had enough money (U.S. General Social Survey, raw data). A survey comparing women in Beijing, Guangzhou, and market-driven Hong Kong illustrates the differences between market and socialist orders within a common cultural environment. This survey found less-educated Hong Kong women less inclined to continue working if they had ample income. And when asked whether it was work or family that was more important in their lives, the percentages of women choosing work were 43 percent in Beijing, 24 percent in Guangzhou, and only 12 percent in Hong Kong (Liu, Liu, and Xiong 1991).[4]

---

4. For a similar choice of work over family (though more a choice of work vs. husband rather than work vs. child) in Russia, see du Plessix Gray (1990).

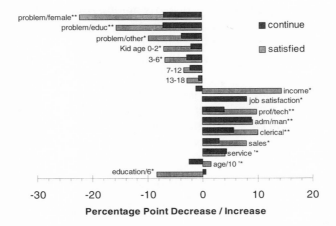

Figure 9.2 Job satisfaction and willingness to continue in job, women, 1991. Notes: Percentage change coefficients are from a probit analysis that also included indicators for village and town origin and province of residence. Percentages for positive response to each of the questions, "Would you continue working if your spouse had enough income to support the family?" and "Are you satisfied with your job?" Among the background conditions, "problem in finding a job" because of gender, education, and other reason is compared with "no problem in finding a job." Having a child in the specified age ranges is compared with having no children aged 0–18. Occupation is compared with manual worker. Income is logged. Age effects are for an extra ten years of age. Education is in six-year units. (*) $p < .05$, with the first * for satisfaction and the second for continuity in job ('* when only the second value is statistically significant). Source: 1991 Women's Survey, urban population.

A detailed analysis of the determinants of job satisfaction and continued work suggests that both demand- and supply-side factors shape Chinese women's perceptions of the quality of their jobs. On the demand side, women are less pleased and more likely to discontinue their jobs when they had difficulties getting one – particularly when the difficulties involved gender discrimination (Fig. 9.2). Again on the demand side, higher-income and higher-status positions increase satisfaction and a desire to continue in the job. On the supply side, both education and the burden of taking care of children reduce women's enthusiasm for their jobs. Thus, both demand and supply factors shape women's attitudes toward their work. Both could combine to help reduce women's likelihood of continuing to work. Particularly among young married women, for whom perceptions of job discrimination are greater and for whom younger children pose more of a burden, the tendency to retreat from the job market produces a more M-shaped curve in women's total labor force participation. One suggestion that this tendency is being realized is that in 1991 women with infants were four percentage points less likely to work than women without infants.[5] In short, both supply-side (more attention to young children) and demand side (more discrimination by employers) conditions could reduce participation in the labor force.

Objective Measures

Several objective measures illustrate the joint significance of demand and supply factors. On the demand side, in the 1988 CHIP data women were more likely to be in paid employment if they lived in cities with high average incomes and with rapid economic growth. Already by 1988 market-induced growth and higher incomes encouraged women to go to work or remain in the paid work force. Moreover, women were also more likely to work when they had more education, suggesting that employers were beginning to reward educational credentials.[6] Thus, with increases in women's education, more women should enter paid work. These all suggest market tendencies that encourage women's work.

However, by 1995 there were also countervailing tendencies, suggesting that demand and supply factors were changing. Drawing on the census data for 1990 and 1995, we can examine whether women now had the autonomy to spend more time in the home when their children were young and whether women in towns experienced less labor demand. Our indicators will be whether in 1995 more women were unemployed and seeking work and whether more women were at home taking care of children and household chores.

5. The effect for infants from newborn to age two was significant at $p < .05$. Other items in the probit equation were education (highly positive), age, age-squared, province, rural/urban origin, husband's work, and husband's education. On average, 93 percent of women were still in market work.
6. The probit equations also included age, age-squared, age-cubed, central city (vs. suburban village) residence, size of city, and marital status. For women aged 25 to 39, large cities and nonsuburban residence encouraged paid work. In 1988, marriage had no effect, which is consistent with the census data for 1990. Marriage began to reduce work only after 1990.

We group women first by age, with those in their early twenties on the far left and those in their late forties on the far right of Figure 9.3. Within each five-year age group, the two left bars are for cities and the two right bars are for towns. Then, within city and town pairs, the 1990 data are on the left and the 1995 data are on the right. If demand for women's labor is decreasing over time, that should appear in the data as more women seeking work in 1995. If women are exercising their new autonomy to take care of their family rather than doing market work, that should appear as more women doing housework. Across both years, if labor demand (relative to supply) is lower in towns, that should appear as more town women seeking work. And, likewise, if there is simply a custom of women being less involved in market work in towns, that should appear as more town women doing housework in both 1990 and 1995.

The data suggest that all of these tendencies occur. There are both place and year effects. By place, paid work was more common in cities in both years. Conversely, housework was more common in towns at both dates. Across years, paid work tended to decline for both city and town women. Older town women remained in paid work at about the same level across years, but among all other groups paid work declined. The decline was related to both increased housework and increased job seeking. These are all tendencies that are consistent with the "pessimistic" view of what happened during market reform. However, we should note again that it is not just that women were forced out of the labor force by declining demand and forced job seeking. Young women with young children were also electing to spend time on housework, which is consistent with lower satisfaction and reduced desires to continue in paid work among that group. Thus, these data suggest multiple consequences of market forces, including the diffusion of messages about proper women's roles from abroad, new freedom to choose not to work in the formal labor force, more job losses and longer periods of job seeking, and the shift of new jobs to smaller towns, where there is less demand for women in paid work.

For the time being, however, we should not overstate the decline in women's work. In cities in China, the decline was modest between 1990 and 1995, and it affected men almost as much as women (Fig. 9.4). With downsizing and more competition for jobs in cities, men's market work declined by about two percentage points for everyone over age thirty. Much as in the previous data that showed younger women being the ones

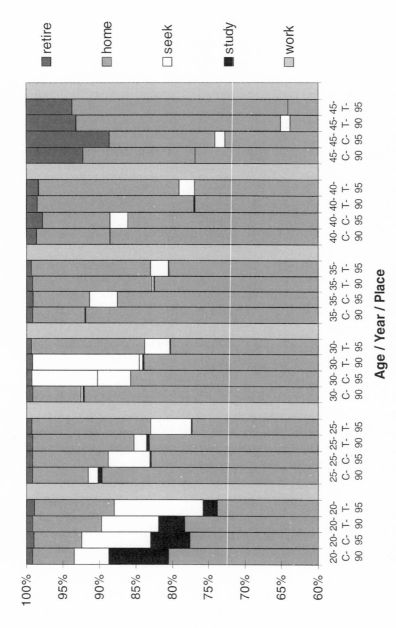

Figure 9.3 Female distribution by occupation, place, and year. Notes: On bottom scale, age in five-year age groups ((20-) 20–24; (25-) 25–29; etc.); (C-) city and (T-) town populations; and census year of 1990 and 1995. National data, including both urban and rural residents. Source: Census Office 1993, tables 4-5, -6; 6-23, -24, -32, -33; Census Office 1997, tables 1-3, -4; 3-7, -8).

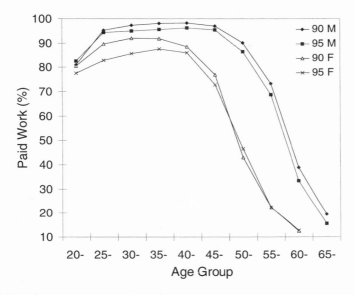

Figure 9.4 Paid work by age, gender, and year. (20-) 20–24; (25-) 25–29; etc. Source: City Census Data (Census Office 1993, tables 4-5, 6-23, 6-32; Census Office 1997, tables 1-3, 3-8).

more likely to stop work for market and family reasons, the biggest decline was for young women, among whom market work declined seven percentage points between 1990 and 1995. Among older women, there was no decline. Thus, in cities, through 1995, market transition reduced women's work only at the margin, and then more among younger than older women. Some of the decline was shared between men and women. And among younger women, part of the decline was voluntary, with many staying home to take care of their children.[7]

7. Anecdotal accounts make much of last-hired, first-fired tendencies among women. The 1995 census data suggest that these tendencies remained weak. Below age 23, single women had less difficulty than men getting a job. After that age, when they married and began to have children, about 1 percent (out of 5% seeking work) more women than men were out of work and seeking a job. Approaching official retirement ages of 50/55 and 55/60 for women and men, with nonmanual work five years later than manual work, both men and women had parallel trajectories. That is, early retirement rates were similar among both men and women. In short, neither job-seeking nor retirement pat-

The shift of manufacturing and other nonfarm jobs out of cities to smaller towns and villages will be one of the greatest influences on women's patterns of work in the future. In towns and villages since 1982, men have begun to retire earlier, and young, single women have flocked to new nonfarm jobs faster than young men. The result of earlier male retirement is that overall, women have gained on men in nonfarm jobs (more below). Among young, single people, women are about as likely as men to get nonfarm jobs. Married women, in contrast, are much less likely to keep those nonfarm jobs, dropping off to only one-fourth or one-third of all nonfarm workers. This, then, produces a mixed pattern. Outside cities, women are gaining on men in nonfarm jobs. However, for married women, that gain falls far short of the very high levels of labor force participation known in cities.[8] Thus, as more nonfarm jobs appear outside cities, Chinese women will experience more of an M-shaped pattern of labor-force participation – high before marriage, low in the initial years of marriage, and then once again high as children begin to leave home. The post-child-rearing labor force participation will be different in quality from the initial participation, being more in self-employment and in agriculture and service jobs that earn lower incomes than the manufacturing and clerical jobs in larger enterprises. Accordingly, it is to the question of quality of jobs that we next turn.

QUALITY OF WORK

While total rates of employment remained high, it could be that there were significant changes in women's quality of work, including shifts into less desirable or lower-paying jobs. We consider first types of jobs and then income levels. For this inquiry we include not just women in cities but all women in nonfarm jobs, regardless of where they live.

terns support alarmist accounts (see Census Office 1997, table 3–8). Consistent with the 1995 census data on job seeking, among youth aged 15 to 19, the percentage of women among unsuccessful job seekers declined from 52 percent in 1982 to only 47 percent in 1995 (Census Office 1985, table 67; 1997, table 3–7).

8. Generalizations based on details from the 1982 and 1990 censuses and raw data on 4,070 nonfarm workers in the 1991 Survey of Chinese Health and Family Behavior conducted by the Carolina Population Center (Chapel Hill: University of North Carolina).

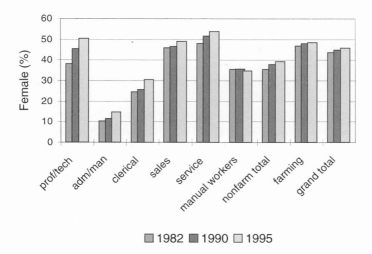

■ 1982 ■ 1990 □ 1995

Figure 9.5 Percent female by occupation and year. Notes: National data, including both urban and rural residents. Sources: Census Office (1985, table 55); (1993, table 6-23); (1997, table 3-2).

Occupations

Contrary to pessimistic predictions, nationwide between 1982 and 1995, women's representation in better jobs increased (Fig. 9.5). As a percentage of the total labor force, women's representation increased from 44 to 46 percent of the total labor force (bars on far right). Except for manual work, which declined, this increase was broadly distributed across all fields. What seems to have occurred is that even while young married women's work was declining, young single women's work increased and men's work decreased at all ages in ways that increased women's percentage of all workers. As just discussed, these tendencies were particularly strong outside cities, in towns and villages. Thus, even while married women outside cities had difficulty keeping better jobs, during economic reform those difficulties were not as great as they were for most men.

Consistent with the optimistic view of the effects of reform, women's proportional increase was greater in nonfarm than in farm work. Also consistent with the optimistic view, women's share in blue-collar, manual work declined, while their share in all types of white-collar work increased. Women remained concentrated in jobs that had less administrative power and were less well paid. Women's underrepresentation in power-wielding administrative and managerial jobs improved only marginally.[9] While the percent female in professional/technical fields showed the most dramatic increases (by over twelve percentage points in thirteen years), this category includes teachers, and women are more likely to be teachers, nurses, cashiers, and accountants than engineers or other high-paid professionals (details not shown). With more women in jobs as teachers, nurses, cashiers, and clerical, sales, and service workers, there are signs of emerging pink-collar ghettos. Nevertheless, in broad occupational categories, women still do not dominate any single category. And compared with the past, many of the new white- or pink-collar jobs represent distinct advances in the quality of work.

An alternate way to view the same data is to ask how men and women separately were distributed across nonfarm jobs in 1982 and 1995. The data suggest that the changes were greater for women than for men (Fig. 9.6). As a proportion of all jobs, women increasingly abandoned manual work for jobs in sales and, to a lesser extent, in professional and technical work. This, of course, fits visual impressions, with women much more prevalent in sales jobs than they were a few years back. This switch to sales and other types of white- and pink-collar jobs suggests that women more than men have broken with the Stalinist tradition. For women, the concentration of work in heavy industry is a thing of the past.

Income

Income is also influenced by forces on both the demand and supply side. On the supply side, women continue to be better educated, and thus potentially could continue to compete for the best jobs. Though some women in cities are taking time off to help raise their young children,

9. In parallel with the small proportion of women in administrative and managerial work, in the late 1980s only 25 percent of urban party members were women (1988 CHIP urban survey raw data). Urban and rural, women constituted 14 percent of all party members, 16 percent of the Fourteenth National People's Congress, and 6 percent of the Party Central Committee. Women made up 21 percent of the National People's Congress and 7 percent of provincial governors and vice governors (Tan 1994). For earlier comparative statistics, see Whyte (1984) and Whyte and Parish (1984).

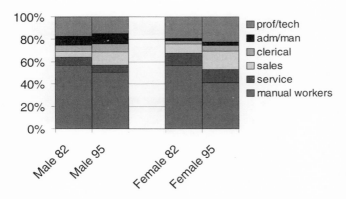

Figure 9.6 Nonfarm occupations by gender and year, for urban and rural residents. Sources: See Fig. 9.5.

most women continue to work full-time. With fewer children, the burdens of child care that might detract from building a career are fewer than in the past. On the demand side, several forces could depress wages. One is that since many of the new jobs are outside the formal, state sector, free of bureaucratic constraints, employers could begin to offer men and women wages that differ even more than in the past. A second force is the incipient concentration of women in gender-segregated ghettos, where many women competing for a limited number of openings will bid down the average wage in these jobs (e.g., Jacobsen 1994, p. 243). A third force is the increasing inequality of rewards in the labor force. Many of the highest rewards go to men who have entered new high-risk private sector positions, with women left behind in less rewarding state and collective sector jobs.

In the space available, we can only illustrate the potential trends. Through the early 1990s, Chinese urban women continued to earn incomes that were close to those of men. In East and South Asia, women earn 51 to 75 percent as much as men, with Japan being on the low and Sri Lanka on the high end. Hong Kong's Chinese population is in the middle, with women earning 63 percent as much as men (ILO 1995, table 16). In most large urban surveys, Chinese women earn at the very top of the Asian ranges. In national city-based surveys for 1988 and 1997, women earned 82 and 80 percent as much as men. In a 1991 study with

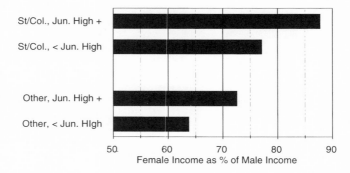

Figure 9.7 Female income share by work unit and education, 1988. Notes: (St/Col) State or urban collective work unit; (Other) other type of work unit (private, joint venture, self-employed, etc.); (Jun. High+) junior high or more education; (< Jun. High) less than junior high education. The percentage estimates are derived from a regression equation of logged income that included average earning levels of city, gender, years of education, and type of work unit, with each of these terms combined with gender. Source: 1988 CHIP Urban Survey.

more towns and villages, in nonfarm work women earned 77 percent as much as men.[10] In comparison with women elsewhere in Asia, then, Chinese women continued to do remarkably well compared with men.[11]

Despite this relative success into the early 1990s, there are signs of potential change. In the 1988 CHIP data, there are mixed signals (Fig. 9.7).

10. Calculations based on raw data from 1988 CHIP survey, 1991 Survey of Chinese Health and Family Behavior (University of North Carolina), and weighted data from the 1997 Quality of Life Survey. In 1988 Chinese females had less education than men and were more likely to be concentrated in collective firms and similar work places. However, controlling for education, age (linear, squared, and cubed), city income, occupation, industry, and work unit ownership increased the female income share only from 82 to 87 percent, leaving 70 percent of the male–female income gap unexplained. This difficulty in attributing the sources of the gender income gap is similar to difficulties in other countries (e.g., Jacobsen 1994, p. 317). Part of the remaining gap may have resulted from the greater assertiveness and bargaining ability of men – note in earlier chapters how, compared with women, men were more likely to report that their income was unfair (Fig. 5.7), that they would slow down at work if dissatisfied (Table 6.2), that they wanted to leave their firm (Table 6.3), and that they had voiced a complaint (Table A7.2).

11. Maurer-Fazio, Rawski, and Zhang (1999) provide a more pessimistic assessment of current wage gaps and trends. Our tentative conclusion is that many of their low estimates are an artifact of method.

With a high-school degree, women in the state or urban collective sector averaged 87 percent as much income as men. Employers in the formal part of the economy have been using a junior high school degree as a minimum threshold for entry into better-paying jobs. With at least this level of education, women gain approximately a ten-percentage-point advantage over women with less education. Because urban women have begun to get almost as much education as men (Chapter 3), the influence of education will help support higher female relative to male income.

However, at the same time, women are falling behind in newly emerging sectors of the economy. In relative income shares, self-employed women and women working for private firms and for joint ventures lag as much as fifteen percentage points behind women who work for older state work units and for urban collective units (Fig. 9.7). Though these other sectors still provide a small minority of all jobs, they are hiring people at a faster rate than the old formal sectors. Thus, in time, the greater tendency to provide different income opportunities by gender in this new sector could exacerbate the gap between men's and women's incomes.

There is also the possibility of an increasing concentration of women in jobs characterized as women's jobs, such as pink-collar clerical, sales, and service jobs or jobs as teachers and nurses.[12] In the West, there are "tipping" patterns, with wages in jobs declining as those jobs move from employing mostly males to employing mostly females (e.g., Goldin 1990, ch. 4; Jacobsen 1994, pp. 226, 241, 479). Figure 9.5 suggests that for China several clerical, sales, and service jobs might be on the verge of tipping in this fashion.[13] To the extent that this tipping occurs, incomes in these jobs could decline dramatically. There was already some evidence of this in the early 1990s. The sales and service sector, which suffered relative income declines in recent years, is increasingly female (cf. Figs. 4.1 and 9.5). Also, in the 1992 firm survey, firms with more females provided

12. As this is being written in early 1998, a group of young executive secretaries gather for a day-long workshop on the first floor of this Beijing hotel. Needless to say, the "executive secretaries," besides being well dressed and expertly groomed, are all female.

13. As yet, China had only modest gender segregation by type of job. Among all the seven occupations in Figure 9.5, 10 percent of men and women would have to change places to obtain a gender-neutral distribution of jobs. This is about the same as in Thailand, but less than in India or Indonesia, where 14 percent would need to change jobs. In Western industrialized countries segregation is higher, at about 40 percent on average (Jacobsen 1994, pp. 377, 425).

lower pay to both male and female employees. Compared with a firm that was only one-quarter female, a firm that was three-quarters female paid employees on average 25 percent less. These are considerable effects, which if intensified by increasing concentrations of women in specific types of jobs and firms could eventually lower women's wages.

Thus, as with work itself, the results for women's income are mixed. Through the 1990s, women's income remained strong relative to men's income. Nevertheless, there are signals of incipient change that could weaken women's income position in the years to come.

CONCLUSION

We end with a mixed picture. On the one side there is ample evidence of great progress. Women's education has continued to increase and both men and women are more likely to get white-collar jobs. Women are increasingly better represented in the best jobs, and few urban women want to quit work. Despite these objective indicators of progress, women perceive that they are increasingly discriminated against. Regardless of the exact reason for this perception, some women with greater education feel that their high expectations are not being met. Ironically, increased rewards for women may be accompanied by an increased sense that those rewards are unjust.

Perhaps more perplexing are the relatively mild effects of economic reform on the socialist contract with women. To the extent that one can tell with aggregate data, the position of women appears to have continued to improve. Women have not beat a retreat to the home, but instead proclaim that they remain enthusiastic about their work. Work is easier to get today for both men and women. This is true in the face of a plethora of anecdotal evidence about the problems women have in the labor force.

Two things may be occurring. One is that this may be the "lull before the storm." As market reform proceeds, many more state firms are going to collapse, and women may be among the first to be fired when firms fold. Moreover, many of the issues for women may well be not in the formal, state sector that we have emphasized due to the types of data that are available. Instead, the most significant issues for women may be in the burgeoning private sector, which will eventually become the dominant sector in urbanized China, in both small towns and large cities. The second thing that may be occurring is that women's consciousness of their condition may be increasing. Given women's increasing education and media attention to women's issues over the last fifteen years, women may be much more critical of conditions that they would have simply accepted in previous decades. If so, it is not so surprising that improved conditions and increasing criticism appear together, much as has occurred in the West.

In short, we might say overall that China is showing the effects of a "Chinese style" market transition, that is, exhibiting some of the trends in women's employment that we expect for a market society, with significant differences. New white-collar clerical jobs are opening up new opportunities for women in the short run, though this may evolve into an underpaid pink-collar segment of the labor force in the future. Women with young children may be discriminated against in favor of younger single women because of employers' new freedom from labor bureau control. While there are data to support both pessimistic and optimistic predictions, on the whole, we agree with the optimistic view of women's continued labor force participation. Chinese women continue to choose to work at high levels compared with Western and other Asian nations, and continue to do well in white-collar jobs. Most important, seen in international comparison, their income as a percentage of male income is extremely high. Overall, Chinese urban women are faring quite well during this transition to market economy with regard to the labor force. How women fare in more private domains is explored in the next chapter.

10

Gender and Family

WILLIAM L. PARISH AND JAMES FARRER

LISTEN to what urban Chinese say at home or in the media today, and you will hear how much marriage and the family have changed under market reform. In this popular discourse, young women looking for husbands have forgotten old standards of "character and honesty" and want to marry only "big monies" (*dakuan*). Extramarital affairs and divorces are described as rampant as husbands and wives seek escape from unsatisfying marriages. In apparently contradictory stories, women are being pushed out of the work force and back into the home while husbands are being "henpecked" by their career-women wives. And – perhaps more predictably – the younger generations are described as increasingly selfish and unwilling to take care of their elderly parents. The purpose of this chapter is to use sample survey data to create an account of the modern urban Chinese family that can sort out these intriguing but confusing popular stories.[1]

Conflicting expectations of marriage are behind some of the confusion in this popular discourse. Claims abound that people, especially young women, have become more mercenary in their marriage choices but also – in an apparent contradiction – that people have become more romantic, with higher emotional expectations of both courtship and marriage. Similarly, Chinese marriages are described as pragmatic arrangements centered on child rearing, yet the media and neighborhood gossip are filled with stories of people who wish for better sex and more

---

1. Since the early 1980s hundreds of women's, family, and youth magazines have barraged readers with articles on these topics. The concerns with "material marriages" appeared early, but became more exaggerated as the market reforms picked up steam. According to editors interviewed by James Farrer (1998), women made up the main readership for such magazines, and more than men, women were influenced by or were more interested in the ideas of romance, companionship, and marital sexual fulfillment promulgated in such media.

romance in marriage, some finding escape through extramarital affairs or divorce.

The other related theme that seems to underlie these ambiguous accounts is that of gender power in the marital relationship. Much is made of shifting power relations in modern Chinese marriage. Urban husbands are sometimes characterized as pathetic, henpecked failures in the market economy. We also hear stories of "strong" career women and "big money" businessmen with housewives and/or kept mistresses. These divergent stories suggest that urban Chinese are sensitive to changes in husband–wife relationships wrought by the market economy. It is the job of this chapter to sort out the sociological evidence on gender relations in the family and describe the structural dynamics underlying changes in these relations, if indeed there are any pronounced changes.

As in other areas of social life, the Chinese family has been strongly affected by socialist policies. While contending trends in gender relations in socialist societies may be puzzling on the surface, we argue that the underlying patterns are simple and familiar ones. Once women gain near equality with men in education, work, and income, and once rapidly falling birth rates reduce the burden of raising children, much else follows in turn. What follows is a typical set of dilemmas for women in industrial societies. There are sharp increases in freedom of choice in marriage, more emphasis on husband–wife companionship, and more equality in decision making between husband and wife. Simultaneously, there is an increase in conflicts over chores. Men become less useful to women, and marital satisfaction for some women declines. Rates of divorce increase.[2]

ISSUES

This chapter examines two major issues: first the role of bargaining and cultural frames in shaping family behavior, and then our issue from earlier chapters of whether socialist and market systems have systematic

2. These effects of industrialization on changes in family functions and gender roles in the family were an early and constant theme in the sociology of the family (e.g., Ogburn 1938; Burgess and Locke 1945; Goode 1963, 1993; Cherlin 1981). The voluminous journal literature on these themes emphasizes the interaction between women's attitudes and marital discord as well as the varying roles of hours of work and relative income (e.g., Guttmann 1993, pp. 10–18; Greenstein 1995).

consequences for family life. At the microsocial level, spousal bargaining and cultural frames compete in the scholarly literature on gender relations, including the sharing of chores and the assertiveness of wives with respect to their husbands. At the macrosocial level, socialist and market systems have a host of secondary consequences, which should in turn affect both bargaining resources and cultural frames.

Bargaining and Culture

Let us first consider the microlevel mechanisms affecting change in the family. One view emphasizes bargaining and exchange between men and women in the family.[3] According to this view, as women receive better education and well-paying work their bargaining positions relative to their husbands should improve. In particular, wives should be able to demand shared housework and better treatment from their husbands as wives' contribution to family income increases (Hochschild and MacHung 1989; Brines 1994). Consistent with this view, if men are resistant to bargaining, we would expect wives' satisfaction with their husbands to decline.[4]

In U.S. research the bargaining perspective has not worked as well as expected in explaining differences in the sharing of chores and other forms of economic sharing between men and women (Pleck 1985; Berado, Shehan, and Leslie 1987; Brines 1994; Presser 1994). It seems that men in the United States are unwilling to spend more time on chores when their wives generate more income. Rather, housework is a female, gendered activity governed by cultural ascriptions of some kinds of work as male and others as female (Berk 1985; South and Spitze 1994).

3. The benign (the voluntary "Dear, let's rationally calculate our respective comparative advantages in market and home work") (Becker 1981) and power or resource (the involuntary "You can't ask me to wash the dishes when I am so tired from bringing home the family's income") (Berk 1985; Coverman 1985) versions of the bargaining hypothesis led to much the same set of predictions about the division of household chores. For debates about bargaining approaches, see Berk and Berk (1983). For application of some of these ideas to a Chinese family system, see Lee, Parish, and Willis (1994).
4. Wives in the European socialist states, particularly in Russia, found husbands with blocked careers and modest incomes to be despondent and wives to see these husbands as unnecessary appendages to their lives (e.g., du Plessix Gray 1990; Goode 1993). One consequence was that wives were increasingly the ones to initiate divorce proceedings (Lapidus 1978). An added byproduct can be increased violence against wives by frustrated, underachieving husbands (e.g., Ishwaran 1989, p. 279).

In opposition to the "money talks" approach, the cultural frames approach suggests that people use a variety of cultural schemas in making judgments about family life.[5] These judgments are often more powerful than what a naive, "rational," economic calculus would lead one to expect. In household chores and relative husband and wife assertiveness in interpersonal interactions, cultural frames about what it means to be male or female often dominate. One example is in the analysis of chores. Julie Brines (1994) draws out some of the implications of each approach. If the "money talks" approach were the only determinant of the sharing of chores, then one of two patterns would emerge. There could be a linear pattern, with wife's chore hours falling and husband's hours rising regularly as the wife's portion of their joint income rose from 0 to 100 percent (Fig. 10.1A). Or, consistent with much U.S. research, there could be more of an S-shaped pattern – with husband and wife moving to near equality once the wife began working and then shifting again only when the wife made almost all their joint income (Fig. 10.1B). If, instead, the cultural frames argument is closer to what actually occurs, then a third pattern might emerge (Fig. 10.1C). Brines labels this a gender display model, because as the wife's income rises above 50 percent of their joint income, the wife's greater earning capacity becomes a threat to both the wife's feminine identity and the husband's masculine identity. To demonstrate that she is really feminine, despite her higher earnings, the wife "displays" her femininity by doing even more of the family chores. To "display" that he is really masculine, the husband does even less of the chores. In Brine's U.S. data, wives follow pattern A, with chores falling regularly as their income shares rise. Husbands follow pattern C, with a husband's chores falling as his wife begins to contribute more than half of all income.

We look for these patterns in China, as well as examine the consequences of income shares for women's assertiveness and marital disagreements. In China, of course, both traditional, presocialist cultural

5. We prefer to use the term "cultural frames" because culture has been shown to be piecemeal, and contingent rather than organized in the holistic "systems" described by earlier anthropologists. People mix and choose from a limited but eclectic vocabulary of cultural frames in social interactions. See, for instance, Swidler (1986) on "culture as a toolkit," Bourdieu (1987) on cultural "practice," or Sewell (1992) on "schemas and resources" for models of culture consistent with the approach here. The emphasis is on how cultural schema enable and also favor certain types of social interactions.

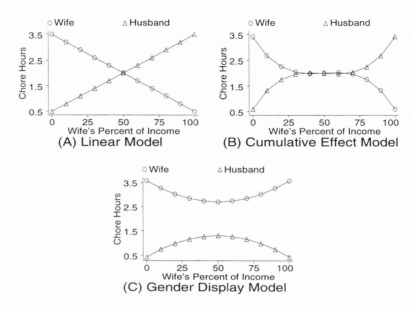

Figure 10.1 Potential relationships between chores and income shares. Notes: Wife's percent of income is $(100 \times \text{wife's income})/(\text{wife's income} + \text{husband's income})$. Models adapted from Brines (1994).

frames of feminine docility and socialist frames of gender equality compete for influence in family life. We want to examine which set of frames wins, and whether there is much of a role for bargaining in spousal relations.

Socialist and Market Institutions

The most important two macrolevel mechanisms for social change in the family are socialist institutions and market institutions. Family patterns before and after economic reform provide a natural experiment in the influence of these institutions on women's role in the family.

Socialist Institutions. Let us first consider the impact of socialist institutions, with attention to both the liberating and restricting tendencies of these institutions. The liberating side includes educational institutions, state-controlled labor markets, and state-sponsored social services (especially childcare). According to Engels's (1884) ideal of the family under socialism, women should enjoy great autonomy vis-à-vis men if the inequalities of capitalist labor markets are eliminated. The known record of socialist states regarding women's status in the family is mixed. In some respects, these states historically did extremely well with regard to women. Compared with other societies, women in socialist states made great gains in health, education, work, and income attainment (e.g., see Jancar 1978; Lapidus 1978; Whyte and Parish 1984; Einhorn 1993; Sorenson and Trappe 1995). These material advantages were joined with an ideology of gender equality, including in China an emphasis on how "women hold up half the sky."

The socialist institutions had negative tendencies as well. Many of these were material in nature. Given the socialist tendency to downplay light industry and services, women were ill served by a system that provided few consumer goods, few appliances, and cramped housing. The result was that the burden of maintaining a family increased. Lines at the market were longer. There was less convenience food. Until recently household appliances were in short supply, and in China many families had to share kitchens and bath facilities with others. Moreover, in China, prior to the 1980 marriage law reform, it was extremely difficult for women to exit unsatisfactory marriages. Divorce was extremely rare. All this should have decreased women's bargaining leverage with respect to their husbands.

Unsurprisingly, then, the record of accomplishments with regard to gender equality was mixed. Great gains in the world of work were combined with modest gains in chores and marital relations. In China freer choice in marriage occurred very rapidly in the 1950s as the initial socialist institutions were introduced (e.g., Five-City Family Research Group 1985; Liu and Xue 1987; Pan 1987; Whyte 1990, 1993). Socialist institutions, however, also created administrative controls over family life that kept a lid on the changes that gender equality might be expected to bring.

In sum, socialism gave women the resources (income, education, childcare facilities) to become more autonomous in their bargaining with husbands over relationship issues such as housework. Socialism also gave women a new set of cultural frames supporting male–female equality. Simultaneously, socialism limited women's abilities to bargain with husbands by restricting their opportunities to exit relationships or to use income to buy labor-saving appliances. The effects of socialist institutions on families in contemporary urban China should therefore occur both directly, through continuing institutions such as child-care facilities, and indirectly as a lagged effect, as women act on the equality they gained under the older socialist system.

Markets. Marketization has produced several often contradictory consequences for women. Increased family incomes should help women absolutely by allowing families to buy labor-saving appliances and generally enjoy a higher standard of living. In the West, the spread of household appliances is often said to be unrelated to hours spent on chores. Expectation about home cleanliness and quality of meals cooked at home kept pace with the increased ease of washing clothes, cooking meals, and sweeping the house (e.g., Jacobsen 1994, p. 129). Nevertheless, in China, with nearly all women in full-time paid work and with few appliances to begin with, the recent spread of appliances might have alleviated time spent on chores somewhat. The only fly in the ointment may be that with increased appliances and larger apartments come higher standards for cleanliness and appearances, fed by advertisers and others. Part of the question, then, is which side is winning in the race between new appliances and new housekeeping standards.

The market has also greatly increased the space for autonomous individual activities, including leisure activities and social interactions in the workplace. The comparison-shopping opportunity that mixed-gender workplaces provide may increase divorce (Greenstein 1990, 1995; South and Lloyd 1995). Increased opportunities for mixed-gender leisure activities such as dancing and karaoke provide additional opportunities to begin affairs.[6]

New cultural frames are associated with the market culture. According to anecdotes, the new market-oriented popular culture may create unrealistic standards of male economic achievement, and for wives a resultant disappointment in husbands' performance exacerbated by traditional expectations that men outperform their wives. As in Eastern Europe, marketization has also meant a great increase in open discus-

6. According to Farrer's ethnographic study, social dance halls in Shanghai are frequented by married men and women, who often leave their spouses at home with the child (Farrer 1998).

sions of sexuality and in sexual representations in the media, especially sexual representations of women (Doelling 1993; Kon and Riordan 1993; Kunz 1996). The market-driven media have also propagated an increasingly relaxed attitude toward both pre- and extramarital sexuality. Radio call-in programs discuss marital sexual problems in some detail, and extramarital affairs are a frequent topic of TV serials. The market thus acts as a mechanism for producing and transmitting new cultural ideals of sexual fulfillment and sexual liberality, which augment individual autonomy in sexual relations.

While marriage autonomy was achieved decades ago, courtship may be changing under the influence of the market economy.[7] The market economy creates new resources (increased income) and new cultural activities (commercial entertainment) which people engage in. Through the commercial media, the market also provides a set of ideologies associating romance with consumption. In China, this cultural diffusion through the market can be extremely rapid because there are producers in Hong Kong and Taiwan speaking the same language (or a close cousin) and sharing cultural practices and values (Zha 1995, pp. 165–99). The popular love stories of the prolific Taiwan novelist Qiong Yao, for instance, are available in bookstores throughout China.

The mechanism of the market is therefore also a mechanism of cultural diffusion of Western ideas into China. One trend that complicates this picture, however, is that "traditional" forms of marital culture may also be revived by these same market forces (or the "traditions" even created by the market).[8] Expensive wedding banquets and fortune-telling are one obvious example of a commercial revival of so-called traditions in the sphere of marriage.

In sum, like socialist institutions, market institutions also affect the microsocial mechanisms of bargaining and cultural frames outlined above. Socialist institutions provided economic, social, and cultural resources that increased equality and autonomy within marriage, but hindered family members from exercising their autonomy. Markets in turn create conditions of autonomy that allow for effective bargaining and

---

7. The market has been associated in the West with a shift from "courting" to "dating," the biggest distinction being the expense and commodification involved in the practices of "dating" or "going out" (see Modell 1983; Bailey 1988).
8. See Tobin (1992) for discussions of the commercial production of "Japanese traditions" and "Western imports" that are often only tendentiously "traditions" or "imports."

acting on autonomous impulses, for instance, by getting divorced or having an affair. The long-term effects of markets, however, may be to reduce women's resources compared with men's and thus weaken their bargaining positions. Both socialist and market institutions may thus provide some impetus and some obstacles to increasing gender equality within the family. It is the purpose of this chapter to estimate the strengths of these different effects.

To deal with these issues, we call on several surveys from the late 1980s and early 1990s. Our primary emphasis is on analysis of the original data from the 1991 women's survey, and the published report from this data set (Sha, Xiong, and Gao 1994). Our Appendix Table A8.1 provides the descriptive material on this data set, as does Appendix B. In addition, we refer here and there to secondary data from a 1990 a nonrandom national sex survey (Liu 1992), a 1993 seven-city survey of family behavior (Shen and Yang 1995), and unpublished reports from a 1996 women's survey by Anqi Xu. Our discussion is organized around the three topics of marriage markets, family roles, and marital satisfaction and divorce, with major emphasis throughout on the relative roles of bargaining and cultural constraints, as shaped by lingering socialist and emerging market forces.

MARRIAGE MARKETS AND EQUALITY

Marriage Autonomy and Romance

Public calls for free choice of marriage partners first became common in China during the May Fourth Movement of the 1910s and '20s. Then, under the influence of the 1950 marriage law, autonomous choice quickly became the norm in urban China (Sha, Xiong, and Gao 1994). Market reforms broadened these choices while changing the nature of the choice process. Changes in marriage practice go along with conditions that favor personal autonomy and romance in selection of marriage partners. One of these changes was a rise in marriage ages. In the 1980s, with female marriage ages remaining near twenty-four and male ages perhaps two years above that, urban marriage ages were sufficiently high that most brides and grooms were already at work and had some degree of independence before they contemplated marriage (Sha, Xiong, and Gao 1994, p. 103; SSB 1995b, p. 20).

Unsurprisingly, then, since the 1960s few urban marriage choices have been decided entirely by parents. In the 1991 urban women's survey, 95 percent of all marriage choices were decided by the couple involved.[9] The emphasis on autonomous choice by the couple is also consistent with the couple's reported desiderata in picking mates. When asked the characteristics that are important in picking a mate, women reply that the most important is character (54%), followed by education (18%), occupation (10%), and appearance (7%). Men have a similar list, though as one might expect their percentages put more emphasis on appearance (15%) and less on education (12%) and occupation (8%) (Sha, Xiong, and Gao 1994, p. 123). There is a continuing utilitarian element, particular in the one-fourth of all women who insist on education and occupation. This fits anecdotal accounts of the role of financial considerations for women in marriage (e.g., Xu 1994a).

However, for most men and women the emphasis is not on family background and political credentials (possible choices in the 1991 survey) but on the personal qualities of individual character or moral standing (*renpin*). All of this is consistent with other accounts of how the companionate ideal has spread in China (Honig and Hershatter 1988). This spread has been accelerated by popular newspaper accounts and talk shows and by movies, love songs, and other types of popular culture from Hong Kong and Taiwan (Lull 1991; Pickowicz 1995). But much of it existed earlier, as suggested by the relative uniformity of mate choice responses by people of different ages.[10] Whatever the exact origins, a

9. Sha, Xiong, and Gao (1994, pp. 99, 114). Three additional notes: (1) In this sample of those who married mostly after 1960, there is only a slight liberalizing trend over time. Both the percentages and the modest post-1960 trend are consistent with post-1960 data in other studies (Pasternak 1986; Pan 1987, p. 65; Whyte 1993; Shen and Yang 1995). (2) For comparison, in early 1980s women's marriages in much more developed Taiwan, channels for meeting the spouse were as follows: 42% on her own (including through work, in school, and in the neighborhood), 42% through friends, 16% through kin, and 8% through a professional matchmaker (Thornton and Lin 1994, p. 152). These percentages are similar to the channels used in China – which were 41% on his or her own, 42% through friends, and 16% through kin. (3) Riley (1994) argues that parental intervention in marriage introductions remains common because of the need to use social networks in Chinese society. Given the basic similarities in social outcomes in China and in other urban settings, we find this kind of explanation not to be particular to urban China.
10. Sha, Xiong, and Gao (1994, pp. 124–25). On the early emergence of the romantic ideal prior to recent diffusion from the West, Hong Kong, or Taiwan, see Jankowiak (1993, p. 221).

1989–90 study of sexual behavior finds ample evidence of the pervasiveness of the romantic ideal in cities, one example being the 88 percent of urbanites who agree that marriage must involve love (Liu
1992).[11]

Popular anecdotes emphasize an increasing materialism among youth
in courtship. In the reform era, dating has become increasingly popular
among Chinese youth, including visits to dance halls and other forms of
commercial entertainment.[12] Dating requires expenditure and forefronts
the economic considerations in courtship. The increase in dating allows
for greater comparison and companionship before marriage and less
supervised intimacy (Farrer 1998). In the West such dating was associated with the emergence of more liberal attitudes toward premarital sexuality and a greater emphasis on consumption as a part of romance
(Bailey 1988). Although still rejected by most married Chinese in 1990,
premarital sex was more likely to be accepted by the young and the
better educated (Sha, Xiong, and Gao 1994). One-fourth of the husbands
and one-sixth of the females reported sex before marriage, though that
sex was usually with an intended spouse (Liu 1992, pp. 315–30).

Contrary to alarmist predictions of Chinese officials and some Western
scholars (e.g., Schell 1988), the market is not a wholesale destroyer of
Chinese traditions. Elements of Chinese tradition are just as amenable
to commercialization as modern Western customs. Marriage rituals
reflect an increased emphasis on ostentatious consumption, including
traditional Chinese banquets. This partly represents a return to traditional patterns in a highly commercial form. Drastically simplified in the
initial decade of socialist rule, these rituals again became elaborate in the
1980s (Pan 1987, p. 92; Honig and Hershatter 1988, p. 143; Whyte 1990,
1993). In the 1960s, about a third of all couples spent significant amounts
on wedding gifts and ceremonies, but by the end of the 1980s, this figure
had climbed to one-half of all couples, with some amounts being con-

11. The sample in this study, based in part on opportunistic samples of marriage and family
magazine subscribers, is clearly biased, particularly toward the more educated and
those in white-collar occupations. Nevertheless, the variation in responses across education and occupation categories is sufficiently small to suggest that the pattern of
responses is not restricted to a small subset of the population.
12. Anqi Xu's 1996 survey of marital quality shows a great increase in the attendance of
commercial leisure activities such as dance halls during courtship among the youngest
cohort of urban couples (personal communication).

siderable.[13] In cities, expenditures were much larger by the husband's than by the wife's family. These rituals reflect traditional elements such as the emphasis on the husband's family's contribution and large banquets but also new elements such as Western-style wedding garb and Taiwan-style wedding portraiture.

What this discussion shows is that socialism laid the foundations for a culture of autonomous dating, but a lack of resources and strict social controls limited the exercise of this autonomy. The market society gave young people more money to spend and more places to go. Parental and community restraints relaxed. Simultaneously, the commercial culture of dating forefronted economic considerations, which explains some of the popular discussion of increasingly mercenary attitudes toward courtship. The market transforms courtship and wedding practices, but does not lead to a wholesale "Westernization" since traditional Chinese practices are just as amenable to commercialization. What the market does seem to produce is a syncretic culture in which individuals are allowed a wider range of choices than ever before.

Income Equality and Marital Equality

As we saw in the last chapter, one effect of socialist policies was to bring women's levels of education and income near to the levels of men. Given the rapid increases in women's education, work, occupational status, and income, one expects husbands and wives to have become more equally matched in social characteristics (Liu and Xue 1987; Pan 1987). The trends in education are clear. In 1991, compared with older women, more younger women had as much or more education than their husbands. The percentage of women having more education than their husbands increased from about 15 to 20 percent. The percentage having as many

13. In a 1988 survey of recent marriages in Tianjin, China's third largest city, average (median) expenditures per son were RMB $5,000 and per daughter were $2,000 (Wang and Pan 1994, p. 186). This was in a year when the average (median) monthly income in Tianjin was only $125. Thus, much of the expenditure was from parental resources. Of course, much of the expenditure included expenses for furniture, bedding, clothing, and so on that would have been needed regardless of whether there were elaborate ceremonies (Pan 1987, pp. 94–95). Nevertheless, the socially acceptable level of expenditures for both ceremonial and household "necessities" escalated rapidly in the 1980s. By the early 1990s, the most expensive weddings were costing $20,000 to $30,000 for grooms and $10,000 to $20,000 for brides (Shen and Yang 1995, p. 389).

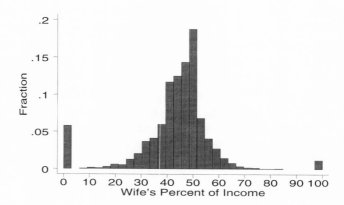

Figure 10.2 Wife's and husband's income, distribution of population. Notes: Wife's percent calculated as $100 \times$ (wife's income/(wife's + husband's income)). Source: 1991 Women's Survey, Urban Sample.

years of education increased from one-fourth to two-fifths. And, conversely, the number of women with less education than their husbands was cut in half, from about one-half down to one-fourth (1991 Women's Survey). Thus, by the early 1990s, in educational qualifications women were much better positioned to hold their own in "bargaining" with husbands and the husbands' parents.

The consequences of increasing educational equality carried over into incomes (Fig. 10.2). By 1991, most wives had nearly as much income as their husbands. Most of these women were tightly bunched in the 40 to 50 percent range of her and her husband's joint income. This modal group, then, had become almost a normative standard for urban society, with nearly all adult women working full time in jobs that paid only slightly less than their husbands' jobs. Very few people fell outside this central, egalitarian range. A few women did not work, either because they were out of the labor force during prime working years (fewer than 5%) or because they had retired in their forties or fifties (about 10% of the 45- to 54-year-old age group). About 2 percent of women earned all of the husband–wife joint income.

There are several reasons why couples are not at the egalitarian middle. Couples at the extreme ends of the income share distribution are older, less educated, and in poorer health (details not shown). At the upper extreme, husbands in poor health are likely to have become house husbands, entirely dependent on their wives for earned income. At the lower extreme, both husband and wife are much less educated. The result is that in income, people at the extremes have only modest incomes. Thus, at either the 100 or 0 percent income share position, the actual advantage of the full-income partner is not very great. For wives the result is that when they are at the 100 percent extreme, they are only moderately satisfied with their jobs. And to some extent, they work only because they have to (details not shown).

Despite the mixed blessing of being the sole provider in the family, we can provide several preliminary findings suggesting that wives' share of income has significant consequences for husband–wife relations. Through the middle ranges, women with a higher share of joint income are receiving higher salaries, and they are more satisfied with their jobs (details not shown). Moreover, the potential bargaining advantage of increasing income shares influences several aspects of the woman's life. One consequence is that women with more income decide more purchases of consumer durables such as televisions and refrigerators. On average, husbands made one-fifth of the purchase decisions, with the other decisions made either by the wife alone (13%), jointly by husband and wife (62%), or by someone else in the household (6%). With ten-percentage-point increase in the wife's income share, the husband's role in decisions diminished by 1.3 percentage points. The increased role of the wife was evident in decisions they made jointly (particularly common when they contributed equal amounts of income) and in purchase decisions that the wife made on her own. Ironically, men "recovered" their decision-making roles only when they made little or no income, becoming the "house husband" who did the shopping while the wife was at work.[14]

Another consequence was that increased income share was associated with stronger gender equality beliefs.[15] In a multivariate analysis, the con-

14. The full model included the following influences that increased wife's joint or sole role in decision making – wife's age, education, Shanghai City residence, grew up in city or town, poor health, and six different durables other than a motorcycle or telephone. Source: 18,036 purchase decisions in the 1991 Women's Survey, for a little over four decisions per couple.
15. The gender equality scale includes the appropriately coded responses to "a wife's career achievements should not exceed her husband's," "females are inferior to males in career and in work," "females can have close male friends after marriage," "a wife

sequences of greater income share were as great as several other background conditions. One way to assess the influence of changes in income share is to ask how many percentage points' change in the wife's income would be needed to have the same effect as a unit's change in some other background condition. These include an extra year of education (10 share points), a year younger in age (1 point), living in the city of Shanghai (13 points), growing up in a city (17 points), and being of an ethnicity other than ethnically Korean (95 points). Thus, except for Korean ethnicity, a wife's share of income compares well with other factors that shape a subset of values about gender equality. Education has a very large effect. And many other effects are very similar to income share – particularly age, which has an almost one-to-one relationship with income share. Again, this suggests that changes in income share are likely to influence a woman's assertiveness and bargaining with her spouse.

FAMILY ROLES

Family Functions

The Chinese family has traditionally involved a long-term contract between parents and children, in which parents raise children with the implicit (and often explicit) assumption that children will reciprocate by taking care of them in their old age. This arrangement supports the bargaining position described above. Moreover, this arrangement has been associated with strong patriarchal cultural frames, such as a Confucian ideology, which emphasize the patrilineal line in residence after marriage.[16] Clearly, both self-interest and culture are at work in the maintenance of this venerable tradition of intergenerational obligations. The weak link in this arrangement has always been young married women

can refuse her husband's sexual demands," and "a wife can initiate sex." The multivariate analysis includes the background conditions listed below plus a term for Hui ethnicity (nonsignificant) and 100 percent of income. The last term is strongly negative, suggesting once again that women who earn all of family income work out of external necessity rather than inner drive.

16. For literature reviews of both traditional practice and changes in the family during the first half of this century, see Lang (1946), Levy (1949), Baker (1979), and Watson and Ebrey (1991). On more recent changes, see Whyte and Parish (1984) and Davis and Harrell (1993).

who may see little gain in living with and/or taking care of her husband's parents instead of living with and taking care of her own (or living neolocally) (Wolf 1972). As young women gain resources compared with their husbands, under the bargaining perspective we would expect some changes in this patriarchal pattern of elder care. More couples should take in the wife's elderly parents. Continuing tendencies toward elderly coresidence with a son, on the other hand, would be evidence of the strength of patriarchal cultural frames.

Another related issue is the perception of children. To borrow the language of economics, some Chinese urban parents are beginning to treat their children not as producer goods (that produce a later return after an initial investment) but as consumer goods (that are simply enjoyed now). This also can be seen as a change either in the intergenerational bargain or in cultural frames about the meaning of children and the meaning of marriage.

Among the currently old, most urban males have a pension. Most females do not (Liu and Xue 1987, p. 363). Having never worked in the state sector, currently old women rely heavily on their spouses and adult children. Both sons and daughters send support.[17] This will change somewhat as the current working population ages. More of the women currently working are in state-sector jobs, where a pension continues to be guaranteed, despite some changes in the system (see Chapter 2). One result is that among men and women currently at work, expectations are that while they may live with children in old age – just as four-fifths of the currently old do – they will not rely on their children financially. When asked what they expect from a son or daughter in old age, fewer than 5 percent say they anticipate financial support from their children.[18] This is surely optimistic, since over one-fifth of all women remain

17. In the 1993 urban family survey, married children are equally likely to send the husband's and wife's parents support, and the wife's parents get 84 percent as much as the husband's parents (Shen and Yang 1995, p. 372). In comparison with Taiwan, these amounts are surprisingly equal between the spouse's parents – which is again consistent with the theme of greater equality between husband and wife. And, at 13 percent of nominal monthly income, the amounts are surprisingly large in comparison with Taiwan (see Lee, Parish, and Willis 1994, p. 1025).

18. Sha, Xiong, and Gao (1994, pp. 478, 485). Despite the higher economic development level and higher rates of saving for old age, a much higher 39 percent of Taiwan city residents say they will need financial support from children in old age (1989 women and family survey, raw data). Thus, the much more extensive pension system in Chinese cities makes a difference in parental perception of future need.

employed in the collective sector, which usually provides no pension. Nevertheless, the low expectations of financial support suggest fewer incentives to emphasize children, particularly sons, as a source of support in old age.

Most couples lived in an apartment by themselves immediately after marriage.[19] When couples could not arrange a residence on their own, living with the husband's parents remained the most common pattern – which, again, is the traditional pattern. This shows that young couples have reduced the need to live with a husband's parents when they were newly married, which was traditionally the period when a new daughter-in-law would be most under pressure from her in-laws (Wolf 1972). This pattern of neolocal residence can thus be interpreted as an increase in the status of women under socialist institutions. However, the tendency to live with the husband's parents when no independent home is available shows the strength of traditional patrilineal cultural frames.[20]

Household Chores

Household labor is one of the most intransigent structures of gender inequality in industrial societies. In both market and socialist societies, wives are caught in a double-bind of market work and house work and have less time for leisure and study than men. As suggested above, several microsocial mechanisms may govern the sharing of household labor. The bargaining – or dependency – theory of marital relations, outlined above, predicts that as women earn more of the family's income their share of housework should decrease. Gender-specific cultural frames seem to keep this from happening (Brines 1994; Berk 1985).

China offers a special case to study this problem. First, as a legacy of socialism there are more households with a nearly equal share of income coming from husbands and wives. This allows for a good test of the bargaining perspective. Second, Chinese households are likely to have other adults present who can also contribute to chores. This complicates but

19. In major cities, with more crowded housing conditions, neolocal residence is only 46 percent (Shen and Yang 1995, p. 35). In Taiwan cities, with private housing, an even smaller 40 percent of newlyweds live separately from parents (Thornton and Lin 1994, p. 341). On trends in China, see Davis-Friedman (1991).
20. Of course as the current generation of parents with a single child matures, residence with a son or daughter will lead to intense negotiation.

adds to the bargaining perspective. Third, the only recent availability of basic household amenities such as natural gas for cooking, refrigerators, and piped water lets us examine whether basic amenities reduced chore time. At the same time, the increasing number of rooms (here indexed by number of bedrooms) could imply an increasing set of household standards that would nullify the effect of more household amenities. Finally, increased education should be associated with greater internalization of gender equality cultural frames, leading to more chores for husbands and fewer chores for wives.

The 1991 women's survey finds men spending 1.4 hours on cooking and laundry compared with women's 2.6 hours.[21] While they still did less housework than Chinese women, Chinese men's chore hours were higher than comparable times for U.S. men (0.6 hours) and men in European socialist and nonsocialist societies (about 1.2 hours).[22] Moreover, much more than men in market societies, Chinese husbands seemed to respond to their wives' proportions of income according to the bargaining or dependency perspective (Fig. 10.3). That is, as the wife's proportion of total family income increased, then the husband's proportion of chore time increased. At the extremes, women's chores increased by an hour when she contributed no income and, conversely, decreased by half an hour when she provided all of the income. The pattern differs slightly for wives and husbands – the wives follow an S-shaped, cumulative effect model while the husbands follow a linear model (see Fig. 10.1).[23] Though the two lines do not cross, much more so than in most societies, both husbands and wives patterns are consistent with a bargaining model. Thus, while gender-specific cultural frames continue to

---

21. We focus on cooking and laundry because there are no other categories in the data set that apply to virtually all families. Child care follows patterns similar to those reported here, but child care is not relevant to families with no young children.

22. The comparative times include a slightly broader definition of chores, which under-states the advantage of Chinese men (Markus 1976, p. 81). A 1984 Chinese study finds men spending 1.5 and women 2.5 hours per day, and about double this time during days off from work (RI 1991, p. 584). A Beijing study finds men spending 2.23 hours compared with women's 3.72 hours (Pan 1987, p. 126). For additional comparisons that favor Chinese men, see Ma et al. (1992) and Sheng, Stockman, and Bonney (1992, p. 211).

23. That is, for husbands, the best-fitting regression line is a single term for income share. For wives, in contrast, the best-fitting line has a term for income share, the square, and the cube of that share (see Brines 1994). The regression equations for both include the set of background characteristics in Figure 10.4.

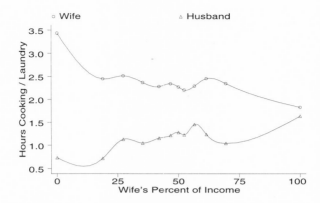

Figure 10.3 Hours doing cooking and laundry by wife's income share. Note: Average (mean) times calculated from log of hours before exponential conversion back to linear hours. Mean points joined by spline curve. See Fig. 10.1 for approximate sample size in each income category. Source: 1991 Women's Survey, Urban Sample.

keep mens' chores below those of women, much more so than in other societies men respond to their wives' income share.[24]

Household conditions other than just bargaining over money and time could underlie the pattern of chores. To check for this, we can also examine bargaining in the context of other household conditions (Fig. 10.4). In this analysis, bargaining remains important. Much as in the previous, descriptive analysis, most of the effects for wives are at the extremes of all or no income. The effects for husbands are more continuous, leading to almost seven more minutes on chores for each ten-percentage-point increase in wives' income share. Either way, a woman's income is important, which fits the bargaining perspective.

Contrary to a common pattern in developed societies, household conveniences provided by new market forces were also important (Fig. 10.4).

24. The bargaining model persists within region, age, education, and mate-choice subgroups. The few exceptions are Jilin Province (no obvious reason except there are many Korean-descent families there, in which husbands do few chores), people aged 50 to 59 (relation right but sample too small to attain significance), college-educated (ceiling effect, with all college-educated husbands doing more chores). Spouse chosen for utilitarian (education, occupation, family connections) versus personalistic (character, temperament, appearance) reasons has no effect on the bargaining relationship.

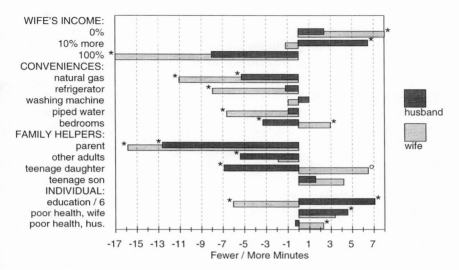

Figure 10.4 Change in daily minutes cooking and laundry by family situation. Notes: Wife's income as percent of husband and wife's joint income, including the effects of her having none, all, and ten percentage points more of the joint income. (Natural gas) Bottled gas, piped gas, and electric cooking fuel (vs. coal or other source); (piped water) piped water in home; (bedrooms) number of bedrooms; parent, teenage daughter, and son coded 1 if any of these in home. Other adults in home coded 1 to 4. Poor health coded 1 to 4. The truncated values for wife's income being either 0 or 100 percent are +51 and −23 minutes. Additional, unshown coefficients for infant, preschool, and primary age children were also included in the regression analysis. (*) $p < .05$; (°) $p < .10$. Source: 1991 Women's Survey, Urban Sample, 4,322 observations.

Cooking could be with either coal or natural gas.[25] Requiring advance lighting before beginning the meal, coal is time-consuming and messy. Natural gas, in contrast, saves men about five minutes and women about eleven minutes. The approximately half of all women who had a refrigerator saved about nine minutes on chores. Washing machines were unimportant and the influence of piped water was statistically

25. In 1991, one-third used coal, including a few who used wood or other kindling. Not quite half used bottled gas, about a fifth used gas piped into the home, and 3 percent used electricity for cooking. Electricity is combined with gas in our tabulations. See Appendix Table A10.1 for the average share of these amenities per household.

insignificant, though the influence was in the expected time-saving direction. Thus, for some but not all modern conveniences, the increased availability of amenities for the home meant a saving in the time spent daily
on cooking and washing.[26] In contrast, more bedrooms means more work
for women, even while men reduce their time when there are more bedrooms. Our interpretation is that more bedrooms are associated with a
new cultural frame, propagated by advertising, which implies that women
are the ones responsible for the new "Chuppie" lifestyle. In this emerging cultural frame, husbands have less responsibility for this new lifestyle
– and accordingly for them more bedrooms are associated with less
housework. If true, for women this new cultural trend – at three extra
minutes a day for each extra bedroom – could help erase the advantages
of more household conveniences (on increasing housing space, see Table
2.1).

The traditional extended nature of Chinese households continued to
help dual-career couples. A little more than 10 percent of households
surveyed in 1991 had a husband's parent or, more rarely, a wife's parent
in the household. When one of these parents was present, chore time
declined thirteen minutes for husbands and sixteen minutes for wives.
As one might expect, husbands were quick to bail out when there were
other adults or teenage daughters in the household to help with chores
(Fig. 10.4). This pattern, together with the wives' continued higher share
of housework, suggests the importance of a cultural frame through which
husbands are still considered secondary "help" in household labor.[27]

The responsibility of husbands varied both with their education and
their wives' needs. For each extra six years of education, husbands con-

26. A new but potentially important effect of the market economy is the increased availability of hired household help for families with enough income. According to one
survey of urban working women, 8 percent of Beijing families and 3 percent of
Guangzhou families hired housekeepers (Liu 1995a, pp. 17–25). With further economic
development, this number could become higher, especially given the large available
pool of cheap rural labor.
27. The sharing of general child-care tasks (a separate category on the survey from educating children) shows a similar pattern to chores. Women spend more time than men
on child care (an average of one hour daily for all women to forty minutes daily for
all men), but as a wife's proportion of income increased, her husband spent more time
on child care. On the other hand, the task of educating children is equally shared. Husbands and wives spend virtually the same amount of time educating children (25
minutes daily for women and 28 minutes daily for men). Cultural frames about the
gendering of domestic labor thus differ by task.

tributed an extra seven minutes – and their educated wives were relieved of a similar quantity of chores. Besides doing more chores when more educated, husbands also did more when their wives were in poor health.[28]

Women's Perceptions of Chore Burdens

The time sharing of chores says little about whether these chores are borne heavily or lightly by the people who do them. Judging the level of the burden in dual-career families requires attention to attitudes and other types of behavior. In both U.S. and Chinese research, women's well-being often suffers from heavy chore responsibilities (e.g., Hochschild 1989; Sheng, Stockman, and Bonney 1992). Just how much they self-consciously suffer depends in part on whether wives perceive other options. Women who have few options other than to rely on their husbands for economic support report less distress with chores (Lennon and Rosenfield 1994).

When asked whether they are happy or unhappy with time spent on chores, urban Chinese women react much like U.S. women (Fig. 10.5). Chinese women are less satisfied with chores when they spend more time on chores. Moreover, women are less satisfied with chores when they are more educated and when they work in higher-status occupations. This is consistent with an account that emphasizes both new cultural frames and possibilities for action offered up by the market economy. When a woman has more education and works in higher-status occupations she is likely to have a higher set of expectations about equal sharing in household tasks. And, in higher-status occupations, she may consider that she has options outside marriage that make her less tolerant of exceptionally heavy chore responsibilities.

These expectations influence a woman's general life satisfaction (Fig. 10.5). Unsurprisingly, women with more education have higher expectations that make them less satisfied. Women are more satisfied with most aspects of life when they earn more income from their own work. And, finally, they are dissatisfied when they continue to have major responsibilities for household chores. Thus, much as in research for other soci-

28. "Poor health" is on a four-point scale. Husband's help increased four minutes for each point on this scale. Thus compared with a wife who was in excellent health, a wife in extremely poor health got an extra 16 minutes' help from her husband every day.

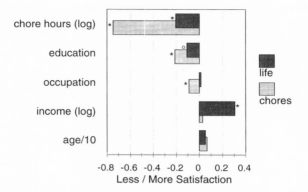

Figure 10.5 Satisfaction with life and chores. Notes: Determinants of satisfaction with time spent on chores and with a combination of recreation, cultural activities, marriage, family life, health, income, and friends. Education is coded 1–4 for primary, junior high, senior high, and college. Occupation is coded 1–4 for manual/sales/service, clerical, administrative/managerial, and professional/technical occupations. Coefficients from two OLS regressions, with 707 and 721 observations each. (*) $p < .05$; (°) $p < .10$. Source: 1988 Quality of Life Survey, subsample of currently married, working women.

eties, Chinese women are quite sensitive to the burden of household tasks. However, the transformation of this dissatisfaction into a new domestic contract for sharing household tasks seems likely to be a slow process, as it has been elsewhere.

MARITAL SATISFACTION AND DIVORCE

Much about Chinese marriage has changed, and like changes in public roles for women, the foundations for this change were laid in the socialist period. Though there are lingering patriarchal tendencies in wedding finance and in grandparent residence, husband and wife are much more likely to have selected one another in free-choice marriages, with personal attraction as a major desideratum. Young wives are more likely to have jobs as good as their husbands' and to make almost as much income as them. Fewer children are in the home to act as a drag on women's labor. Given the micro- and macrosocial mechanisms outlined above, these changes lead to several predictions about marital satisfaction.

First, there is the mechanism of changing cultural frames, especially the spread of a companionate, romantic ideal of marriage through the media during the reform era. This might lead to greater expectations of marriage, which reduce marital satisfaction for educated people most exposed to these ideas. Then, there is the mechanism of resource-based bargaining between husbands and wives, which implies that women with a greater share of resources under their own control might have less reason to tolerate unsatisfying relationships. On the macrosocial level, a freer social life in the reform era is also likely to make more comparisons with other men and women possible, which may lower satisfaction with the current spouses. First, we review these arguments.

As in the West, the spread of the companionate, romantic ideal, accompanied by a decline in other economic and welfare functions of the family, should have made families less stable. The nature of the companionate, romantic ideal makes it inherently more difficult to gain information about each other before marriage – particularly in areas where dating practices are only beginning to emerge – and the content of companionate expectations is more likely to shift over time (Goode 1963; Shorter 1975; Becker 1981). As a result, self-conscious marital dissatisfaction and divorce should increase.

The bargaining perspective emphasizes changing shares of marital resources and shares of family burdens. With all women working full time, and having few chances to work part time, the sharing of household chores should have become more of an issue. And with greater earnings equality compared with husbands, women who have more possibility of supporting themselves should more frequently apply for divorce (e.g., Hannan, Tuma, and Groenveld 1978; Trent and South 1989; Cherlin 1992; Edwards et al. 1992; Greenstein 1995). This continues the theme of options from our discussion of chores. Women who have options will be less resigned to their existing situation (e.g., Lennon and Rosenfield 1994). Having more options leads to more attempts at bargaining, this literature suggests.

Marital Satisfaction

The bargaining perspective implies that women are likely to have higher demands of husbands as they themselves earn more of the family's income. The 1991 women's survey asked about complaints, or about areas

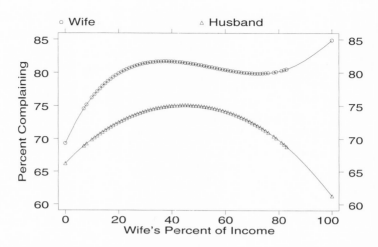

Figure 10.6 Wife's and husband's complaints about spouse by income share. Notes: "Complaint" includes any area where one of the spouses thinks the other could improve (*gaijin*). Data smoothed using predictions from a probit analysis based on the simple, squared, and (for wife) cubed value of wife's income percent. Actual data are available only where there is a circle or triangle. See Fig. 10.2 for the density of data by wife's percent of income. Observations number 4,411. Source: 1991 Women's Survey, Urban Sample.

where the spouse could improve (*gaijin*), and questions about disagreement (*maodun*), or areas of conflicts. The former survey item reflects attitudes about the spouse's deficiencies in specific areas, while the latter reflects perceptions of the occurrence of disagreements. Though most women had complaints about their husbands, economically dependent women had the fewest complaints (Fig. 10.6). Women who earned all the income, and had house husbands, had the most complaints. This is consistent with a bargaining perspective, which suggests that as women's income resources rise they become more assertive relative to their husbands. To a considerable extent, husbands' responses to their wives' incomes mirrored those of their wives (Fig. 10.6). As the wife's income contribution neared 100 percent, his complaints about her diminished in all areas. Our interpretation is that, much like economically dependent wives, economically dependent husbands accepted the tradeoff between economic and other kinds of services from wives.

A difference between husbands and wives was, however, evident in their attitudes toward a dependent spouse. Men were less likely to have complaints if their wives earned less than themselves, while women were more likely to complain if they earned more than their husbands. Though based on very few observations, the level of wives' complaints rose as they reached 100 percent of family income. Our interpretation is that men perceive a wife's financially dependent status as normal, while wives see a dependent husband as a burden.[29] Again, this shows the influence of cultural expectations, but also may reflect the reality that dependent husbands are more of a burden for wives than vice versa, given women's lower levels of pay and men's lower contributions to household chores.

For household disagreements, the pattern is more complex but revealing. The data are based on responses to a request to list up to three areas that caused disagreements or conflicts (*maodun*) with the spouse. Disagreements of any sort are least common when the wife earns no income, all the family income, or exactly half of all income (Fig. 10.7). Statistically, this pattern is clearest for women who earn half the joint income, since for these people there are sufficient observations to establish statistical significance. Our tentative interpretation of this "emerging valentine" pattern is as follows. As before, there is a tendency for disagreements to increase as her income share rises. This is consistent with the hypothesis that wives become more assertive as they earn more, and that men feel ignored by busy wives.[30] However, in the middle range where there is equal income, both husbands and wives report fewer disagreements (Fig. 10.7), though they have more complaints in this range (Fig. 10.6). Our tentative interpretation of this discrepancy is that while partners both feel entitled to complain in more equal relationships, partners in these more equal relationships are more willing to compromise on expectations, and fewer conflicts (*maodun*) arise. Reported disagreements are therefore fewer in the most equal relationships, evi-

---

29. This interpretation is supported by the fact that wives making 100 percent of income are significantly more likely to report disagreements about income (see Fig. 10.7).

30. Of course, the causal influences are not simply from income to assertiveness. More assertive women are probably also likely to get better jobs and more income. Conversely, the minority of women who are completely out of the labor force in part decided to remain at home and take care of children and household chores voluntarily – adopting a traditional cultural frame of the good housewife. Even with shared decisions about work, chores, and complaining, the point about the relation between work, income equality, and assertiveness in marital relations remains.

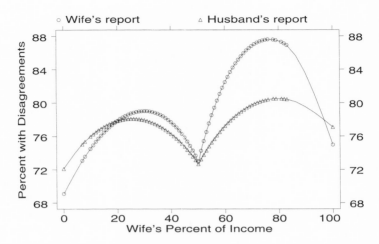

Figure 10.7 Disagreements by wife's income share. Notes: Data show the percent with any disagreement (*maodun*) with spouse. The data are smoothed using predictions from a probit analysis based on the simple, squared, and (for wife) cubed value of wife's income percent plus the absolute distance from equality in incomes. Source: 1991 Women's Survey, Urban Sample.

dence that these relationships are perceived by both partners as more harmonious.

At the extremes of the income share distribution, the predictions of the bargaining perspective hold. At the extreme low end, the wife recognizes her dependent position (and does most of the housework; see Fig. 10.3) and open disagreements decline. At the extreme upper end of the income share distribution, the opposite occurs. The nonearning husband, recognizing his dependent position, makes fewer demands on the wife's time (the wife's proportion of housework declines; see Fig. 10.3) and disagreements decline. According to both spouses, then, open disagreements decline in situations in which one spouse has no income at all. Disagreements are most likely when both spouses have income, but one spouse is making much more than the other. This is likely because the couples in these ranges usually have one spouse who is earning a high income (see Fig. 10.2), giving the high-earning spouse more bargaining leverage and creating more conflicts. This is especially true when the woman is the high-earning spouse. Thus, though the

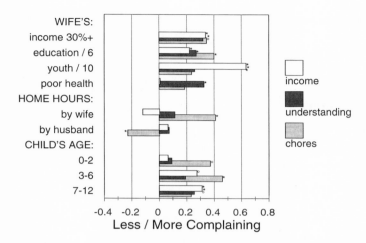

Figure 10.8 Specific complaints by wife's characteristics. Notes: The "complaints" are for the main way (better job or income, more mutual understanding, and more help with chores) that a husband could improve (*gaijin*). High values mean more complaining about specific issues. Wife's earning 30 percent or more of income is compared with wives earning only 0 to 29 percent of the couples' joint income. The education bar shows the consequence of an additional six years of education. The youth bar shows the effect of being ten years younger. Home hours is the logged sum of time spent on cooking, laundry, child care, and child instruction. Coefficients are from a single multinomial logit analysis. Observations number 4,028. (*) $p < .05$; (°) $p < 1.0$. Source: 1991 Women's Survey, Urban Sample.

pattern is more complex than we anticipated, the bargaining perspective is supported. The complexity may be explained by a cultural norm that relationships should be essentially equal, reflected in the finding that these relationships produce markedly fewer conflicts.

When asked where their husbands might improve, women were particularly likely to mention mutual understanding and mutual considerateness (39%), better job or income (30%), and help with chores (12%). Thus, there was evidence of an emphasis both on companionate marriage and on expectations for utilitarian help with income and chores. As in the simpler analysis of complaints, detailed complaints varied in predictable ways (Fig. 10.8). Women who contributed more to family income were more assertive in their complaints, as were younger women and

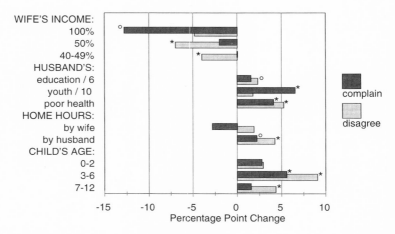

Figure 10.9 Husbands' reports of complaints and disagreements. Notes: About three-fourths of husbands have any complaint or disagreement with their wives. The presence or absence of that complaint or disagreement is analyzed here in two separate probit analyses. Wife's income percent is compared with all other possible income percentages. Observations number 4,190 and 4,206. Also see notes to Fig. 10.7. (*) $p < .05$; (°) $p < .10$. Source: 1991 Women's Survey, Urban Sample.

women with more education. Women also complained more when their burdens were greater. Poor health increased complaints, particularly about husbands' degree of understanding. Long hours spent on child care, cooking, and laundry increased complaints about help with chores. More help from husbands on these same tasks helped diminish complaints about chores. The burdens of raising children increased complaints, not only about chores but also about income and to a lesser extent about understanding. Thus, the lingering socialist tendency to increase women's education, work, and income all had an effect. The dual burden of raising children and tending house while working full time increased women's various discontents with their husbands.

Husbands also show a predictable pattern of complaints. Husbands have more complaint and disagreement issues both when they have greater burdens and when they have higher expectations (Fig. 10.9). The issue-inducing burdens include young children, longer hours of work on household tasks, and poor health.[31] Expectation-raising tendencies include youth and more education. The positive effects of education and youth on husbands' complaints show that in the reform era both husbands and wives may have increased expectations and therefore lower thresholds for expressing dissatisfaction with marriage. This is further evidence of changing cultural expectations. Net of these effects, complete economic dependency reduces the husband's complaints. Full or near equality in incomes mitigates disagreements, showing that husbands also perceive a state of equality as more harmonious. All of this again suggests complex negotiation processes between husbands and wives involving both bargaining and cultural expectations.

Women's special situation in dual-career families also shaped their pattern of disagreements with husbands. In the 1991 survey, women could mention as many as three specific areas of disagreement. The most common areas were disagreements over children (46%), chores (34%), and income (17%).[32] The pattern of disagreements is not precisely the same as with complaints (Fig. 10.10). Instead of diminishing disagreements, more help by the husband at home has just the opposite effect. The reason, we suspect, is that when wives and husbands share more tasks around the home, there are more chances to disagree on how to cook the food, wash the clothes, or tend the children. Another differing pattern is that instead of increasing disagreement, education reduces disagreement over things such as income. This may be because education gives couples cultural tools to reduce conflict. Youth both reduces disagreements over children (more energy?) and increases disagreements over income. Except for these partially differing, and largely plausible patterns, the pattern of results is much the same as for complaints.

For wives, increased burdens such as tending young children, long hours in taking care of things around the home, and poor health all increase disagreements with husbands (Fig. 10.10). Except at the equal-

31. Wives' work on chores helps mitigate these burdens. The wife's and husband's home hours effects are statistically different from one another at $p < .05$.
32. This percentage order is the same order as that of potential responses listed in the questionnaire, which probably influenced responses. Since it is the patterning of responses rather than their absolute level that is of greatest concern, we do not find this probable "interview design" effect disturbing. Chore conflicts also rank second (21%) after child conflicts (34%) in the 1993 family survey (Shen and Yang 1995, pp. 360, 365). In the 1989–90 sex survey, chore conflicts rank fourth (9%) after children, daily affairs, and personality conflicts (Liu 1992, p. 563).

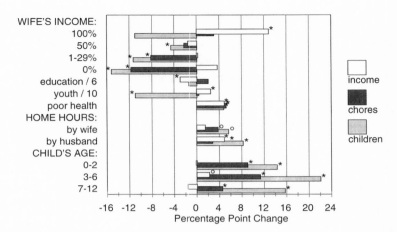

Figure 10.10 Wife's reports of disagreements by background characteristics. Notes: Percentage point changes derived from three separate probit analyses. High values indicate a higher probability of disagreeing over a specific issue. Reported effects of 0, 1–29, 50, and 100 percent of income are in comparison with all intermediate percentages. Observations number 4,210. (*) $p < .05$; (°) $p < .10$. Source: 1991 Women's Survey, Urban Sample.

ity point of 50 percent, more income increases assertiveness and conflict. Economic dependency, with incomes less than 30 percent of total income, reduces assertiveness and conflict. At the very top end, wives making all the family income have conflictual relations with their husbands over income. Thus, again, these patterns are consistent with an account that emphasizes both the problems of a dual burden of work without and within the home and the opportunities of a new willingness to speak out about these burdens as women continue to work and gain more resources compared with their husbands.

Sexual Satisfaction

More evidence for changing cultural frames is increased expectation of sexual fulfillment in marriage, especially for women (Jankowiak 1993, p. 234). Consistent with the increasing emphasis on romance, sexual behavior is again a publicly accepted topic, supported in part by letters-to-the-editor columns, call-in talk shows, and newly published advice manuals (e.g., Ruan 1991). A 1989–90 survey of couples reports an increasing acceptance of the ideal of sexual satisfaction for both husbands and wives, particularly among those who are young, more educated, and in higher-status, white-collar occupations (Liu 1992, pp. 309, 410). Reported frequencies of sexual intercourse in marriage seem not that different from American studies (Laumann et al. 1994). Nevertheless, tight housing conditions, with many people sharing the same room or bed and with thin walls between rooms and apartments, limits full expression of new ideals.[33] One result is that extensiveness of reported foreplay and duration of intercourse seems shorter in China than in the United States.[34] For women, frequency of orgasm is similar in the two societies – about one-fourth frequently or always experience orgasm during intercourse. For men, orgasm is more frequent in the United States than in China – three-fourths versus one-half usually or always experience orgasm. In reported sexual satisfaction, U.S. husbands and wives report comparable levels of extreme satisfaction (about 40%), while in China the levels of extreme satisfaction diverge (29% for males vs. 17% for females). Again, the most important factor in this seeming convergence of ideals of sexual fulfillment is the market economy, which has worked through the media to propagate new ideals of sexual satisfaction, many of which are directly translated from Western sources, including Alfred Kinsey. Levels of wealth have not risen to the point, however, that these ideals can be put into practice in the crowded housing conditions in which many Chinese couples find themselves.

Divorce

Our final question is whether all the trends listed so far lead to a higher probability of divorce. When writing about rising divorce in European socialist societies and developed market societies, scholars offer a variety

33. In the 1989–90 sex survey, 47 percent had children or other family members sleeping in the same room with the married couple. Only 29 percent reported good sound insulation between their room and adjoining rooms, and 14 percent reported poor sound insulation. Sexual satisfaction was more affected by sound insulation than by children in the same room (Liu 1992, pp. 478–85). Also see Jankowiak (1993, p. 231) on China, and du Plessix Gray (1990, p. 73) for the same problem in Russian housing.
34. In China, half report no more than five minutes' foreplay. Though not precisely comparable, so few (16%) of U.S. couples report less than fifteen minutes' total duration of last intercourse that duration must be considerably longer in the United States.

of explanations. Consistent with the bargaining perspective is the idea that socialist societies accelerate the tendencies toward lower birth rates and women's work in ways that free women from family dependency and give them financial autonomy and the ability to abandon tortured marital relationships. These explanations are consistent with explanations of how women's work and equality promote divorce in market societies (e.g., Cherlin 1992; Edwards et al. 1992). A complementary line of bargaining explanation suggests that divorce increases when spouses offer fewer advantages. Those advantages decline when men and women have similar rather than complementary roles (Becker 1981) or when males cannot gain stable employment – the typical ghetto problem in the United States (Wilson 1987; Oppenheimer 1988). The issue is whether similar trends are appearing in China. For a long time, divorce was highly constrained in China by extensive legal barriers that tied couples to relationships (e.g., Whyte and Parish 1984). However, since the new marriage law of 1980, rules for divorce have been liberalized, the right to divorce has been promoted in the media, and divorces have begun to increase.

Though divorce is driven by substantial problems within relationships, changing cultural frames have undoubtedly played a role in the increase in divorce rates. These changes appear in statistics on the acceptability of divorce. In 1991, when presented with the question of what a couple should do when they were emotionally incompatible, 84 percent of young wives said the couple should divorce or separate. Even among older wives, 67 percent said the couple should divorce or separate.[35] In short, across all age groups, most people thought divorce or separation was an appropriate response.

Similarly, in the 1992 Urban Survey when presented with separate questions about whether a child, wife, and husband would benefit or suffer from divorce, the percentage saying a wife or husband would benefit was sharply higher among the young. Doubts about the consequences for children remained high even among young respondents. But for adults, there was much more confidence in beneficial results of

---

35. Men gave similar responses (Sha, Xiong, and Gao 1994, p. 374). Though potentially biased by a general East Asian tendency to acquiesce to any opinion, taken at face value, Chinese were more approving of divorce than American respondents, only 47 percent of whom approved and 21 percent of whom were indifferent on the issue of whether divorce was the best solution when a couple could not seem to work out their marriage problems (Davis and Smith 1994, p. 591).

divorce. Besides the percentage saying benefits would be positive, the percent saying the benefits were uncertain doubled from about 10 to about 20 percent. Thus, among the youngest respondents opinion had sharply changed. By the early 1990s, two-thirds of all young people – who were the most likely to divorce – either thought divorce could have beneficial effects for the adults involved or were uncertain about whether the effects would be positive or negative. In short, opinion had radically changed. In the past, pressure for staying married supported an official policy of keeping couples together. But by the 1990s, this community pressure had weakened significantly, following a reversal in government policy and propaganda.[36] Socialist institutions and ideals seem to have laid the groundwork for this change, although administrative controls delayed their expression in behavior.

Divorce rates have shot up with the relaxation of these controls. Nationwide, including both urban and rural populations, divorce was previously quite rare.[37] In 1980, for every 1,000 total population, there were only .35 divorces. By 1996, this rate had more than doubled to .82. This implies that about 10 percent of all marriages could eventually end in divorce. In cities, of course, rates were much higher. In Beijing and Shanghai, for example, the 1996 divorce rate per 1,000 population was about 1.7, implying that about one-fifth of all marriages could end in divorce.[38] Though unexceptional by U.S. and Northern European standards, these rates are exceptional by developing country standards. The average non-Muslim country at China's level of development has a divorce rate of .15 per 1,000 population (United Nations 1991; Goode

36. The weakening was most rapid among women, the educated, and those in big cities such as Shanghai and Beijing (details not shown). For comparison, in the United States, people are not much more likely to say that a divorce is good (57%) or of uncertain benefit (24%) for the wife. U.S. residents, however, are much more likely to say that when a marriage is in trouble divorce benefits the child (Davis and Smith 1994, p. 586).

37. More precisely, divorce was rare in the late 1950s and then again in the late 1960s through the 1970s. In urban areas, divorce was even more common than today when the new 1950 marriage law and marriage law campaigns encouraged couples to escape marriages arranged before 1949. And there was an uptick in divorce in the early 1960s. For historical summaries, see PRI (1987, p. 504), Meijer (1971), and Xu (1994a).

38. SSB (1997, pp. 739–40). Note that we use not the yearbook figure of number of people divorcing but the more common divorces per 1,000 population. For unknown reasons, divorce was also very common in the northeast (Manchuria). And, in common with a pattern elsewhere in the world, divorce was common in Muslim-dominated provinces such as Xinjiang, Ningxia, and Qinghai.

1993; Parish 1995). Thus, China, along with other socialist societies, now has a relatively high divorce rate.

The bargaining perspective is also supported by several other patterns in divorce and remarriage. Consistent with the increasing status of women, women file for perhaps two-thirds of all divorces.[39] And in most regions, women also remarry at least as quickly as men.[40] Reputed reasons for males not remarrying any more quickly include the high level of male wedding expenditures that make remarriage too costly and the more frequent descent of males into drink, gambling, and other social maladies that make them unfit mates (Xu 1994a). Or, in short, if this analysis is correct, Chinese men are repeating patterns found among Russian men (Lapidus 1978; du Plessix Gray 1990). Also, consistent with the comparison-shopping opportunities provided by female work, extra-marital affairs are a frequent complaint in court cases, at least by husbands against wives. Also, consistent with aggression by frustrated, underachieving men, physical abuse is a common complaint by women in divorce cases (Xu 1994a).[41]

DISCUSSION AND CONCLUSION

We began the chapter with two issues: whether an attention to bargaining or cultural frames provided the best purchase on gender and family behavior, and whether socialist and market systems had systematic consequences for family life. Let us consider each issue in turn.

39. The percentage of applications by women varies from a high of 89 percent in the Northeast (Manchuria), where divorce rates are high, to a more common figure of 60 to 70 percent in the major cities (Liu 1992, p. 539; Zhou 1992, p. 62).
40. The only exceptions are three Muslim provinces (Xinjiang, Ningxia, and Qinghai), where men are still greatly advantaged in remarriage. Men are also slightly advantaged in the south-central provinces of Hubei, Hunan, and Guangdong. Everywhere else, women and men remarry about in proportion to the overall sex ratio, except that on the east coast women are advantaged in Shanghai City and the three provinces of Jiangsu, Zhejiang, and Shandong (PRI 1993. p. 36).
41. In the 1993 seven-city study of families, 15 percent report physical blows, with husbands contributing 11 percent to this total (Shen and Yang 1995, p. 361). In another Shanghai study, almost one-fifth report blows (Xu 1995). These percentages are less than in American results, where one-fourth report blows sometime during the married couple's history (Straus et al. 1980) – though questionable wording may have contributed to some difference in results.

Bargaining and Culture

There are ample examples of the influence of cultural frames, both old and new. Let us focus on family form, chores, and marital relations.

Family Form. Much as in the rest of East Asia, grandparents continue to reside with sons. This intergenerational contract continues to hold, reflecting a pragmatic bargain that retains its usefulness to families. In China, with more ample pensions, some of the impetus toward coresidence is weakened. Nevertheless, half of today's elderly mothers still have no pensions, and old age homes are scarce. Long-term care of the elderly infirm remains familized rather than institutionalized. And, in turn, dual-career parents need elderly grandparents to help with shopping, cooking, and child care. The most perplexing thing about continued grandparent coresidence is that it is with sons, despite some perceived practical advantages of daughters dealing with their own mothers. This shows that even the most fundamental family bargains are mediated by durable cultural categories. In time, as the one-child generation comes of age, and couples have two sets of parents to take care of without sharing their responsibility with siblings, urban China will provide the social laboratory for testing new arrangements for caring for aging parents and also testing the flexibility and durability of the cultural frames on which this intergenerational bargain is based.

Chores and Marital Relations. There is also ample evidence of the role of traditional cultural frames in shaping chores. Even when husbands approach wives in the amount of work done around the home, husbands never completely catch up with women. Also, when it comes to complaints about one's spouse, men gladly accept the dominant position – which is consistent with the traditional practice of women marrying up and men marrying down. Women complain when this pattern is reversed.

Despite these cultural continuities, the most striking thing about the Chinese data on chores, decision making, and complaints is the considerable responsiveness of men to women's increasing incomes. The data on household chores and purchasing decisions show that women with more of the family income can strike better bargains with their husbands

in housework and household purchasing decisions. The data on complaints suggest that women with more resources are more assertive.

Chinese housework patterns are perhaps best understood as reflecting
a process of bargaining against variable resources, but a bargain that is
judged against a norm of a statistically and culturally "typical" modern
urban Chinese family: both husband and wife working, both earning
roughly equal incomes, and both contributing to household labor, at
levels less equal than their incomes, but more equal than in most industrial societies. This suggests a process by which the norms governing the
household division of labor in China have gradually changed to match
the relative equality of income. Perhaps we can conclude from this discussion that changes in the family are most likely to occur when these
mechanisms work in the same direction, as they did during the early
reform period in which bargaining, cultural frames, socialist institutions,
and the market all produced conditions conducive to more equal sharing
of housework between men and women (equal incomes, ideas of gender
equality, socialized child-care facilities, more appliances). This may
explain the relatively high levels of equality we see in China, despite very
deep patriarchal traditions (which are still evident in neighboring Hong
Kong and Japan) (Ma et al. 1992; Liu 1995a).

Socialist and Market Systems

Our second issue in the chapter was whether socialist and market
systems had systematic social consequences. There are two answers to
this question. One is that socialism had many consequences for women,
and that in particular socialism increased the bargaining power of
women within the home. The second answer is that China is experiencing multiple transitions. This helps explain the confusing melee of public
discourse on the developments in the Chinese family, with which we
began this chapter. One way of looking at these divergent tales is to recognize that China is perhaps unique in undergoing two simultaneous
macroeconomic processes we are familiar with in different regions of the
world economy. One is the buildup and then slow collapse of state socialist institutions that we have observed in Eastern Europe. Although
socialism brought many benefits to women that are still important today
(education, employment, etc.), the dissolution of the Chinese state
economy may now be bringing many of the same family problems to

China that we saw in the former Soviet Union, including despondent middle-aged husbands and spousal abuse. This may explain popular concerns about the status of husbands and the dissatisfaction wives report in their husbands' economic performances.

On the other hand we are also seeing the social patterns more typical of the emergence of another "Asian tiger," patterns evocative more of changes in Taiwan twenty years ago than of Eastern Europe today. These are the cultural and social consequences of rapid economic growth and bubble economics. Occasionally these consequences reinforce those of the collapse of socialist institutions. Both processes result in increased individual autonomy for women and youth and in increased divorce rates. Furthermore, the "economic miracle" syndrome in Asia has typically brought with it an emphasis on male economic performance that exacerbates the status anxieties of husbands still working in inefficient state industries. On the other hand, the market provides a growth in white-collar and service jobs that keep women in the work force rather than send them back into the home as would be expected from the collapse of socialist institutions. Young educated women have especially benefited from these new opportunities and can demand more from their husbands. Families benefit from increased standards of living. A more companionate nuclear family may be the long-term result, but the immediate consequence is the continuing reliance of the poor elderly on their increasingly affluent offspring. The consumer society has brought with it new practices of dating, but also reinforced older "commodifiable" traditions such as the Chinese wedding banquet. The *nouveau riche* culture of money carries over into these marriage practices whereby weddings have become venues for ostentatious consumption. Finally, the increased commodification and exploitation of sexuality has been a public component of the East Asian economic miracle economies, and in China we have described several consequences in the increased emphasis on sexual fulfillment in marriage and in more sexual possibilities both before and outside marriage. We have not had the space or data to describe some of the negative consequences of these patterns, which include widespread commercial sex and the commercial exploitation of sexual imagery, particularly of women. These are patterns that may have negative consequences for women and children, particularly those drawn into the sex industry.

The impact of these macrosocial processes on the family is predictably mixed. The market economy has brought women more opportunities for individual fulfillment, but to some extent has made relationships with men seem more problematic or less satisfying. As described in the preceding chapter, improved education, work, and income have many benefits for women by increasing their options. Today urban women in the formal sector have a much better chance of supporting themselves on their own, and much greater security in the face of family mishaps such as the loss of a husband through death or divorce. The market, by increasing the space for autonomous socializing and providing resources and cultural frames for articulating dissatisfaction, has allowed family members more autonomy in challenging traditional patterns, allowing the open expression of dissatisfaction and increased divorce, but also creating pressures for more mutually beneficial and mutually satisfying relationships.

Part IV

COMPARISONS AND CONCLUSIONS

11

Taiwan and China Compared

THROUGHOUT this book, we have examined the consequences of moving from a redistributionist communitarian socialist contract to a more individualist market social contract. Most of this examination has been through comparisons across time or among subgroups within China – for example, pre- and postreform behavior, people near and far from the rapidly developing coastal sunbelt, and producers (managers, entrepreneurs) and redistributors (administrators). In this chapter, we want to extend these comparisons.

Taiwan provides a final example of how society can look very different under a market-based social contract. It also provides some indication of China's future under the new market social contract. To some extent, Taiwan provides a controlled experiment. It shares a common cultural origin, and to a limited extent a common Leninist political origin in the organization of the Nationalist (KMT) state. Although its market-based, export-led growth has produced much higher levels of prosperity and social outcomes that now contrast with China, this growth arguably could presage China's subsequent development. Though now with a per capita gross national product that is twenty-eight times China's current level, Taiwan arrived at this level only recently, as its labor force moved in four short decades from being 60 percent agricultural in 1952 to being only 11 percent agricultural in 1995. This rapid transformation was created by rates of economic growth that China is now beginning to emulate.[1]

---

1. The debate between situational and systemic factors provides competing explanations for the economic gap between the two societies. One side of the debate sees Taiwan's strength as compared with the mainland in systemic factors, such as a capitalist economy, ideological diversity, and political pluralism (Friedman 1962; Metzger & Myers 1991), while the other view sees it in situational factors, such as the island's small scale, the positive legacy of a half-century of Japanese colonial rule, and a high per capita level of U.S. aid (Cohen 1991).

The comparison with Taiwan provides us a chance to revisit many of the conclusions of the previous chapters. In those chapters, we suggested that the socialist contract had a host of systematic consequences for people's lives – including patterns of education, jobs, income, political participation, and gender equality. Conversely, we suggested that a return to a market social contract would reverse many of the socialist patterns, leading to new sets of education, job, income, political, and gender opportunities, and many differences in popular responses to these new opportunities. If these suggestions are correct, then Taiwan, epitomizing a particular market path, should be very different from China. To set the stage for this comparison, let us begin with a little history.

HISTORICAL DEVELOPMENT

Until it became a colony of Japan from 1895 to the end of the World War II, the island of Taiwan was one of China's frontier provinces. Originally from the nearby Minnan- and Hakka-speaking regions of China, the numerically dominant Taiwanese population represents one of many minor cultural variants of larger Chinese civilization.[2] To some extent this shared civilization was strengthened after 1945, when the Japanese returned Taiwan to China, and even more so after 1949 when the Nationalist Kuomintang (KMT) party under Chiang Kai-shek fled to Taiwan. The Nationalists brought an accompanying influx of mainlanders from various parts of China. Coming to constitute about one-sixth of the total population, and reinforced by an educational system that emphasized Mandarin as the sole language of instruction (just as in China) and textbooks that celebrated traditional Confucian values, these new settler elites attempted to create a uniform "national" Chinese culture with many traditional overtones (e.g., Wilson 1970). Supported by both customary practice in Taiwan and a continuing school and media emphasis on traditional Confucian values regarding respect for the family, the elderly, and authority, much that was traditional persisted for a time. Given the extremely rapid increase in urbanization, education, and media exposure, though, things soon began to change.[3]

2. Of course, movements to increase local cultural pride and ethnic political mobilization can sometimes enlarge on these differences, producing bitter scholarly and popular debate about national and cultural identity (e.g., Murray and Hong 1994).
3. E.g., Hsiao, Cheng, and Chan (1989) and Thornton and Lin (1994).

In the economy, Taiwan's early path of development presages some aspects of China's current development. Partially because so many Japanese-owned enterprises had been taken back from the Japanese, publicly owned (*gongying*) state enterprises dominated the Taiwanese economy in the 1950s. But with the switch to more laissez-faire policies and a switch to export-led development in the 1960s, the private sector began to outpace the public sector. This was not just any private sector, but one dominated by small informal enterprises, located initially in the countryside and run not by the previously favored 1949 immigrants from the mainland but by the original local population. In time, as these enterprises prospered, they increasingly moved to cities, overwhelming the formal sector. Though most enterprises remained very small, with frequent openings and closings and with high rates of mobility among work sites in the informal and small enterprise sector, a few firms got much larger and began to take on more formal characteristics (Lin 1995a). Nimbleness in production allowed the Taiwan economy to respond rapidly to changes in international market demand, thereby producing one of the highest economic growth rates in the world. As a result of this extremely rapid transformation of the economy, many people moved from farmer to urban worker and entrepreneur in a single generation. At the same time, even while supplying the vital oil, petrochemical, cement, and other products consumed by the informal, small-scale sector, the surviving state sector became less important in the total economy.[4]

With about a three-decade lag, China seems to be retracing several parts of this development path. Those parts include an initial emphasis on a formal sector dominated by state-owned enterprises controlled by an urban elite. In both China and Taiwan this initial state dominance was followed not so much by a selling off of the state sector – though both societies dispersed stock from some or all of the state sector – as by the growing up of a massive informal sector out of an initially excluded second-class native citizenry that began mostly in the countryside. What was different in Taiwan is that the "bamboo wall" penning people in the countryside never existed, so that urbanization and the growth of a vibrant private sector could occur much earlier and more smoothly.

---

4. E.g., Galenson (1979), Amsden (1985), Hamilton (1991), and Ranis (1992).

However, the initial pressures and processes of the transformation seem in some ways remarkably similar.[5]

Politically, Taiwan evolved only gradually toward a democratic system – again suggesting potential paths that China might follow. In part because of a 1920s shared history, when they collaborated in joint state-building efforts guided in part by advisers from the Soviet Union, both the Nationalists and the Communists adopted a Leninist-style one-party government. Even after retreating to Taiwan, one-party dominance continued under an episodically harsh martial law.[6] Despite the firm top-down control, supported by tightly controlled media in turn supported by a large security apparatus and large military, there were local village and township elections. In these local elections, the ruling Nationalist Party lost as much as 30 percent of all contests over the years. This provided the basis for a nascent opposition party. Finally, in 1986, the opposition that had been trained in the hothouse of local elections formally organized itself as the Democratic Progressive Party (DPP). Following the lifting of martial law in 1987, the number and freedom of the print media expanded rapidly. Electoral laws were methodically, if haltingly, relaxed. Popular elections were held for the national parliament. Televised legislative debates between the opposition DPP and the dominant Nationalists (KMT) heated up, involving at times a circus of fistfights before an island-wide audience. A host of betel-chewing radicals led local demonstrators in a year-round parade of special- and general-interest street protests before government offices. Calm in the midst of this storm of protest was maintained by an increasingly professionalized civil service, staffed at the top by American trained Ph.D.s and in the localities by a host of college- and high school-educated personnel selected and promoted through uniform civil service exams.[7] Finally, in 1996,

5. For references to rural small-scale industrialization in Taiwan and China, see Blank and Parish (1990) and Parish (1994). On the rapid movement out of the countryside, even when rural industrialization was successful and the urban–rural income gap modest, see Speare, Liu, and Tsay (1988).

6. On the early consequences of this one-party hegemony for political socialization in both schools and the family, see Wilson (1970). Samuel Huntington (1991) refers to this East Asian-style one-party, strong bureaucratic, paternalistic government as a Confucian Leninist state.

7. The critic will be quick to note the loopholes in the system, including special privileges for people who transfer in laterally from the military, for those with KMT party seniority, and for those with family and other special connections. For histories of social and political developments, see Gold (1986), Moody (1992), and Tang (1996b).

Taiwan had its first American-style presidential campaign and the first popularly elected president.[8]

In China, of course, there is some distance to go in many of these developments. The shift to an educated, professionalized civil service began only in the 1980s. Election to offices above the urban district level remain indirect, and elections below that level often remain minimally contested and often involve disinterested and involuntary voting. All of this we have discussed. Nevertheless, there are similarities. Although voters had limited choices, contested elections for village leaders were held. Candidates were competing for votes quite intensively (IRI 1994). It was common for candidates to host dinners for villagers or even offer cash to buy votes (Shi 1996). In Taiwan as well, open voting for competing candidates began from below, in elections for local office. Historically in Taiwan many candidates were picked because of family and other connections, using clientelist networks rather than universalistic principles.[9] The tantalizing possibility is that even this type of flawed democracy provides a training and organizing ground for later, more openly competitive politics.

One can think of dozens of objections to this kind of broad comparison. It ignores hordes of details. Nevertheless, if one is to concede at least some heuristic value to the comparison, in survey data for urban China and urban Taiwan, we are capturing two societies with similar cultures at very different points of a shared historical trajectory. By turning to a more open, export-oriented development path with a considerable dependence on a marketized informal sector, China is at the beginning steps of that process. Much as in Taiwan of the 1960s, most of China's informal sector remains in small towns and villages, and thus out of the purview of our urban, formal sector samples. Our comparison, thus, is between a Chinese urban society dominated by a largely formal, only partially marketized state sector, with many traditional socialist legacies still in place, and a Taiwan urban society that is dominated by a highly fluid, highly marketized private sector, still consisting of many small and informal economic activities. In the comparisons of political culture, we are also comparing a China that is at only the early stages of profes-

---

8. See Chao and Myers (1998) for a comprehensive discussion of the democratization process in Taiwan.
9. E.g., Wu (1987) and Liu (1991).

sionalization and liberalization and a Taiwan in the midst of a raucous transformation to a free-wheeling, open democracy. Economically, of course, despite rapid development in the early 1990s, Chinese cities remained at least two decades behind cities in Taiwan. Thus, as in most natural experiments, this is a flawed comparison. Still, the comparison is better than many, involving as it does a shared culture, shared initial political form, and shared beginning emphasis on state industry. If ideas about strong systemic differences between market and planned societies are correct, then, many of those differences should be found in comparisons between Taiwan and China in the early 1990s.

Why there should be systematic differences between Taiwan and China, despite the shared origins, should be obvious by now. Thus, let us move directly to specific substantive areas, with an emphasis on material conditions and reactions to these conditions, political participation, and gender. The material for these comparisons comes from several previous data sources, the 1990 Chinese census, the 1988 CHIP survey, and the 1992 China urban survey. In addition, for Taiwan, we use the 1990 census, the 1990 labor force survey, the 1990 Social Change Survey, and the 1989 Taiwan Women and Family Survey (see Appendix B for details). These all provide society-wide data that allow systematic comparison between the two locales.

MATERIAL REWARDS

We begin with the types of material rewards that help shape people's reactions to their life situations. With an emphasis on jobs and income, this analysis repeats some of the themes about life chances and redistributor/producer class interests from Chapters 3 and 4. Over the last thirty years, life chances in Taiwan were much more fluid and individualistic than in China. Much as in China, education opportunities increased rapidly for both males and females (census figures). With the higher levels of urbanization and higher gross national product per capita, urban education levels in Taiwan were higher than in comparable Chinese cities. Thus, both males and females in Taiwan were well qualified to assume the new jobs in manufacturing and other activities that blossomed with an expanding, export-led economy. Much of this education growth also applied to people from the countryside. With no artificial barriers between city and countryside, farmers and the sons of farmers flooded into cities to take new jobs. By 1990, sons of farmers constituted almost half of all manual workers in Taiwan (1990 Social Change Survey). Thus, this was a highly fluid system, quite different from Chinese cities which until the 1980s kept farmers out of city, with the result that less than half of the working class in Chinese cities came from a farm background. Instead, in China, most manual workers were simply repeating their father's status (see Chapter 3). Now, of course, things are beginning to change, and in time Chinese cities will begin to look more similar to those in Taiwan. But as of the 1990s, there was still less fluidity in lower-status occupations in China.

Taiwan also seemed more fluid in mobility across sectors. Given the paucity of large firms with established internal labor markets, most people could not begin low in an organization and then gradually move up the career ladder of the same or related firms. One result was considerable midcareer movement out of firms into self-employment and entrepreneurship (1989 Taiwan Women and Family Survey). Again, this is a pattern toward which Chinese cities may be moving. The growth of the small self-employed (*geti*) and private (*siying*) sector is now becoming more acceptable (1995 Private Enterprise Survey). However, as of the early 1990s, most people were still responding to an occupational system that was less individualist, and which tied people much more to work units and supervisors than did the employment system in Taiwan. Our chapter on workers suggested that personalistic dependency caused worker dissatisfaction and the potential for protest.

Blocked Mobility

Macrolevel data on patterns of employment are consistent with the initial impressions of the two very different employment systems. We begin with the data for Taiwan (Fig. 11.1). In Taiwan, there are some interesting subpatterns among different age groups. There are very few people in administrative and managerial positions, and most of these positions are achieved in the middle to later part of one's career. Clerical work is more common among the young. Sales and service work are more common among the old, for two reasons – among the young, education provides better jobs, and among the old there is midcareer movement into small family-owned shops and workshops.

The more significant pattern in the figure, however, is the considerable

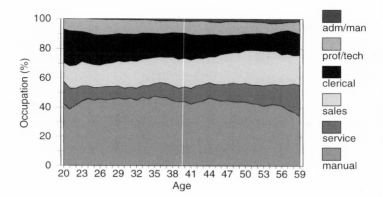

Figure 11.1 Occupation by age, Taiwan 1990. Notes: Nonfarm occupations, including administrative/managerial, professional/technical, clerical, sales, service, and manual work. Islandwide data. Observations number 20,298. Source: May 1990 Labor Force Survey.

constancy in the manual/nonmanual divide in occupations. From the very start of a person's career, over half (55%) of new job entrants begin in white-collar jobs. Seniority has only modest influence on movement across these gross occupational divides. The split between blue- and white-collar remains largely constant, until blue-collar workers begin to leave the labor force in their late fifties. This Taiwan data is consistent with a labor force that puts less emphasis on seniority and more on education and other achieved characteristics. Or, broadly speaking, in labor market characteristics, while China is similar to Japan, with considerable mobility being internal within large work units or economic systems, Taiwan is similar to the United States, with considerable mobility being interfirm among work units.

Comparisons of other societies' data with Chinese data is difficult. In the Chinese data, the upper white-collar occupations (administrator/ manager, professional/technical, and clerical) are classified in unusual ways, leading to a bloating of the first two categories and understatement of the final category (see Appendix A1). Nevertheless, the patterns are sufficiently strong for us to tentatively draw the following conclusions (Fig. 11.2). Much as we suggested earlier, administrators and managers remain abundant compared with comparable groups in Taiwan. The

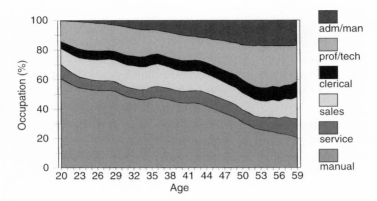

Figure 11.2 Occupation by age, China 1995. Notes: For administrative/manage-
rial, professional/technical, clerical, sales, service, and manual work. National
data. Farmers excluded. Source: 1995 Census (Census Office 1997).

efforts to trim the size of the bureaucracy in firms and government still
left many administrators and managers in place (see Chapter 7). Also,
despite a recent growth in sales and service jobs, these jobs remained
scarce compared with Taiwan, which itself did not have as many as some
other developing countries (see Fig. 3.7). The Nationalist's socialist policy
of disparaging commerce and promoting manufacturing continued to
have a lingering effect. Finally, and this is potentially the most important,
over half of all workers began their careers in blue-collar, manual work
(55%). It is only with seniority that people could escape their blue-collar
situation. Despite the partial recovery from the Cultural Revolution
period, when over 60 percent began as blue-collar workers, this work
remained a common destiny for many young people (see Fig. 3.6).

These patterns contribute to very striking differences between Taiwan
and China (Figs. 11.1 and 11.2). While life chances remain largely constant by seniority in Taiwan, in China life chances vary greatly by seniority.[10] Whether this makes one feel better or worse about one's job and

10. The pattern is more than just a quirk of the 1995 census, and it is not just a cohort
    effect – i.e., not just better jobs for people who entered the labor market in more lush
    times, though it is partly that (see Fig. 3.7, bottom right panel). The pattern was also
    present in the 1982 census, and it is present in samples that are restricted to urban areas
    (such as the urban half of the 1988 CHIP survey). One is cautioned that after about

life situation is not clear. In Taiwan, because of few chances to move up within large organizations, many people exit jobs in small family-owned enterprises for life as entrepreneurs. In China, in time, if one remains in the good graces of one's superior, one can move up the organizational ladder or, with a proper set of recommendations, to another large organization in the same line of work.

The Chinese pattern could lead to considerable dissatisfaction. Our study of workers suggested that workers did not like being dependent on supervisors (Chapter 6). Moreover, young workers aren't like they used to be. It is true that administrators and managers became more educated in recent years (Chapter 7). However, workers also became educated, and given the compression of education levels in urban China, the gap in education between young worker and older supervisor is increasingly small (see Chapter 3 on trends). By the early 1990s, when compared with administrators and managers twenty years older, younger workers lagged in education by only two-thirds of a single year.[11] This meant that there were many workers who equaled their supervisors in education. One could imagine that this produced many "young turks" who begrudged their supervisors and the larger bureaucratic establishment. It would also be consistent with the pattern we have observed so far, of a sharp divide in participatory patterns – with a group of well-connected, older people who work through established channels and a group of more poorly connected but well-educated younger workers who contemplate more direct action outside established channels (see Chapters 6 and 8). The bifurcation between the young, educated, and waiting for advancement and those in administration and management seems sharper in China than in Taiwan. Whether this leads to frustration is a topic that we return to later.

Income

Our earlier discussion of income patterns considered issues of bargaining and the emergence of patterns of reward that were more consist-

age 45, the decline in manual jobs is exaggerated by first women and then men taking early retirement from those jobs.

11. 1992 China Urban Survey, wherein manual workers aged 25 to 34 average 10.3 years of education and administrators aged 45 to 54 average 11.0 years of education (weighted).

ent with a market-based economy (Chapter 4). We found some evidence of both patterns. On the market transition side of the transition/bargaining debate, younger workers were making more gains as a result of more human capital (education), managers were gaining on administrators, and economic firms had higher rewards than government work units. On the bargaining side, higher-level work units and party members were paid more. Fitting neither side of the debate, people in public organizations (health, education, etc.) made major gains after 1993. In addition, we noted that most of the advantages either by type of organization or by occupation were modest in comparison with those in market societies. Thus, while conceding that bargaining could continue for long periods (as it does in "actually existing" market societies) and that signs of market-based rewards were beginning to occur, we suggested that much of the debate was undertheorized.

Here we want to add materials to the rethinking of the issues around this debate. Taiwan is an important case. Except for the publicly owned upstream firms in cement, petroleum, metals, and so on, Taiwan is an economy of highly competitive small firms. There are few areas where a "core" sector can wall itself off from competition in ways that would permit paying workers above the prevailing wage. One sign of that competition is the low returns to education, which at a modest 4 percent for each year of education are among the lowest observed in market societies. Guthrie (2000) suggests that much of the empirical exploration of market transition is wrong-headed because it assumes greater market competition will increase incomes for producers. If competition is truly intense, Guthrie suggests, the result of more competition may well be to depress incomes. If this is indeed what occurs, then Taiwan, with few protected sectors, should have only modest incomes for producers closest to the market.

For this comparison we used large surveys from around 1990. The income is expressed in log form, allowing comparison across societies. The resulting coefficients can be read as essentially percentage effects. For comparison, we consider economic enterprises in China to be similar to public enterprises in Taiwan, and public organizations in China to be similar to education, health, and related organizations in Taiwan. The small private sector in China, consisting in 1988 mostly of small, family-owned stores, restaurants, and small workshops, is similar to the self-

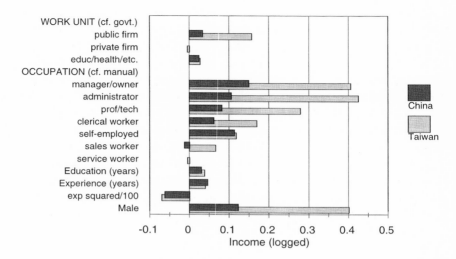

Figure 11.3 Income determinants, China, 1988, and Taiwan, 1990. Notes and source: OLS regression coefficients based on 16,525 observations from the city portion of the May 1990 Taiwan Labor Force Survey ($R^2 = .45$) and 17,669 observations from the 1988 Urban CHIP Survey, China ($R^2 = .44$). Except for Chinese sales work and Taiwan service work, private firms, and education, health, etc. organizations, all coefficients statistically significant at $p < .05$. Coefficients not shown include average income level of city and missing work unit status (China) and hours of work (Taiwan). See text for additional notes.

employed in Taiwan. In Taiwan, owner-managers and hired managers are similar to managers in China (Fig. 11.3)

What then do the comparative patterns reveal? First, true to the image of Taiwan as a highly competitive economy, wages across different types of work units are quite even (Fig. 11.3, top portion). Except for large, publicly owned upstream firms, income across sectors is quite similar. This suggests, first, that bargaining occurs. As the critics in Taiwan's opposition party suggest, large public firms may be inefficient, paying salaries above market rates. Indeed, relatively speaking, these privileged firms pay even more than comparable firms in China. Private firms, in contrast, pay no more than the government and marginally less than education, health, and other types of organizations. Thus, an active market promotes not higher incomes for those close to production, but (with the exception of public firms) the same income as everyone else. This is consistent with the Guthrie caution about expecting higher incomes among people close to the market in a truly competitive economy. The results are also consistent with our suggestion that most of the gains to bargaining are modest in China. Compared with public firms in Taiwan, publicly owned enterprises in China do not pay very much.

Second, compared with manual workers, upper white-collar workers in Taiwan are well paid, particularly in comparison with similar workers in China.[12] All this leads to several conclusions. First, as already suggested, much of the prior research on income differences in China, regardless of whether taking the bargaining or market transition perspective, has been making a big fuss over a very small income gap. One is struck by how much of the old, egalitarian ethos remained through 1988. In urban China, upper white-collar workers continued to do only marginally better than blue-collar workers there. Despite complaints from workers (Chapter 6), in urban areas, the workers' state had not disappeared. Conversely, among upper white-collar workers who increasingly met or heard about their comparable workmates in Taiwan and elsewhere in East Asia, their modest position relative to blue-collar workers must have been increasingly galling in the late 1980s and early 1990s. More generally, the first conclusion that one is tempted to draw from these statistics is that neither bargaining nor market forces had much effect through the late 1980s. It was only in the early 1990s, with the resumption of rapid reform, that income inequalities and greater rewards for upper white-collar workers began to appear (Fig. 4.1).

Second, the producers/redistributors analogy for managers and administrators again fails us. Much as in Guthrie's suggestion for the homogenizing effects of an openly competitive market economy, managers and owners in Taiwan are marginally less successful than administrators. This is precisely the opposite of what a simple, binary producer/redistributor model would predict for highly marketized Taiwan. Thus, again, we need another test of market transition. Relative incomes alone will not do.

12. The exact figures in these comparisons vary depending on what else is considered in the analysis. If there is nothing else in the analysis – only occupation and not gender, education, experience, etc. – then the percentage advantages over manual labor still favor most upper white-collar occupations in Taiwan over those in China. Specifically, the Taiwan/China percentages are as follows: managers and owners (64/46), administrators (88/36), professional and technical (37/23), clerical workers (17/17). In the United States, the percentage advantages are more than double the Taiwan figures (see notes to Chapter 4).

Third, human capital continued to be rewarded differently in China. Income returns to education remained smaller in China, while returns to seniority remained larger. Thus, much as in the last graph on jobs by age, a major way people in Chinese cities got income increases was simply by being persistent. Seniority paid off in China to a greater extent than in Taiwan. In ten to twenty years of work, one's relative income advantage compared with a worker in Taiwan was ten to twenty percentage points higher in China. Thus, again, despite attempts to get people to retire earlier and to honor education credentials, one is struck by the persistence of a system that gave great reward to institutionalized promotion based on seniority.

Finally, males had a much greater advantage in Taiwan (Fig. 11.3). The coefficients translate into females making 89 percent as much as males in China, net of other influences – some of which would exaggerate the gender gap. In Taiwan, the coefficient translates into females making only 67 percent as much as men, net of other influences. Thus, again, the old egalitarian social contract that promised women more income advantages in China continued to have some effect. All of this is again consistent with our chapters on women's work and income.

In short, through the late 1980s and into the early 1990s, the labor markets in China and Taiwan continued to be very different. Those differences do not fit easy generalizations about the incomes of producers and redistributors. If anything, the Taiwan figures suggest that when it comes to bargaining, that state firms in China might come and take some lessons from managers of public firms in Taiwan. Or, more generally, the results suggest that the use of income differences to examine the speed of market transition has just about outrun its utility. We need more direct indicators of market competition in different portions of the labor force.

More significant, the comparative income figures and the figures on mobility and age suggest that upper-status workers in China are under-rewarded, while older, high-seniority workers in China are overrewarded. Moreover, we have inferred that workers in Chinese cities are more beholden to large organizations and to their superiors, in ways that could produce discontent – particularly among younger, more educated workers. In an economy of large organizations, workers will have less freedom to make adjustments based primarily on their own volition — which in turn could lead to more frustration. If these respective groups of workers are indeed using these kinds of standards to judge their economic and social success, then this should appear in comparisons of satisfaction with pay, economic opportunity, and general well-being. It is to this issue that we now turn.

In this section we revisit issues about responses to reform and the economy. In the earlier discussion, we suggested that strong class interests were at work. Even while being optimistic about their own life situations, people in upper white-collar jobs were more likely to want to accelerate the pace of reform and to complain about rates of pay and the inability of individuals to get ahead based on their own efforts (Chapter 5). The complaints were particularly intense among professionals and technicians. Professionals and technicians seemed to be aggrieved because they lacked direct access to channels of authority. Unfortunately, because we had no directly comparable data, we could not tell whether this whining is just part of the "naturally given" role of intellectuals in society or whether intellectuals in China were somehow more aggrieved – because of the Cultural Revolution and other political campaigns against them, or because the socialist system, which was supposed to be run by intellectuals, had not led them into the halls of power. We approach the problem of comparison by providing similiar survey items from Taiwan and China.

In addition, we want to examine the role of "generation." In China, different generations had very different experiences as they approached adulthood and entered the labor market. Those who came of age in the 1950s encountered an optimum situation. There were many posts to be filled, and few qualified people to fill them (Chapter 3). In contrast, during the Cultural Revolution decade when most people had to take blue-collar jobs, there were few good job opportunities, and even those that were available could be entered only after years in the countryside or in menial roles in factories.

A literature on early life experiences suggest that there should be lingering cohort effects for people who had these contrasting types of experiences. These include studies of the lasting impact of the Great Depression in the United States and of the relative affluence or poverty of times when people grow up (e.g., Elder 1974; Ingelhart 1990). Detecting these influences is problematic because they are confounded with age. Older people typically adjust their expectations downward, making the same old situation seem more acceptable than it once did. By comparing people of different cohorts in China and Taiwan, we adjust for some of the age effect. If the effect is primarily one of diminishing expectations with age, then the pattern of responses by cohort should be similar in the two societies. If early cohort experiences (and the current conditions for people of different age) are important, then intersocietal differences should emerge.

We consider the 1950s and early 1960s periods of rapid expansion and opportunity in China. Despite a downward dip in the Great Leap Forward, this was a time of rapid expansion and new job opportunities (see Chapter 3). In Taiwan, there were some of the same opportunities as the society rebuilt from the exit of the Japanese colonialists and the end of the Civil War. Thus, some of the 1950s spurt of opportunity that came from rebuilding a society was shared between the two societies. The next period diverged, however. In Taiwan, growth accelerated in the 1966–76 period, as export-led growth took off. This was the very time that labor market conditions deteriorated in China. Then, we consider the period of early reform, 1977–84, and late reform, 1985 and afterward. Comparisons are to the 1966–76 period.

In aggregate statistics on job and income success, it is difficult to discern any lasting impact of the Cultural Revolution period. One example is the statistics on current jobs held by people of different ages (Fig. 11.2). There is no clear downward dip for people who would have turned twenty and entered the labor market during the Cultural Revolution decade, except that there may be fewer professional and technical workers among this group (approximately the group aged 39 to 49 in 1995). Many of the effects could appear in attitudes, however. To examine attitude effects by cohort and class, we include cohort, current occupation, and gender in the analysis. Our scales are constructed by combining Taiwan and China samples and then doing the analysis across both societies. We report both the gross difference between the societies and the patterns among specific groups in each society.

Reasonable Income

Are the two societies entirely different worlds? Or, to amend a verbiage common in China, are these two societies of "one culture, but two

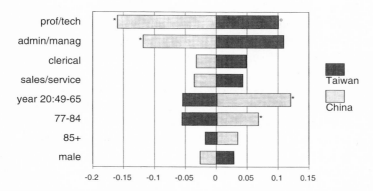

Figure 11.4 Is income reasonable relative to one's abilities? Notes: "Year 20" is the year respondent turned age twenty, when jobs were most likely to be secured. Years reported are compared with 1966–76, the Cultural Revolution decade in China and the decade of initial export-led growth in Taiwan. Occupations are compared with manual worker. Bottom scale shows proportion change co-efficients from a probit analysis of whether one's income is fair, coded 1 (fair) and 0 (not fair). Thus a coefficient of –.10 suggests that a person is ten percentage points more likely to think income fair. The overall average percent finding their income fair is 48 percent, and the Taiwan percent is 15 percent greater than in China ($p < .05$). (*) $p < .05$; (°) $p < .10$. Sources: 1990 Taiwan Social Change Survey; 1992 China Urban Survey.

systems"? If the answer is accurately reflected in responses to the question of whether one's income is reasonable given one's abilities, then it is clear. These are two diametrically opposed systems (Fig. 11.4). When a group answers high in Taiwan, then the same group answers low in China, and vice versa.

Overall, respondents in Taiwan are fifteen percentage points more likely to say that their income is reasonable. This provides an answer to the question we asked earlier, which was whether people find material rewards more satisfactory when they have ample freedom to move among jobs on an individualistic basis and when rewards at the start of the career were commensurate with rewards later on. The answer appears to be that they prefer the freedom of voluntaristic movement and opportunities for rewards early in the work career.

Second, there are distinct differences among subgroups as well. From income statistics, we suggested that white-collar workers in China might well perceive themselves as underpaid. This is clearly the case. Upper white-collar workers in Taiwan were generally happy with their pay. Upper white-collar workers in China in 1992 were distinctly unhappy with their pay. To them, the egalitarianism of the old redistributive system seemed unfair.

These perceptions were colored by early cohort experiences. This is not just an aging effect. Though statistically not significant, cohorts from earlier generations, now older, were less satisfied with income in Taiwan. In contrast, people who had grown up in the golden age of early socialism in China and who now enjoyed the benefits of seniority (Fig. 11.2) were twelve percentage points more likely to be pleased with their income – as well they should be. Again, this was not just an age effect, for compared with the Cultural Revolution generation, the 1977–84 early reform generation was more pleased with its income. The upturn in career opportunities caused greater income satisfaction. All this suggests that the geological layering of Chinese socialist history in labor markets continues to have a lingering effect on people's perception of their situations.

Economic Efficacy

Though in more muted fashion, the story of "two systems" is repeated in judgments of individual economic efficacy (see Chapter 5 and Appendix A5 for survey items). On a four-point scale, Taiwan respondents were .36 points more likely than Chinese respondents to say that individuals could succeed by their own efforts. This is, again, consistent with a society that is economically more open, where one is less beholden to superiors in large organizations and where people are less likely to perceive that one needs special connections to government officials who control access to scarce resources. In specific questions, the response patterns were as follows, with the higher percentage representing those from Taiwan who give the individualistic effort answer to the question "A person can succeed if they work hard" (64/72). "Family background is not essential for success" (48/63). Last, do you need special family connections to schools, job opportunities, financing, supplies to get ahead? When given a long list of possible causes for a person being poor, the respondent chose not luck or poor personal network connections but instead said he or she was lazy, dumb, had little education, or that there were other individualistic explanations (41/71).

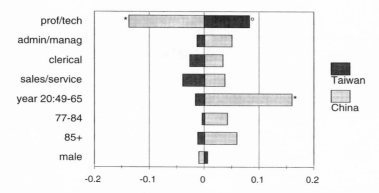

Figure 11.5 Economic efficacy by place. Notes and sources: OLS regression coefficients, with Taiwan being .36 ($p < .05$) more likely to agree with economic efficacy statements. Also see Fig. 11.4. (*) $p < .05$; (°) $p < .10$.

In addition to the overall differences between the two societies, professional and technical personnel in the two societies split on economic efficacy (Fig. 11.5). The elite group in Taiwan judged that a person could get ahead by individual effort. The comparable elite group in China made just the opposite judgment. Cohort effects also diverged. In Taiwan, cohort effects were nonexistent. In China, compared with the Cultural Revolution generation, everyone else thought individuals could get ahead by their own efforts. This opinion was particularly strong and significant among the generation that came of age in China's golden age of the 1950s and who by now had risen to positions of authority by dent of seniority.

Optimism

When asked not about income and success but instead about optimism concerning current conditions, the two societies were similar (see Chapter 5 for specific items). This is much as in our earlier analysis, where intellectuals and other white-collar workers were very critical of the pace of reform but then content with their life situations. Feelings of inadequate income are apparently assuaged by other kinds of rewards, including quality of work and beliefs that their lives are on an upward trajectory (Fig. 11.6). The other unstated point here, of course, is that the

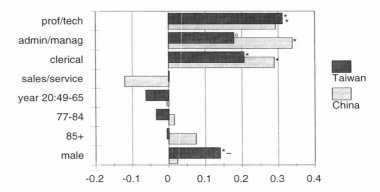

Figure 11.6 Hope about life. Notes and sources: Coefficients from OLS regression analysis. Taiwan is .14 points higher on the hope scale ($p < .05$). The constant is $-.24$. (*) $p < .05$; (°) $p < .10$. For China/Taiwan differences in magnitude of coefficients, ($\sim$) $p < .05$. Also see Fig. 11.4.

manual workers in the statistical comparison group were not very optimistic about their current situation. These are tendencies that are shared between the two societies. Upper white-collar workers in both societies are more optimistic than their manual and lower white-collar brethren.

There are two remaining differences between the two societies. One is that on the four-point optimism scale, people in Taiwan are a marginally .14 points more hopeful ($p < .05$). Thus, the greater openness and higher absolute incomes in Taiwan continue to have a modest effect on these types of "well-being" measures, even if the difference is not large. Finally, males in Taiwan are significantly more optimistic. This repeats our theme about greater gender equality in China. This is a part of the old socialist contract that has yet to disappear.

POLITICAL ATTITUDES

This section has two tasks. One is to see whether the rapidly evolving political atmosphere in Taiwan led to rapid changes in people's attitudes, and whether, therefore, people in Taiwan were much more optimistic about helping to shape political decisions. Our second task is to see whether the extreme differences in modes of contacting are really that distinct compared with market settings. In the chapters on workers, intellectuals, and participation, we found a sharp bifurcation between younger, more educated and older, better educated workers (Chapter 6). This bifurcation was repeated in the analysis of responses to nonwork grievances (Chapter 8). We want to see whether that sharp bifurcation is unique to the structural situation in China – with its sharp bifurcation between older workers who have risen to positions of authority and younger workers who are stuck in lower positions (Fig. 11.2). We have a small amount of information on this topic in the Taiwan and China surveys for 1990 and 1992.

One set of questions concerned individual political efficacy. On both the questions that we can use, the Taiwan respondents were again more likely to say that the individual can make a difference. The items were as follows, with the second figure being the percent agreeing in Taiwan: "Individuals can affect society" (32/73). "Citizens can affect government" (26/68). These percentage point differences are extremely large, suggesting that the recent political opening encouraged a sense of political opportunity in Taiwan.[13] The 1989 events and other incidents discouraged these kinds of attitudes in China.

The individual items can be combined into a single scale, using the full range of responses, from very strongly agree through slightly agree to very strongly disagree. On this four-point scale, the Taiwan tendency toward an optimistic individualist response is again large, at .72 ($p < .05$). In addition, there are some strong intergroup differences (Fig. 11.7). As in our earlier analysis, professional and technical workers remain very pessimistic about individuals making a difference in government policy decisions. This is very different from similar elite groups in Taiwan, where pessimism about political influence had waned by 1990. In Taiwan, professional and technical intellectuals were no different from other occupation groups in their attitudes about political efficacy.

In China, while the intellectuals were pessimistic, the golden age generation was equally optimistic about political efficacy. The comparison

---

13. We want to underline the word "recent." As recently as 1985, Taiwan attitudes were much closer to those on the mainland (see Parish and Chang 1996). The years 1986 to 1987 constituted a tipping point. The audacity of the opposition DPP to declare itself a party in that year and the rescission of martial law were watershed events that tremendously increased public confidence in the ability to affect policy decisions. This fits with our theme throughout that market transition is often as much an episodic political event as a gradual erosion by market forces (Parish and Michelson 1996).

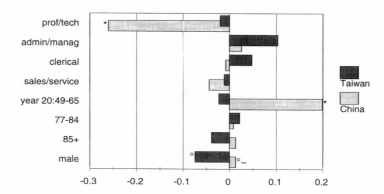

Figure 11.7 Citizen political efficacy. Notes and sources: OLS regression coefficients. Also see Fig. 11.4.

with Taiwan suggests that this was not just an age effect. It is not just that old people are more complacent about the potential of political influence. There was something special about this generation in China, including the era in which they grew up and the connections they acquired by eventually rising to positions of authority through the strong seniority system in China. Once again, these patterns are consistent with the strong bifurcation between older, well-connected people in author-ity and young, educated people who are out of authority, and therefore convinced that they can have little influence on political decisions.

Despite shared cultural and, to some extent, political origins, the strong bifurcation between young and old, establishment and nonestablishment intellectuals has not persisted in Taiwan. Our inference is that the dif-ferences in the system of occupational achievement and promotion help create this divergence. The emphasis on seniority in China means that the young must wait their turn, which creates frustration and a sense of being left out, particularly among young intellectuals who see themselves as at least as well qualified as those who are in positions of influence.

GENDER AND FAMILY

In the two previous chapters on women, work, and family, we suggested that the legacy of socialism continued to improve women's chances for equality in education, jobs, income, and the sharing of family chores. The only issue was whether these tendencies could persist as more state enterprises are replaced by small, informal enterprises, many of them coming out of the countryside, where gender equality norms have made less progress. By comparing Taiwan, we hope to get more sense of potential development paths. In Taiwan, an informal sector of small enterprises coming out of the countryside eventually overtook the formal, state sector. Thus, there may be lessons that can be learned from the Taiwan experience.

Also, in the previous chapter we suggested that women's near income equality with husbands provided a bargaining leverage over chores and family decision making that was rare among previously studied societies. It also led to a set of raised expectations and additional assertiveness that contributed to a rising divorce rate. One of the questions that we ended with was whether this bargaining power was the result of a unique combination of socialist gender ideals and socialist employment opportunities. By comparing a society with a common Chinese cultural origin, we can begin to get more of a sense of the role of traditional cultural frames and new socialist frames in shaping the consequences of income equality and bargaining.

Moreover, as noted in the previous chapter, many of the new cultural frames adopted in China's major cities have a Taiwan origin. Romance novels, love songs, and pop heros now come from Taiwan. Thus, by going to the source of part of this new popular culture, we can again get a better sense of where Chinese gender and family practice might be headed. To deal with these issues, we have data on work, jobs, income, and household chores.

Market Work

In the 1950s and 1960s, Taiwan shared with the rest of East Asia an M-shaped pattern of labor force participation. Young, unmarried women worked but then retreated to the home when they married and began to have children. Only once the children began to mature did women return to the labor force, often in less well-paid jobs.

To a greater extent than in Japan or South Korea, Taiwan overcame this pattern. Because Taiwan's small firms were highly labor-intensive, employers exhausted the supply of males and single females and by the early 1980s had to turn to married women to staff stores and factories.

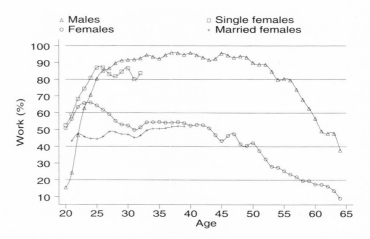

Figure 11.8 Work by age, gender, and marital status, Taiwan, 1990. Notes: Work includes both remunerated and unremunerated work for family-owned stores and factories. Data for cities. Single female data shown only for when there were at least fifty underlying observations. Married female data not shown for ages when total female and married female data are essentially the same. Two-year (forward-looking) averages for all data points. See Fig. 9.3 for comparable data for China. Source: 1990 Taiwan Labor Force Survey.

Gradually, Taiwan's female market labor pattern began to take on the shape of an inverted U (see Brinton, Lee, and Parish 1995). The transformation was less than complete, however. Even in 1990, there was a sharp divergence in the employment of single and married women (Fig. 11.8). In that year, almost 90 percent of single women worked – a figure rivaling that of young men.[14] However, with marriage, this figure was cut in half, to about 45 percent, and the recovery in women's labor force participation never exceeded 50 percent.

In short, despite great change over the past and despite advantages compared with other East Asian (not Southeast Asian) societies, there were sharp discrepancies between single and married women's labor force participation. Both for traditional cultural frame reasons (married women should devote themselves to their children, husbands, and parents-in-law) and because of employers' desires to avoid perceived

14. Men's labor force participation was delayed in part by universal military service obligations.

health costs and loss of time and energy by women with competing family demands, married women were much less involved in the labor market.

This is in sharp contrast to women's behavior in Chinese cities, where through the mid-1990s, almost twice as many women remained in the labor market (cf. Fig. 9.3). Nevertheless, the situation in Taiwan could in part represent China's future. Already, women are much less likely to be in the labor market and instead to be home taking care of household chores and children when they live in towns as opposed to cities (Fig. 9.4). Anecdotal case evidence suggests that as one moves away from larger towns, this tendency is even more extreme (interviews, summer 1996). Outside the major cities there are plenty of young, unmarried women available to work. In major cities, given the lingering restraints on migration, employers must still hire married women (see Chapter 2). In small towns and cities, given the bounty of underemployed labor, employers can be more discriminating (in the multiple senses of that word). Given the difficulty of regulating the new, private entrepreneurs in these small, out-of-the-way places, many of the practices of Taiwan should begin to dominate the Chinese nonfarm labor market. China, we infer, should begin to appear much more like Taiwan, with most women working outside the home before marriage but with as many as half returning to the home to do unpaid home work after marriage. At least, this will be the tendency, though the slow demise of the large, formal state-owned sector and regulatory intervention may well soften the trend.

Jobs

The types of jobs available to women also differ between the two societies. Earlier, we suggested that a pink-collar ghetto had yet to emerge in China's cities. The comparison of women by occupation suggests the possible trend (Fig. 11.9). Compared with Taiwan, in all occupations but one, women in China are more likely to make up a higher percentage of workers in an occupation. This fits what we know about overall labor force participation. However, in clerical jobs, women are much more important in Taiwan. This fits a more "standard" market economy, where women occupy half of all secretarial jobs and other similar types of pink-collar clerical work. Because this sector is more important in Taiwan than

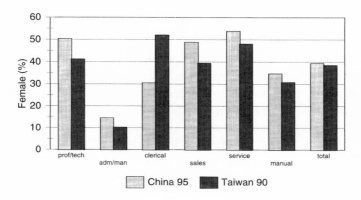

Figure 11.9 Percent female by occupation and place. Notes: Data for all nonfarm occupations. Sources: 1990 Taiwan Labor Force Survey; SSB (1997a, table 3-2).

in China (Figs. 9.1 and 9.2), the net result is that the male–female gap in nonfarm jobs is not all that great (Fig. 11.9, last set of bars).[15] The larger point here is that as one looks ahead to the future of women's work in China's cities the probable changes include not only many married women dropping out of the labor market but also the women who remain being more concentrated in pink-collar jobs, particularly in clerical work and also in sales, service, and the professional/technical jobs involved with human services (nurses, teachers, etc.). This ghettoization of female roles, then, provides more opportunities for income discrimination – a discrimination supported by the natural process that occurs when women crowd into the same field, thereby causing more competition among themselves for the same jobs, and when, collectively and individually, males more proactively pursue their incomes and other interests (see Tables 6.2, A7.2, A7.3; Jacobsen 1994).

One can make a counterargument, which goes as follows: Chinese women show a strong desire to work in responses to survey questions and may not be willing to go back to the home. Maybe the high divorce rates will keep them scared in this respect. It is also possible that men's

15. The Taiwan–China percent female gap in all types of nonfarm work is greater when one considers only cities, wherein the percent female in China is 42 and in Taiwan it remains at 38 percent. Some surveys also find more female participation in Chinese cities – e.g., see the 1988 CHIP results in Appendix Table A1.1.

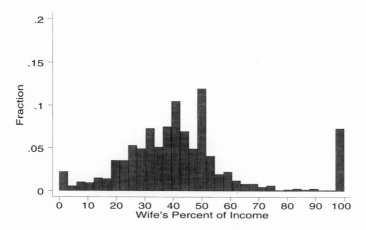

Figure 11.10 Wife's and husband's income distribution, Taiwan, 1996. Notes: For working wives only, excluding the 42 percent of wives not in the market labor force. For China patterns using the same display format but including all wives, working and nonworking, see Fig. 10.1. Source: 1996 Taiwan Social Change Survey.

incomes are insufficient in most cases to support a housewife. Having tasted the "freedom" of employment will they so easily return to domestic servitude? We also have the one-child policy which limits child rearing. Thus, the effects of socialism could continue to linger. The answer to this uncertainty may well be that there will be two quite distinct groups of women: Urban women, for whom employment will remain strong, and rural and small-town women, who will more closely approximate women in Taiwan.

Income Inequality

As one would expect, ghettoization of female jobs in a labor market consisting mostly of small, weakly regulated firms leads to considerable female income inequality (see section on income above). The lower rates of pay then play into husband and wife income inequality. A full 42 percent of married women in Taiwan are not in market work. Even when we exclude them from the calculations, Taiwan wives make much less than their husbands (Fig. 11.10). The income-earning wives in Taiwan are not concentrated in the 40 to 50 percent range, which is the pattern in China (cf. Fig. 10.1). Instead, most working wives in Taiwan are dispersed more broadly over the 30 to 50 percent range. In short, compared with wives in China, wives in Taiwan have significantly smaller income shares.

Chores and Bargaining

The lower income share puts Taiwan wives in a disadvantaged bargaining position relative to their husbands. Thus, compared with women in China, wives in Taiwan should be less demanding and less able to get help with chores. In addition, of course, there may be other people in the household to help with chores. Use of paid help seems modest, with only 5 percent having a maid or other nonkin helper. Though they can be a burden in later years of declining health, Taiwan families are more likely to have a coresident parent-in-law or other senior kin to help (29% in Taiwan vs. only 5% in China).[16] Thus, assuming that husbands are the helpers of last resort, the unconstrained migration of parents from village to city and the expensive private housing market that forces people to double up could help ensure that husbands can escape many household chores.

The inequality in income might be a moot point if the same bargaining principles did not apply in Taiwan. The relative success of bargaining in China could be the result of a socialist ideological framing, which gave greater primacy to gender equality. If so, Taiwan patterns might be similar to patterns in the United States, where the husband's help with chores changes little relative to the wife's income share. Or Taiwan might even provide an extreme example of "gender display," with high income share wives doing even more of chores and their husbands doing even fewer chores than in egalitarian households. If so, then, wife's chore hours would follow a concave pattern and husband's hours a convex pattern (see Fig. 10.1).

The simple answer is that the Taiwan chore hours follow a gender display model, and that husbands are largely unresponsive to changes in wife's relative income (Fig. 11.11). Even as women's income approaches half of their joint income, wives still sustain the lion's portion of house-

16. Data from the 1996 Taiwan Social Change Survey and the 1992 China Urban Social Survey.

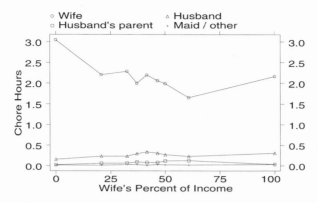

Figure 11.11 Household chores by wife's income share, Taiwan, 1996. Notes: Husband's and wife's reports on daily hours of chores (grocery shopping, cooking, washing dishes, laundry, house cleaning, and household repair work). "Husband's parent" figure includes a small amount of help from wife's parent. Children's help, not shown, is similar to husband's figure. Hour figures are exponentiated from average of log hours. See Fig. 10.3 for comparable information for China. Source: 1996 Social Change Survey.

hold chores. Husbands' help nudges up only slightly. At even higher income shares, wives' hours once again increase and husbands' hours retreat somewhat before moving up slightly when the wife provides all their joint income.[17] Also, despite high rates of coresidence (about a third of the families in the middle-income share range have a coresident older kinsmen in the household), older kin help only slightly in the average household. They are not replacing the husband's absent help. Nor are hired maids substituting for the husband.

The answer to our earlier query about whether late socialism created a special atmosphere which assisted wives in bargaining with their husbands is that it did indeed. Socialist and market systems have distinct consequences for bargaining over household chores. In Taiwan, not only are most wives concentrated on the left-hand side of the income share

17. The curvilinear, "gender display" pattern is sustained in separate multivariate analyses for husband and wife – i.e., both income share and the square of income share are statistically significant in analyses that include age, age squared, education, gender of respondent, adult kin in household, and children in household (+ for wife, – for husband).

graph, making little or no income. In addition, even in the middle ranges of income share, they are largely unsuccessful in getting their husbands to assume a significant portion of household chores.[18] Then, when wives' income shares rise above 50 percent they do exactly what the "gender display" model predicts. They perform not less but more hours of chores, while their husbands do less. Again, this suggests a dramatic difference between the two social systems. Where Chinese couples approximate bargaining models much more closely than we have seen elsewhere in the world, Taiwan couples approximate gender display models much more clearly than we have seen elsewhere in the world (cf. Figs. 10.1, 10.3, and 11.11).

Divorce

Finally, we want to put the Chinese divorce rates in perspective by including comparisons with most societies in the world, including Taiwan. In Taiwan, divorce rates rose rapidly over the last three decades – starting from a rate of .38 in 1966 and rising to a rate of 1.57 by 1995. However, even with this rapid rise, Taiwan divorce rates were only average for that country's level of economic development (Fig. 11.12). With the exception of Muslim societies (short line in upper left), market societies follow a regular pattern. As the level of economic development rises, divorce rises in a linear fashion. Urbanization, lower birth rates, women's financial autonomy, and greater individuation are among the mechanisms that scholars suggest promote this type of pattern (e.g., Goode 1993). Socialist societies follow the same trajectory, only at a much higher level. By the early 1990s, China was on this common socialist trajectory. Our interpretation of the unique socialist trajectory is that the high proportion of women at work, their more equal incomes, modest socialist birth rates, and an ideology of gender equality all contribute to women's

---

18. There is an additional complexity, which is that as income proportion rises, the number of wives reporting that their husband gives significant help with chores rises from 10 to 35 percent (1989 Taiwan Women and Family Survey). This is consistent with an approach that emphasizes different cultural frames, with Taiwan women simply having much lower expectations of husbands. We lack space to develop the point, but much like women in China, economically dependent women in Taiwan are less likely to report spousal conflict and less likely to have contemplated divorce – based on an analysis of 990 wives, with age, education, city, and town status in the equation. 1996 Social Change Survey, East Asian Social Survey module.

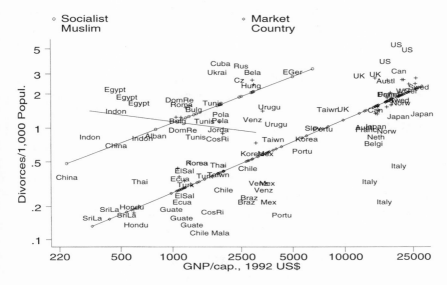

Figure 11.12 Divorce, economic development, and type of society. Notes: Divorces per 1,000 total population in about 1970, 1980, and 1990. Gross national product per capita in 1992 calculated back to earlier dates through use of growth rates. The lines are regression slopes for Muslim, socialist, and market societies. Sources: United Nations (1991), DGBAS (1996), SSB (1997a).

assertiveness and the rise of divorce rates in socialist states. Thus, again, there is a sharp distinction in family and gender behavior between socialist and market societies.

CONCLUSION

We began the comparison of Taiwan and China in order to deal with the question of whether market and socialist systems are really different in their consequences for everyday life. We need to keep reminding the reader that there are many variants of socialism, with China's more idealistic version having more drastic consequences for people's mobility opportunities during the Cultural Revolution decade, and many variants of market societies, with Taiwan's being much more on the individualistic mobility side, with ample mobility among firms and work units.

With that caution in mind, by now the obvious answer to the question of whether market and socialist systems make a difference in people's lives is that the systems make a great deal of difference. Taiwan has more individualistic opportunities for farmers to move to cities, for dissatisfied workers to leave work units to go work on their own, for people to be rewarded on the basis of their education credentials, for people to be rewarded for their abilities at an early age rather than waiting for mid-career recommendations by superiors who one cannot afford to offend while waiting for the recommendation, and for higher income rewards to people who do rise to senior posts. All of this has the consequence of convincing Taiwan residents that economic success is a matter of individual effort, that pay levels are fair, and that they can be optimistic about their life situations.

The contrast between responses in China and Taiwan is particularly strong for professional and technical workers, who in China in the early 1990s felt that they were an abused class – that they as intellectuals had been wronged by the party-state.[19] With an articulate group of alienated intellectuals, the government of China faced a potent ideological counterforce that could be used against them. The income reforms of 1993 sharply raised the incomes of Chinese intellectuals in public organizations, one suspects in part to help quell the grousing of intellectuals (see Chapter 4). Whether that rise in income and benefits was enough to dampen intellectual complaints is a topic to which later research should return.

The two systems had other consequences as well. Given its sharply different mobility opportunities for different generations, China had a geologically layered sense of opportunity. Groups who had come of age in the "golden" 1950s, and who had since risen through seniority to higher-level posts, remained uniquely optimistic. They were convinced that one could get ahead by one's own efforts and convinced that "ordinary people" could influence government policy decisions. They repeat, and explain more clearly than we have seen before, why there is such a sharp bifurcation in political attitudes and behavior between young, educated workers and older workers who feel that they can work within the system. The Taiwan–China comparisons show that this bifurcation is not just a simple old/young divide but one uniquely shaped by China's economic and political history. Children (really, teenagers) of the Cultural

19. E.g., Link (1992).

Revolution decade, of course, hold diametrically opposed views, often being much more pessimistic about chances of individual economic opportunity and fairness of pay. For them, much as for children of the Great Depression in the United States, there is a lingering effect of early life experiences.

Some of the sharpest differences between the two social and economic systems were in gender equality and familial bargaining. In common with many other developing market economies, married women have far fewer job opportunities than young, unmarried women. One result is that married women contribute far less to family income. A secondary consequence is that they have little bargaining leverage with their husbands over household chores. Combined with a cultural frame that makes gender equality normative – in the sense that it is both "average" or "normal" and that legacies of old socialist rhetoric linger on – women in China are more successful in getting their husbands to contribute to household chores. Thus both in the market and at home, there is more gender equality in China than in Taiwan. Despite all the shortfalls that one can rightfully point to in China, in cities, the consequences for women are more favorable than in most market societies.

Now all of this could change. As China begins to emulate Taiwan, with rural small industries growing much more rapidly than large state firms, married women's opportunities are declining. If this tendency continues, then, in the not too distant future, women's position in small towns in China could begin to approximate that in Taiwan. That can be seen as a test of how different systems of economic organization have very different economic consequences for women.

12

Conclusion

O U R introductory chapter began with two questions – the question of whether socialist and market social contracts have a host of systematic consequences for life chances, work, interest articulation, gender, and attitudes, and the question of who wins in the politics of market transition. Let us return to each issue in turn.

SYSTEMATIC CONSEQUENCES

We suggested that this issue could be seen as a debate between the Hungarian economist Janos Kornai, who argues for a host of systemic consequences, and Alex Inkeles, who argues that education, media exposure, and work in complex organizations tend to homogenize social life, regardless of economic and political system. We have found ample examples of the Inkeles position. Throughout, more educated respondents were far more critical. They were less accepting of current reform conditions, of their work situations, and of the chances for political participation. In participation, they were much more likely to suggest modes of participation outside corporatist channels. As personified among professional and technical workers, educated, nonestablishment intellectuals, while complaining mightily about low pay and lack of economic or political efficacy, were among the few groups who became more proactive in pursuing their interests between the late 1980s and early 1990s (Chapters 5, 6, 8, and 11). All this suggests that education has the potential to produce proactive, participant citizens who make additional demands on modernizing social systems. This is much as Inkeles, Huntington, and Almond, and many others have suggested. In addition, within the home, the educated were more likely to share chores evenly, in ways that others writing about the modernization of the family propose (e.g., Goode 1963).

Also, once freed of extreme top-down controls, people in the southern sunbelt, close to the diffusion chain of messages from Hong Kong and Taiwan in the form of songs, television, and satellite programming, have attitudes that are different from the rest of the population. This, again, fits the Inkeles model, though with more of an emphasis on diffusion than on an internally generated critical consciousness. The result may well be the same: that once people are exposed to a wider variety of media, it is difficult to reverse people's ideas and expectations.

That said, we still find ourselves closer to Kornai's position on systematic consequences. More so than we realized when we began this research, we are impressed by the panoply of differences between pre- and postreform attitudes and behavior. The final review of differences between socialist and market social contracts in our comparison of Taiwan and China further drives home this message. Whether it be economic attitudes (fair pay, individual economic efficacy), gender and family behavior (women's work, bargaining over chores), or political efficacy, we are impressed by the striking differences between Taiwan and China. At least in their specific versions of the socialist and market social contract, there is a panoply of secondary consequences that affects many aspects of people's lives. Much of the contrast between individual initiative and reliance on communal and work unit collectivities echoes differences that Karl Polanyi and others suggest occurred at the start of the commercial and, then, the industrial revolution in the West. We are impressed with how China's version of socialism in many ways froze society in time or even reversed modernizing, individualizing processes that were already under way.

Dependency and Authoritarianism

One of the ways that Chinese society was frozen in time or even reversed was in increasing vertical dependency on superiors in work units. Much as in accounts of European socialism by Chirot (1972), Wiles (1977), Jowitt (1983), Kaminski (1992), Kornai (1992), and others, people became beholden to superiors in work units. The symptoms of this dependency included interest articulation through corporatist channels both at work and outside work. It also included principled particularism, with superiors free to reward those who promised to toe the administrator's line. In China, with its extreme emphasis on seniority and overall equality, the result was sinking morale, with feelings that pay was not reasonable, that one could not get ahead by one's own effort, and that personalistic connections with one's superior were necessary for promotion. These symptoms of dependency remind one of Karl Marx's description of what was wrong with the industrial revolution. By moving people off the farm and out of small artisan shops, where people heretofore controlled the pace and quality of their work, workers developed a sense of estrangement or alienation from their work. They no longer controlled their work but instead were beholden to the owner and his appointed supervisors. What socialist systems did – and particularly China, which controlled interfirm and residential mobility much more tightly than in European socialist states – was to create extreme versions of the very conditions that Marx railed against. There was no way to escape the control of arbitrary superiors, unless one waited long enough without causing trouble and became a supervisor oneself. Some political campaigns tried to modify aspects of this system. The Cultural Revolution was the most extreme of these movements, allowing frustrated young turks to attack their all-controlling superiors and promoting many of these "young turks" helicopter-fashion into positions of authority (e.g., Oksenberg 1970; Lee 1978). However, by bringing even more resources under administrative control, the Cultural Revolution exacerbated the "estranging" dependency situation. With a further weakening of the market, a reduction in housing and consumer goods that could be bought freely, and a reduction of rules that could be appealed to when people were promoted in an orderly fashion, personalized dependency was exacerbated.

We have seen the lasting consequences in the data on how people pursue their interests. Reflecting the cellularized nature of work units, and the many resources that these work units came to control by the end of the Cultural Revolution, most people continued to think of going first to superiors at their work unit when they had a problem either outside or at work (see Chapters 6 and 8). These tendencies affected not only lower-level workers but also their supervisors. Even the best-intentioned supervisors spent vast amounts of time on settling complaints about housing and other matters that had little to do with technocratic production issues. If current proposals about marketizing housing and other fringe benefits are carried through, one of the groups that will be liberated are the supervisors, who will no longer have to be social workers and complaint mediators. For the average worker personalized decision making about everyday benefits and promotion created a sense that people were getting ahead because of special connections. In the 1980s, this led to a pervasive popular belief that everyone was using connections (e.g., Yang 1994; Yan 1995). It is not surprising that when asked in the early 1990s whether a person could get ahead by his or her own efforts, most people thought not (Chapters 5 and 11).

China is now moving away from this system. We see the possible changes not only in the comparisons with Taiwan, where workers are much more likely to say that one can get ahead by one's own efforts. We also see some of these tendencies in China. Already by the early 1990s, those in the private sector and in the fast-growing southern sunbelt are more likely to say that people could get ahead by their own efforts, that they would make contacts outside work to solve their problems, and that they would not or did not vote because it was of no use to them. While people in China's old rustbelt remained stuck in personalistic, dependency relations, people elsewhere were moving toward more individualistic solutions. This repeats an early pattern in the industrializing West, where greater mobility, more goods in the open market, and an urban lifestyle led to people becoming far more individualistic (e.g., Simmel 1903a, b). In China's version of the socialist system, these natural tendencies were stalled. Now they are emerging once more.

Once China begins to move away from an institutionalized system of dependency, it will also solve some of the "authoritarianism" issues that critics note in socialist societies. Most of the authoritarianism issues that affect people's lives are not ones that begin with a capital "A." As we saw in popular reactions to reform, freedom of speech and other related democracy issues are low on most people's agendas. They are more concerned about stability of prices, real incomes, and government corruption. The authoritarianism that affects most people's lives is spelled with a small "a," and involves mostly the smaller dependency issues that we have been discussing. This kind of small "a" authoritarianism extended beyond the workplace to store clerks who arbitrarily served or did not, depending on the whim of the moment. This too is passing, as customer service becomes a watchword. There may also be gradual change in larger democratic issues. We saw that the small, family-business entrepreneurs were already more independent-minded than ordinary folk working in large state-run enterprises. In time, as the private sector grows, this population will not only be more independent-minded but also have the financial resources to use in mobilizing opinion and organizations against established government institutions and policies.

Not all these changes will occur just as a simple result of market forces. In the West, the move away from personal dependency on arbitrary supervisors occurred not merely as the result of a more open market with greater mobility among employers who provided more enlightened labor–management relations. Instead, it relied heavily on labor strikes and strife, with governments finally intervening to force employers to recognize unions, and with these unions engaging in collective labor agreements that published rules in ways that limited the arbitrary authority of supervisors (e.g., Dahrendorf 1959; Crozier 1964; Edwards 1979). The Chinese government is trying to circumvent this tumultuous process by establishing government mediation committees that often rule in favor of workers. However, so long as work rules remain opaque and the officially sanctioned union remains more beholden to management than to the workers, much of the old history of the West will be repeated.

Life Chances

One of our beginning concerns was whether socialist systems lived up to their promised equality and security for everyone, including the promise to help the previously disadvantaged. We saw that significant parts of the promise were fulfilled. By quieting strong urban interest groups that typically get governments in developing market societies to spend too much money on university education and too little on basic education, China provided middle levels of junior and senior high school education for most people, including females. Simultaneously, however, China's emphasis on heavy industry and the forced affirmative action and leveling policies of the Cultural Revolution destroyed mobility opportunities for most people. Educated parents in most societies are able to pass along advantages to their children, with better education and credentials for appointment to better jobs being one of the major ways for achieving continued high status for elite families (e.g., Parkin 1979). For a time, during the Cultural Revolution, China destroyed much of this typical pattern. The costs were high, with much of a generation lost to the idealism of the Cultural Revolution and with parental hopes for children's achievement dashed by the utopian visions of radical leaders. With a return to a more individualistic system with exams and educational credentials now tracking people into different careers, many of the parental influences are returning. Much as in China before the period of socialist idealism or in market societies, parents' education and status have a strong influence on child's educational and occupational achievement. The pattern is illustrated by an encounter with a family in recent years. The daughter had just passed the entrance exam to get into a famous school. This is the very school that the daughter's uncle would have qualified for a generation before had he not been excluded because he was of the wrong class origin and the school was being downsized to meet the dictates of the Cultural Revolution. The uncle immediately sent a congratulatory note, suggesting that the niece would now realize the dream that had once absorbed his life. This again illustrates the steep U-shaped curve in education and job trajectories, with the return to more open, exam-based competition, and the return of many more sales, service, and other kinds of white-collar jobs providing more opportunities for people to move up in society. Thus, even more than in other socialist societies, the emphasis on a managed economy and managed mobility was counterproductive for most people. The return to the market, though perhaps overly influenced by interest group lobbying for a strong role for educational credentials, creates new opportunities for occupational mobility and for the rewarding of individualistic effort through open competition in exams and in the market.

Job Satisfaction

The consequences of the socialist social contract for job satisfaction are, by now, obvious. Particularly in China, with its extreme emphasis on seniority and principled particularism, young workers were often dissatisfied. The dependency-inducing consequences of this system weakened morale not only among blue-collar workers but also up and down the occupational ladder. We saw this in the statistics on satisfaction among bureaucrats, with junior bureaucrats often being dissatisfied along with junior blue-collar workers. Indeed, during the Cultural Revolution, it was the frustration of these junior bureaucrats that often led to the most violent actions against senior leaders (e.g., Lee 1978).

That simmering frustration continued into the 1980s. With rapidly increasing basic education, junior bureaucrats and junior workers often approached their superiors in levels of education. However, the junior workers still had to wait for their turn in the seniority system to get the housing, benefits, and authority that went with eventual promotion (Chapters 4 and 11). Indeed, when we showed the Taiwan chapter to one of our Chinese colleagues now in the United States, his response was that we had it perfectly right. One of the major reasons he left China was that when he calculated how long it would take to rise to a sufficient rank to get housing, other benefits, and authority the time was longer than he felt he could tolerate. As he put it, he decided he "didn't want to live in a gerontocracy."

Parts of this system are changing. The emphasis on mandatory retirement is having some effect. Educated young people have many high-income, high-responsibility opportunities in joint ventures and in the growing private sector. Nevertheless, our figure on jobs by age from the 1995 census suggests that in many parts of China the role of seniority remained strong through the mid-1990s (Chapter 11).

Another source of dissatisfaction was in the modest incomes for upper-level white-collar workers. Lenski (1994) suggests that one of the reasons socialist systems collapsed in Europe was that income gaps were too modest. We believe that we have illustrated that principle for China. Regardless of whether they are in or out of government, in or out of the party, administrators, managers, professionals, and technicians all say that they are paid too little and that pay has little relation to merit. Part of this weak link to merit, we suggest, is because of the undue emphasis on seniority. The other, we suggest, is the low pay of upper white-collar workers relative to manual workers. Given the increased contact with peers from Asia and elsewhere, upper white-collar workers know that they are relatively underpaid. Modest pay, with more of an emphasis on basic living standards provided by subsidized housing and other benefits, is counterproductive, leading in turn to fewer incentives for performance in one's work.

THE POLITICS OF MARKET TRANSITION

We began by suggesting that the spate of literature on market transition is undertheorized. The simple distinction between redistributors (e.g., administrators) and producers (e.g., entrepreneurs) is inadequate to fit the reality of what is happening in China. We have accumulated a long list of why the usual accounts are inadequate. Near the top of that list is that both in cash and in kind, the economic rewards to government administrators, enterprise managers, and others in responsible positions are all too low. Compared with similar workers in actually existing market societies, these people are not very well paid. This has the unfortunate result of decreasing morale, and tempting government administrators to engage in corruption in order to bring the living standards of their spouses and children up to what they perceive to be an acceptable level. Thus, we suggest, one of the surest signs of successful market transition will not be that administrator salaries fall far behind the levels of entrepreneurs and others but that they remain close to the salaries of people with similar levels of training and experience. Only then will the most capable administrators continue in public administration and eschew the temptations to cheat on the administrative system. Only then will the costs of doing business in the market decline and the rules of the market become more predictable.

Guthrie (2000) suggests that with increased market competition the incomes of those close to the market may well fall. Consistent with this perspective, we find that in the highly competitive, small business sector of Taiwan managers and owners average less income than administrators. While some Taiwan owners and managers are much richer than administrators, on average, managerial and ownership positions do not lead to huge incomes. Or, more properly, in actually existing market societies, there are sharp cleavages in the incomes of those close to production. Much as in Róna-Tas's (1994) examination of different types of entrepreneurs in post-socialist Hungary, entrepreneurs are often of two types. The "erosion from below" types of small entrepreneurs often come from humble backgrounds and remain at modest income levels. The "erosion from above" entrepreneurs are more likely to come from higher-level backgrounds, to own or manage firms with current and prior connections to the state, and to have higher incomes. Whether the small (from below) or large (from above) firms dominate depends on the political economy of specific market economies. For example, in Taiwan, given its particular political history, small firms dominate. In Japan and South Korea, with their particular political and social histories, large firms dominate (Hamilton and Biggart 1988; Hamilton 1991; Orru, Biggart, and Hamilton 1997). All this suggests that we need a much more developed political economy of types of firms, with attention to path dependence (Stark 1992), before making predictions about whether entrepreneurs, managers, and administrators will have the highest incomes as a result of market transition.

Our results also suggest that the competing bargaining school of transition is too simplistic (e.g., Bian 1994a, b). This applies both to the original versions of this argument that suggested administrators, high-rank firms, and party members were winning in the bargaining over resources and to more recent versions which suggest that there are ample rewards for both producers and redistributors (e.g., Bian and Logan 1996). Whether in the original or revised version, the bargaining argument seems too simplistic for some of the reasons already listed. Compared with actually existing market societies, the income gaps between elite and manual work positions are extremely modest. Through the early 1990s, neither group was winning very much in the struggle for income and benefits. Where administrators were winning in housing, in monetary terms that victory was a hollow one. Moreover, the tendency to take one's benefits in kind when direct monetary payments are low is a pattern shared with actually existing market societies. Thus, it is unclear whether this pattern is worthy of extensive comment.

Also, the bargaining by type of work unit seems quantitatively unexceptional. The one-fifth to one-fourth income gain that comes from working for high-rank firms is about the same income boost that comes from working for core as opposed to periphery firms in developed market societies. State-owned firms in China are actually less advantaged than government-owned firms in marketized Taiwan. Thus, again, we need a more developed political economy of interfirm differences if we are to detect patterns that are unique to China (see Walder 1992; Guthrie 2000). The contentious literature on segmented labor markets and differences in benefits between core and periphery firms in the West provides the cautious note that many of the theoretical debates about the sources of differential benefits are difficult to adjudicate with existing data sets (e.g., Smith 1990; Baron 1994). The same debates will be difficult to adjudicate in China. The more general conclusion is that quantitative differences among types of firms in China look very similar to the differences we know from actually existing market societies.

Our results are more consistent with the Róna-Tas's (1994) suggestion of technological continuity, with the added proviso that the technocratic

turn in China has several additional twists. Consistent with Róna-Tas's
suggestion, technocrats or people with applied technical experience are
beginning to move out of the public into the private sector. Once there,
the technocrats have more economic success than simple administrators,
suggesting that it is not just social capital (special network connections)
but human capital (technocratic experience) that helps them in their new
jobs. Equally important, within government administration, virtuocrats
are being replaced by educated technocrats. Thus to compare administrators and entrepreneurs today with people having the same labels
twenty years ago is somewhat like comparing apples and oranges. Moreover, one of the most important changes has been to get political operatives out of economic enterprises. The reactions of bureaucrats to these
types of moves show a differentiated set of interests and responses
that belies any attempt to treat bureaucrats (managers, administrators,
political operatives of different rank) as a single undifferentiated whole.
Already, by the late 1980s, bureaucrats close to production were optimistic about their prospects. Those far from production and closer to the
virtuocratic, political operative work of the past were pessimistic about
their prospects. This set of differences in attitudes tells us more than
incomes about the progress of market transition.

GENDER

Finally, we should return to the issue of gender, and whether women are
losing out in the transition to the market. There is ample reason to think
that they would be losing. Employers have more autonomy to discriminate, and married women are exposed to new messages from abroad
about the good housewife and mother who stays at home to tend her
children. We find some of these tendencies, and we suggest that the
growth of many new nonfarm jobs in towns and villages will promote a
typical East Asian M-shaped pattern of labor force participation, with
most women working before marriage, many dropping out of the labor
force at marriage, and then returning to lesser jobs once their children
begin to mature. Also the increasing concentration of women in new
pink-collar clerical and service jobs will help reduce pay in these jobs.

Despite these market-accelerated tendencies, we are more impressed
by the continuing gains of women. At least for the time being, urban
women continue to gain on men in education, jobs, and, seemingly,

bargaining power at home. Combined with education, job, and income advantages, the new autonomy and household appliance advantages provided by the market give women an unusual set of bargaining advantages relative to their husbands. In our comparison society of Taiwan, women continue to lag behind men in jobs and income and, in turn, in their ability to bargain their husbands into more help with chores. For Taiwan, the "gender display" model of household chores continues to describe patterns of chore sharing. In Chinese cities, in contrast, where gender equality has become more of the behavioral and ideological norm, "effective bargaining" is the order of the day. With this effective bargaining, many traditional and modern cultural norms about male and female roles are weakened, even though they never completely fade away.

In short, then, much more than we have seen in other settings, including in comparisons to European socialist states, the comparisons of attitudes and behavior in urban China and Taiwan demonstrate that socialist and market societies can lead to distinct differences in the lives of men and women. This fits with the larger theme of this final chapter, suggesting that old and new social contracts have a host of systematic consequences for the lives of urban residents.

Appendix A

Supplementary Materials

APPENDIX A1. OCCUPATION CLASSIFICATIONS

Though there is variation among surveys, the following definitions typically hold:

- managers (*yewu ganbu*). Managers of stores, factors, and similar economic units.
- administrators (*xingzheng ganbu*). Includes both ordinary government administrators and senior party and political operatives in economic enterprises (stores, factories) and public organizations (hospitals, schools, institutes) (see Table A1.1).
- professional and technical workers. Split equally across economic enterprises and public organizations, the professionals include doctors, teachers, engineers, and pilots. The technical workers include a broad spectrum of accountants, cashiers, and lower-level engineering assistants. The low end can reach quite far down, and often includes a high proportion of female lower-level school teachers (professionals) and store cashiers (technical workers).
- clerical workers. Secretarial and routine office workers, with many in economic enterprises and some in government and public organizations (Table A1.1).
- sales/service workers. Sales clerks, barbers, cleaning personnel, etc. This group is sometimes combined with manual workers (as was done in the 1988 CHIP survey).
- manual workers. Blue-collar production workers.
- private entrepreneurs. Through the early 1990s, these remained mostly small family stores and workshops, though a few larger private enterprises were beginning to emerge.

Several tendencies cause instability in classification across surveys. The three official pay scales for bureaucrat (administrator/manager), technician (professional/technical), and worker (manual and service) greatly influence how the respondent, the interviewer, and the survey coder think about occupations. Thus, by International Labor Office and United

317

Table A1.1. *Type of Work Unit by Occupation, 1988*

	Type of work unit (%)			
	Economic enterprise	Public organization	Government	Total
Manager	94.2	3.5	2.3	100.0
Administrator	43.3	15.5	41.2	100.0
Professional/technical worker	44.7	50.0	5.4	100.0
Clerical worker	68.2	11.5	20.3	100.0
Private entrepreneur	88.2	5.2	6.6	100.0
Manual, sales, service worker	96.0	3.2	.9	100.0
Total	81.9	10.8	7.3	100.0

Notes: Economic enterprises are factories, stores, banks, etc. Public organizations are hospitals, schools, research institutes, etc.
Source: 1988 CHIP urban survey, approximately 1,800 income earners.

Nations standards, the administrator/manager, professional/technical, and manual worker categories are often inflated. Examples of administrator/manager inflation are found in the 1987–91 ESRIC and 1992 urban surveys (Table A1.2). The 1988 CHIP survey seems to suffer from inflation in the professional/technical category, with many sales workers reclassified as professional/technical and service workers reclassified as manual (of the Census and CHIP columns in Table A1.2).

These classification issues are separate from the question of sample bias, wherein interviewers tend to interview more upper white-collar workers and fewer manual workers than there are in the population (see Appendix B). In descriptive statistics, our strategy is to use weights to make the reported results more closely reflect the actual population characteristics. As for the classification results, there is little we can do except to warn the reader that precise comparison of occupations across surveys and survey organizations can be difficult, and that for some occupations (e.g., administrators, technical workers) the categories can reach further down the hierarchy of jobs than one might normally expect.

Finally, a few words on the typical characteristics of different occupa-

Table A1.2. *Occupation Distribution by Survey*

	CHIP urban 1988	Census, cities 1990	ESRIC Quarterly 1987–91	Urban Survey 1992
Administrator/manager	5.4	6.2	11.6	12.8
Professional/technical worker	11.2	17.2	7.7	6.2
Clerical worker	21.8	6.7	16.4	18.2
Private entrepreneur	1.7	—	3.1	4.4
Sales/service worker		18.1	8.2	6.2
Manual worker	59.9	51.6	53.1	52.2
Total	100.0	100	100.1	100

Notes: All samples are weighted by the 1990 Census education distribution (see Appendix B).
Sources: See Appendix B on the respective surveys.

tions. Adopting the 1988 CHIP definitions of occupation, it is only the administrators and managers who are dominated by party members (Table A1.3). To get ahead in these leadership roles, party membership is a near necessity. It takes time to rise into an administrator or manager role, with people in these two roles being older than any other group (Chapter 11). Education among administrators increasingly rivals that among professional and technical workers (see also Chapter 7 on this issue). Though rare in administrative and managerial roles, females are well represented in most other occupations (Chapter 9).

APPENDIX A2. STATISTICS

Throughout the book, we present the results of multivariate statistical analysis in several different forms, depending on the nature of the phenomenon being explained (the dependent variable) and the characteristics that help provide an explanation (the independent variables). For different types of dependent variables, we provide the following kinds of analyses:

Table A1.3. *Occupation Characteristics, 1988*

	Distribution (%)	Age (yrs)	Education (yrs)	RMB$ per year	Party (%)	Female (%)
Manager (of economic enterprise/firm)	1.6	46	10.1	2,338	77	13
Administrator	3.8	48	10.8	2,137	83	16
Professional/ technical worker	11.2	41	11.9	1,869	32	51
Clerical worker	21.8	40	10.1	1,760	39	44
Private entrepreneur	1.7	43	7.1	1,533	11	53
Manual, sales, service worker	59.9	36	8.4	1,482	7	55
Total	100.0	38	9.3	1,615	21	50

Notes: Weighted results (see Appendix B on weighting). RMB (*renminbi*) or Chinese currency denominated income includes imputed values for housing and fringe benefits. Average (mean) values of income calculated from the exponent of logged income.
Source: 1988 CHIP urban survey, approximately 1,800 income earners.

- continuous variables – e.g. income – for which we present regression coefficients from an ordinary least squares (OLS) regression analysis,
- binary variables – e.g. voted, planning to exit an enterprise – for which we present proportional change or odds ratios from a probit or logit analysis, and
- trichotomous variables – e.g., institutional contacting, work slow down, or no action in response to work grievances (Table 6.2) – for which we present multinomial logit coefficients.

For most independent variables we present a single coefficient that shows the effect of a single unit's change in the variable – e.g., the effect of an extra year of age or of an extra year of education. Sometimes these variables are dichotomous, and thus coded 0 or 1 – e.g., for being male or a party member. The results are read much as for the continuous variables.

At other times, the independent variables come in sets. A common example is for occupation, where each occupation – professional, administrator, managers, etc. – is coded 0 and 1. In these sets, one of the 0/1 variables becomes the comparison variable. In the analysis of occupation, the comparison variable is usually manual labor. Thus, all the other occupation results indicate whether the other occupation has more or less of the observed characteristic when compared with manual workers.

In the analysis of continuous variables, a regression coefficient indicates the amount of change on the dependent variable for each unit change of an independent variable. For example, in Figure 5.7, the regression coefficient of economic efficacy for private sector workers is .20. We know from Table A5.2 that the range of economic efficacy is 2.59 (minimum value is −1.47 and maximum value is 1.12). As a proportion of this full range, then, .20/2.59 = .08. In a sense, then, compared with public sector manual workers, private sector workers felt 8 percent more economic efficacy, which is a sizable effect. When the dependent variable is logged, as in the income analysis in Chapter 4, the coefficients can be read as approximations of percentage effects. Thus, in the analysis of total income in Table 4.2, the economic enterprise coefficient of .06 implies that compared with people in government agencies people in economic enterprises earn 6 percent more income.

For binary variables, we often present the results as proportion change coefficients, which multiplied by 100 become percentage change coefficients. The proportion change coefficients show the effect on the dependent variable of each unit change of the independent variable, when all variables are at their mean (average). In Figure 11.4, for example, when asked whether their income was fair, Taiwan professionals were 10 percent more likely to think their income was fair compared with manual workers there. In contrast, mainland professionals were 16 percent less likely to think their income was fair compared with manual workers there.

The analysis of binary variables can also be presented as odds ratios from a logistic analysis. Most readers are familiar with there ratios from media reports of medical research – the statement "If you eat cauliflower three times a day your risks of colon cancer are cut in half" is an example of this type of analysis. Intuitively, they report how the odds of a particular outcome change with a one-unit increase in the size of each independent variable. A coefficient of 1.00 indicates a neutral relationship, meaning that the odds of a given outcome are neither increased nor decreased by a given background condition. A coefficient of 2.00 indicates the odds are doubled, while a coefficient of .50 indicates that the odds are cut in half. For example, in Table A8.2, administrators and managers were twice more likely to voice their complaints (odds ratio = 2.04) than manual workers.

For trichotomous variables, the multinomial logit coefficients indicate the increased or decreased log odds of an outcome relative to a comparison outcome. Thus, in the analysis of responses to grievances at work, the coefficients indicate the relative chances of acting either by institutional contacting or slowing down at work in comparison with the option of doing nothing at all (Table 6.2). In this analysis we are more interested in the size and direction of the effects than in giving them a ready intuitive interpretation.

To help us both with intuitive interpretations and to know whether our results could occur by chance alone, we also report tests of statistical significance. These tests depend on the size of both the underlying coefficients and the sample within each cell. Probability values indicate the frequency with which a coefficient could result from chance alone, with the results indicated as follows:

- $p < .01$, less than 1 time in 100,
- $p < .05$, less than 5 times in 100, and
- $p < .10$, less than 10 times in 100.

Or, to invert the terminology, $p < .10$ means with more than 90 percent assurance we would get the same result if the sample were redrawn and $p < .01$ indicates with more than 99 percent assurance we would get the same result if the sample were redrawn.

All analyses were done in the statistical package STATA. For additional references the reader can consult the STATA manuals or most basic statistical texts (e.g., Blalock 1960; Aldrich and Nelson 1984; Fox 1984; StataCorp 1995).

APPENDIX A3. EDUCATION STATISTICS, 1988

	Mean	Standard deviation	Minimum	Maximum
Enrolled in school	.549	.50	0	1
Father's work unit				
Type				
Economic enterprise	.702	.46	0	1
Public organization	.163	.37	0	1
Other/unknown	.010	.10	0	1
Government agency (cf.)				
Ownership				
Central government	.480	.50	0	1
Regional government	.384	.49	0	1
Neighborhood collective	.113	.32	0	1
Other	.010	.10	0	1
Private (cf.)	.012	.11	0	1
Father's personal attributes				
Occupation				
Professional/technical	.192	.39	0	1
Administrator	.128	.33	0	1
Manager	.047	.21	0	1
Clerical	.273	.45	0	1
Entrepreneur	.017	.13	0	1
Manual, sales/service (cf.)				
Party member	.482	.50	0	1
Education	10.253	3.45	0	16
Income (log)	7.669	.33	6.2	9.8
City attributes				
High economic growth	.452	.50	0	1
Average income	7.378	.18	6.9	8.2
Central city	.888	.32	0	1
Youth attributes				
Son	.509	.50	0	1
Siblings age 5–21	1.052	.81	0	4
×daughter	.556	.82	0	4

(cont.)

	Mean	Standard deviation	Minimum	Maximum
Age				
16	.187	.39	0	1
17	.194	.40	0	1
18	.188	.39	0	1
19	.167	.37	0	1
20	.151	.36	0	1
21 (cf.)				
Missing data flags				
Father's				
Income	.011	.10	0	1
Ownership	.002	.04	0	1
Party membership	.010	.10	0	1
City economic growth	.069	.25	0	1

Note: Sample size is 3,341; (cf.) comparison groups.
Source: 1988 CHIP Urban Survey, youth aged 16–21.

APPENDIX A4. INCOME STATISTICS, 1988

	Mean	Standard deviation	Minimum	Maximum
Dependent variables				
Housing space (sq. meters)	3,379	.49	.7	5.9
Base wage, log	6.981	.42	1.6	9.7
Other income, log	6.121	1.13	.0	10.3
Total income, log	7,405	.45	4.5	10.3
Work unit attributes				
Type				
Economic enterprise	.767	.42	0	1
Pubic organization	.139	.35	0	1
Other	.008	.09	0	1
Government agency (cf.)	.085	.28	0	1
Ownership				
Central government	.389	.49	0	1
Regional government	.390	.49	0	1

(cont.)

	Mean	Standard deviation	Minimum	Maximum
Neighborhood collective (cf.)	.203	.40	0	1
Joint venture	.003	.06	0	1
Foreign	.0004	.02	0	1
Other	.005	.07	0	1
Private	.009	.09	0	1
Personal attributes				
Occupation				
Manager	.018	.13	0	1
Administrator	.047	.21	0	1
Professional/technical	.158	.36	0	1
Clerical	.234	.42	0	1
Entrepreneur	.013	.11	0	1
Manual, sales/service (cf.)	.530	.50	0	1
Party member	.237	.43	0	1
Male	.523	.50	0	1
Education, years	10,380	2.84	0	16
Experience, years	20,796	11.12	0	64
Experience^2/1,000	.056	.05	0	.4
Average income of city	7.387	.18	6.9	8.2

Notes: Based on sample of 17,493; (cf.) comparison groups.
Source: 1988 CHIP Urban Survey, income earners.

APPENDIX A5. VARIABLES IN FIGURES 5.4–5.9 AND
ATTITUDE SCALES

Tables A5.1 and A5.2 list the summary statistics for variables used in Figures 5.4–5.9. The attitude scales used in Figures 5.5–5.8 were constructed as follows: "Hope" includes five agree/disagree items. It is the inverse of a normal anomie scale, which would indicate a loss of values and standards to live by. The last two items in the scale are shared with the "reform good" scale.[1] With their original variable numbers, the items

1. The standard "mental well being" scale was modified to emphasize a reform element at the time the questionnaire was redesigned in Beijing – hence our inclusion of two items in both scales.

Table A5.1. *Reform Reaction, 1987–91 (Variables in Figs. 5.4 and 5.5)*

	Number of observations	Mean	Standard deviation	Minimum	Maximum
Dependent variables					
Satisfaction scale	15,332	–.01	.91	–1.83	2.21
Pace of reform					
Too slow	15,931	.23	.42	0	1
Too fast	15,931	.37	.48	0	1
Just right	15,931	.32	.47	0	1
Don't know	15,931	.08	.27	0	1
Independent variables					
City characteristics					
Inflation rate (for 1988–91)	11,055	.16	.06	.02	.30
Income per cap.					
(square root)	15,931	.55	.13	.25	.95
Population (logged)	15,931	4.93	.98	2.97	6.66
Location					
Guangzhou	15,931	.01	.11	0	1
Shanghai	15,931	.05	.21	0	1
Southeast	15,931	.09	.28	0	1
Beijing	15,931	.05	.22	0	1
Tianjin	15,931	.05	.22	0	1
Southwest	15,931	.05	.23	0	1
Remainder of China (cf.)					
Personal characteristics					
Income, personal (categ.)	15,931	4.27	2.32	1	9

Occupation

Private sector	15,931	.02	.14	0	1
Sales/service work	15,931	.06	.24	0	1
Professional/technical	15,931	.09	.28	0	1
Administrator/manager	15,931	.12	.33	0	1
Clerical worker	15,931	.15	.36	0	1
Manual worker (cf.)	15,931	.35	.48	0	1
Student	15,931	.01	.12	0	1
Not employed	15,931	.06	.23	0	1
Retired	15,931	.12	.33	0	1
Other occupation	15,931	.01	.11	0	1
Occupation unknown	15,931	.02	.14	0	1
Education	15,931	3.43	1.06	1	5
Youth $(80 - age)/10$	15,931	3.92	1.48	0	6.6
Male	15,931	.53	.50	−1	0
Party member	15,931	.26	.44	0	1

Date of interview

May 1987	15,931	.16	.36	0	1
October 1987	15,931	.15	.36	0	1
May 1988	15,931	.16	.37	0	1
October 1988	15,931	.13	.34	0	1
May 1989	15,931	.13	.34	0	1
October 1989	15,931	.12	.33	0	1
September 1991	15,931	.15	.36	0	1

Notes: (cf.) Comparison group.

Table A5.2. *Reform Reactions, 1992 (Variables in Figs. 5.6–5.9)*

	Number of observations	Mean	Standard deviation	Minimum	Maximum
Dependent variables					
Hopefulness	2,143	.006	.73	-1.90	2.19
Reform, optimistic attitude	2,134	-.0002	.68	-1.97	1.97
Economic efficacy	2,092	-.014	.66	-1.47	1.12
Income fair	2,327	.398	.49	0	1
Acquisitiveness	2,083	-.007	.76	-1.65	2.25
Regional characteristics					
City					
Income growth	2,143	.60	.46	-.50	1.91
Light industry/services (% of GNP, logged)	2,143	2.52	.24	1.54	2.71
City population (logged)	2,159	13.69	1.15	11.45	15.83
Weak neighbor ties (index)	2,159	.004	.72	-2.21	1.61
Locale (reported in figures)					
Guangdong Region	2,143	.09	.28	0	1
Shanghai City	2,143	.05	.21	0	1
Tianjin City	2,143	.04	.20	0	1
Beijing City	2,143	.04	.20	0	1
Yangzi Delta Region	2,143	.07	.25	0	1
Locale (not reported)					
North Central	2,143	.21	.41	0	1
Central	2,143	.22	.41	0	1
Fujian Province	2,143	.02	.13	0	1

	Observations				
Southwest	2,143	.04	.20	0	1
Sichuan Province	2,143	.02	.15	0	1
Northeast (cf.)					
Personal characteristics					
Family income, per cap.	2,143	4.64	.50	2.44	7.09
Occupation					
Professional/technical	2,143	.12	.32	0	1
Administrator (govt.)	2,143	.08	.27	0	1
Manager (firm)	2,143	.07	.26	0	1
Clerical worker	2,143	.22	.42	0	1
Sales/service	2,143	.05	.22	0	1
Private sector	2,143	.03	.18	0	1
None/other	2,143	.04	.18	0	1
Manual worker (cf.)					
Age/10 (youth inverted)	2,143	4.18	1.46	1.6	8.2
Male	2,143	.52	.50	0	1
Education (years)	2,143	10.95	3.20	0	18
Party member	2,143	.31	.46	0	1
Never married (not reported)	2,143	.15	.35	0	1
Income missing (not reported)	2,143	.01	.12	0	1

Notes: (cf.) Comparison group. "Not reported" items are in equation though not in figures in text. Observations based on the equation for "hope."
Source: 1992 Urban Social Survey.

in the summary scale are as follows: (92) "People's thoughts are constantly changing. One really doesn't know what one can hold on to." (93) "With so many decisions to be made in life, sometimes one really doesn't know what one should do." (94) "Life is really meaningless." (95) "Society is changing too fast now. Life is much more difficult than before reform." (96) "Reform has caused change in many aspects of life, providing people many more opportunities to develop."

"Reform," or the "happy with reform" measure, includes five agree/disagree items: (95) "Society is changing too fast now. Life is much more difficult than before reform." (96) "Reform has caused change in many aspects of life, providing people many more opportunities to develop." (97) "Reform has caused many things to change for the worse. It is still not as good as in the past when everyone was about the same, going to work to get a salary without worry." (98) "Regardless of how society changes, I am convinced that compared with others I will not end up on the bottom rung." (99) "Today in society there are more and more people who don't respect the rules." Items 96 and 98 enter the summary scale with a negative loading compared with the other items in the scale.

"Economic efficacy" is a four-item scale emphasizing the role of individual effort in economic success. (66) "One only needs to be willing to exert oneself and then one will surely succeed." Literally, the phrase for effort is "be willing to eat bitterness." (70) "If one wants to become a leader, then one must have a very good family background." The implication is to be born of a high-status family with good connections, and the item enters the summary scale in a reverse direction from other items. (76) "Under current conditions, in your opinion the main reason a person's income lags behind others is mainly because of: (a) laziness, (b) bad luck, (c) inability, (d) bad fate, (e) social injustice, (f) personally risky activities, (g) poor education, (h) wrong family background, (i) poor health, (j) disinterest in money, (k) bad character, (l) poor money management, (m) fears losing face, (n) other. Responses of laziness, inability, risk adverseness, poor education, poor health, disinterest in money, bad character, poor money management, and fear of losing face were coded 1 for high on personal responsibility. The rest were coded 0 for low in personal responsibility. (100) "In your opinion, if a person wants to succeed today this depends mostly on: (a) willingness to take risks, (b) scholarship, (c) ability, (d) willingness to exert oneself, (e) willingness to manipulate others, (f) family background, (g) good at making friends

with all kinds of people, (h) good at building good relations with superiors, (i) good at seizing opportunities, (j) good luck, (k) other. Responses
of taking risks, scholarship, ability, and exertion were coded as high in
individual initiative.

"Income fairness" is based on the question "Is your income reasonable or fair relative to your ability?"

"Monetary acquisitiveness" includes seven items, with the first five
having a possible response of strongly agree, agree, disagree, strongly
disagree, and don't know or "not clear." After giving the "not clear"
response the mean (average) score for that item, all items were combined. The individual items were as follows: (67) "As long as one doesn't
steal or kill, any means of making money is fine." (68) "Work is merely
for earning money to get by." (71) "One only needs to have money to
gain respect from others, and it makes no difference how one got the
money." (72) "Generally speaking, tranquility alone is wealth. One
needn't be too concerned with fortune, fame, and success." (75) "An individual's earning of money is always beneficial to society." In short, does
one believe in Adam Smith? (77) "Two people, A and B, are looking for
work. A is looking for a job with prestige that is not so highly paid. B is
looking for a job lacking in prestige but with pay twice as high. If it were
you, what kind of work would you choose?" (79) "There are three
people, A, B, and C. A says the more money one has the better. Moreover if he got a lot of money, he wouldn't work again. B says money is
not a good thing. Having a lot is pointless. C says one can't get by without
money. But one just needs a little to get by. With which manner of speaking do you most agree?" As should be obvious from the wording, items
72 and 77 enter the summary scale with weighting inverse of the other
items.

APPENDIX A6. VARIABLES IN FIGURES 7.1 AND 7.2 AND CIVIL SERVANT SCALES

Table A6.1 shows the summary statistics for variables in Figures 7.1 and
7.2. The attitude scales used for civil servants in Chapter 7 were constructed as follows.

1. *Separation.* One important policy of civil service reform has been
the separation of the party from the state. We have a question in the
survey related to the role of party in enterprise: "Enterprises should

Table A6.1. Statistics for Bureaucrats (for Figs. 7.1 and 7.2)

	Number of observations	Mean	Standard deviation	Minimum	Maximum
Dependent variables					
Separation of politics/economics	964	2.189	.83	1	3
Political operatives to business	966	2.042	.83	1	3
Satisfaction with job	965	.574	.49	0	1
Secure job anticipated during reform	945	2.031	.49	1	3
Gain anticipated during reform	943	−.016	1.28	−3	3
Independent variables					
Occupation					
Technical specialist	965	.089	.29	0	1
Enterprise					
Manager	965	.037	.19	0	1
Clerical worker	965	.315	.46	0	1
Government					
Administrator	965	.057	.23	0	1
Clerical worker	965	.122	.33	0	1
Other job					
Administrator, public org.	965	.028	.16	0	1
Political operative, govt., high	965	.046	.21	0	1
Political operative, govt., low	965	.102	.30	0	1
Political operative, enterprise	965	.181	.39	0	1
Political operative, pub. org.	965	.023	.15	0	1
Education (primary, J.H., H.S., college)	965	4.282	.80	1	4
Youth ((65 − age)/10)	965	2.489	.96	0	4.7
Male	965	.717	.45	0	1

Source: 1987 Civil Service Survey.

abolish full-time political and party officers." The respondent had a choice of (1) bad idea, (2) hard to say, or (3) good idea. A high value indicates support for less party influence.

2. *Cadres and business.* We also want to examine how cadres in different subgroups react to the policy of allowing political cadres to be involved in business: "Party and political cadres should be allowed to change their job and do business." The answers included (1) bad idea, (2) hard to say, and (3) good idea. High value indicates support for political cadres doing business.

3. *Satisfaction.* A simple dichotomy, with 1 = satisfied with work, 0 = dissatisfied.

4. *Security.* The cadres surveyed were also asked whether they thought they would be cut from their jobs during organizational and personnel streamlining. They could answer either "possible," "hard to say," or "not possible." Overall, only 16 percent gave the "not possible," completely secure response.

5. *Gain.* In the 1987 survey, the respondents were asked whether the political reform proposed during the thirteenth party congress in 1987 would affect their interests. Interests included status, power, and benefits.[2] The three items – status, power, and benefits – were summed.[3] The resulting index of the total gain or loss during reform ranges from –3 to 3.

APPENDIX A7. POLITICAL PARTICIPATION ITEMS

Table A7.1 shows the summary statistics for variables in Figures 8.1–8.5. Tables A7.2 and A7.3 present results of multivariate logistic regression on complaint behavior and voting. The key questions in the 1987 Political Participation Survey are as follows.

II. In regard to wage raise, promotion, housing assignment, work assignment, leadership style, etc.,
 A. Have you had any opinions, dissatisfaction, complaints?
 B. If yes, have you ever expressed it?

2. The effect could be positive (coded 1), no change (coded 0), or negative (coded –1). Missing values are coded as 0.
3. The three items are highly correlated, as shown in the factor loadings of .75 (status), .72 (power), and .59 (benefits).

Table A7.1. *Political Participation Statistics, 1987*

	Number of observations	Mean	Standard deviation	Minimum	Maximum
Channels of voicing complaints					
Work unit leader	2,415	.11	.31	0	1
Government bureau	2,415	.10	.30	0	1
Media	2,415	.02	.14	0	1
Personal connection	2,415	.01	.08	0	1
Local people's deputy	2,415	.03	.17	0	1
Other	2,415	.01	.11	0	1
Work-related complaint					
Complaint	2,378	.79	.41	0	1
Voiced	1,949	.54	.50	0	1
Responded	1,881	.28	.45	0	1
Solved	1,874	.10	.30	0	1
Nonwork complaint					
Complaint	2,390	.86	.35	0	1
Voiced	2,058	.33	.47	0	1
Responded	2,058	.13	.34	0	1
Solved	2,056	.05	.21	0	1
Electoral behavior					
Voted	2,390	.88	.33	0	1
Voted voluntarily	2,357	.29	.45	0	1
Knowledge of candidate (n/y)	2,371	.55	.50	0	1

Occupation

	N	Mean	SD	Min	Max
Administrative/managerial	2,415	.11	.32	0	1
Government clerk	2,415	.11	.32	0	1
Company/firm clerk	2,415	.08	.28	0	1
Professional/technical	2,415	.20	.40	0	1
Sales/service workers	2,415	.09	.29	0	1
Manual workers	2,415	.16	.37	0	1
Private	2,415	.05	.21	0	1
Other	2,415	.05	.22	0	1
Retired	2,415	.06	.24	0	1
Student	2,415	.08	.27	0	1
Other characteristics					
Party member	2,384	.43	.50	0	1
Education[a]	2,403	2.13	.82	1	3
Age	2,379	38.74	12.69	15	76
Age (18+)	2,376	38.77	12.67	18	76
Male	2,381	.63	.48	0	1
Beijing resident	2,415	.12	.33	0	1
Income[b]	2,377	6.66	.49	1.67	9.21

Notes: [a] Junior high or less coded 1; senior high and technical coded 2; college and more coded 3. [b] Logged family per capita income (missing = mean).

Source: 1987 Political Participation Survey.

Table A7.2. *Complaint Behavior, 1987*

	Complaint	Voiced	Response	Solved
Occupation				
Administrator/manager	.72	2.04*	3.48*	2.50*
Clerical (government)	.80	1.55*	2.08*	2.37*
Clerical (firm)	.70	1.12	.02	.66
Professional/technical	.54*	.85	1.23	.75
Sales/service	.50*	.76	.58	.17#
Private	.30*	.93	1.75	2.17
Other	.60	.81	1.15	.81
Retired	.51*	.83	1.01	1.08
Student	1.70	1.42	1.60	2.41
Manual worker (cf.)				
Income	1.02	1.06	1.13*	1.74*
Age	1.00	1.05*	1.02*	1.03*
Beijing resident	1.26	1.12	.68	.68
Education	1.44*	.98	.99	.78
Male	1.21	1.23#	1.06	.92
Pseudo R^2	.04	.07	.06	.07
Observations	2,320	1,999	1,996	1,994

Note: Nonwork complaints. Odds ratios from a logistic regression. Right three columns only for those who voiced a complaint. (Cf.) Comparison group; (*) $p < .05$; (#) $p < .10$.
Source: 1987 Political Participation Survey.

(a) If yes, through which of the following channels did you express? Please choose one.
1. work unit leaders,
2. mass organizations, such as labor unions,
3. government bureau,
4. newspaper, television station, etc.,
5. personal connection,
6. people's deputy,
7. other.

Table A7.3. *Voting Behavior, 1987*

	Voted	Voted voluntarily	Knowledge of candidates[a]
Occupation			
Administrator/manager	1.11	3.51*	1.89*
Clerical (government)	1.70#	2.02*	1.23
Clerical (firm)	1.28	1.40	1.34
Professional/technical	1.57#	2.17*	1.66*
Sales/service	1.23	1.01	.83
Private	.44*	1.72*	1.12
Other	.55*	1.58#	.64#
Retired	.25*	1.23	.92
Student	3.24*	3.76*	1.83#
Manual worker (cf.)			
Income	1.16	.86	.95
Age	1.04*	1.03*	1.02*
Beijing resident	2.24*	.82	1.31*
Education	.75*	.73*	.84*
Male	.62*	.95	.82*
Pseudo R^2	.05	.05	.02
Observations	2,318	2,289	2,302

Notes: [a] Some/much knowledge coded 1; no knowledge coded 0. Odds ratios from logistic regressions. Population age 18+. (cf.) Comparison group; (*) $p < .05$; (#) $p < .10$.
Source: 1987 Political Participation Survey.

(b) Comparatively speaking, which of the above channels do you think is the most effective?
(c) If not expressed, what was the reason? Please choose one.
1. did not know to whom,
2. no use even if I did,
3. feared revenge,
4. too many opinions, wouldn't make a splash if I did,

      5. unrelated to my interest,

      6. other.

  C. Did you ever get any response?

  D. Was your problem solved?

III.   In regard to price policy, public transportation, living environment, management of public affairs, etc. [A–D same as above]

XI.   Did you participate in the 1987 local people's congress election?

  A. If yes

      1. was/is required by your work unit leaders?

      2. because everyone else did,

      3. voluntarily participated.

  B. If no

      1. formality, not interested,

      2. wanted, but had other obligation.

XII. Did you know about the candidates in your district?

      1. basically yes,

      2. some,

      3. no.

1989–1992 Survey Item

"When you are dissatisfied with certain aspects of social life, what would be your most likely action?" The respondent was given seven choices: (a) talk to government officials, (b) talk to the media, (c) complain, (d) protest publicly, (e) go through illegal channels, (f) seek change through own effort and ideas, (g) do nothing. To simplify the analysis, we grouped these choices under three categories, (1) official channels (a and b), (2) self-initiated channels (d–f), and (3) no action (c and g).

1992 Urban Survey Items

Political Action is a summary scale including responses to the following three items:

- "What would you do if something happens that hurts everyone's interest at work or in your neighborhood? Would you (a) lead a petition to the relevant government office and official, (b) lead the petition if asked, (c) would not lead, but follow the crowd, or (d) avoid trouble?" The first two choices were coded 1 and other choices were coded 0.

- "What would you do if your supervisor made a wrong decision related to work?" The respondent was asked to choose among (a) obey, (b) silently disobey, or (c) tell the supervisor he or she is wrong. The last choice was coded 1 and the other two answers coded 0.
- "In recent years, have you made suggestions or expressed your opinions about workplace reform, innovation, and the improvement of management?" The answers included (a) yes, often, (b) sometimes, (c) only when asked, (d) only talked to friends and colleagues about it, (e) never. The first two choices were coded 1. The other answers were coded 0.

APPENDIX A8. GENDER AND FAMILY STATISTICS

	Mean	Standard deviation	Minimum	Maximum	Number of observations
Dependent variables					
Cooking/laundry hours					
By wife	2.55	1.14	0	9	4,322
By husband	1.43	1.12	0	6	4,126
By wife (logged)	1.21	.34	0	2.3	4,322
By husband (logged)	.77	.50	0	1.9	4,126
Wife's main complaint					
Understanding	.39				
Husband's income/job	.27				
Chores	.11				
Care of parents	.02				
None	.20				4,312
Wife, disagreements over					
Husband's income/job	.17	.37	0	1	4,417
Chores	.34	.47	0	1	4,417
Children	.46	.50	0	1	4,417
Husband's attitudes					
Complaints	.74	.44	0	1	4,396
Disagreements	.75	.43	0	1	4,415

(cont.)

Independent variables

	Mean	SD	Min	Max	N
Wife's share of income					
% of joint income	43.35	14.91	0	100	4,424
0%	.06	.23	0	1	4,424
30%+	.90	.30	0	1	4,424
45–49%	.22	.41	0	1	4,424
50%	.13	.34	0	1	4,424
100%	.01	.11	0	1	4,424
Wife's characteristics					
Education (years/6)	1.64	.48	0	3.7	4,424
Youth (60– age)/10	2.36	.80	0	4	4,424
Poor health	1.50	.60	1	4	4,421
Husband's characteristics					
Education (years/6)	1.78	.51	0	3.8	4,414
Youth (70– age)/10	3.14	.88	.2	5	4,424
Poor health	1.39	.56	1	4	4,421
Home hours					
By wife	3.93	1.80	0	14.5	4,380
By husband	2.41	1.68	0	11.5	4,246
By wife (logged)	1.53	.38	0	2.7	4,380
By husband (logged)	1.09	.55	0	2.5	4,246

(conti.)

	Mean	Standard deviation	Minimum	Maximum	Number of observations
Conveniences					
Natural gas	.66	.47	0	1	4,423
Refrigerator	.52	.50	0	1	4,410
Washing machine	.67	.47	0	1	4,420
Piped water	.86	.34	0	1	4,421
Bedrooms	2.30	1.07	0	6	4,344
Family members/help					
Parent	.13	.34	0	1	4,386
Other adults	.55	.92	0	4	4,424
Children aged 0–2	.16	.36	0	1	4,424
Children aged 3–6	.22	.41	0	1	4,424
Children aged 7–12	.32	.47	0	1	4,424
Daughter aged 13–18	.12	.33	0	1	4,424
Son aged 13–18	.14	.35	0	1	4,424

Note: Sample sizes approximate for analysis in text.
Source: 1991 Women's Survey, Urban Sample.

Appendix B

Surveys, Sampling Biases, and Weighting

CHINA

ESRIC Surveys, 1987–92

For China, we rely heavily on a series of surveys conducted by the Economic System Reform Institute of China (ESRIC) (see Table B1). This includes the 1987 Political Participation Survey (Chapter 8), the 1987 Civil Service Surveys (Chapter 7), the 1987–91 Semiannual Surveys (Chapter 5), the 1988 Quality of Life Survey (Chapter 10), and the 1992 Urban Social Survey (various chapters.). Eventually disbanded after the events of 1989, the Economic Reform Institute for a time ran high-quality surveys using a national sample drawn from China's largest cities (see Table B2). A government think tank designed to give top policy-makers advice on the pace of economic reform, the Institute assembled some of the top survey talent in China.

Samples. The Institute's samples were based on cluster sampling. Cities were stratified into large, medium, and small cities according to their population. In addition to Beijing, Tianjin, and Shanghai, 37 cities were randomly selected from the three categories, ranging down to a minimum of 93,800 (Zhangshu) municipal population. Spread over 23 provinces, about 40 cities were included in most surveys (see Table B2 for a typical list of sample cities).

Within each city, sampling was with probability proportional to size (PPS) – which means that larger neighborhoods had a greater probability of being selected. Three neighborhoods were sampled in each city, except in Beijing, Tianjin, and Shanghai, where six neighborhoods were sampled. Within each neighborhood, one subneighborhood (residents' committee) was randomly sampled, and within each subneighborhood

343

Table B1. *Description of Surveys*

	Organization/principal investigator	Month/year of survey	Number of observations	Sample sites[b]
Political Participation Survey	ESRIC[a]	7/1987	2,415	8 cities[b]
Civil Service Reform Survey (cadre)	ESRIC	12/1987	988	8 cities
Civil Service Reform Survey (mass)	ESRIC	12/1987	1,562	8 cities
Quality of Life Survey	ESRIC	8/1988	2,321	37 cities
Semiannual Survey	ESRIC	5/1987	2,576	40 cities
Semiannual Survey	ESRIC	10/1987	2,438	37 cities
Semiannual Survey	ESRIC	5/1988	2,577	39 cities
Semiannual Survey	ESRIC	10/1988	2,176	35 cities
Semiannual Survey	ESRIC	5/1989	2,143	35 cities
Semiannual Survey	ESRIC	10/1989	2,020	33 cities
Semiannual Survey (with module on housing reform)	ESRIC	9/1991	2,520	39 cities
Quality of Life Survey	ESRIC	8/1988	2,325	40 cities
Urban Social Survey	ESRIC	6/1992	2,370	44 cities
Economic Enterprise (Firm) Survey	Labor Institute of China	11/91–1/92	8,071	7 prov.
Economic Enterprise (Firm) Survey	Li et al. (1996)	Fall 1992 to Winter 1993	9,397	422 firms in 12 prov.
Chinese Household Income Project (CHIP) (urban)	Griffin and Zhao (1993)	3–4/1989	9,009	10 prov.
Women's Survey	CASS[c]	1991	4,509	6 prov.
Taiwan Social Change Survey I & II	Academia Sinica	1990	2,531	Islandwide

Notes: [a](ESRIC) Economic System Reform Institute of China. [b]Specifically, the eight largest cities: Beijing, Shanghai, Tianjin, Guangzhou, Shenyang, Wuhan, Chongqing, and Harbin. [c](CASS) Chinese Academy of Social Sciences.

Table B2. *Sample Cities in ESRIC Surveys and Coding for Regions*

Regions	Cities	Provinces
Beijing	Beijing	
Tianjin	Tianjin	
Shanghai	Shanghai	
East	Hangzhou	Zhejiang
	Jiaxing	Zhejiang
	Wuxi	Jiangsu
Guangzhou	Guangzhou	Guangdong
Central	Wuhan	Hubei
	Xiangfan	Hubei
	Kaifeng	Henan
	Xinxiang	Henan
	Sanmenxia	Henan
	Jinan	Shandong
	Zibo	Shandong
	Zaozhuang	Shandong
	Linyi	Shandong
	Lianyungang	Jiangsu
Northeast	Shenyang	Liaoning
	Dalian	Liaoning
	Benxi	Liaoning
	Wafangdian	Liaoning
	Harbin	Heilongjiang
	Daqing	Heilongjiang
	Jiamusi	Heilongjiang
	Qiqihar	Heilongjiang
	Yichun	Heilongjiang
	Jilin	Jilin
South Central	Liuzhou	Guangxi
	Duyun	Guizhou
	Ganzhou	Jiangxi
	Sanming	Fujian
North Central	Taiyuan	Shanxi
	Xian	Shaanxi
	Wuhai	Inner Mongolia
	Chifeng	Inner Mongolia
Northwest	Lanzhou	Gansu
	Yinchuan	Ningxia
Southwest	Chongqing	Sichuan
	Peiling	Sichuan
	Kunming	Yunnan

20 households were randomly sampled. This produced a total of 60 households in each city – except for the three largest cities, which had 120 households. Within the household, interviewers rotated in succession from asking about the oldest male, youngest female, oldest female, and youngest male – returning to ask about the oldest male in the fifth household interviewed. The ages produced by this method ranged from 14 to 99, with a concentration in the 18 to 74 age range. When no one could be found at homes, interviewers could substitute an adjacent household.

The Political Participation Survey and the two Civil Service Reform surveys were conducted in eight large cities (Beijing, Shanghai, Tianjin, Guangzhou, Shenyang, Wuhan, Chongqing, and Harbin). The sample for the Civil Service Reform Survey was obtained by drawing a probability sample of all people using the techniques described above, and retaining the first 1,000 cadres in the sample. To ensure adequate observations for statistical analysis, the Political Participation sample was stratified by occupation. Occupations with small proportions in the total population, such as administrators, clerical workers, professionals, and those in the private sector, were oversampled. Other occupations with large proportions in the population (manual workers and retirees) were undersampled.

1991 Firm Survey

What we have titled the 1991 Firm Survey or, more properly, the Economic Enterprise Survey, is based on a self-administered questionnaire of workers and staff in factories and stores (Chapter 6). Funded by the China National Social Science Research Fund (roughly comparable to the National Science Foundation in the U.S.), the survey was conducted between November 1991 and January 1992. Under the direction of principal investigator Tongqing Feng, the survey was a collaborative effort of the Labor Institute of China, the All-China Federation of Labor Unions, and the Institute of Sociology at the Chinese Academy of Social Sciences. The sample included 8,071 employees in 100 economic enterprises in seven provinces: Yunnan, Guangdong, Zhejiang, Hubei, Shanghai, Gansu, and Heilongjiang.

The questionnaire included 320 questions, covering a wide range of issues such as ownership, management, industrial sector and profitability of the enterprise, individual family and work history, income, job satisfaction, morale, labor relations, and other attitudinal questions. The respondents, who were randomly selected from enterprise payrolls, were not only workers but also managers, technicians, and cadres. In most cases, the respondents from an enterprise gathered in one large room in several groups during work time. They were asked to fill out a questionnaire under the supervision of trained interviewers from the Labor Institute and the Institute of Sociology. Their answers were assured confidentiality. The data set contains some errors which were caused by respondents who did not complete all the questions. There are also problems with questionnaire coding and data entry. Nevertheless, the final data set, with 7,790 usable observations, provides valuable information.

1992 Firm Survey

We used this data set to validate the findings from the 1991 Firm Survey. This fall 1992/winter 1993 survey was based on self-administered questionnaires distributed to enterprises in twenty-six widely dispersed cities. Enterprises included firms in manufacturing, construction, transportation, and wholesale and retail services. In each city, a representative of the local bureau of labor was trained to randomly select seven enterprises from each of the three sectors of state-owned, collectively owned, and joint venture enterprises (Li et al. 1996).

Sampling Biases and Weighting

One issue with the ESRIC samples and the worker survey is sampling bias. The level of education in each sample was higher than the 1990 census figure (Table B3). One reason was that the ESRIC samples were drawn from the household registration system which excludes the urban "floating" population (currently 10 to 20 percent of the urban population). Most of the excluded were rural surplus laborers with less education and occupying many of the more menial construction and service jobs in Chinese cities. However, because the census excludes many of the same types of people, there must be other reasons for the discrepancy between census and survey education levels.

More important, some interviewers had to conduct the survey in several households simultaneously. Without adequate assistance from the interviewer, the more educated respondents were more likely to

Table B3. *Education Distributions and Sample Biases* (%)

Education	1990 census[a]	USS sample[b]	Semiannual sample[c]	Civil reform[d]		PART. sample[e]	Taiwan sample[f]	Taiwan census[g]
				Mass	Cadre			
Junior college or more	9	22	16	12	47	41	23	17
Senior high	23	37	33	35	35	30	28	27
Junior high	36	29	34	34	15	24	17	18
Primary	23	10	13	16	2	4	26	32
None	10	2	5	4	1	1	8	8
Total	100	100	100	100	100	100	100	100

Notes:

[a] 1990 census data for cities, 16–64, see Census Office 1993.

[b] 1992 Urban Social Survey.

[c] 1987–1991 Semiannual Surveys (7 surveys combined).

[d] 1987 Civil Service Reform Survey (mass and cadre subsamples).

[e] 1987 Political Participation Survey.

[f] 1990 Taiwan Social Change Survey.

[g] Raw data from DGBAS, 1990 Labor Force Survey.

complete the questionnaire. This would also result in more valid cases among the more educated. The problem with the worker samples could be caused by missing temporary workers and others who were not officially on the enterprise payroll, and who were mostly less-educated rural workers.

To correct this problem, we weighted samples by the education level of the urban population as reported in the 1990 population census of China. For the worker sample, we weighted by the education level of the urban enterprise work force in the same 1990 population census. Therefore, throughout the book, all descriptive statistics using these surveys are based on adjusting education to the 1990 census for cities. By weighting, these descriptive statistics should reflect the true population more closely. For example, in the 1992 urban social survey, for the question "Is your income fair compared with your ability?" the unweighted percentage of those who answered "not fair" was 47 percent, reflecting an upward bias due to the larger educated and thus more dissatisfied group in the sample. After weighting, however, it dropped to only 40 percent. In multivariate analyses which typically include the education variable, we assume that the inclusion of the education variable resolves most of the sampling bias problem.

1988 CHIP Survey

Conducted in the spring of 1989, with questions about income in 1988, the CHIP Survey is based on a State Statistical Bureau sample of 9,009 urban households in Beijing, Shanxi, Liaoning, Jiangsu, Anhui, Henan, Hubei, Guangdong, and Yunnan. The 9,009 respondents in the survey reported on a total of 31,287 household members (including themselves) and 17,493 income earners – which is the subsample that we use in Chapter 4. Questionnaire design was by a joint U.S./Chinese Academy of Social Science (CASS) research team, with funding from the Ford Foundation, the Institute of Economics of CASS, the East Asian Institute of Columbia University, and the City University of New York. Within each province, a subsample was drawn using the existing State Statistical Bureau urban sampling framework. The research team signed a contract with each sampled province or city to administer the questionnaire. The questionnaires were mailed and collected from each of the ten provincial contractors directly. Further description of the survey can be found in Griffin and Zhao (1993). The data set is available from Inter-University Consortium for Political Science Research in Michigan.

1991 Women's Survey

Directed by the Population Institute at the Chinese Academy of Social Sciences, the 1991 Women's Survey was supported by the United Nations Population Fund and the Academy of Social Sciences and involved collaboration with the East-West Center in Hawaii. The survey used probability sampling of intact husband–wife families in six province-level units (Shanghai City, Guangdong, Shandong, Jilin, Shanxi, and Ningxia) to produce a total sample of 4,509 urban couples. Cities of different size were included. Both husband and wife were interviewed separately, producing a total of 4,509 wife and 4,509 husband interviews. Prior publications from the survey include Sha, Xiong, and Gao (1994) and Sha et al. (1995).

TAIWAN

In comparing Taiwan and China, Chapter 11 relies on several additional surveys from Taiwan. From both government and other sources, the surveys were as follows.

1990 Taiwan Labor Force Survey

The Labor Force Survey is conducted annually in May by the Directorate General of Budget, Accounting and Statistics (DGBAS; *zhuji chu*), an organization roughly equivalent to Beijing's State Statistical Bureau. The survey is based on an islandwide probability sample drawn from Taiwan's continuous household register, which in 1990 produced a sample of 18,220, which in turn included a total of 56,895 household members, young and old. Our analysis is of the adult, working-age members living in towns and cities. By 1990, most members lived in either a city (61 percent) or town (33 percent). Thus, there were ample observations to work with in this sample, and its distribution is close to census results for the same year.

1990 Taiwan Social Change Survey

This is an annual survey, directed at the time by the principal investigator, Hei-yuan Chiu, of Academia Sinica, Taiwan's premier research institute. It is based on a probability sample drawn from the continuous household register so as to represent the total working-age (15–64) population. The interviewers were students with formal training in social science and research methods. Distributions of the data on age, education, and occupation show this data set to be basically representative of the total adult population in Taiwan. From this sample, we drew respondents from the five administrative municipalities and the urbanized counties abutting the largest municipalities. This provided a 1,549-person sample approximately as urban as the mainland urban social survey. In comparisons with Taiwan, we also limited respondents in China to those below age 65.

1996 Taiwan Social Change Survey

Part of the same series as the above survey, this version used an East Asian Social Survey module which eventually will provide comparisons with South Korea and China. Based on an islandwide sample of 2,831 people 25 to 60 years of age, the survey provides information on work, family, and political participation.

1989 Taiwan Women and Family Survey

A collaborative effort of the University of Chicago, Taiwan National University, and Academia Sinica, this 3,803-woman survey provides data on women and the husbands of married women. It is based on a probability sample drawn from the islandwide continuous household register. Interviewers were social workers, who were mostly female.

References

Aberbach, Joel D., and Bert Rockman. 1994. "They Don't Get No Satisfaction (Or Do They?): The Senior U.S. Federal Executive 1970–1992." Paper presented at the Conference on "Ten Years of Change." University of Manchester, Manchester, England, September.

Aldrich, J. H., and F. D. Nelson. 1984. *Linear Probability, Logit, and Probit Models.* Newbury Park, CA: Sage Publications.

All-China Federation of Labor Unions. 1986. *Zhongguo Zhigong Duiwu Zhuangkuang Diaocha* (A Study of Chinese Workers). Beijing: Workers Publishing House.

All-China Federation of Labor Unions. 1993. *Zouxiang Shehui Zhuyi Shichang Jingji de Zhongguo Gongren Jieji* (Chinese Working Class Marching Toward Socialist Market Economy). Beijing: China Social Science Publishing House.

All-China Federation of Labor Unions, Policy Research Office. 1992. *Zhongguo Gonghui Tongji Nianjian* (China Labor Union Statistical Yearbook). Beijing: Workers Publishing House.

Almond, Gabriel A. 1991. "Capitalism and Democracy." *PS: Political Science and Politics* 24:467–74.

Almond, Gabriel A., and Sidney Verba. 1963. *The Civic Culture: Political Attitudes and Democracy in Five Nations.* Princeton: Princeton University Press.

Amsden, Alice H. 1985. "The State and Taiwan's Economic Development." Pp. 78–106 in Peter Evans, Dietrich Rueschemeyer, and Theda Skocpol, eds., *Bringing the State Back In.* Cambridge, Eng.: Cambridge University Press.

Arendt, Hannah. 1951. *Origins of Totalitarianism.* New York: Harcourt, Brace.

Ashwin, Sarah, and Elaine Bowers. 1997. "Do Russian Women Want to Work?" Pp. 21–37 in Mary Buckley, ed., *Post-Soviet Women.* Cambridge, Eng.: Cambridge University Press.

Bachman, David. 1991. *Bureaucracy, Economy, and Leadership in China: The Institutional Origins of the Great Leap Forward.* Cambridge University Press.

Bahry, Donna, and Brian D. Silver. 1990. "Soviet Citizen Participation on the Eve of Democratization." *American Political Science Review* 84, no. 3, Sept.: 821–47.

Bailey, Beth A. 1988. *From Front Porch to Back Seat: Courtship in Twentieth Century America.* Baltimore: Johns Hopkins University Press.

Baker, Huge D. R. 1979. *Chinese Family and Kinship.* New York: Columbia University Press.

Banerji, Arup, et al. 1995. "The Political Economy of Formal Sector Pay and Employment in Developing Countries." Policy Research Working Paper no. 1435. Washington, D.C.: World Bank.

Banfield, Edward C. 1963. *City Politics.* Cambridge, Eng.: Cambridge University Press.

Barme, Geremie, and John Minford, eds. 1989. *Seeds of Fire: Chinese Voices of Conscience.* New York: Noonday Press.

Barnes, Samuel H., and Max Kaase, eds. 1979. *Political Action: Mass Participation in Five Western Democracies.* Beverly Hills, Calif.: Sage Publications.

Baron, James N. 1994. "Reflections on Recent Generations of Mobility Research." Pp. 384–93 in David B. Grusky, ed., *Social Stratification.* Boulder: Westview.

Bates, Robert H. 1981. *Markets and States in Tropical Africa.* Berkeley: University of California Press.

Bauer, John, et al. 1992. "Gender Inequality in Urban China." *Modern China* 18, no. 3:333–69.

Baum, Richard. 1996. *Burying Mao.* Princeton University Press.

Becker, Gary S. 1981. *A Treatise on the Family.* Cambridge, Mass.: Harvard University Press.

Berado, Donna, Constance Shehan, and Gerald Leslie. 1987. "A Residue of Tradition: Jobs, Careers, and Spouse's Time in Housework." *Journal of Marriage and the Family* 49:381–90.

Berg, Ivar. 1971. *Education and Jobs: The Great Training Robbery.* Boston: Beacon.

Berk, Richard A., and Sarah Fenstermaker Berk. 1983. "Supply-Side Sociology of the Family: The Challenge of the New Home Economics." *Annual Review of Sociology* 9:375–95.

Berk, Sarah Fenstermaker. 1985. *The Gender Factory: The Appointment of Work in American Households.* New York: Plenum.

Berliner, Joseph S. 1994. "Conclusion: Reflections on the Social Legacy of Communism." In James R. Millar and Sharon L. Wolchik, eds., *The Social Legacy of Communism.* New York: Cambridge University Press.

Bettleheim, Charles. 1976. *Economic Calculations and Forms of Property.* London: Routledge and Kegan Paul.

Bialer, Seweryn. 1980. *Stalin's Successors: Leadership, Stability, and Change in the Soviet Union.* New York: Cambridge University Press.

Bian, Yanjie. 1994a. *Work and Inequality in Urban China.* Albany: State University of New York Press.

——— 1994b. "*Guanxi* and the Allocation of Urban Jobs in China." *China Quarterly* no. 140:971–98.

——— et al. 1995. "Work Units and Housing Reform in Two Chinese Cities." Manuscript.

1997. "Bringing Strong Ties Back In: Indirect Ties, Network Bridges, and Job Searches in China." *American Sociological Review* 62:366–85.

and John R. Logan. 1996. "Market Transition and the Persistence of Power: The Changing Stratification System in Urban China." *American Sociological Review* 61:739–58.

Blake, Judith. 1989. *Family Size and Achievement.* Berkeley: University of California Press.

Blalock, Hubert M. 1960. *Social Statistics.* New York: McGraw-Hill.

Blanchard, Olivier, et al. 1993. *Post-Communist Reform: Pain and Progress.* Cambridge, Mass.: MIT Press.

Blank, Grant, and William L. Parish 1990. "Rural Industry and Nonfarm Employment." Pp. 109–39 in Reginald Kwok, William Parish, and Anthony Yeh, eds., *Chinese Urban Reform.* Armonk, N.Y.: M. E. Sharpe.

Block, Peter. 1987. *The Empowered Manager.* San Francisco: Jossey-Bass.

Bourdieu, Pierre. 1987. *Outline of a Theory of Practice.* Cambridge, Eng.: Cambridge University Press.

Braun, Michael, J. Scott, and D. F. Alwin. 1994. "Economic Necessity or Self-Actualization? Attitudes Toward Women's Labour Force Participation in East and West Germany." *European Sociological Review* 10:29–48.

Braun, Juan, and Norman V. Loayza. 1994. "Taxation, Public Services, and the Informal Sector in a Model of Endogenous Growth." *Policy Research Working Paper* no. 1334. Washington, D.C.: World Bank.

Breslauer, George 1984. "On the Adaptability of Soviet Welfare-State Authoritarianism." In Erik Hoffman and Robbin Laird, eds., *The Soviet Polity in the Modern Era.* New York: Aldine.

Brines, Julie. 1994. "Economic Dependency, Gender, and the Division of Labor at Home." *American Journal of Sociology* 100:652–88.

Brinton, Crane. 1938. *The Anatomy of Revolution.* New York: Prentice-Hall.

Brinton, Mary. 1993. *Women and the Economic Miracle: Gender and Work in Postwar Japan.* Berkeley: University of California Press.

Brinton, Mary, Yean-ju Lee, and William L. Parish. 1995. "Married Women's Employment in East Asia." *American Journal of Sociology* 100:1099–130.

Broaded, C. Montgomery, and Chongshun Liu. 1996. "Family Background, Gender and Educational Attainment in Urban China." *China Quarterly*, no. 145:53–86.

Buckley, Mary, ed. 1992. *Perestroika and Soviet Women.* Cambridge, Eng.: Cambridge University Press.

Burawoy, Michael. 1979. *Manufacturing Consent: Changes in the Labor Process under Monopoly Capitalism.* Chicago: University of Chicago Press.

and Pavel Krotov. 1992. "The Soviet Transition from Socialism to Capitalism: Worker Control and Economic Bargaining in the Wood Industry." *American Sociological Review* 57:16–38.

and Janos Lukacs. 1992. *The Radiant Past.* Chicago: University of Chicago Press.

Burgess, Ernest W., and Harvey J. Locke. 1945. *The Family: From Institution to Companionship.* New York: American Book Company.

Burns, John. 1989. "Chinese Civil Service Reform." *China Quarterly*, no. 120:739–70.

Butler, David, and Donald Stokes. 1969. *Political Change in Britain.* New York: St. Martin's Press.

Calhoun, Craig. 1994. *Neither Gods nor Emperors: Students and the Struggle for Democracy in China.* Berkeley: University of California Press.

Carnaghan, Ellen, and Donna Bahry. 1990. "Political Attitudes and the Gender Gap in the USSR." *Comparative Politics.* Pp. 379–99.

Census Office (Quanguo renkou chouyang diaocha bangong shi), ed. 1997. *1995 Quanguo 1% Renkou Chouyang Diaocha Ziliao.* Beijing: China Statistics Press.

Census Office, State Council (and State Statistical Bureau, Department of Population Statistics). 1993. *Tabulation on the 1990 Population Census of the People's Republic of China.* Beijing: China Statistics Press (in Chinese and English).

Census Office, State Council (and State Statistical Bureau, Department of Population Statistics). 1985. *1982 Population Census of China.* Beijing: China Statistics Press (in Chinese and English).

Chang, Kai. 1995. "Gongyou zhi qiye zhong nu zhigong de shiye ji zai jiuye wenti de diaocha yu yanjiu." *Shehuixue yanjiu* 57, no. 3:83–93.

Chao, Linda, and Ramon Myers. 1998. *China's First Democracy.* Baltimore: Johns Hopkins University Press.

Cheek, Timothy. 1994. "From Priests to Professionals: Intellectuals and the State Under the CCP." In Jeffrey N. Wasserstrom and Elizabeth J. Perry, eds., *Popular Protest and Political Culture in Modern China*, 2nd edition. Boulder: Westview Press. Pp. 124–45.

Chen, Jo-hsi. 1978. *The Execution of Mayor Yin, and Other Stories from the Great Proletarian Cultural Revolution.* Bloomington: Indiana University Press.

Chen, Xiangming, and Xiayuan Gao. 1993a. "China's Urban Housing Development in the Shift from Redistribution to Decentralization." *Social Problems* 40:266–83.

Chen, Xiangming, and Xiaoyuan Gao. 1993b. "Urban Economic Reform and Public-Housing Investment in China." *Urban Affairs Quarterly* 29:117–45.

Chen, Xiangming, and William L. Parish. 1996. "Urbanization in China: Reassessing an Evolving Model." In Josef Gugler, ed., *The Urban Transformation of the Developing World.* Oxford University Press.

Chen, Yueliang. 1995. "Social Security in 1994–1995." Pp. 202–11 in Jiang Liu, Xueyi Lu, and Tianlun Shan, eds., *1994–1995 Zhongguo Shehui Xingshi Fenxi yu Yuce* (1994–95 China Social Trends Analysis and Forecast). Beijing: China Social Sciences Press.

Cherlin, Andrew J. 1981. *Marriage, Divorce, Remarriage.* Cambridge, Mass.: Harvard University Press.

1992. *Marriage, Divorce, Remarriage.* Revised edition. Cambridge, Mass.: Harvard University Press.

Chi, Hsi-sheng. 1991. *Politics of Disillusionment: The Chinese Communist Party Under Deng Xiaoping, 1978–1989.* Armonk, N.Y.: M. E. Sharpe.

CHIP codebooks (1988 Chinese Household Income Project, Keith Griffin and Zhao Renwei, 1993). ICPSR 9836. Ann Arbor, Mich.: Inter-University Consortium for Political and Social Research. Photocopy and electronic files.

Chirot, Daniel. 1972. "The Corporatist Model and Socialism." *Theory and Society* 9, no. 2 (March): 363–82.

Cohen, Paul A. 1991. "Situational versus Systemic Factor in Societal Evolution," in Thomas A. Metzger and Ramon H. Myers, eds., *Two Societies in Opposition: The Republic of China and the People's Republic of China After Forty Years.* Stanford: Hoover Institution Press.

Collier, Ruth Berins, and David Collier. 1991. *Shaping the Political Arena: Critical Junctures, the Labor Movement, and Regime Dynamics in Latin America.* Princeton: Princeton University Press.

Collins, Randall. 1979. *The Credential Society.* New York: Academic Press.

Connor, Walter D. 1979. *Socialism, Politics, and Equality: Hierarchy and Change in Eastern Europe and the USSR.* New York: Columbia University Press.

1988. *Socialism's Dilemmas: State and Society in the Soviet Bloc.* New York: Columbia University Press.

1991. *The Accidental Proletariat: Workers, Politics, and Crisis in Gorbachev's Russia.* Princeton University Press.

1996. *Tattered Banners: Labor, Conflict and Corporatism in Postcommunist Russia.* Boulder: Westview Press.

Conway, M. Margaret. 1991. *Political Participation in the United States.* Washington, D.C.: Congressional Quarterly.

Cook, Linda J. 1993. *The Soviet Social Contract and Why It Failed: Welfare Policy and Workers' Politics from Brezhnev to Yeltsin.* Cambridge, Mass.: Harvard University Press.

Coverman, Shelley. 1985. "Explaining Husband's Participation in Domestic Labor." *The Sociological Quarterly* 26:81–97.

Crowley, Stephen. 1994. "Barriers to Collective Action: Steelworkers and Mutual Dependence in the Former Soviet Union." *World Politics* 46:589–615.

Crozier, Michel. 1964. *The Bureaucratic Phenomenon.* Chicago: University of Chicago Press.

Dahl, Robert A. 1985. *A Preface to Economic Democracy.* Berkeley: University of California Press.

Dahrendorf, Ralf. 1959. *Class and Class Conflict in Industrial Society.* Stanford: Stanford University Press.

Dallin, Alexander. 1995. "Where Have All the Flowers Gone?" Pp. 245–62 in Gail Lapidus, ed., *The New Russia: Troubled Transformation.* Boulder: Westview Press.

Dalton, Russell J. 1988. *Citizen Politics in Western Democracies.* Chatham, N.J.: Chatham House Publishers.

Daniels, Robert V. 1971. "Soviet Politics Since Khrushchev." Pp. 16–25 in John W. Strong, ed., *The Soviet Union Under Brezhnev and Kosygin*. New York: Van Nostrand Reinhold.

Davis, Deborah, 1988. "Unequal Chances, Unequal Outcomes: Pension Reform and Urban Inequality." *China Quarterly* 114:223–42.

————. 1990. "Urban Job Mobility." Pp. 85–108 in Deborah Davis and Ezra F. Vogel, eds., *Chinese Society on the Eve of Tiananmen: The Impact of Reform*. Harvard.

————. 1992a. "Job Mobility in Post-Mao Cities: Increases on the Margins." *China Quarterly* no. 132:1062–85.

————. 1992b. "'Skidding': Downward Mobility Among Children of the Maoist Middle Class." *Modern China* 18:410–37.

————. et al., eds. 1995. *Urban Spaces in Contemporary China*. Washington, D.C.: Woodrow Wilson Center Press.

————. and Stevan Harrell. 1993. *Chinese Families in the Post-Mao Era*. Berkeley: University of California Press.

Davis, James A., and Tom W. Smith. 1994. *General Social Surveys, 1972–1994: Cumulative Codebook*. Chicago: National Opinion Research Center.

Davis-Friedman, Deborah. 1991. *Long Lives: Chinese Elderly and the Communist Revolution*. 2nd edition. Stanford, Calif.: Stanford University Press.

Deng, Xiaoping. 1988. "On Reforming the Leading Organizations of the Party and the State." Pp. 19–21 in ESRCC, 1988, *Ten Years for Economic System Reform of China*. Beijing: Jingji Guanli Chubanshe.

Deng, Zhong, and Donald J. Treiman. 1997. "The Impact of the Cultural Revolution on Trends in Educational Attainment in the People's Republic of China." *American Journal of Sociology* 103:391–428.

DeSoto, Hernando. 1989. *The Other Path*. New York: Harper.

DGBAS (Directorate-General of Budget, Accounting and Statistics). 1996. *Social Indicators in Taiwan Area of the Republic of China, 1995*. Taipei: Executive Yuan, Republic of China.

DiFranceisco, Wayne, and Zvi Gitelman. 1984. "Soviet Political Culture and 'Covert Participation' in Policy Implementation." *American Journal of Political Science* 78:603–21.

Djilas, Milovan. 1957. *The New Class*. New York: Holt, Rinehart and Winston.

Dobson, Richard B. 1980a. "Socialism and Social Stratification." Pp. 88–114 in Jerry G. Pankhurst and Michael Paul Sacks, eds., *Contemporary Soviet Society: Sociological Perspectives*. New York: Praeger.

————. 1980b. "Education and Opportunity." Pp.115–37 in Jerry G. Pankhurst and Michael Paul Sacks, eds., *Contemporary Soviet Society: Sociological Perspectives*. New York: Praeger.

————. 1994. "Communism's Legacy and Russian Youth." Pp. 229–51 in James R. Millar and Sharon L. Wolchik, eds., *The Social Legacy of Communism*. New York: Cambridge University Press.

Doelling, Irene. 1993. "'But the Picture Stays the Same . . .' The Image of Women in the Journal *Fuer Dich* Before and After the 'Turning Point.'" In Nanette

Funk and Magda Mueller, eds., *Gender Politics and Post-Communism: Reflections from Eastern Europe and the Former Soviet Union.* London: Routledge.

Dore, Ronald. 1976. *The Diploma Disease: Education, Qualification and Development.* Berkeley: University of California Press.

Dornbusch, Rudiger, and Sebastian Edwards. 1989. *The Macroeconomics of Populism in Latin America.* World Bank.

du Plessix Gray, Francine. 1990. *Soviet Women: Walking the Tightrope.* New York: Doubleday.

Duch, Raymond M. 1993. "Tolerating Economic Reform: Popular Support for Transition to a Free Market in the Former Soviet Union." *American Political Science Review* 87:590–608.

Editorial Group. 1990. *Zhigong Laobao Fuli Yiqian Ti Wenda.* Beijing: Science and Technology Press.

Edwards, John N., T. D. Fuller, S. Vorakitphokatorn, and S. Sermsri. 1992. "Female Employment and Marital Instability: Evidence from Thailand." *Journal of Marriage and the Family* 54:59–68.

Edwards, Richard. 1979. *Contested Terrain: The Transformation of the Workplace in the Twentieth Century.* New York: Basic Books.

Einhorn, Barbara. 1993. *Cinderella Goes to Market: Citizenship, Gender and Women's Movements in East Central Europe.* London: Verso.

Eisenstadt, S. N., and Luis Roniger. 1981. "Clientelism in Communist Systems." *Studies in Comparative Communism* 14:233–45.

and Luis Roniger. 1984. *Patrons, Clients, and Friends.* Cambridge, Eng.: Cambridge University Press.

Ellman, Michael. 1989. *Socialist Planning.* 2nd ed. Cambridge, Eng.: Cambridge University Press.

Engels, Friedrich. 1884 [1972]. *The Origin of the Family, Private Property and the State.* New York: International Publishers.

Erickson, Robert, and John H. Goldthorpe. 1994. "Trends in Class Mobility: The Post-War European Experience." Pp. 289–316 in David B. Grusky, ed., *Social Stratification.* Boulder: Westview.

ESRCC (Economic System Reform Commission of China). 1986. *Gaige: Women suo Mianlin de Tiaozhan he Xuance* (Reform: Challenges and Choices). Beijing: Economics Publishing House.

ESRIC (Economic System Reform Institute of China). 1991. Semiannual Survey. September.

Fairbank, John King. 1986. *The Great Chinese Revolution 1800–1985.* New York: Harper & Row.

Farrer, James. 1998. " 'Kaifang': Sexuality and Market Reforms in China." Ph.D. diss., University of Chicago.

Featherman, David L., F. Lancaster Jones, and Robert M. Hauser. 1975. "Assumptions of Mobility Research in the United States." *Social Science Research* 4:329–60.

Finifter, Ada W., and Ellen Mickiewicz. 1992. "Redefining the Political System of the USSR: Mass Support for Political Change." *American Political Science Review* 86:857–74.

Fischer, Claude. 1982. *Personal Networks in Town and City*. Chicago: University of Chicago Press.

Fish, M. Steven. 1995. *Democracy from Scratch: Opposition and Regime in the New Russian Revolution*. Princeton: Princeton University Press.

Fitzpatrick, Sheila. 1976. "Social Mobility in the Late Stalin Period: Recruitment into the Intelligentsia and Access to Higher Education, 1945–1953." Paper presented at Kennan Institute Conference on "USSR in the 1940s."

1979. *Education and Social Mobility in the Soviet Union 1921–1934*. New York: Cambridge University Press.

1994. *Stalin's Peasants: Resistance and Survival in the Village After Collectivization*. New York: Oxford University Press.

Five-City Family Research Group (Wu Chengshi Jiating Yanjiu Xiangmu Zu). 1985. *Chinese Urban Families: Five-City Family Survey Report and Compiled Materials* (Zhongguo Chengshi Jiating). Jinan, China: Shandong People's Press.

Foster, George. 1965. "Peasant Society and the Image of the Limited Good." *American Anthropological Review* 67:293–315.

Fox, John. 1984. *Linear Statistical Models and Related Models*. New York: John Wiley.

Friedman, Milton. 1962. *Capitalism and Freedom*. Chicago: University of Chicago Press.

Friedrich, Carl J., and Z. K. Brzezinski. 1966. *Totalitarian Dictatorship and Autocracy*. New York: Praeger.

Fu, Zhengyuan. 1993. *Autocratic Tradition and Chinese Politics*. New York: Cambridge University Press.

Galenson, Walter, ed. 1979. *Economic Growth and Structural Change in Taiwan*. Ithaca: Cornell University Press.

Ganzeboom, Harry B. G., and Donald J. Treiman. 1993. "Preliminary Results on Educational Expansion and Educational Attainment in Comparative Perspective." Pp. 467–506 in Henk A. Becker and Piet L. J. Hermkens, eds., *Solidarity of Generations: Demographic, Economic, and Social Change and Its Consequences*. Amsterdam: Thesis Publishers.

George, Vic, and Nick Manning. 1980. *Socialism, Social Welfare, and the Soviet Union*. London: Routledge and Kegan Paul.

Gill, Ernest. 1986. "Foreigners in Their Own Land." *New York Times Magazine*, Feb. 16, pp. 46ff.

Gilmartin, Christina K., Gail Hershatter, Lisa Rofel, and Tyrene White, eds. 1994. *Engendering China: Women, Culture, and the State*. Cambridge, Mass.: Harvard University Press.

Gold, Thomas B. 1986. *State and Society in the Taiwan Miracle*. Armonk, N.Y.: M. E. Sharpe.

Goldin, Claudia. 1990. *Understanding the Gender Gap: An Economic History of American Women*. New York: Oxford University Press.

Gong, Ting. 1994. *The Politics of Corruption in Contemporary China: An Analysis of Policy Outcomes.* New York: Praeger.

Goode, William J. 1963. *World Revolution and Family Patterns.* New York: Free Press.

1993. *World Changes in Divorce Patterns.* New Haven: Yale University Press.

Granick, David. 1990. *Chinese State Enterprises.* Chicago: University of Chicago Press.

Greenhalgh, Susan. 1985. "Sexual Stratification: The Other Side of 'Growth with Equity' in East Asia. *Population and Development Review* 11:265–314.

Greenstein, Theodore N. 1990. "Marital Disruption and the Employment of Married Women." *Journal of Marriage and the Family* 52:657–76.

1995. "Gender Ideology, Marital Disruption, and the Employment of Married Women." *Journal of Marriage and the Family* 57:31–42.

Griffin, Keith, and Renwei Zhao, eds. 1993. *The Distribution of Income in China.* London: Macmillan.

Grusky, David B., and Robert M. Hauser. 1984. "Comparative Social Mobility Revisited: Models of Convergence and Divergence in 16 Countries." *American Sociological Review* 49:19–38.

Gudin, Gregory E., and Aiden Southall, eds. 1993. *Urban Anthropology in China.* Leiden: Brill.

Guthrie, Douglas. 2000. *Dragon in a Three-Piece Suit: Foreign Investment, Rational Bureaucracies, and Market Reform in China.* Princeton: Princeton University Press.

Guttmann, Joseph. 1993. *Divorce in Psychological Perspective.* Hillsdale, N.J.: Lawrence Erlbaum.

Hamilton, Gary G., ed. 1991. *Business Networks and Economic Development in East and Southeast Asia.* Hong Kong: Hong Kong University Press.

and Nicole Woolsey Biggart. 1988. "Market Culture and Authority: A Comparative Analysis of Management and Organization in the Far East." *American Journal of Sociology* 94 supplement: S52–S94.

Hannan, Michael T., Nancy B. Tuma, and L. P. Groenveld. 1978. "Income and Independence Effects on Marital Dissolution: Results from the Seattle and Denver Income-Maintenance Experiments." *American Journal of Sociology* 84:611–33.

Harding, Harry. 1987. *China's Second Revolution.* Washington, D.C.: Brookings Institute.

Harris, Peter. 1986. "Socialist Graft: The Soviet Union and the People's Republic of China – A Preliminary Survey." *Corruption and Reform* 1:13–32.

Hauser, Robert M., and David B. Grusky. 1988. "Cross-National Variation in Occupational Distributions, Relative Mobility Chances, and Intergenerational Shifts in Occupational Distributions." *American Sociological Review* 53:723–41.

Hauslohner, Peter A. 1984."Managing the Soviet Labor Market: Politics and Policy-Making Under Brezhnev." Ph.D. diss., University of Michigan.

Havel, Vaclav, et al. 1985. "The Power of the Powerless." Pp. 23–96 in John Keane, ed., in *The Power of the Powerless Citizens Against the State in Central-Eastern Europe*. London: Hutchinson.

Hayek, Friedrich A. 1944. *The Road to Serfdom*. Chicago: University of Chicago Press.

He, Mingsheng, and Tang Kuiyu. 1989. *Zhongguo Xiaofei zhi Mi* (China's Consumption Craze). A booklet in the compendium by Yunkang Pan, ed., *Shehui Xuezhe dui Shehui de Jinggao* (Warnings About Society from Sociologists). Beijing: Chinese Women's Publishing House.

Hewett, Ed A. 1988. *Reforming the Soviet Economy: Equality versus Efficiency*. Washington, D.C.: Brookings Institution.

Higley, John, and Richard Gunther, eds. 1992. *Elites and Democratic Consolidation in Latin America and Southern Europe*. Cambridge, Eng.: Cambridge University Press.

Hochschild, Arlie Russel. 1989. *The Second Shift: Working Parents and the Revolution at Home*. New York: Viking.

Hollander, Paul. 1973. *Soviet and American Society: A Comparison*. Chicago: University of Chicago Press.

Honig, Emily, and Gail Hershatter. 1988. *Personal Voices: Chinese Women in the 1980s*. Stanford, Calif.: Stanford University Press.

Hough, Jerry F. 1969. *The Soviet Prefects, The Local Party Organs in Industrial Decision-Making*. Cambridge, Mass.: Harvard University Press.

    1976. "Political Participation in the Soviet Union." *Soviet Studies* 28:3–20.

    1977. *The Soviet Union and Social Science Theory*. Cambridge, Mass.: Harvard University Press.

Hsiao, Hsing-Huang Michael, Wei-Yuan Cheng, and Hou-sheng Chan. 1989. *Taiwan: A Newly Industrialized State*. Taipei: Department of Sociology, National Taiwan University.

Huang, Yasheng. 1990. "Economic Bureaucracies and Enterprises During Reforms." *China Quarterly*, no. 123, September:431–58.

Hummon, David M. 1990. *Commonplaces: Community Ideology and Identity in American Culture*. Albany: SUNY Press.

Huntington, Samuel P. 1968. *Political Order in Changing Societies*. New Haven: Yale University Press.

    1991. *The Third Wave*. Norman: University of Oklahoma Press.

    and Joan M. Nelson. 1976. *No Easy Choice: Political Participation in Developing Countries*. Cambridge, Mass.: Harvard University Press.

Ikels, Charlotte. 1996. *The Return of the God of Wealth: The Transition to a Market Economy in Urban China*. Stanford, Calif.: Stanford University Press.

ILO (International Labor Office). 1995. *Yearbook of Labor Statistics*. Geneva: International Labor Office.

Inglehart, Ronald. 1990. *Culture Shift*. Princeton: Princeton University Press.

1997. *Modernization and Postmodernization: Cultural, Economic, and Political Change in 43 Societies.* Princeton: Princeton University Press.

Inkeles, Alex. 1950. *Public Opinion in Soviet Russia.* Cambridge, Mass.: Harvard University Press.

1960. "Industrial Man: The Relation of Status to Experience, Perception, and Value." *American Journal of Sociology* 66:1–31.

1968. *Social Change in Soviet Russia.* Cambridge, Mass.: Harvard University Press.

1974. *Becoming Modern: Individual Change in Six Developing Countries.* Cambridge, Mass.: Harvard University Press.

1976. "The Modernization of Man in Socialist and Nonsocialist Countries." In M. G. Fields, ed., *Social Consequences of Modernization in Communist Societies.* Baltimore: Johns Hopkins University Press.

and Raymond Bauer. 1959. *The Soviet Citizen: Daily Life in a Totalitarian Society.* Cambridge, Mass.: Harvard University Press.

IRI (International Republican Institute). 1994. *People's Republic of China: Election Observation Report.* May 15–31.

Ishwaran, K., ed. 1989. *Family and Marriage: Cross-Cultural Perspectives.* Toronto: Wall & Thompson.

Jacka, Tamara. 1990. "Back to the Wok: Women and Employment in Chinese Industry in the 1980s." *Australian Journal of Chinese Affairs* 24:1–23.

Jacobsen, Joyce P. 1994. *The Economics of Gender.* Cambridge, Eng.: Blackwell.

Jagannathan, N. Vijay. 1986. "Corruption, Delivery Systems, and Property Rights." *World Development* 14:127–32.

Jancar, Barbara Wolfe. 1978. *Women Under Communism.* Baltimore: Johns Hopkins University Press.

Jankowiak, William R. 1993. *Sex and Hierarchy in a Chinese City: An Anthropological Account.* New York: Columbia University Press.

Jefferson, Gary H., and Thomas G. Rawski. 1994. "How Industrial Reform Worked in China: The Role of Innovation, Competition, and Property Rights." Annual Bank Conference on Development Economics, April 28–29, The World Bank, Washington, D.C.

and Yuxin Zheng. 1992a. "Growth, Efficiency, and Convergence in China's State and Collective Industry." *Economic Development and Cultural Change* 40(2):239–65.

and Yuxin Zheng. 1992b. "Innovation and Reform in Chinese Industry: A Preliminary Analysis of Survey Data." Unpublished paper.

Jennings, M. Kent. 1983. "Gender Roles and Inequalities in Political Participation: Results from an Eight Nation Study." *Western Political Quarterly* 36:364–85.

Jia, Hao, and Zhimin Lin, eds. 1994. *Changing Central-Local Relations in China: Reform and State Capacity.* Westview Press.

Jiang, Liu, Xueyi Lu, and Tianlun Shan, eds. 1995. *1994–1995 Nian Zhongguo Shehui Xingshi Fenxi yu Yuce.* Beijing: China Social Sciences Press.

Jowitt, Ken. 1983. "Soviet Neo-Traditionalism: The Political Corruption of a Leninist Regime." *Soviet Studies* 35:275–97.

1992. *New World Disorder: The Leninist Extinction.* Berkeley: University of California Press.

Judd, Ellen R. 1994. *Gender and Power in Rural North China.* Stanford, Calif.: Stanford University Press.

Kalleberg, Arne L., and Mark E. Van Buren. 1996. "Is Bigger Better? Organization Size and Job Rewards," *American Sociological Review* 61:47–66.

Kaminski, Antoni Z. 1992. *An Institutional Theory of Communist Regimes.* San Francisco: ICS Press.

Kant, I. 1970. *Kant's Political Writings,* H. Reiss, ed. Cambridge, Eng.: Cambridge University Press.

Kanter, Rosabeth. 1972. *Commitment and Community: Communes and Utopias in Sociological Perspective.* Cambridge, Mass.: Harvard University Press.

Kennedy, Michael, D. 1991. *Professionals, Power, and Solidarity in Poland: A Critical Sociology of Soviet-Type Society.* Cambridge, Eng.: Cambridge University Press.

and Irerneusz Bialecki. 1989. "Power and the Logic of Distribution in Poland." *Eastern European Politics and Societies* 3:300–328.

Kerr, Clark, and Abraham Siegel. 1954. "The Inter-Industry Propensity to Strike." In Arthur Kornhauser et al., eds., *Industrial Conflict.* New York: Wiley.

Kinder, Donald R., and Roderick D. Kiewiet. 1979. "Economic Discontent and Political Behavior: The Role of Personal Grievances and Collective Economic Judgments in Congressional Voting." *American Journal of Political Science* 23:495–527.

1981. "Sociotropic Politics: The American Case." *British Journal of Political Science* 11 (April):129–41.

Kirkby, R. J. R. 1985. *Urbanization in China.* New York: Columbia University Press.

Kligman, Gail. 1994. "The Social Legacy of Communism: Women, Children, and the Feminization of Poverty." Pp. 252–70 in James R. Millar and Sharon L. Wolchik, eds., *The Social Legacy of Communism.* Woodrow Wilson Center Series. New York: Cambridge University Press.

Kluegel, James, and Petr Mateju. 1995. "Egalitarian vs. Inegalitarian Principles of Distributive Justice." Pp. 209–38 in James R. Kluegel et al., eds., *Social Justice and Political Change: Public Opinion in Capitalist and Post-Communist States.* New York: Aldine De Gruyter.

Kohn, Melvin L., and Kazimierz M. Slomczynski. 1990. *Social Structure and Self-Direction: A Comparative Analysis of the United States and Poland.* Cambridge, Mass.: Blackwell.

Kojima, Reitsu. 1987. *Urbanization and Urban Problems in China.* I.D.E. Occasional Paper Series No. 22. Tokyo: Institute of Developing Economies.

Kon, Igor, and James Riordan. 1993. *Sex and Russian Society.* Bloomington: Indiana University Press.

Konrad, Gyorgy, and Iván Szelényi. 1979. *The Intellectuals on the Road to Class Power.* New York: Harcourt Brace Jovanovich.

Kornai, Janos. 1980. *Economics of Shortage.* Amsterdam: North-Holland.

   1992. *The Socialist System: The Political Economy of Communism.* Princeton University Press.

   1995. *Highways and Byways: Studies on Reform and Post-Communist Transition.* Cambridge, Mass.: MIT Press.

Kornblum, William. 1974. *The Blue Collar Community.* Chicago: University of Chicago Press.

   1959. *The Politics of Mass Society.* New York: The Free Press.

Kristof, Nicholas, and Sheryl Wudunn. 1994. *China Wakes: A Struggle for the Soul of a Rising Power.* New York: Times Books.

Kunz, Jean Lock. 1996. "From Maoism to *Elle*: The Impact of Political Ideology on Fashion Trends in China." *International Sociology* 11(3):317–35.

Kwok, R. Yin-wang, William L. Parish, and Anthony gar-on Yeh, eds. 1990. *Chinese Urban Reform.* Armonk, N.Y.: M. E. Sharpe.

Laaksonen, Oiva. 1988. *Management in China During and After Mao.* New York: Walter de Gruyter.

Lane, David. 1985. *Soviet Economy and Society.* New York: New York University Press.

Lang, Olga. 1946. *Chinese Family and Society.* New Haven: Yale University Press.

Lapidus, Gail W. 1978. *Women in Soviet Society.* Berkeley: University of California Press.

   1983. "Social Trends." Pp. 186–249 in Gail W. Lapidus, ed., *After Brezhnev: Sources of Soviet Conduct in the 1980s.* Bloomington: Indiana University Press.

Laumann, Edward O., et al. 1994. *The Social Organization of Sexuality: Sexual Practices in the United States.* Chicago: University of Chicago Press.

Lavely, William, Xiao Zhenyu, Li Bohua, and Ronald Freedman. 1990. "The Rise in Female Education in China: National and Regional Patterns." *China Quarterly*, no. 121:61–93.

Lee, Hong Yung. 1978. *The Politics of the Chinese Cultural Revolution.* Berkeley: University of California Press.

   1991. *From Revolutionary Cadres to Party Technocrats in Socialist China.* University of California.

Lee, Peter Nan-Song. 1990. "Bureaucratic Corruption During the Deng Xiaoping Era." *Corruption and Reform* 5:29–47.

Lee, Yean-Ju, William L. Parish, and Robert J. Willis. 1994. "Sons, Daughters, and Intergenerational Support in Taiwan." *American Journal of Sociology* 99:1010–41.

Lee, Yok-shiu, 1988. "The Urban Housing Problem in China." *China Quarterly*, Sept., no. 115.

Leem, Kyung Hoon. 1996. "Labor Solidarity and Militancy in Post-Communist Russia: Coal Miners and Railroad Workers in Kuzbass and Vorkuta." Ph.D. diss., University of Chicago.

Leff, Nathaniel H. 1964. "Economic Development Through Bureaucratic Corruption." *American Behavioral Scientist* 8:8–14.

Lehmbruch, Gerhard, and Philippe C. Schmitter, ed. 1982. *Patterns of Corporatist Policy-Making*. Beverly Hills: Sage.

Lennon, Mary Clare, and Sarah Rosenfield. 1994. "Relative Fairness and the Division of Housework: The Importance of Options." *American Journal of Sociology* 100(2): 506–31.

Lenski, Gerhard. 1994. "New Light on Old Issues: The Relevance of 'Really Existing Socialist Societies' for Stratification Theory." Pp. 55–61 in David B. Grusky, ed., *Social Stratification: Class, Race, and Gender in Sociological Perspective*. Boulder, Colo.: Westview.

Levy, Marion J. 1949. *The Family Revolution in Modern China*. Cambridge, Mass.: Harvard University Press.

Lewis-Beck, Michael. 1988. *Economics and Elections: The Major Western Democracies*. Ann Arbor: University of Michigan Press.

———. 1991. "Introduction." In Helmut Norpoth, Michael S. Lewis-Beck, and Jean-Dominique Lafay, eds., *Economics and Politics: The Calculus of Support*. Ann Arbor: University of Michigan Press.

Li, Elizabeth, Yuanchen Dai, Ernst Stromsdorfer, and Dongqi Chen. 1996. "Codebooks and Marginal Distributions of Variables for Chinese Labor Market Research Project." Department of Economics, Miami University, Hamilton, Ohio. Photocopy.

Li, Fang. 1993. "Recent Administrative Reform in China." in Miriam K. Mills and Stuart S. Nagel, eds., 1993. *Public Administration in China*. Westport, Conn.: Greenwood Press.

———. 1997. "The Social Organization of Entrepreneurship: The Rise of Private Firms in China." Ph.D. diss., University of Chicago.

Li, Hanlin. 1995. "Power, Resources, and Exchange in the Chinese 'Work Unit Society.'" *International Journal of Sociology and Social Policy* 15:309–28.

Li, Xueju. 1994. *Zhongguo Chengxiang Jiceng Zhengquan Jianshe Gongzuo Yanjiu* (A study of Chinese urban basic level government construction). Beijing: China Sociology Press.

Liang, Zai, and Michael J. White. 1994. "Market Transition, Government Policies, and Interprovincial Migration in China, 1983–88." Paper presented at the annual meeting of the Population Association of America.

———. 1996. "Internal Migration in China, 1950–1988." *Demography* 33:375–84.

Lieberthal, Kenneth. 1995. *Governing China: From Revolution Through Reform*. New York: W. W. Norton.

——— and David Lampton, eds. 1992. *Bureaucracy, Politics, and Decision Making in Post-Mao China*. University of California Press.

——— and Michel Oksenberg. 1988. *Policy Making in China*. Princeton: Princeton University Press.

Lim, Edwin, and Adrian Wood. 1985. *China: Long-Term Development Issues and Options*. Baltimore: Johns Hopkins University Press.

Lin, Anchi. 1995a. "Social and Cultural Bases of Corporate Expansion: The Formation of Business Groups (Jituan) in Taiwan." Ph.D. diss., Harvard University.

Lin, Nan. 1995b. "Institutional Capital, Human Capital, and Work Attainment: A Study of Urban China." Unpublished manuscript.

    and Yanjie Bian. 1991. "Getting Ahead in Urban China." *American Journal of Sociology* 97:657–88.

Lin, Yimin. 1992. "Between Government and Labor: Managerial Decision-making in Chinese Industry." *Studies in Comparative Communism* 25: 381–403.

Lindblom, Charles. 1977. *Politics and Markets*. New York: Basic Books.

Link, Perry. 1992. *Evening Chats in Beijing*. New York: Norton.

    Richard Madsen, and Paul G. Pickowicz. 1989. *Unofficial China: Popular Culture and Thought in the People's Republic*. Boulder, Colo.: Westview.

Lipset, Seymour M., Martin Trow, and James Coleman. 1956. *Union Democracy: The Inside Politics of the International Typographical Union*. New York: Free Press.

Lipset, Seymour Martin. 1961. *Political Man*. New York: Doubleday.

Liu, Binyan. 1983. *People or Monsters? And Other Stories and Reportage from China after Mao*. Bloomington: Indiana University Press.

Liu, Bohong. 1995a. "Cong Beijing, Guangzhou, Xianggang zaizhi nuxing jiuye diaocha kansandi zhiye funu jiaose chongtu zhuangkuang." *Jiaose yu kunhuo yu nuren de qulu*. Tong Shaosu, ed. Hangzhou: Zhejiang renmin chuban she.

    1995b. "Zhongguo nuxing jiuye zhuangkuang." *Shehuixue Yanjiu* 56:39–48.

Liu, Dalin. 1992. *Sexual Behavior in Modern China: A Report of the Nation-wide "Sex Civilization" Survey on 2,000 Subjects in China*. Shanghai: San Lian Shudian.

Liu, Xiaocong, Bohong Liu, and Yumei Xiong. 1991. "Beijing, Guangzhou, Hsiangkang nuxing renkou jiuye bijiao yanjiu." Pp. 555–67 in *Almanac of China's Population, 1991*. Population Research Institute, CASS. Beijing: Economic Management Press.

Liu, Yih-Jun. 1991. "The Election-Driven Democratic Transformation: A Comparative Perspective." Ph.D. diss., University of Chicago.

Liu, Ying, and Su-zhen Xue, eds. 1987. *Chinese Marriage and Family Research* (Zhongguo Hunyin Jiating Yanjiu). Beijing: Social Science Literature Press (Shehui Kexue Wenxian Chubanshe).

Loayza, Norman V. 1994. "Labor Regulations and the Informal Economy." *Policy Research Working Paper* no. 1292. Washington, D.C.: World Bank.

Logan, John R., and Yanjie Bian. 1993. "Inequalities in Access to Community Resources in a Chinese City." *Social Forces* 72(2):555–76.

Lu, Jianhua. 1991. "Chinese Workers' High Expectations of Enterprise Managers." *International Sociology* 6:37–49.

Lu, Xueyi, and Li Peilin, eds. 1997. *Zhongguo Xinshi qi Shehui Fazhan Baogao, 1991–1995*. Shenyang: Liaoning Renmin Chubanshe.

Lull, James. 1991. *China Turned On: Television, Reform, and Resistance*. London: Routledge.

Ma, Youcai, Ying Liu, Xuewen Sheng, Chen Meng. 1992. *Funujiuye yu jiating – Zhongri bijiaoyanjiu diaocha baodao*. Beijing: China Social Sciences Press.

MacKuen, Michael B., Robert S. Erickson, and James A. Stimson. 1992. "Peasants for Bankers? The American Electorate and the U.S. Economy." *American Political Science Review* 86:597–611.

Manion, Melanie. 1993. *Retirement of Revolutionaries in China*. Princeton: Princeton University Press.

Mare, R. D. 1979. "Social Background Composition and Educational Growth." *Demography* 16:55–72.

1980. "Social Background and School Continuation Decisions." *Journal of the American Statistical Association* 75:295–305.

Markus, Maria. 1976. "Women and Work." Pp. 76–90 in Andras Hegedus et al., eds., *The Humanisation of Socialism: Writings of the Budapest School*. London: Allison and Busby.

Marsh, Alan. 1990. *Political Action in Europe and the USA*. London: Macmillan.

Mason, David S. 1995. "Justice, Socialism, and Participation in the Postcommunist States." Pp. 49–80 in James R. Kluegel et al., eds., *Social Justice and Political Change: Public Opinion in Capitalist and Post-Communist States*. New York: Aldine De Gruyter.

Matthews, Mervyn. 1982. *Education in the Soviet Union: Programs and Institutions Since Stalin*. Boston: Allen & Unwin.

Maurer-Fazio, Margaret. 1994. "An Analysis of the Emerging Labor Market in the People's Republic of China and Its Effect on Rates of Return to Investments in Education." Ph.D. diss., University of Pittsburgh.

Thomas G. Rawski, and Wei Zhang. 1999. "Inequality in the Rewards for Holding Up Half the Sky: Gender Wage Gaps in China's Urban Labour Market, 1988–1994." *The China Journal* 41:55–88.

McAdam, Doug. 1982. *Political Process and the Development of Black Insurgency, 1930–1970*. Chicago: University of Chicago Press.

McKendreick, Neil, John Brewer, and J. H. Plumb. 1982. *The Birth of Consumer Society: The Commercialization of Eighteenth-Century England*. London: Europa Publications.

Meijer, M. J. 1971. *Marriage Law and Policy in the Chinese People's Republic*. Hong Kong: Hong Kong University Presss.

Meisner, Maurice. 1986. *Mao's China and After: A History of the People's Republic*. New York: The Free Press.

Metzger, Thomas A., and Ramon H. Myers. 1991. "Two Diverging Societies." In *Two Societies in Opposition: The Republic of China and the People's Republic of China After Forty Years*. Stanford: Hoover Institution Press.

Michelson, Ethan, and William L. Parish. 2000. "Gender Differentials in Economic Success: Rural China in 1991." In Barbara Entwisle and Gale

Henderson, eds., *Re-Drawing Boundaries: Work, Household, and Gender in China*. Berkeley: University of California Press.

Millar, James R., and Elizabeth Clayton. 1987. "Quality of Life." Pp. 31–57 in James R. Millar, ed., *Politics, Work, and Daily Life in the USSR*. Cambridge, Eng.: Cambridge University Press.

Millar, James R., and Sharon L. Wolchik. 1994. "Introduction: The Social Legacies and the Aftermath of Communism." Pp. 1–30 in James R. Millar and Sharon L. Wolchik, eds., *The Social Legacy of Communism*. New York: Cambridge University Press.

Miller, Arthur H., William M. Reisinger, and Vicki L. Heslie. 1996. "Understanding Political Change in Post-Soviet Societies: A Further Commentary on Finifter and Mickiewicz." *American Political Science Review* 90, no. 1 (March): 153–66.

Mincer, Jacob. 1974. *Schooling, Experience, and Earnings*. New York: National Bureau of Economic Research.

Ministry of Labor. 1995. *Laodong Neican* (labor references). No. 1.

Ministry of Public Health. 1991. *Selected Edition on Health Statistics of China 1978–1990*. Beijing.

Modell, John. 1983. "Dating Becomes the Way of American Youth." In Leslie Moch, ed., *Essays on the Family and Historical Change*. College Station: Texas A&M University Press.

Moody, Peter R. 1992. *Political Change on Taiwan: A Study of Ruling Party Adaptability*. New York: Praeger.

Moore, Barrington. 1958. *Political Power and Social Theory*. Cambridge, Mass.: Harvard University Press.

———. 1966. *The Social Origins of Dictatorship and Democracy*. New York: Beacon.

Murray, Stephen O., and Keelung Hong. 1994. *Taiwanese Culture, Taiwanese Society: A Critical Review of Social Science Research Done on Taiwan*. Lanham, Md.: University Press of America.

Nathan, Andrew. 1985. *Chinese Democracy*. New York: Knopf.

Naughton, Barry. 1995. "Cities in the Chinese Economic System: Changing Roles and Conditions for Autonomy." Pp. 61–89 in Deborah S. Davis et al., eds., *Urban Spaces in Contemporary China*. New York: Cambridge University Press.

Nee, Victor. 1989. "A Theory of Market Transition: From Redistribution to Markets in State Socialism." *American Sociological Review* 54:663–81.

———. 1991. "Social Inequalities in Reforming State Socialism: Between Redistribution and Markets in China." *American Sociological Review* 56:267–82.

———. 1992. "Organizational Dynamics of Market Transition: Hybrid Forms, Property Rights, and Mixed Economy in China." *Administrative Science Quarterly* 37:1–27.

———. 1996. "The Emergence of a Market Society." *American Journal of Sociology* 101:908–49.

Nelson, Joan M. 1990. *Economic Crisis and Policy Choice: The Politics of Adjustment in the Third World*. Princeton: Princeton University Press.

Nove, Alec. 1983. *The Economics of Feasible Socialism*. London: George Allen & Unwin.

NPC (National People's Congress). 1994. *Labor Law of People's Republic of China*. Presidential Order No. 28.

Nunberg, Barbara. 1995. *Managing the Civil Service: Reform Lessons from Advanced Industrialized Countries*. World Bank Discussion Papers, no. 204. Washington, D.C.: World Bank.

O'Brien, Kevin J. 1992. "Bargaining Success of Chinese Factories." *China Quarterly* no. 132:1086–100.

O'Donnell, Guillermo A. 1979. *Modernization and Bureaucratic-Authoritarianism: Studies in South American Politics*. Berkeley: Institute of International Studies, University of California.

　1988. *Bureaucratic Authoritarianism: Argentina, 1966–1973, in Comparative Perspective*. Berkeley: University of California Press.

O'Donnell, Guillermo, Phillipe C. Schmitter, and Laurence Whitehead, eds. 1986. *Transitions from Authoritarian Rule*. Baltimore: Johns Hopkins University Press.

Ogburn, William. 1938. "The Changing Family." *Family* 19:139–43.

Ogden, Suzanne, et al. 1992. *China's Search for Democracy: The Student and the Mass Movement of 1989*. Armonk, N.Y.: M. E. Sharpe.

Oksenberg, Michel. 1970. "Getting Ahead and Along in Communist China: The Ladder of Success on the Eve of the Cultural Revolution." In John Wilson, ed., *Party Leadership and Revolutionary Power in China*. Cambridge, Eng.: Cambridge University Press.

Oppenheimer, Valerie Kincaid. 1970. *The Female Labor Force in the United States: Demographic and Economic Factors Governing Its Growth and Changing Composition*. Berkeley: University of California, Institute of International Studies.

　1988. "A Theory of Marriage Timing." *American Journal of Sociology* 94:563–91.

Orru, Marco, Nicole W. Biggart, and Gary G. Hamilton. 1997. *The Economic Organization of East Asian Capitalism*. Thousand Oaks, Calif.: Sage.

Osborn, Robert J. 1970. *Soviet Social Policies*. Homewood, Ill.: Dorsey.

Oshima, Kazutsugu. 1990. "The Present Condition of Inter-regional Movements of the Labor Force in Rural Jiangsu Province, China." *Developing Economies* 28:202–20.

Pan, Yunkang, ed. 1987. *Marriage and Family in Urban China* (Zhongguo Chengshi Hunyin yu Jiating). Jinan, China: Shandong People's Press.

　1989. *Shehui Xuezhe dui Shehui de Jinggao* (Warnings about Society from Sociologists). Beijing: Chinese Women's Publishing House.

Parish, William L. 1979. "The View from the Factory." Pp. 183–200 in Ross Terrill, ed., *The China Difference*. New York: Harper.

1984. "Destratification in Chinese Society." Pp. 84–120 in James Watson, ed., *Class and Stratification in China*. Cambridge, Eng.: Cambridge University Press.

1987. "Urban Policies in Centralized Economies: China." Pp. 73–84 in George S. Tolley and Vinod Thomas, eds., *The Economics of Urbanization and Urban Policies in Developing Countries*. Washington, D.C.: World Bank.

1990. "What Model Now?" Pp. 109–39 in Reginald Kwok, William Parish, and Anthony Yeh, eds., *Chinese Urban Reform*. Armonk, N.Y.: M. E. Sharpe.

1994. "Rural Industrialization: Fujian and Taiwan." Pp. 119–40 in Thomas P. Lyons and Victor Nee, eds., *The Economic Transformation of South China*, Cornell East Asia Series, no. 70. Ithaca: Cornell East Asia Program.

1995. "World Divorce Patterns: Commentary on William J. Goode." Paper presented at Annual Meeting of the American Sociological Association, Washington, D.C.

and Chi-hsiang Chang. 1996. "Political Values in Taiwan: Sources of Change and Constancy." In Hung-mao Tien, ed., *Taiwan's Electoral Politics and Democratic Transition*. Armonk, N.Y.: M. E. Sharpe.

and Ethan Michelson. 1996. "Politics and Markets: Dual Transformations." *American Journal of Sociology* 101:1042–59.

and Martin King Whyte. 1978. *Village and Family in Contemporary China*. Chicago: University of Chicago Press.

and Robert J. Willis. 1993. "Daughters, Education and Family Budgets: Taiwan Experiences." *Journal of Human Resources* 28:863–98. Reprinted in T. Paul Schultz, ed., *Investment in Women's Human Capital*. Chicago: University of Chicago Press, 1995.

and Xiaoye Zhe. 1995. "Education and Work in Rural China: Opportunities for Men and Women." In Hsiao-hung Nancy Chen, Yial-ling Liu, and Mei-O Hsieh, eds., *Family, Human Resources, and Human Development*. Taipei, Taiwan: Department of Sociology, National Chengchi University.

Parkin, Frank. 1979. *Marxism and Class Theory: A Bourgeois Critique*. London: Tavistock.

Pasternak, Burton. 1986. *Marriage and Fertility in Tianjin, China: Fifty Years of Transition*. Population Institute Paper no. 99. Honolulu, Hawaii: East-West Center.

Payne, Lynn Webster. 1994. "Progress and Problems in China's Educational Reform." Pp. 113–142 in William A. Joseph, ed., *China Briefing, 1994*. Boulder, Colo.: Westview Press.

Pepper, Suzanne. 1990. *China's Education Reform in the 1980s: Policies, Issues, and Historical Perspectives*, China research monograph no. 36. Berkeley: Institute of East Asian Studies.

Perkins, Dwight. 1990. "The Influence of Economic Reforms on China's Urbanization." Pp. 78–108 in Reginald Kwok, William L. Parish, and Anthony Yeh, eds., *Chinese Urban Reform*. Armonk, N.Y.: M. E. Sharpe.

Pickowicz, Paul G. 1995. "Velvet Prisons and the Political Economy of Chinese Filmmaking." Pp. 193–220 in Deborah S. Davis, R. Kraus, B. Naughton, and

E. J. Perry, eds., *Urban Spaces in Contemporary China.* Cambridge, Eng.: Cambridge University Press.

Pilkington, Hilary. 1996. *Gender, Generation and Identity in Contemporary Russia.* London: Routledge.

Pleck, Joseph. 1985. *Working Wives/Working Husbands.* Beverly Hills, Calif.: Sage.

Polanyi, Karl. 1944. *The Great Transformation.* New York: Reinhart.

Portes, Alejandro. 1976. "On the Sociology of National Development." *American Journal of Sociology* 82:55–85.

———. 1994. "The Informal Economy and Its Paradoxes." Pp. 426–52 in Neil J. Smelser and Richard Swedberg, eds., *The Handbook of Economic Sociology.* Princeton: Princeton University Press.

Presser, Harriet B. 1994. "Employment Schedules Among Dual-Earner Spouses and the Division of Household Labor by Gender." *American Sociological Review* 59:348–64.

PRI (Population Research Institute, CASS). 1987, 1991, 1993. *Zhongguo Renkou Nianjian, 1986, 1991, 1993, 1996* (Almanac of China's Population, 1987, 1991, 1993, 1996). Beijing: Economic Management Press.

Przeworski, Adam. 1991. *Democracy and the Market.* Cambridge, Eng.: Cambridge University Press.

Psacharopoulos, George. 1973. *Returns to Education.* New York: Jossey-Bass.

———. 1994. "Returns to Investment in Education: A Global Update." *World Development* 22:1325–43.

Pye, Lucian. 1988. *The Mandarin and the Cadre.* Ann Arbor: University of Michigan Press.

Ranis, Gustav. 1992. *Taiwan: From Developing to Mature Economy.* Boulder, Colo.: Westview.

Rawls, John. 1971. *A Theory of Justice.* Cambridge, Mass.: Harvard University Press.

Rawski, Thomas G. 1992. "Reform Without Privatization." Unpublished paper.

RI (Research Institute, All China Women's Federation, and Research Office, Shaanxi Provincial Women's Federation). 1991. *Statistics on Chinese Women, 1949–1989.* Beijing: China Statistics Press.

Richman, Barry M. 1967. *A Firsthand Study of Industrial Management in Communist China.* Los Angeles: Graduate School of Business Administration, University of California.

Riley, Nancy E. 1994. "Interwoven Lives: Parents, Marriage, and Guanxi in China." *Journal of Marriage and the Family* 56:791–803.

Riskin, Carl. 1987. *China's Political Economy: The Quest for Development Since 1949.* New York: Oxford University Press.

Robinson, Jean. 1985. "Of Women and Washing Machines: Employment, Housework, and the Reproduction of Motherhood in Socialist China." *China Quarterly* 101:32–57.

Róna-Tas, Ákos. 1994. "The First Shall Be Last? Entrepreneurship and Communist Cadres in the Transition from Socialism." *American Journal of Sociology* 100:40–69.

Rosen, Stanley. 1991. "Women, Education, and Modernization." In Ruth Hayhoe, ed., *Education and Modernization: The Chinese Experience.* Oxford: Pergamon.

———. 1993. "Women and Reform." *China News Analysis*, no. 1477, Jan. 15.

Rousseau, J. J. 1950. *The Social Contract and Discourses.* New York: Dutton.

Ru, Xin, Xueyi Lu, and Tianlun Shan. 1998. *1998 Zhongguo Shehui Xingshi Fenxi yu Yuce. (Shehui Lanpi Shu).* Beijing: Social Science Materials Press.

Ruan, Danqing, et al. 1997. "On the Changing Structure of Social Networks in Urban China." *Social Networks* 19:75–90.

Ruan, Fang Fu. 1991. *Sex in China.* New York: Plenum.

Rueschemeyer, Dietrich, and Peter B. Evans. 1985. "The State and Economic Transformation: Toward an Analysis of the Conditions Underlying Effective Intervention." In Peter B. Evans, Dietrich Rueschemeyer and Theda Skocpol, eds., *Bringing the State Back In.* New York: Cambridge University Press.

Sabel, Charles F., and David Stark. 1982. "Planning, Politics and Shop-floor Power: Hidden Forms of Bargaining in Soviet-Imposed State-Socialist Societies." *Politics and Society* 11:439–75.

Salaff, Janet. 1981. *Working Daughters of Hong Kong.* New York: Cambridge University Press.

Sandbrook, Richard. 1986. "The State and Economic Stagnation in Tropical Africa." *World Development* 14:319–32.

Schell, Orville. 1988. *Discos and Democracy: China in the Throes of Reform.* New York: Pantheon.

Schmitter, Philippe C. 1974. "Still the Century of Corporatism?" *Review of Politics* 36, no. 1 (Jan.): 85–131.

Schor, Juliet B. 1992. *The Overworked American: The Unexpected Decline of Leisure.* New York: Basic Books.

Scott, James C. 1976. *The Moral Economy of the Peasant.* New Haven: Yale University Press.

Seeberg, Vilma. 1990. *Literacy in China.* Bochum: Brockmeyer.

Sewell, William H. 1992. "A Theory of Structure: Duality, Agency and Transformation." *American Journal of Sociology* 98:1–29.

Sha, Jicai, Yu Xiong, and Jialing Gao, eds. 1994. *Sampling Survey Data of Women's Status in Contemporary China.* Institute of Population Studies, Chinese Academy of Social Sciences. Beijing: International Academic Publishers.

———. Qiming Liu, and Shuqing Sun, eds. 1995. *Dangdai Zhongguo Funu Jiating Diwei Yanjiu* (Women's Domestic Status in Contemporary China). Tianjin: Tianjin People's Press.

Shapiro, Robert Y., and Harpreet Mahajan. 1986. "Gender Differences in Policy Preferences: A Summary of Trends from the 1960s to the 1980s." *Public Opinion Quarterly* 50:42–61.

References 373

Shaw, Victor N. 1996. *Social Control in China: A Study of Chinese Work Units.* Westport, Conn.: Praeger.

Shen, Chonglin, and Shanhua Yang. 1995. *Dangdai Zhongguo Chengshi Jiating Yanjiu: Qi Chengshi Diaocha Baogao he Ziliao Huibian* Beijing: China Statistics Press.

Sheng, Xuewen, Norman Stockman, and Norman Bonney. 1992. "The Dual Burden: East and West (Women's Working Lives in China, Japan and Great Britain)." *International Sociology* 7:209–223.

Shi, Tianjian. 1996. "Direct Elections in Rural China." Paper presented at the annual meeting of Association for Asian Studies, Honolulu, Hawaii.
1997. *Political Participation in Beijing.* Cambridge, Mass.: Harvard University Press.

Shirk, Susan L. 1993. *The Political Logic of Economic Reform in China.* Berkeley: University of California Press.

Shorter, Edward. 1975. *The Making of the Modern Family.* New York: Basic Books.

Silver, Brian. 1987. "Political Beliefs of the Soviet Citizen: Sources of Support for Regime Norms," in *Politics, Work, and Daily Life in the USSR*, James Millar, ed. New York: Cambridge University Press.

Simmel, Georg. 1903a [1971]. "Group Expansion and the Development of Individuality." Pp. 251–93 in Donald Levine, ed., *On Individuality and Social Forms*. Chicago: University of Chicago Press.
1903b [1971]. "The Metropolis and Mental Life." Pp. 324–39 in Donald Levine, ed., *On Individuality and Social Forms*. Chicago: University of Chicago Press.

Siu, Helen F., and Zelda Stern, ed. 1983. *Mao's Harvest: Voices from China's New Generation.* New York: Oxford University Press.

Skilling, H. Gordon. 1971. *Interest Groups in Soviet Politics.* Princeton: Princeton University Press.

Skinner, G. William. 1977. *The City in Late Imperial China.* Stanford: Stanford University Press.
and Edwin A. Winckler. 1969. "Communist China: A Cyclical Theory." In Amitai Etzioni, ed., *A Sociological Reader on Complex Organizations*, 2nd ed. New York: Holt, Rinehart and Winston.

Smith, Hedrick. 1976. *The Russians.* New York: Quadrangle.

Smith, Michael R. 1990. "What Is New in the 'New Structuralist' Analyses of Earnings?" *American Sociological Review* 55:827–41.

Solinger, Dorothy J. 1995a. "China's Urban Transients in the Transition from Socialism and the Collapse of the Communist "Urban Public Goods Regime." *Comparative Politics* 27, no. 2.
1995b. "The Floating Population in the Cities: Chances for Assimilation?" Pp. 113–42 in Deborah S. Davis et al., eds., *Urban Spaces in Contemporary China*. New York: Cambridge University Press.
1999. *Contesting Citizenship in Urban China.* Berkeley: University of California Press.

Sorenson, Annemette, and Heike Trappe. 1995. "The Persistence of Gender Inequality in Earnings in the German Democratic Republic." *American Sociological Review* 60:398–406.

South, Scott J., and Kim M. Lloyd. 1995. "Spousal Alternatives and Marital Dissolution." *American Sociological Review* 60:21–35.

and Glenna Spitze. 1994. "Housework in Marital and Nonmarital Relations." *American Sociological Review* 59:327–47.

Speare, Alden, Paul K. C. Liu, and Ching-lung Tsay. 1988. *Urbanization and Development: The Rural-Urban Transition in Taiwan.* Boulder, Colo.: Westview Press.

SSB (State Statistical Bureau). 1985, 1989, 1992a, 1993a, 1994a, 1995a, 1996, 1997a, 1998a. *Zhongguo Tongji Nianjian* (China Statistical Yearbook). Beijing: China Statistical Publishing House.

SSB (State Statistical Bureau). 1992b, 1993b, 1994b, 1995b, 1998c. *Zhongguo Renkou Tongji Nianjian* (China Population Statistical Yearbook). Beijing: China Statistical Publishing House.

SSB (State Statistical Bureau). 1997b, 1998b. *Zhongguo Tongji Zhaiyao* (China Statistical Abstract). Beijing: China Statistical Publishing House.

Stacey, Judith. 1983. *Patriarchy and Socialist Revolution in China.* Berkeley: University of California Press.

Stark, David. 1986. "Rethinking Internal Labor Markets." *American Sociological Review* 51:593–604.

1992. "Path Dependence and Privatization Strategies in East Central Europe." *East European Politics and Societies* 6:17–54.

StataCorp. 1995. *Stata Statistical Software.* College Station, Tex.: Stata Corporation.

State Council. 1993. *Jiguan Gongzuo Renyuan Gongzi Gaige Fangan* (Preliminary Regulations of State Employee Wage Reform). No. 79, Nov. 15.

Stepanek, James B. 1991. "China's Enduring State Factories: Why Ten Years of Reform Have Left China's Big State Factories Unchanged." Vol. 2, pp. 440–54 in U.S. Congress Joint Economic Committee, *China's Economic Dilemmas of the 1990's: Problems of Reforms, Modernization, and Interdependence.* Washington: Government Printing Office.

Straus, Murray, et al. 1980. *Behind Closed Doors: Violence in the American Family.* New York: Anchor/Doubleday.

Swidler, Ann. 1986. "Culture in Action: Symbols and Strategies." *American Sociological Review* 51:273–86.

Szalai, Erzsebet. 1990. *Gazdasag es hatalom* (Economy and Power). Budapest: Aula.

Szelényi, Iván. 1978. "Social Inequalities in State Socialist Redistributive Economies." *International Journal of Comparative Sociology* 19:63–87.

1988. *Socialist Entrepreneurs: Embourgeoisement in Rural Hungary.* Madison: University of Wisconsin Press.

1994. "Post-Industrialism, Post-Communism, and the New Class." Pp. 723–29 in David B. Grusky, ed., *Social Stratification.* Boulder: Westview.

1996. "Cities Under Socialism – and After." Pp. 286–317 in Gregory Andrusz, Michael Harloe, and Iván Szelényi, *Cities After Socialism*. London: Blackwell.

Szelényi, Iván, and Eric Kostello. 1996. "The Market Transition Debate: Toward a Synthesis?" *American Journal of Sociology* 101:1082–96.

Tan, Shen. 1994. "Analysis and Predictions of the Women's Situation in Contemporary China" (Dangdai Zhongguo Funu Zhuangkuang). *Sociological Research* (Shehuixue Yanjiu) 51:69–77.

Tang, Wenfang. 1992. "Rural Industrialization and the Dilemma of Reform in China." *China Report* 5, no. 3:8–21. Washington, D.C.: Washington Center for China Studies.

——— 1993. "Workplace Participation in Chinese Local Industries." *American Journal of Political Science* (Aug.): 920–40.

——— 1996a. *Dangdai Zhongguo Qiye Juece* (Enterprise Decision Making in Contemporary China). Hong Kong: Oxford University Press.

——— 1996b. "Housing Reform in Urban China." *China Rights Forum*, Summer, pp. 8–10.

——— 1996c. "Taiwan Minzhu Hua yu Zhongguo Dalu Zhengzhi Gaige" (Taiwan's Democratization and China's Political Reform). Pp. 57–68 in Xiaoming Huang, ed., *Taiwan: Politics, Policy and Society*. Hong Kong: Center for Social Science Services.

——— 1999a. "Party Intellectuals' Demand for Reform in Contemporary China." Hoover Essays in Public Policy. Hoover Institution, Stanford University.

——— 1999b. "Nurture Seeds of Democracy in China." *Los Angeles Times*, March 22, B5.

——— and William Parish. 1996. "Social Reaction to Urban Reform in China." *Problems of Post-Communism*, Sept., pp. 35–47.

Taylor, Jeffrey R. 1988. "Rural Employment Trends and the Legacy of Surplus Labor, 1978–86." *China Quarterly* 116 (Dec.):736–66.

Thogersen, Stig. 1990. *Secondary Education in China After Mao*. Aarhus: Aarhus University Press.

Thomas, Hugh, ed. 1980. *Comrade Editor: Letters to the People's Daily*. Hong Kong: Joint Publishing.

Thompson, E. P. 1971. "The Moral Economy of the English Crowd in the Eighteenth Century." *Past and Present* 50:76–136.

Thornton, Arland, and Hui-Sheng Lin. 1994. *Social Change and the Family in Taiwan*. Chicago: University of Chicago Press.

Tidrick, Gene, and Jiyuan Chen, eds. 1987. *China's Industrial Reform*. New York: Oxford University Press.

Tilly, Charles. 1975. "Food Supply and Public Order in Modern Europe." Pp. 380–455 in Charles Tilly, ed., *The Formation of National States in Western Europe*. Princeton: Princeton University Press.

——— 1978. *From Mobilization to Revolution*. Reading, Mass.: Addison-Wesley.

Tilly, Chris, and Charles Tilly. 1994. "Capitalist Work and Labor Markets." Pp. 283–312 in Neil J. Smelser and Richard Swedberg, eds., *The*

Handbook of Economic Sociology. Princeton, N.J.: Princeton University Press.

Tilly, Louise A., and Joan W. Scott. 1978. *Women, Work, and Family*. New York: Holt, Rinehart and Winston.

Titma, Mikk, and Nancy Brandon Tuma. 1993. "Stratification in a Changing World." Pp. 225–54 in Jacek Szmatka, Zdzislaw Mach, and Janusz Mucha, eds., *Eastern European Societies on the Threshold of Change*. Lewiston: Edwin Mellen Press.

Tobin, Joseph, ed. 1992. *Re-Made in Japan: Everyday Life and Consumer Taste in a Changing Society*. New Haven: Yale University Press.

Tolley, George S. 1991. *Urban Housing Reform in China: An Economic Analysis*. World Bank Discussion Papers no. 123. Washington, D.C.: World Bank.

Treiman, Donald J. 1977. *Occupational Prestige in Comparative Perspective*. New York: Academic Press.

____ and Kim-Bor Yip. 1989. "Education and Occupational Attainment in 21 Countries." Pp. 373–94 in Melvin L. Kohn, ed., *Cross-National Research in Sociology*. Newbury Park, Calif.: Sage.

Trent, Katherine, and Scott J. South. 1989. "Structural Determinants of the Divorce Rate." *Journal of Marriage and the Family* 51:391–404.

Tsui, Kai-yuen. 1997. "Economic Reform and Attainment in Basic Education in China." *China Quarterly* 149:104–27.

Turner, Ralph. 1960. "Sponsored and Contest Mobility in the School System." *American Sociological Review* 25:855–66.

United Nations, Statistical Office. 1991. *Demographic Yearbook*. New York: United Nations.

U.S. Department of Commerce. 1995. *Statistical Abstract of the U.S., 1995*. Washington, D.C.: U.S. Government Printing Office.

U.S. Department of Commerce, Bureau of the Census. 1976. *Statistical Abstract of the U.S.* Washington, D.C.: U.S. Government Printing Office.

U.S. GSS. United States General Social Survey. Various years. Chicago: University of Chicago.

Verba, Sidney. 1978. "The Parochial and the Polity." Pp. 3–28 in Sidney Verba and Lucian W. Pye, eds., *The Citizen and Politics: A Comparative Perspective*. Stamford, Conn.: Greylock Publishers.

____ Norman H. Nie, and Jae-on Kim. 1978. *Participation and Political Equality*. Chicago: University of Chicago Press.

Walder, Andrew G. 1986. *Communist Neo-Traditionalism: Work and Authority in Chinese Industry*. Berkeley: California University Press.

____ 1987. "Wage Reform and the Web of Factory Interests." *China Quarterly* 109:22–41.

____ 1989. "Factory and Manager in an Era of Reform." *China Quarterly* 118:242–64.

____ 1990. "Economic Reform and Income Distribution in Tianjin, 1976–1986." Pp. 135–56 in Deborah Davis and Ezra Vogel, eds., *Chinese Society on the Eve of Tiananmen*. Cambridge, Mass.: Harvard University Press.

1992. "Property Rights and Stratification in Socialist Redistributive Economies." *American Sociological Review* 57 (Aug.):524–39.

1995. "Career Mobility and the Communist Political Order." *American Sociological Review* 60:309–28.

Wang, Shaoguang. 1994. "Central-Local Fiscal Politics in China." Pp. 91–112 in Jia Hao and Lin Zhimin, eds., 1994. *Changing Central-Local Relations in China: Reform and State Capacity*. Boulder: Westview Press.

1995a. "The Rise of the Regions: Fiscal Reform and the Decline of Central State Capacity in China." In Andrew G. Walder, ed., *The Waning of the Communist State: Economic Origins of Political Decline in China and Hungary*. Berkeley: University of California Press.

Wang, Hui, and Yunkang Pan, eds. 1994. *Tianjin Shi Qianhu Chengshi Jumin Hujuan Diaocha* (Tianjin City 1,000 Household Residents' Interview Survey). Tianjin: Tianjin Academy of Social Sciences.

Wang, Xiaoyi. 1995b. "Change in Rural-Urban Relations in 1994." Pp. 152–62 in Liu Jiang, Xueyi Lu, and Tianlun Shan, eds., *1994–1995 Nian Zhongguo Shehui Xingshi Fenxi yu Yuce*. Beijing: China Social Sciences Press.

Wank, David. 1995. "Bureaucratic Patronage and Private Business: Changing Networks of Power in Urban China." Pp. 153–83 in Andrew G. Walder, ed., *The Waning of the Communist State: Economic Origins of Political Decline in China and Hungary*. Berkeley: University of California Press.

Watson, Rubie S., and Patricia Buckley Ebrey, eds. 1991. *Marriage and Inequality in Chinese Society*. Berkeley: University of California Press.

Weakliem, David L. 1990. "Relative Wages and the Radical Theory of Economic Segmentation." *American Sociological Review* 55:574–90.

Wen, Shengtang. 1995. "Anti-Corruption in 1994." Pp. 136–51 in Liu Jiang, Xueyi Lu, Tianlun Shan, eds., *Analysis and Forecast of 1994–1995 Social Situation in China*. Beijing: China Social Science Press.

WGBH Educational Foundation. 1983. "The Russians Are Here." *Frontline*, WGBH, June 13, 1983.

Whyte, Martin King. 1974. *Small Groups and Political Rituals in China*. Berkeley: University of California Press.

1984. "Sexual Inequality Under Socialism: The Chinese Case in Comparative Perspective." Pp. 198–238 in James L. Watson, ed., *Class and Social Stratification in Post-Revolution China*. Cambridge, Eng.: Cambridge University Press.

1990. "Changes in Mate Choice in Chengdu." Pp. 181–214 in Deborah Davis and Ezra Vogel, eds., *Chinese Society on the Eve of Tiananmen*. Cambridge, Mass.: Harvard University Press.

1993. "Wedding Behavior and Family Strategies in Chengdu." Pp. 189–216 in Deborah Davis and Steven Harrell, eds., *Chinese Families in the Post-Mao Era*. Berkeley: University of California Press.

and William L. Parish. 1984. *Urban Life in Contemporary China*. Chicago: University of Chicago Press.

Wiles, P. J. D. 1977. *Economic Institutions Compared*. New York: John Wiley.

Williams, Oliver. 1993. "An Outsider's Perspective." Pp. 145–53 in Miriam K. Mills and Stuart S. Nagel, eds., *Public Administration in China*. Westport, Conn.: Greenwood Press.

Wilson, Richard W. 1970. *Learning to Be Chinese: The Political Socialization of Children in Taiwan*. Cambridge, Mass.: MIT Press.

Wilson, William Julius. 1987. *The Truly Disadvantaged: The Inner City, the Underclass, and Public Policy*. Chicago: University of Chicago Press.

Wolf, Margery. 1972. *Women and the Family in Rural Taiwan*. Stanford: Stanford University Press.

1985. *Revolution Postponed: Women in Contemporary China*. Stanford: Stanford University Press.

Woo, Margaret Y. K. 1994. "Chinese Women Workers: The Delicate Balance between Protection and Equality." Pp. 279–98 in Christina K. Gilmartin, Gail Hershatter, Lisa Rofel, and Tyrene White, eds., *Engendering China: Women, Culture, and the State*. Cambridge, Mass.: Harvard University Press.

World Bank. 1994. *China – Disease Prevention Project*, December. http://www.worldbank.org.

World Bank. 1995. *World Development Report 1995*. New York: Oxford University Press.

Wu, Nai-teh. 1987. "The Politics of Regime Patronage: Mobilization and Control within an Authoritarian Regime." Ph.D. diss., University of Chicago.

Xie, Bai-san. 1991. *China's Economic Policies, Theories and Reforms Since 1949*. Shanghai: Fudan University Press.

Xie, Yu, and Emily Hannum. 1996. "Regional Variation in Earnings Inequality in Reform-Era Urban China." *American Journal of Sociology* 101:950–92.

Xu, Songtao, and Jianliang Hou. 1993. *Guojia Gongwuyuan Zhanxing Tiaoli Shiyi* (A Study of the Temporary Civil Service Regulations). Beijing: People's Publishing House.

Xu, Anqi. 1994a. "Zhongguo lihun xiankuang, tedian ji qi qushi." *Shanghai Kexue Yuan Xueshu Jikan* (2):156–65.

1995. "Jiating baoli de faduan:Shanghai fuqi gongji xingwei de xiankuang ji tejeng." *Shehui Xue Yanjiu* 55 (1):86–91.

Xu, Xinyi. 1994b. "Organizational Control in Chinese Work Units." *International Sociology* 9:463–74.

Yan, Yun-xiang. 1995. "Everyday Power Relations: Changes in a North China Village." Pp. 215–41 in Andrew G. Walder, ed., *The Waning of the Communist State: Economic Origins of Political Decline in China and Hungary*. Berkeley: University of California Press.

Yang, Jianbai, and Xuezeng Li. 1980. "The Relations Between Agriculture, Light Industry and Heavy Industry in China." *Social Sciences in China*, no. 3:19–40.

Yang, Lu, and Yukun Wang. 1992. *Zhufang Gaige* (Housing Reform). Tianjin: Tianjin People's Publising House.

Yang, Mayfair Mei-hui. 1994. *Gifts, Favors, and Banquets: The Art of Social Relationships in China*. Ithaca, N.Y.: Cornell University Press.

Yuan, Yue, and Wen Fang. 1998. "1997–98 Survey on Hot Issues in Urban China." Pp. 181–201 in Xin Ru, Xueyi Lu, and Tianlun Shan, eds., *1998 Zhongguo Shehui Xingshi Fenxi yu Yuce* (1998 China Social Trends Analysis and Forecast). Beijing: China Social Sciences Press.

Zaks, Jeffrey S. 1994. "Human Capital in a Worker's Paradise: Returns to Education in Urban China." Working Paper 94–7. Boulder: University of Colorado.

Zaslavsky, Victor. 1995. "From Redistribution to Marketization: Social and Attitudinal Change in Post-Soviet Russia." Pp. 115–42 in Gail W. Lapidus, ed., *New Russia: Troubled Transformation*. Boulder, Colo.: Westview Press.

Zdravomyslova, Olga. 1995. "The Position of Women in Russia." Pp. 190–98 in David Lane, ed., *Transition: Politics, Privatisation and Inequality*. New York: Longman.

ZGCZNJ. 1996. *Zhongguo Caizheng Nianjian* (China Finance Yearbook). Beijing: Zhongguo Caizheng Zazhishe.

ZGFLNJ. 1990, 1993, 1994. *Zhongguo Falu Nianjian* (China Legal Yearbook). Beijing: China Legal Yearbook Publishing House.

Zha, Jianying. 1995. *China Pop: How Soap Operas, Tabloids and Bestsellers Are Transforming a Culture*. New York: The New Press.

Zhang, Bingyin. 1992a. *Renda Gongzuo de Lilun yu Shijian* (Theory and Practice of the People's Congress). Beijing: Legal Publishing House.

Zhang, Ning. 1992b. "A Conflict of Interest: Current Problems in Educational Reform." In Andrew Watson, ed., *Economic Reform and Social Change in China*. London: Routledge.

Zhe, Xiaoye. 1989. *Chengshi zai Zhuanzhedian Shang* (Cities at a Turning Point). A booklet in the compendium by Yunkang Pan, ed., *Shehui Xuezhe dui Shehui de Jinggao* (Warnings About Society from Sociologists). Beijing: Chinese Women's Publishing House.

Zhou, Qing. 1992. *Marriage, Family, and Population Growth in Contemporary China* (Dangdai Zhongguo Hunyin Jiating yu Renkou Fazhan). Beijing: China Population Press.

Zhou, Xueguang. 1995. "Partial Reform and the Chinese Bureaucracy in the Post-Mao Era." *Comparative Political Studies* 28:440–68.

Zhou, Xueguang, Nancy B. Tuma, and Phyllis Moen. 1996. "Stratification Dynamics Under State Socialism." *Social Forces* 74:759–96.

1997. "Institutional Change and Job Shift Patterns in Urban China, 1949 to 1994." *American Sociological Review* 62:339–65.

Index

acquisitiveness (*see also* consumption): 103, 107, 119, 121–22

administrators (*see also* bureaucrats; civil servants; corruption; technocrats): advantages of, 51, 56, 64, 65, 68, 81, 87–88, 90–91, 93–94, 95, 97, 99; ages of, 174–75; attitudes of, 115–18, 169–72, 177–78; and civil service regulations, 167; and corruption, 313; definition of, 317; differential fate of, 315; education of, 61, 62, 68–69, 168; income of, 95, 174, 181, 182, 183, 284–86; and income, 95, 284–86; and interest articulation, 197, 198–200, 202; as new class, 51n; quality of, 173–75; and seniority, 280–81; in Taiwan, 276, 280–82, 284–87, 289, 291, 292, 294; in transition, 163, 165; types of, 167–72, 315

affirmative action, 10, 52, 55, 57, 65, 74–75, 78, 310

age (*see also* seniority): and assertiveness with spouse, 259–61; and attitudes about bureaucracy, 170, 172; and divorce attitudes, 264; and expectations, 282; and interest articulation, 204, 282; and optimism, 120; and political attitudes, 294; and reform attitudes, 115–18; 125–27; in Taiwan, 294; and work, 216, 219, 221–23, 311, 312

alienation, 5, 11, 136n, 308–11

Almond, Gabriel, 6–7, 306

appliances, and women's chores, 237, 238, 250–52

assertiveness, individual: and age, 259–61; and cultural framing, 302n; delayed, 307; and education, 259–60, 306; female, 259–62; individualism, 311; male, 172, 228n, 202–3, 204 fig.; in private sector, 197, 204 fig., 309; with spouse, 302n; in Taiwan, 302n; of workers, 146, 153–54

attitudes (*see also* assertiveness;

expectations; satisfaction): 14–15; attitude scales, 325–31; about bureaucrats, 169–73, 180; by cohort, 287–94; determinants of reform attitudes, 104–7; and material conditions, 104, 110; satisfaction with reform, 108–14; spillover effect, 114; in Taiwan, 288–94

authoritarianism (*see also* dependency): 9, 23, 185, 309; fragmented, 166n, 309

autonomy, in marriage, 238, 240

backyard steel mills, *see* Great Leap Forward

bamboo curtain, *see* migrants

bargaining (*see also* intergenerational bargaining; spousal bargaining; work units, bargaining among; worker bargaining): 10, 12, 13, 14, 16; individualistic, 186–87

bargaining school (*see also* administrators, advantages of; firms, types of; market transition, debates about; party members, advantages of; work units, bargaining among): 12–13, 51, 80–81, 99–100, 314

Baron, James, 53n, 314

Becker, Gary, 15

Berk, Sarah, 15, 234n

Bian, Yanjie, 13, 51, 52, 55, 56, 57, 60, 69, 71, 80, 81, 82, 83, 84, 85n, 92, 98, 100, 131, 194, 314

blue-collar workers, *see* manual workers; workers

Brines, Julie, 15, 234, 235, 248

Burawoy, Michael, 80, 130, 135

bureaucracy (*see also* principled particularism; retirement, mandatory): 7; bureaucratic control, 70, 124, 164; centralization, 104, 110, 166; decentralization, 179; in Taiwan, 276

women's education (*cont.*)
216, 217, 220; and son preference, 56, 68; trends in, 61, 62
women's health, 211; and jobs, 216
women's income, 85, 86, 211, 217, 219, 284 fig., 286; in Asia, 227–28; and husband's income, 244–45; private sector and, 229; in Taiwan, 284 fig., 286, 299–300; trends by year, 226–30
women's work, 209–31; age patterns in, 221–24; demand for, 212, 219–20, 226–27; Hong Kong comparisons, 218; and job concentration, 297–98; and job satisfaction, 218–20; M-shaped curve in, 214, 220, 224, 295, 315; and managerial discrimination, 212, 213, 214–15, 223n; and Muslim provinces, 217; and perceived discrimination, 216–18; quality of, 224–30; regional variation in, 215, 217, 224; rural, 215; supply of, 213, 219–20, 226–27; in Taiwan, 295–99; United States comparisons, 218; and willingness to continue working, 218–20
work, *see* job mobility; jobs
work units (*see also* firms; private sector; state sector): 29; bargaining among, 80–81, 87–90, 93–95, 100, 110, 284–85; and education bargaining, 56, 69; and elections, 194; and interest articulation,
192–93; and job recruitment, 71; and systematic consequences, 307; types of, 137
worker bargaining (*see also* strikes): 10, 128; and age, 134, 161; channels, 134, 148–54; and cooptation devices, 130, 134, 144–45, 153, 155; and dependency, 128–30, 144, 150–53, 161; determinants of, 150–54; and disciplinary measures, 137–39; and education, 134, 161; and exit tendencies, 155; by historical period, 131–34; and in-kind benefits, 129–30, 134, 145–46, 161; and managerial authority, 133–34, 141–43, 150–53, 159, 161; in Russia, 129; and shared residence, 131, 132; and single-industry cities, 129; and skilled workers, 130–31; and social networks, 131–32, 140–41, 153, 160; and soft-budget constraints, 130, 133–34; and supervisors, 135; types of, 134–35; and unemployment rate, 130, 134; in the U.S., 129
workers (*see also* manual workers; unemployment): complaints by, 139–40; decision-making authority, 140, 141 fig.; and kin in firm, 140–41; and labor contracts, 35, 137, 159; and laggard behavior, 139

youth (*see also* age), 26